SECOND EDITION

Novel Destinations

Novel Destinations

A Travel Guide *to*
Literary Landmarks
From Jane Austen's Bath *to*
Ernest Hemingway's Key West

Shannon McKenna Schmidt & Joni Rendon
Foreword by Matthew Pearl

NATIONAL
GEOGRAPHIC
WASHINGTON, D.C.

Published by National Geographic Partners, LLC.
Copyright © 2008, 2017 Shannon McKenna Schmidt and Joni Rendon
Foreword Copyright © 2017 Matthew Pearl

ISBN: 978-1-4262-1780-7

The Library of Congress has cataloged the 2008 edition as follows:

Schmidt, Shannon McKenna, 1971-
  Novel destinations : literary landmarks from Jane Austen's Bath to Ernest
Hemingway's Key West / Shannon McKenna Schmidt and Joni Rendon.
     p. cm.
  Includes index.
  ISBN 978-1-4262-0277-3
  1. Literary landmarks--United States--Guidebooks. 2. Literary landmarks-
-Great Britain--Guidebooks. 3. Authors, American--Homes and haunts-
-United States--Guidebooks. 4. Authors, English--Homes and haunts--Great
Britain--Guidebooks. 5. United States--Intellectual life--Guidebooks. 6. Great
Britain--Intellectual life--Guidebooks. I. Rendon, Joni, 1972- II. Title.
PS141.S36 2008
823.009'358209--dc22
                                                                    2008000295

Since 1888, the National Geographic Society has funded more than 12,000 research, exploration,
and preservation projects around the world. National Geographic Partners distributes a portion
of the funds it receives from your purchase to National Geographic Society to support programs
including the conservation of animals and their habitats.

National Geographic Partners
1145 17th Street NW
Washington, DC 20036-4688 USA

Become a member of National Geographic and activate your benefits today
at natgeo.com/jointoday.

For information about special discounts for bulk purchases, please contact
National Geographic Books Special Sales: specialsales@natgeo.com

For rights or permissions inquiries, please contact National Geographic
Books Subsidiary Rights: bookrights@natgeo.com

Interior design: Cameron Zotter/Nicole Miller

Printed in China
17/RRDS/1

Contents

Part One:
TRAVEL BY THE BOOK

The best literary experiences at home and abroad

Part Two:

JOURNEYS BETWEEN THE PAGES

The pages of literature come to life in the following 11 locales,
immortalized by famed novelists.

Foreword

My first week in college, I fell in with a group of freshmen already down to business. They were searching for the bridge Quentin Compson jumped off of in *The Sound and the Fury*. We looked the whole day, Cambridge being all bridges. One unapproachable member of the group recited whole passages as we walked. Finally, our reward: a brick-size plaque marking the bridge with a *Sound and the Fury* quote. Much later, I heard that Faulkner had never actually been to Cambridge, Massachusetts, before writing that scene. The geography in the book had been approximated, fogged over; the plaque was a bridge of a different kind, a bridge between fiction and a real destination.

What I wouldn't pay for my poker buddy Kevin's literary stint to boast about. Davy Byrnes pub in Dublin, Ireland, is where the everyman hero of modern fiction, Leopold Bloom, has lunch (a Gorgonzola sandwich) in Joyce's *Ulysses*. Kevin was Davy Byrnes' bartender . . . for a day. The manager was tipped off to the fact that Kevin may have embellished his bartending credentials when Kevin couldn't change a keg. No problem: Kevin had lived in *Ulysses* for a day, and served a few beers in it.

Joyce bragged that if Dublin were ever destroyed, it could be rebuilt by reading *Ulysses*. Some of our favorite texts do not fold out into a map. Looking for the spot where the *Pequod* sinks in a whale and

Ahab swirl? Where exactly did Didi and Gogo hang around for Godot? Luckily, universes can fit on a head of a pin, and the pins are worth honoring, too. Beckett might have thought of the idea for *Waiting for Godot* on *this* bar stool. Poe pictured the raven landing in *this* room. And out of the top-floor window of Herman Melville's Arrowhead, his home in western Massachusetts, doesn't that view make the top of Mount Greylock look very much like a . . . whale?

Sometimes a book invites a journey, sometimes we invite ourselves. We can cross through rugged mental landscapes. A physical place can map out a mental one; the mental one can prompt a new physical one. If the Dante house in Florence cannot conclusively be declared the home of Dante Alighieri, that hardly lessens its impact on visitors.

No one is worse with directions than I am. I spent four years of college lost. (Does the Charles River need to curve so much?) When I returned to the area, I was writing a novel and armed with a Boston map circa 1865. I was using it for researching a book and a past, but it made me feel at home in the present for the first time. I grew up in Florida and liked to say I had become a native of Boston, at least of 19th-century Boston. With "obsolete" maps, I have entered the lives of Longfellow, of Emerson, of Poe, of Thoreau, of Dante, of Kafka, whether the buildings remain or long ago vanished. Writers infuse their work with a sense of place because a sense of place is what often orients our ideas.

Searching for Faulkner's bridge was the kind of thing I had probably imagined I would do at college. Looking back, maybe it had something to do with my becoming an English major and, eventually, a writer. I don't remember actually caring much that afternoon whether or not we would ever find that bridge. I had found my first camaraderie in a new place.

—MATTHEW PEARL
Author of *The Dante Club*, *The Poe Shadow*, *The Last Dickens*,
and *The Last Bookaneer*
www.matthewpearl.com

Introduction

I FELT AS IF I'D GOT INTO A NOVEL while going about in the places I'd read so much of," Louisa May Alcott wrote in her journal after seeing the sights of Dickensian London in 1865. Though it's been more than 150 years since the writer penned those words, her sentiment still strikes a chord with many a modern-day traveler—including us, two lifelong voracious readers who share an equally passionate appetite for exploration.

During one of our many transatlantic phone calls (Shannon lived in New Jersey at the time and Joni had recently moved to London), the conversation turned to our two great loves: reading and travel. Shannon had just visited Louisa May Alcott's home in Concord, Massachusetts, with her family, while Joni was preparing for an upcoming trip to Dublin—not by reading guidebooks but by delving into the works of famed Irish scribes Wilde, Joyce, and Beckett.

It was during this conversation that the inspiration for *Novel Destinations* struck. We realized that in our travels near and far, we've not only looked to novels to provide a new dimension to our travel experiences, but equally, we've sought out the literary places in our travels that will give us a deeper perspective on the books we cherish.

We suspect we're not the only ones for whom the mere mention of Ernest Hemingway's Key West or Victor Hugo's Paris is enough to inspire a mad dash to book an airline ticket, pack a bag, and set off for some novel exploration. After all, it's through the eyes of authors like these that many of us came to know the places we're eventually able to visit firsthand.

Whether it's having afternoon tea at Bath's Pump Room, which Catherine Morland frequented in *Northanger Abbey*, seeing the room where the Alcott girls (and their *Little Women* counterparts) "took to the boards" to act out homespun theatrical productions, or sipping a pint in the pub where James Joyce and *Ulysses'* Leopold Bloom once did the same, traveling off the page is a thrilling way to see the world.

Even celebrated writers such as John Steinbeck felt the allure of following in the footsteps of the authors they admired. Steinbeck once dreamed of making like Jack London and sailing across the Pacific on a freighter. As he later professed in his memoir, *Travels with Charley,* "No two journeys are alike"—whether the final destination lies within the pages of a favorite book or across the expanse of the open road ahead.

—SHANNON MCKENNA SCHMIDT AND JONI RENDON

Part One:

TRAVEL BY THE BOOK

The best literary experiences at home and abroad

Read 'Em and See:

AUTHOR HOUSES AND MUSEUMS

What conditions are necessary for the creation of works of art?" Virginia Woolf pondered in *A Room of One's Own.* For Henry David Thoreau, it was the primitive surroundings of a one-room cabin stripped of all but the bare necessities; for Edith Wharton, it was a grand manse embraced by lushly landscaped gardens. However humble or majestic, each writer's most intimate places—the private worlds where they dreamed, dozed, drew inspiration, and spent their most creative hours—give readers a rare glimpse into the ephemeral moment of artistic creation.

Whether uncovering Sherlock Holmes's London, roaming the Spanish countryside where Don Quixote battled windmills, gazing at the typewriter on which Margaret Mitchell tapped out *Gone with the Wind,* or exploring the Hudson Valley where the Headless Horseman galloped into Washington Irving's imagination, it's easy to follow a trail of ink drops to the places where the stories got their start.

ALL THE WOR(L)D'S A STAGE:

SHAKESPEARE'S ENGLAND

· ·

SHAKESPEARE'S GLOBE THEATRE, LONDON

21 New Globe Walk • Tel: (44) 207 902 1400

• *www.shakespearesglobe.org*

• Globe season runs May through October

• Sam Wanamaker Playhouse open year-round

"England's shrine to its national idol would never have been built if it weren't for an American guy from Chicago," says Jon Edgley-Bond, who leads tours of the theatre's interior. He's referring to Sam Wanamaker, the actor and director who led the charge to reconstruct the open-air Elizabethan playhouse where the Bard once plied his craft. A stray cannonball spark ignited the thatched roof of the original Globe during a production of *Henry VIII*, burning the theatre down to the ground in 1613. (It was subsequently rebuilt, and then destroyed by Puritans three decades later.)

Today the new Globe—thatched roof and all—has been faithfully restored to its Tudor-style glory on the south bank of the River Thames. Modern-day "groundlings," much like their counterparts 400 years ago, can pay a mere pittance (then just a penny and today only £5) to stand in the pit surrounding the stage during performances. Some would

THE MYSTERIOUS MARLOWE: Born the same year as the Bard, fellow Elizabethan playwright Christopher Marlowe wrote blank verse dramas such as *Tamburlaine* and *Doctor Faustus*, which provided inspiration for some of Shakespeare's early works. The good-natured rivalry between the two was cut short when Marlowe was mysteriously murdered in 1593. Since then, it has been speculated that Marlowe faked his death and was the real author of the plays today attributed to Shakespeare. Marlowe is commemorated on the stained-glass window in **Westminster Abbey's Poets' Corner**, with a question mark beside the date of his death.

argue groundlings have the best "seats" in the house, but those with weary legs can watch the action unfold from the wooden balcony stalls in the O-shaped amphitheater.

Performances run during summer months only, but an informative exhibition on the Globe's history is open year-round in conjunction with tours of the theatre. Also open year-round is the **Sam Wanamaker Playhouse**. The replica Jacobean playhouse stages works of the period as they would have originally been performed—lit by flickering candlelight. The small, wood-paneled space, with two snug galleries embracing the pit and stage, brings spectators up close to the performers.

Shakespeare's brother, Edmund, is buried in an unmarked grave near the Globe at **Southwark Cathedral** (*www.southwark .anglican.org/cathedral*). The playwright is thought to have worshiped at London's oldest Gothic church, and his memory is preserved by a recumbent alabaster statue under a stained-glass window depicting characters from his plays.

OPEN-AIR THEATRE, REGENT'S PARK, LONDON

Inner Circle, Regent's Park • Tel: (44) 844 826 4242 • www.openairtheatre.org

• Season runs June through September

Established in 1932, this leafy, intimate amphitheater—set amid trees twinkling with fairy lights—may well be the most magical spot in the world to catch one of the Bard's works. The theatre is the resident venue of the New Shakespeare Company, whose productions each year include a Shakespeare play, a musical, and a children's performance. Arrive early to soak up the atmosphere by picnicking on the inviting lawn surrounding the theatre. Barbecue and other dining options are available before each evening performance, so have a bite and order up a glass of bubbly at the crescent-shaped bar that stretches the length of the auditorium.

"Over hill, over dale. Thorough bush, thorough brier, Over park, over pale, . . . I do wander everywhere."
—A MIDSUMMER NIGHT'S DREAM

STRATFORD-UPON-AVON, ENGLAND

Shakespeare Birthplace Trust • Tel: (44) 178 920 4016 • www.shakespeare.org.uk

Bard fans have been making a pilgrimage to this picturesque Tudor town in western England for hundreds of years to pay homage to the country's iconic wordsmith.

SHAKESPEARE'S BIRTHPLACE

Henley Street

In 1564, young Will Shakespeare drew his first breath in a low-ceilinged bedroom on the second floor of a rambling half-timbered house in the center of Stratford. It is thought that after spending his youth here, the playwright continued to live at the house with his bride, Anne Hathaway, before subsequently moving to London. The house's original and replica furnishings from his era provide a fascinating glimpse into Elizabethan life and times. Colorful jewel-tone decorative cloths, hand-dyed in the traditional Tudor fashion, hang from beds and adorn the walls. Shakespeare's father operated a glovemaking business, and his workshop is laid out with tools and skins as if in preparation for the day's work.

Charles Dickens and John Keats were among the early sightseers to one of England's first tourist attractions. A facsimile copy of a visitors' book with their signatures is on display, while a glass windowpane bears the etched signatures of other literati, including Thomas Carlyle and Sir Walter Scott.

At the rear of the house is a stunning traditional English garden planted with many of the trees, flowers, and herbs mentioned in Shakespeare's works, while an adjacent exhibition center illuminates the Bard's life.

Descendants of the dramatist lived in the house until the early 19th century, after which advocates like Charles Dickens helped secure the funds to acquire it in 1847. In later years, the Shakespeare Birthplace Trust was established, which today oversees the area's five Shakespeare-related properties.

MARY ARDEN'S HOUSE

Wilmcote, 3 miles northwest of Stratford

In a case of mistaken identity worthy of a Shakespearean plot, a picturesque wood-beamed farmhouse with sloping floors (today known as Palmer's Farm) was erroneously thought to be the home of Shakespeare's mother, Mary Arden, for more than two centuries. Only in the past decade were deeds uncovered revealing that Arden, the daughter of a prosperous local farmer, had in fact lived in the neighboring abode (which dates back 50 years earlier but was refaced with red brick during Victorian times). Today both properties and their surrounding outbuildings, including a dovecote and a stone cider press, have been combined into a historic site showcasing Tudor rural life.

ANNE HATHAWAY'S COTTAGE & GARDENS

Shottery, 1 mile west of Stratford

An enchanting thatch-roofed, lattice-windowed cottage surrounded by hollyhocks and climbing roses was the fairy-tale setting where Shakespeare likely wooed his future wife, Anne Hathaway. The sizable 500-year-old cottage not only survived a potentially devastating fire in modern times but also remarkably still contains many items dating back to the Hathaways' occupancy. Among the well-preserved furnishings are the carved oak, four-poster bed on which Anne Hathaway is thought to have been born, an elm-boarded settle on which the Bard may have courted his bride, and another Tudor-era bed that some scholars believe is the infamous "second best bedde" that Shakespeare bequeathed to Anne in his will. (Whether the bequest itself was actually intended as a slight remains shrouded in controversy.)

NEW PLACE AND NASH'S HOUSE

Chapel Street

The grand brick and timber dwelling described in Shakespeare's will as "the newe place wherein I nowe dwell" was the only home Shakespeare ever owned. With five gables, 20 rooms, and 10 fireplaces, New Place was the second largest building in Stratford during Shakespeare's time. It was purchased by the prosperous playwright in 1597, and he may have written his later plays, including *The Tempest*, at the home.

New Place was substantially altered by a later owner and then razed to the ground in 1759 by an eccentric clergyman, Francis

See page 99 for information on **Holy Trinity Church**, the Bard's final resting place.

Gastrell, in a row over taxes. Gastrell had already invoked the ire of Stratford residents for cutting down Shakespeare's famed mulberry tree after becoming annoyed at curious sightseers.

The hallowed grounds of New Place have recently been reimagined, and an illuminated reflecting pool now marks its foundations. An Elizabethan knot garden and elements of Shakespeare's Great Garden have also been restored. Next door at **Nash's House**, the former home of Shakespeare's granddaughter, an exhibit tells the story of the Bard as family man, businessman, landowner, and writer. Among the items on display are mementos of the first Shakespeare festival held in Stratford in 1769 and relics carved from the infamous mulberry tree.

HALL'S CROFT
Old Town Street

This 500-year-old gabled Tudor dwelling was once the domain of Shakespeare's beloved eldest daughter, Susanna, and her esteemed husband, medical practitioner Dr. John Hall. The doctor's consulting room, which displays ointment jars and cringe-worthy medical implements from the 16th and 17th centuries, provides an enlightening look at the primitive field of medicine during the Bard's time. The walled garden contains many of the plants, flowers, trees, and herbs mentioned in Dr. Hall's medical notebooks, which he would have used to treat patients.

THE PLAY'S THE THING: Dating back to 1879, Britain's Royal Shakespeare Company (*www.rsc.org.uk*) stages several productions a year at its three Stratford theatres: **The Royal Shakespeare Theatre,** located on the banks of the River Avon; the adjacent **Swan Theatre,** a modernized circular Elizabethan-style venue; and **The Other Place,** a 200-seat studio theatre. In addition to playgoing, visitors can take in the view from atop a tower or learn about the theatre world on various tours—including one given after dark.

Other Places to See Shakespeare

LENOX, MASSACHUSETTS (*www.shakespeare.org*)

A former artists' colony in the Berkshire Mountains, Lenox has been home to the Elizabethan-modeled **Shakespeare & Company** ensemble since 1978. The company operates year-round and stages performances in numerous venues, including the tented Rose Footprint Theatre, a partial reconstruction of Shakespeare's first London theatre.

NEW YORK, NEW YORK (*www.publictheater.org*)

Shakespeare in the Park is an annual summer rite of passage for New Yorkers, who line up early each performance day to score coveted tickets for the free performances held in Central Park's open-air Delacorte Theater. Those with limited time and deep pockets can obtain tickets in advance by making a donation.

ASHLAND, OREGON (*www.osfashland.org*)

This Pacific Northwest town on the edge of the California border boasts one of the oldest and largest professional nonprofit theatres in the United States. Founded in 1935, the **Oregon Shakespeare Festival** stages an eight-and-a-half-month season of 11 Shakespearean and classic plays in three venues, including an outdoor Elizabethan-style amphitheater.

CEDAR CITY, UTAH (*www.bard.org*)

The **Utah Shakespeare Festival** was founded in 1961, partly as after-hours entertainment for the plethora of summer tourists visiting the area's national parks. The Tony Award–winning festival stages plays June through October, and one of its two theatres is modeled on Shakespeare's Globe in London.

STRATFORD, ONTARIO (*www.stratfordfestival.ca*)

Set on—where else?—the River Avon, this town of ultimate Bard buffs in eastern Canada boasts the largest classical repertory theatre in North America, and its annual **Stratford Festival** draws more than 600,000 during its April to October season. Stroll the Shakespeare Gardens after taking in one of the plays offered at Stratford's four theatres.

More Playful Destinations

SHAW'S CORNER, HERTFORDSHIRE, ENGLAND

Ayot St. Lawrence, near Welwyn • Tel: (44) 143 882 1968 • *www.nationaltrust.org* *.uk/shaws-corner* • Open late March through October

A Dubliner by birth, Nobel Prize–winning dramatist George Bernard Shaw spent most of his life in England. In 1906, the playwright and his wife, Charlotte, settled in Ayot St. Lawrence, a small village north of London. Although Shaw moved there to escape the spotlight, he also intended his home to become a place of pilgrimage for his many admirers. He wrote dozens of his plays there, including *Man and Superman* and *Pygmalion* (which became the basis for the musical *My Fair Lady*).

A life-size statue of Shaw is on display at the **National Gallery of Ireland** in Dublin. In his will he left a third of his royalties to the art museum, the "cherished asylum" of his boyhood.

Every day in all weathers, Shaw would cross the garden to work in his revolving writing hut, ingeniously built to follow the sun's light throughout the day. Upon the playwright's death in 1950, the house and all of its contents—from his clothes and stationary exercise bike to his Oscar statuette for the screenplay of *Pygmalion*—were bequeathed to the National Trust. The result is a living shrine to the eccentric dramatist, who died shortly after a fall while pruning an apple tree on the property. His ashes were scattered in the large garden, where performances of his plays are held during summer months.

ABBEY THEATRE, DUBLIN, IRELAND

26 Lower Abbey Street • Tel: (353) 18 78 72 22 • *www.abbeytheatre.ie*

"We hope to find in Ireland an uncorrupted and imaginative audience," wrote poet and playwright W. B. Yeats in his 1897 manifesto for the establishment of what eventually became the Abbey Theatre. Yeats and the theater's co-founders wanted to bring to the stage works that reflected "the deeper thoughts and emotions of Ireland" while fostering new voices like J. M. Synge and Sean O'Casey. The

Abbey's curtain was first raised on December 27, 1904, and the theater thereafter became a symbol of the Irish literary revival, a movement that cultivated a renewed sense of national identity through pride in Gaelic culture. Although the original building that housed it burned to the ground in 1951 and a new structure was built to replace it a decade later, the Abbey of today still regularly stages plays from the Irish repertoire alongside performances of international classics.

James Joyce's only play, *Exiles,* was turned down by W. B. Yeats acting on behalf of the Abbey Theatre. To experience Joyce's Dublin, see pages 272–82.

IBSEN MUSEUM, OSLO, NORWAY

Henrik Ibsen's Gate 26 • Tel: (47) 40 02 36 30 • *www.norskfolkemuseum.no/en*
• Closed Mondays in winter

Ibsen's dying words—uttered from the bed in his spacious Oslo apartment on May 23, 1906—were "On the contrary," an appropriate farewell from the controversial playwright known for works that shattered Victorian moral codes. Regarded as a founding father of modern drama, he earned renown by plumbing the depths of the human psyche and delivering scathing social commentary in plays like *A Doll's House* and *Hedda Gabler.* After a stroke in 1900 left Ibsen increasingly immobilized, zealous fans would sometimes linger on the street below his apartment hoping for a glimpse of the bearded, white-haired playwright in the window.

HONORING IBSEN: Although he spent 27 years in self-imposed exile from his native land, the playwright is beloved by Norwegians and the country boasts two additional Ibsen museums outside Oslo. Ibsen was born in the port town of Skien, and the farmhouse where he spent much of his boyhood is today the **Ibsen Museum in Skien** (*www.telemarkmuseum.no*). At 15, Ibsen left home, later becoming assistant to an apothecary housed in what is now the **Ibsen Museum in Grimstad** (*www.gbm.no/en/ibsenmuseet*), which opened in 1916. The chemist's shop where Ibsen worked is as it was a century ago, next to the living quarters where he wrote his first play, *Catilina.*

Subsequent to the deaths of Henrik and his wife, Suzannah, many of their possessions were dispersed in museums throughout the country, but the playwright's 2006 centenary brought the restoration of his apartment along with the return of its contents. The focal point of the restored apartment is the study where Ibsen wrote his final dramatic works, *John Gabriel Borkman* and *When We Dead Awaken.* Other rooms on display include the library, dining room, and opulent blue living room. Admittance is via guided tours that take place hourly; an adjacent exhibit, "On the Contrary!," illuminates surprising elements of Ibsen's life such as his talent as an artist: Several of his paintings, cartoons, and stage sketches are on display.

MONTE CRISTO COTTAGE, NEW LONDON, CT

325 Pequot Avenue • Tel: 860-443-5378 • *www.theoneill.org/monte-cristo-cottage* • Open Memorial Day through Labor Day; limited hours

Overlooking the Thames River in a picturesque seaside town is a gingerbread-trimmed house whose cheerful exterior belies the tortured lives of its occupants at the turn of the 19th century. Then the summer home of the boy who would become America's only Nobel Prize–winning playwright, Eugene O'Neill, the house took its name from the dramatist's father, a touring stage actor in *The Count of Monte Cristo.* O'Neill would later use Monte Cristo Cottage as the setting for both his comedic play *Ah, Wilderness!* and his tragic autobiographical masterpiece, *Long Day's Journey Into Night,* which featured unflattering portrayals of his penny-pinching father, his morphine-addicted mother, and his alcoholic brother.

"O'Neill's set directions were very precise in those plays," says Sally Thomas Pavetti, the curator who played an instrumental role in the meticulous years-long restoration of the national historic landmark, which is owned by the Eugene O'Neill Theater Center. "In addition, O'Neill drew a three-by-three-inch first-floor plan of the house for his notes of *Long Day's Journey Into Night,* remembering exactly where the tables, bookcases, chairs, and piano were placed. We followed his notes as precisely as possible in our renovation of the Monte Cristo Cottage."

Although few of the O'Neills' original possessions remain in the museum, the playwright's bedroom contains the simple desk at which he wrote his early Pulitzer Prize–winning drama, *Anna Christie*, while working for the Provincetown Players.

Due to the similarities of the fictional Tyrone family in *Long Day's Journey Into Night* to his own family members, O'Neill stipulated that the play, penned in 1942, should not be published until 25 years after his death. His third wife, Carlotta, later controversially claimed he had a change of heart and she had the play published in 1956, just three years after the dramatist died.

TAO HOUSE
AT THE EUGENE O'NEILL
NATIONAL HISTORIC SITE

Outside of Danville, CA

• Tel: 925-838-0249 • *www.nps.gov/euon*

Open Wednesday through Sunday

East of San Francisco, in the San Ramon Valley, the National Park Service preserves Tao House, where O'Neill and his third wife, Carlotta, lived in relative seclusion from 1937 to 1944. The itinerant O'Neill—who had lived in more than 35 places by the time of his move to Danville—called the remote refuge his *"final home and harbor."* The O'Neills built the two-story, three bedroom house from the ground up, combining Spanish and Oriental influences and furnishing it with Chinese antiques like the playwright's teak bed—a former opium couch. Several of the dwelling's architectural features, such as its serpentine walkway to ward off evil spirits, reflect principles of Taoism, a philosophy that greatly influenced O'Neill's work. He penned many of his most critically acclaimed plays, including *Long Day's Journey Into Night*, *The Iceman Cometh*, and *Moon for the Misbegotten*, at Tao House before his degenerative neurological condition necessitated a move to San Francisco for medical care.

An eight-foot-tall bronze sculpture inscribed with a passage from *Long Day's Journey Into Night* is located in Danville across from the public library.

The Eugene O'Neill National Historic Site is a gated property not open to private vehicles. Transportation is provided via a free shuttle service from Danville and includes a guided tour of the house. (Advance booking required except on Saturdays.)

Atmospheric Literary Landscapes

Sir Walter Scott's Scottish Border Country

ABBOTSFORD

Melrose, Roxburghshire • Tel: (44) 189 675 2043

• *www.scottsabbotsford.com*

• Open daily March through November

"It is a kind of Conundrum Castle to be sure," Sir Walter Scott wrote of his beloved Abbotsford. The turreted, castle-like manor house with its sumptuous antique furnishings, wood-paneled interiors, and decorative coats of arms could have been taken straight from one of his popular swashbuckling tales such as *Ivanhoe* or *Rob Roy*. Fittingly, the man known as the Father of the Historical Novel was also an avid collector of historic relics. Suits of armor stand sentry in Abbotsford's Gothic entrance hall, and an entire room is devoted to weaponry such as Rob Roy's gun and broadsword.

Located on the banks of the River Tweed in the gentle green Scottish border country, the manse and surrounding gardens—every detail of their design personally supervised by Scott himself— were several years in the making. But the expense of this lavish "conundrum castle" and the bankruptcy of Scott's publishing company nearly forced him to relinquish

Washington Irving paid a visit to Abbotsford in 1817, noting, "The huge baronial pile . . . was just emerging . . . the walls, surrounded by scaffolding, already had risen." Fifteen years later, Scott's friend William Wordsworth visited the "sorrow-stricken" home as Scott's health declined. See pages 84–86 for Irving and pages 19–20 for Wordsworth.

the property. "My heart clings to the place I have created," Scott wrote mournfully in 1825. "The pain of leaving it is greater than I can tell."

To pay off his debts, he cranked out prose at a feverish pace, but exhaustion took its toll and a series of strokes culminated in his death on September 21, 1832, at age 61. Just five months later, the house—its possessions intact—opened as one of the world's first literary museums. In the 19th century, everyone from Queen Victoria to Charlotte Brontë pilgrimaged to the enchanted abode, whose very name, as Brontë noted, "possesses music and magic."

Visitors can take in the drawing room swathed in hand-painted chinoiserie wallpaper, the 7,000-volume library with intricately molded ceilings replicated from Scotland's famed Rosslyn Chapel, and the writer's cozy study, where hundreds more books line shelves in an upper gallery. Scott's worn armchair is still at his desk, where after his death a secret compartment of letters was found.

A visitor center features intriguing items such as design books related to the house's construction and the egg timer Scott used to set the pace of his writing while attempting to write his way out of debt. Best reached by car, Abbotsford is 37 miles southeast of Edinburgh and 80 miles southeast of Glasgow.

DRYBURGH ABBEY AND SCOTT'S VIEW

Grave site, 4 miles southeast of Melrose • www.discovertheborders.co.uk

This eerie, ruined 12th-century abbey, embraced by the River Tweed, is the writer's final resting place. Nearby is Scott's View, the writer's favorite scenic vista, which looks out over the Tweed Valley.

SELKIRK COURTHOUSE / SIR WALTER SCOTT'S COURTROOM

Selkirk village, 6 miles south of Melrose • www.visitscotland.com

In addition to his prolific writing career, Scott held a law degree and occupied the post of sheriff in Selkirk County for more than 30 years. Today, the Selkirk Courthouse where he worked houses an exhibition of his life and writings.

TIBBIE SHIELS INN

St. Mary's Loch • www.tibbieshiels.com

This historic 19th-century stagecoach inn on the banks of St. Mary's Loch, 19 miles west of Selkirk, has served up drams to Sir Walter Scott, Robert Louis Stevenson, and Thomas Carlyle.

SIR WALTER SCOTT WAY

www.sirwalterscottway.com

This 92-mile walkway from South Central Scotland to the southeast Scottish coastline runs through lowland valleys, lochs, and sheep farms, connecting various locales that inspired Scott.

Anne of Green Gables Land, Prince Edward Island, Canada

GREEN GABLES HERITAGE PLACE

8619 Route 6 • Cavendish • Tel: 902-963-7874 • www.pc.gc.ca • Open daily, May 1 through October 31

Anne . . . gazed out into the June morning, her eyes glistening with delight. Oh, wasn't it beautiful? Wasn't it a lovely place? Suppose she wasn't really going to stay here! She would imagine she was. There was a scope for imagination here. — L. M. Montgomery, *Anne of Green Gables*

Instead of the orphan boy Marilla Cuthbert and her brother, Matthew, sought to adopt to help out on their farm, 11-year-old Anne Shirley whirlwinds into their lives. She arrives too late in the evening to be sent back to the orphanage, and by the next day she has a permanent place on the Prince Edward Island farm.

Smart, spirited, and sporting bright red pigtails, Anne's harsh childhood hasn't dimmed her zest for life. A chatterbox given to flights of imagination and comic mishaps, she quickly endeared herself to readers when *Anne of Green*

The original schoolhouse where Montgomery taught is part of **Avonlea Village** (www.avonlea.ca), along with shops and restaurants housed in replica structures from Anne's era.

Gables by L. M. Montgomery was published in 1908. An instant best seller, it even made a fan of curmudgeonly Mark Twain. He called the book "charming" and told a friend, "In *Anne of Green Gables* you will find the dearest and most moving and delightful child since the immortal Alice" of Wonderland.

A musical version based on *Anne of Green Gables* has been staged annually at the **Charlottetown Festival** on Prince Edward Island since 1965 (*www.charlottetownfestival.com*).

Anne's scenic home, Green Gables, was inspired by a real-life farm belonging to relatives of Montgomery's grandfather. The author grew up nearby, raised by her grandparents from an early age after her mother died of tuberculosis. Located in Cavendish (the town that served as the stand-in for the novel's Avonlea), the property is now the **Green Gables Heritage Place** and part of Prince Edward Island National Park.

Rooms in the house have been restored to reflect how they're described in the novel. In Anne's bedchamber, fans will be familiar with the floral-adorned wallpaper (including apple blossoms) and pale-green muslin curtains. Hanging on the closet door is a brown dress with puffed sleeves like the one she receives as a Christmas gift from kind-hearted Matthew.

On display in the visitor reception center is Montgomery's black Empire typewriter, with well-worn lettering on the keys, on which she turned out the Anne of Green Gables series and other works. Elsewhere at the lively Heritage Place are opportunities to join a Sunday picnic with old-fashioned games and ice cream–making or attend a ceilidh with live folk music hosted by characters from the book. An "Anne-imator" is on site every day so that visitors can meet much-loved heroine Anne Shirley in person.

HAUNTED WOOD TRAIL

Enamored with Green Gables' natural beauty, Anne bestows fanciful names on places around the property (a proclivity shared by Montgomery). By the farmhouse is a swath of forest Anne dubs the Haunted Wood. She finds the area beautiful by day but frightening after dark, imagining a woman in white and a headless man roaming around. The ghost-free **Haunted Wood Trail** passes near the **Cavendish Cemetery**, where Montgomery is buried, and connects the Green Gables Heritage Place to the site where she lived with her grandparents. A second pathway on the property, the **Balsam Hollow Trail**, begins at Lover's Lane (also named by Anne) and winds through woodlands and beside a brook.

SITE OF LUCY MAUD MONTGOMERY'S CAVENDISH HOME

Route 6 • Tel: 902-963-2231 • *www.peisland.com/lmm* • Open mid-May through mid-October

Anne's adventures were put to paper in Montgomery's childhood home, where she returned at age 23 to care for her widowed grandmother. Although the house no longer exists, placards illuminate Montgomery's connections to the picturesque site.

ANNE OF GREEN GABLES MUSEUM

4542 Route 20 • Park Corner • Tel: 800-665-2663 • *www.annemuseum.com* • Open mid-May through mid-October

While growing up, Montgomery spent summers with relatives at their Prince Edward Island home, which she called the "wonder castle of my childhood" and refashioned as Silver Bush in the novels *Pat of Silver Bush* and *Mistress Pat*. House tours include the parlor, where Montgomery married in front of the fireplace in 1911. Visitors can also take a carriage ride around the property and see the pond that inspired Anne's Lake of Shining Waters.

LUCY MAUD MONTGOMERY BIRTHPLACE

Intersection of Routes 6 and 20 • New London • Tel: 902-886-2099 (summer); 902-836-5502 (winter) • *www.lmmontgomerybirthplace.ca* • Open mid-May through Thanksgiving

Montgomery was born in this cottage in Clifton (now New London) on November 30, 1874. On display is a replica of her wedding dress, scrapbooks, letters, and other personal effects.

William Wordsworth's Lake District, England

WORDSWORTH HOUSE

Main Street, Cockermouth • Cumbria • Tel: (44) 190 082 4805 • *www.nationaltrust* *.org.uk/wordsworth-house* • Open April through October; closed Fridays

English Romantic poet William Wordsworth, who composed much of his poetry on foot and is said to have walked more than 175,000 miles in his lifetime, was born in a two-story Georgian town house alongside the Lake District's River Derwent in 1770. The poet's lifelong love of nature began in his "sweet childish days," which were spent exploring his family's backyard garden and scrambling down its Terrace Walk to play on the banks of his "fairest of all rivers." Memories of the poet's early years feature heavily in his verse. Today the Wordsworth home re-creates the atmosphere of his middle-class Georgian childhood with period furnishings and tours given by costumed guides.

"Of Cockermouth that beauteous River came, Behind my Father's House he pass'd close by, Along the margin of our Terrace Walk. He was a Playmate whom we dearly lov'd."
—WORDSWORTH, "THE PRELUDE"

DOVE COTTAGE AND THE WORDSWORTH MUSEUM

Grasmere • Cumbria • Tel: (44) 153 943 5544 • *www.wordsworth.org.uk* • Open daily February through December; cottage shown by guided tour

After many years spent wandering, Wordsworth returned to his native Lake District in November 1799 on a "picturesque tour" with his sister, Dorothy, and their good friend, poet Samuel Taylor Coleridge. While at Grasmere, a tiny village nestled beside a glittering lake—"the loveliest spot that man hath ever found"—the poet spotted Dove Cottage, a vacant inn then known as the Dove and Olive Branch. The simple stone house with a slate roof became his and Dorothy's "nest in a green dale" for the

"My mind is much set upon accepting your flattering invitation to the Lakes," novelist Sir Walter Scott wrote Wordsworth in March 1805. During his visit with the teetotaling poet that summer, Scott became a regular patron in the bar at the **Swan Hotel**, a 17th-century inn that Wordsworth immortalized in his poem "The Waggoner." Visitors can still dine and doze at the historic hotel (*www.macdonaldhotels.co.uk/swan*). For more on Scott, see pages 14–16.

next decade. His years there of "plain living, but high thinking" were the most productive of his career, and he composed many of his sonnets, lyric poems, and odes during rambles around the lake. In 1802, the siblings were joined by Mary Hutchison, the poet's bride, and the first three of the couple's five children were subsequently born at Dove Cottage.

Save for the addition of electricity and plumbing, the cottage remains little changed; its small rooms contain a handful of the Wordsworths' possessions, including the poet's marital bed. An adjacent museum displays portraits, Mary Wordsworth's wedding ring, and manuscripts of verse, including the original draft of the famed poem "Daffodils."

RYDAL MOUNT AND GARDENS

Rydal (near Ambleside) • Cumbria • Tel: (44) 153 943 3002 • *www.rydalmount .co.uk* • Open daily March through October; Wednesday through Sunday, November, December, February (closed January)

After a decade of profitable writing, Wordsworth moved his family into Rydal Mount, a spacious 16th-century Tudor cottage outside Grasmere. Set amid four acres of landscaped gardens, the property became a much-loved family refuge from 1813 through the present day, when it is still occasionally occupied by the poet's descendants. Wordsworth's time at Rydal Mount was marked by both great joy and crippling sadness—he was awarded the title of Poet Laureate in 1843, but four years later, his beloved daughter, Dora, died of tuberculosis, and the traumatic event stilled his pen.

In March 1850, the 80-year-old poet caught a cold while on one of his long country walks; he died at Rydal Mount a few weeks later. Wordsworth was laid to rest at St. Oswald's Churchyard in Grasmere.

In the third floor attic study, added to the house by Wordsworth, are his inkstand, manuscripts, and books such as an encyclopedia and Bible. Also displayed is a sword that belonged to his brother John, recovered from the shipwreck in which he perished.

The house's surrounding terraced gardens remain much as the green-thumbed poet designed them. At their edge lies the rustic wood and stone "summer house" where he composed verse in warmer months.

The Lady of the Lakes

WORDSWORTH WASN'T THE LAKE DISTRICT'S only creative prodigy. Beatrix Potter, a Londoner by birth, spent many childhood summers in the area, drawing inspiration for her cuddly illustrations from the region's flora and fauna. With the proceeds from her wildly successful first book, *The Tale of Peter Rabbit*, Potter purchased **Hill Top** (*www.nationaltrust.org.uk/hill-top*), a 17th-century slate and stone farmhouse, in 1905. The ivy-clad farm and surrounding village of Near Sawrey were immortalized in the pages of her later works. Upon her death in 1943, Potter—an avid conservationist—bequeathed the property and 4,000 acres of surrounding land (upon which she had raised prize-winning sheep) to the National Trust, stipulating that Hill Top remain exactly as she had left it. In addition to her rustic oak furniture, including a carved bedstead, desk, and dresser, each perfectly preserved room contains something that appeared in her books, such as the kitchen stove on which mouse pie was cooked in *The Tale of the Pie and the Patty-Pan*.

MORE PLACES TO POTTER ABOUT

Jemima Puddleduck waddled past the **Tower Bank Arms** (*www.tower bankarms.co.uk*), a charming 17th-century Lakeland inn that still offers refreshing pints, hearty meals, and cozy rooms.

Many of Potter's original watercolors can be seen at the nearby **Beatrix Potter Gallery** (*www.nationaltrust.org.uk*) in Hawkshead, located on the premises of her husband's former law offices—better known as Tabitha Twitchit's shop in *The Tale of the Pie and the Patty-Pan*.

The Tale of Timmy Tiptoes and *The Tale of Pigland Bland* were illustrated while Potter stayed at Lindeth Howe overlooking Lake Windermere. Then a summer home that Potter and her family frequently rented, Potter eventually purchased the grand house for her mother, and today it's the **Lindeth Howe Country House Hotel** (*www.lindeth-howe.co.uk*).

The 17th-century **Yew Tree Farm** (*www.yewtree-farm.com*) was rescued from developers by Potter, who encouraged the tenants to open a tearoom. The writer furnished the quaint eatery with antiques and curios that remain there today.

Thomas Hardy Country, Dorset, England

HARDY'S COTTAGE

Higher Bockhampton (near Dorchester)
• Tel: (44) 130 526 2366 • *www.nationaltrust.org.uk/hardys-cottage* • Open Wednesday through Sunday, March through October

"The town man finds what he seeks in the novels of the country," wrote Thomas Hardy, who achieved fame for immortalizing the bucolic farms, green rolling hills, and thatched villages of his native Dorset. In the pages of his dark, fatalistic novels, his rural Dorset landscapes were thinly disguised as the "partly real, partly dream country" of Wessex. "It was in the chapters of *Far From the Madding Crowd* . . . that I first attempted to adopt the word *Wessex* from the pages of early English history and give it a fictitious significance," he explained of his invocation of the region's ancient Saxon name.

In a tiny hamlet surrounded by woodlands, the author was born on June 2, 1840, inside a thatch-roofed cottage built by his great-grandfather. Hardy lived there for most of his first 34 years, initially toiling as an architect while harboring dreams of becoming a writer. Portions of his early novels *Under the Greenwood Tree* and *Far From the Madding Crowd* were penned in his second-floor bedroom. A short walk from the cottage on the edge of Thorncombe Wood lies a visitor center shedding light on the author's life and works.

MAX GATE

Alington Avenue, Dorchester • Tel: (44) 130 526 2538 • *www.nationaltrust.org.uk/max-gate* • Open Tuesday through Sunday afternoons, March through September

"We have no boilers, no gas, we use oil-lamps and candles for lighting and have no bathroom even," Florence Hardy, the writer's second wife, complained of the primitive conditions at her husband's beloved Max Gate. In the 1880s, the author-architect had designed the turreted redbrick Victorian villa on a windswept heath near the town of his birth. His two controversial masterpieces, *Tess of the d'Urbervilles* and *Jude the Obscure,* were penned in the study, where he started work each day punctually at 10 a.m.

An intensely private man who burned most of his notebooks and correspondence to thwart biographers, Hardy spent long days writing and walking on nearby country lanes. Despite his reclusiveness, the author enjoyed hosting visitors for tea in the drawing room, which saw an unending stream of guests during his twilight years. Virginia Woolf, who visited in 1926, noted in her diary that the "little puffy cheeked cheerful old man" had impressed her with "his freedom, ease and vitality"; E. M. Forster was less enthusiastic, finding Hardy "a very vain, conventional, uninteresting old gentleman."

After the 1895 publication of *Jude the Obscure* caused a furor by challenging Victorian conventions of marriage and sexuality— reviewers called it "Jude the Obscene" and a bishop publicly burned a copy—Hardy primarily stuck to writing poetry. Today regarded as one of England's finest novelists, he passed away at Max Gate in 1928.

THE DORSET COUNTY MUSEUM

High West Street, Dorchester • Tel: (44) 130 526 2735 • *www.dorsetcounty museum.org* • Open Monday through Saturday year-round

"Casterbridge announced old Rome in every street, alley and precinct. It looked Roman, bespoke the art of Rome, concealed dead men of Rome," penned Hardy in *The Mayor of Casterbridge.* Roman ruins and Tudor houses rub shoulders in the ancient market town of Dorchester, the fictional Casterbridge in Hardy's novel. The original manuscript is housed in the Dorset County Museum, where Hardy's Max Gate study has been relocated in its entirety.

STINSFORD

This tiny village became Mellstock in Hardy's early novel *Under the Greenwood Tree*. Hardy was christened at Stinsford's 13th-century church and his parents and his wives are buried in the churchyard. The author wanted to be laid to rest in his beloved Dorset countryside, but in a morbid compromise, his wishes were only

For more about the London cathedral Westminster Abbey, see page 99.

partly granted. As a distinguished man of letters, his ashes were interred in Westminster Abbey, while his heart was buried at St. Michael's Churchyard in Stinsford.

BERE REGIS

Disguised as Kingsbere in *Tess of the D'Urbervilles,* Bere Regis was home to the aristocratic Turberville family, from whose name Hardy derived the ancestral moniker of his ill-fated heroine, Tess. At **St. John the Baptist Church**, Tess and her family take refuge underneath the beautiful 16th-century stained-glass Turberville window after being evicted from their cottage. The Turberville family vault lies underneath the south aisle of the church.

GEORGE SAND'S MAJORCA, SPAIN

CARTUJA DE VALLDEMOSSA MONASTERY

Valldemossa • Majorca • *www.cartujadevalldemossa.com* • Open daily except Sundays in December and January

"We are planted between heaven and earth," French feminist scribe George Sand wrote of the 14th-century monastery where she and her lover Frédéric Chopin and her two small children settled in December 1838. "The clouds cross our garden at their own will and pleasure, and the eagles clamor over our heads," she wrote of the austere place. The foursome had left Paris for the winter, traveling to the Spanish isle of Majorca, in hopes the temperate climate would benefit Sand's sickly son and Chopin's consumption.

But their rustic, if charming, abode in the remote village of Valldemossa was no safe harbor. The stone walls of the monastery conferred a bone-chilling damp, exacerbated by Spartan furnishings and a lack of proper heating. Even worse, a vengeful winter mistral soon set in, bringing lashing gales of wind and endless rains. "Fifty days had passed without being able to descend to the plain; the roads had become torrents, and we did not see the sun," wrote Sand.

Chopin's physical and mental condition deteriorated, rendering him housebound and prone to fits of terror in the dank monastery. The isolated couple found themselves shunned by locals, who were terrified of contagion and scandalized by the pair's unconventional lifestyle. As winter advanced, Sand became gripped by sadness, noting, "Death seemed to hover over our heads to seize one of us, and we were alone in contending with him for his prey." The specter of Chopin's demise forced them to flee the island on a steamboat carrying pigs a mere 98 days after their arrival. Sand lamented bitterly, "There is no other way of leaving this cursed country." Although the composer survived, his health—and his relationship with Sand—never fully recovered from the strains of the ill-fated Majorca winter. The centuries-old monastery that Sand once called "the most romantic abode in the world" is now a museum set amid a vista of orange, olive, and cypress trees.

Sand's stay on the island became the subject of her memoir, *Winter in Majorca*. See page 136 for information on her French château.

Lining its soaring, arched corridors, which had once "delighted themselves of [Chopin's] melodies," are various monks' cells, the most famous being numbers 2 and 4, occupied by the author and composer. In a December 1838 letter to a friend, Chopin seemed less than enthusiastic about the simple accommodations, describing his cell as being "in the shape of a coffin, high, and full of dust on the vault." Today the rooms house mementos from their stay, including some of Sand's manuscripts, Chopin's notes, and the composer's beloved Pleyel piano, which had been arduously transported up the mountain by donkey just two weeks prior to their sudden departure.

Jack London's Sonoma Valley, California

Literature meets nature at the 1,400-acre **Jack London State Historic Park**. Visitors can picnic, hike, bike, and horseback ride, as well as view London's homes and grave site. Guided tours are given on weekends, or an audio tour app is available for download.

"I ride over my beautiful ranch . . . The air is wine. The grapes on a score of rolling hills are red with autumn flame . . . The afternoon sun smolders in the drowsy sky. I have everything to make me glad I am alive."
—JOHN BARLEYCORN

JACK LONDON STATE HISTORIC PARK

2400 London Ranch Road • Glen Ellen • Tel: 707-938-5216

• *www.jacklondonpark.com* • Open daily

"Next to my wife, the ranch is the dearest thing in the world to me," Jack London confided to his editor in October 1914. Nine years earlier, the then 29-year-old writer had purchased the first parcel of what was to become 1,400 acres of Sonoma Valley ranch land. With monies earned from his best-selling adventure novels, including *The Call of the Wild* and *The Sea-Wolf,* the onetime hobo, sailor, itinerant laborer, and world traveler had embarked on a journey of a different kind—the creation of a bucolic Eden. Newly married to his second wife, Charmian, he threw himself into his agrarian dream. With customary gusto, he set out to make **Beauty Ranch** a shining example of a "ranch of good intentions" by using organic and sustainable agriculture techniques to cultivate vegetables, grains, and livestock.

Kenwood Vineyards (*www.kenwoodvineyards.com*) owns the grapevines that were once part of Beauty Ranch, and they are used to produce a Jack London series of wines. Each bottle bears a wolf etching similar to that used on the frontispiece of the author's books.

"I have pledged myself, my manhood, my fortune, my books, and all I possess to this undertaking," he once declared. And until his untimely demise in 1916, he dedicated himself to Beauty Ranch, "devoting two hours a day to writing and ten to farming." Though he continued to churn out a thousand words a day, the quality of his writing deteriorated and he readily admitted, "I write a book for no other reason than to add . . . to my magnificent estate."

JACK LONDON COTTAGE

Open daily, afternoons

In 1911, the writer purchased a modest wood-frame bungalow—formerly the headquarters of an abandoned winery—in the midst of his sprawling acreage. There he penned dozens of articles, stories, and books, including *John Barleycorn,* an autobiographical account of his struggle with alcoholism. Although the cottage was intended as an interim residence during the building of London's dream home, Wolf House, the cruel hand of fate intervened when the latter burned to the ground in an inexplicable blaze. The 40-year-old writer mysteriously passed away three years later after falling into a coma on the cottage's sun porch during the night of November 21, 1916. His cause of death was attributed to kidney failure.

Although the cottage fell into ruin after Charmian London's death in 1955, it has since been restored with both real and replica artifacts belonging to the Londons, including the writer's rolltop desk, Dictaphone, and souvenirs from the couple's two-year South Pacific sail.

WOLF HOUSE RUINS

"My house will be standing, act of God permitting, for a thousand years," London proclaimed of the magnificent dream home he was having built on Beauty Ranch. The 15,000-square-foot mansion, hewn from volcanic stone and redwood trees, ironically went up in smoke just days shy of its completion in 1913. At the time, the Londons believed arson was to blame, but later experiments determined the blaze was likely caused by oily rags that spontaneously combusted. Today, only the moss-covered ruins of the stone walls remain as an eerie memorial to Wolf House's ephemeral existence.

HOUSE OF HAPPY WALLS MUSEUM

Open daily

Three years after her husband's death, Charmian London built this stone house as her Beauty Ranch residence. As her will directed, the house later became a memorial to the writer with photographs and exhibits depicting his life of adventure. Other objects on display include custom-designed furnishings the Londons had originally intended to use in Wolf House and a scale model of the *Snark,* the yacht on which they sailed the South Pacific.

SCENIC TRAILS

The park's trail network ranges from back country hikes to easily accessible pathways leading to Wolf House and sites around Beauty Ranch, including London's self-designed circular Pig Palace, which gave each porcine family its own "apartment," and a grove of 81,000 eucalyptus trees the writer had planted on bad investment advice.

WINERY RUINS

In the summer, the ruins of an old winery building are the site of musical revues and concerts staged by Broadway Under the Stars (*www.transcendencetheatre.org*).

GRAVE SITE

The ashes of Jack and Charmian London are buried in a simple grave marked by a large red boulder on a knoll overlooking the valley.

Southern Comfort

MARGARET MITCHELL HOUSE

Atlanta, GA • 990 Peachtree Street • Tel: 404-249-7015 • *www.margaretmitchell house.com* • Open daily

While Margaret Mitchell was convalescing from an injured ankle in 1926, her husband presented her with a portable typewriter and the declaration, "Madam, I greet you on the beginning of a great new career." Concealing her endeavor from family and friends, Mitchell spent the better part of a decade writing the sweeping Civil War–era saga *Gone with the Wind*.

The Margaret Mitchell House is located in a Tudor Revival mansion that during the author's tenure was an apartment building where she and her husband occupied a small, ground-floor unit from 1925 to 1932. Along with guided and self-guided tours of Mitchell's apartment, the museum includes three exhibits. "Margaret Mitchell: A Passion for Character" illuminates her life from childhood to her years as a

The typewriter Mitchell used to write *Gone with the Wind* is on view in the **Margaret Mitchell Exhibit** at the Atlanta-Fulton Public Library (1 Margaret Mitchell Square; 404-730-1700) along with her Pulitzer Prize, her library card, and other memorabilia.

reporter for the *Atlanta Journal* to the frenzy that erupted after the publication of her only novel, which garnered a Pulitzer Prize and inspired a blockbuster movie. "The Making of a Film Legend: *Gone with the Wind*" features two notable props—a life-size portrait of Vivien Leigh as Scarlett O'Hara and the doorway to the O'Hara plantation, Tara—while "Stars Fall on Atlanta" focuses on the 1939 film premiere. Also on display is the suitcase purchased by a book editor to transport Mitchell's voluminous manuscript.

The Margaret Mitchell House is owned and operated by the Atlanta History Center, which regularly hosts author lectures and other events.

FLANNERY O'CONNOR CHILDHOOD HOME

Savannah, GA • 207 East Charlton Street • Tel: 912-233-6014 • *www.flannery oconnorhome.org* • Open Friday through Wednesday afternoons

In the history-rich coastal town of Savannah, the oldest city in Georgia, Mary Flannery O'Connor was born on March 25, 1925. She spent her first 13 years residing in a town house bordering Lafayette Square, one of 21 picturesque squares in this city distinctive for its antebellum architecture and abundant gardens.

The rooms on the two main floors of the Flannery O'Connor Childhood Home

Another historic dwelling on Lafayette Square is the **Hamilton-Turner Inn** (*www .hamilton-turnerinn.com*), where rooms are named for famous figures with Savannah ties. The Flannery O'Connor Room features bright blue walls, a decorative iron bed, and French doors opening onto a courtyard patio.

LITERARY LODGING: As a young debutante, Margaret Mitchell scandalized the Junior League with an evocative dance routine during a ball at **The Georgian Terrace** hotel, which led to her being blackballed by the organization. It was also at The Georgian that Mitchell handed over the manuscript of her soon-to-be-famous novel to an editor. Later the hotel hosted Clark Gable, Vivien Leigh, and other Hollywood stars attending the premiere of the big-screen version of *Gone with the Wind* (*www.thegeorgianterrace.com*).

have been restored to their appearance at the time the future scribe and her family occupied the residence. (Then a single family home, the top floors and basement are now private apartments.) The house contains original furnishings, including a crib and a child's tea table in O'Connor's bedroom.

While living in this Savannah home, five-year-old O'Connor developed a lifelong affinity for domestic birds. A news organization once sent a photographer to take a picture of her pet chicken, which could perform the unusual feat of walking either forward or backward. O'Connor later called the event "the high point in my life." She added, "Everything since has been anticlimax."

FLANNERY O'CONNOR'S ANDALUSIA FARM

Milledgeville, GA • 2628 North Columbia Street • Tel: 478-454-4029 • www.andalusiafarm.org • Open Thursday through Sunday

Best known for her short story collections *A Good Man Is Hard to Find* and *Everything That Rises Must Converge*, O'Connor also penned the novels *Wise Blood* and *The Violent Bear It Away*. Her southern gothic fiction often used rural Georgia as its backdrop and combined themes of religion with dark comedy. "My subject in fiction," she once said, "is the action of grace in territory held largely by the devil."

On her mother's family farm outside Milledgeville in central Georgia, Flannery O'Connor devoted herself to two great loves: writing and raising peacocks, swans, chickens, and other birds. She spent the last of her 39 years, before dying of complications from lupus, amid Andalusia's pastoral beauty, which inspired the settings for such stories as "A Circle in the Fire," "Good Country People," and "The Displaced Person."

FLANNERY FACTS: The **Flannery O'Connor Room** at the museum of her alma mater, Georgia College and State University (221 North Clarke Street; 478-445-4391), in Milledgeville, displays memorabilia such as her writing desk, typewriter, and a painting she created. (Friends once speculated she would be an artist rather than a writer.)

O'Connor is buried by her parents in Milledgeville's **Memory Hill Cemetery** (300 West Franklin Street; *www.friendsofcems.org/memoryhill*).

After O'Connor passed away, her mother moved to a house in Milledgeville and left Andalusia and its contents behind. The white farmhouse at the center of O'Connor's world is "a time capsule," says Craig R. Amason, former director of the Flannery O'Connor-Andalusia Foundation. "It's like walking back into the 1960s." Tours include a view of the writer's ground-floor bedroom, which doubled as her writing space. The sparsely decorated room contains O'Connor's bed and the aluminum crutches she relied upon as her disease advanced and her mobility deteriorated. "It's a very poignant scene for a lot of people," says Amason.

Visitors can watch the PBS movie adaptation of "The Displaced Person" (filmed at the farm in 1976) and walk the grounds—basking, as O'Connor did, in Andalusia's tranquility.

SMITH-MCCULLERS HOUSE MUSEUM

Columbus, GA • 1519 Stark Avenue • Tel: 706-570-8464 • *www.mccullerscenter .org* • Advance booking required

A craftsman-style bungalow on a quiet street in Columbus was the childhood home of novelist, playwright, and short story writer Carson McCullers (born Lula Carson Smith on February 19, 1917).

The Smith-McCullers House is part of Columbus State University's Carson McCullers Center for Writers and Musicians and is a combination museum and venue for writers' receptions, literary discussions, and other educational and cultural programming. The museum collection includes an array of items owned by McCullers such as her typewriter, portable phonograph, ashtray and cigarette lighter, personal stationery, eyeglasses, and trunks used during her travels, which included several European sojourns. Visitors to the house are shown original film footage of the writer,

Carson McCullers spent much of her life in and around New York City. In 1944 she moved with her mother and sister to Nyack, New York, a town along the Hudson River that she called her adopted home. The **Carson McCullers House**, a Victorian dwelling at 131 South Broadway, is part of the Carson McCullers Center for Writers and Musicians and hosts author readings and other events. McCullers is buried in Nyack's **Oak Hill Cemetery** (140 North Highland Avenue; *www.oakhillcemetery nyack.com*).

including a home movie of her 1937 wedding to Reeves McCullers, whom she married in the house's parlor.

Best known for her novels *The Heart Is a Lonely Hunter* and *The Member of the Wedding,* McCullers's life was marked by ill health. Due to a misdiagnosed and untreated childhood case of rheumatic fever, she suffered a series of cerebral strokes (the first one at 24) and died at the age of 50.

Due to its McCullers connection, Columbus—reminiscent of *The Heart Is a Lonely Hunter*'s mill town setting—is part of the **Southern Literary Trail** (*www.southernliterarytrail.org*), which highlights literary landmarks in Alabama, Georgia, and Mississippi.

EUDORA WELTY HOUSE

Jackson, MS • 1119 Pinehurst Street

• Tel: 601-353-7762 • www.eudorawelty.org

• Open Tuesday through Friday; guided tours only; reservations recommended

The house was on a slight hill . . . covered with its original forest pines, on a gravel road then a little out from town, and was built in a style very much of its day, of stucco and brick and beams in the Tudor style.

—Eudora Welty, *One Writer's Beginnings*

"Human life is fiction's only theme," asserted Eudora Welty. A writer, photographer, gardener, and world traveler, the various aspects of her multifaceted life are evident in the home that served as her primary residence for more than 76 years, from the age of 16 until her death in 2001. The Eudora Welty House (which Welty bequeathed to the state of Mississippi) displays her possessions much as she left them, including furniture, artwork, and a voluminous collection of books. The dwelling is "one of the most intact literary houses in America," says Mary Alice White, the writer's niece and former director of the Eudora

Welty and her mother were avid gardeners, and references to plants and gardening abound in Welty's works. The now-restored Welty House gardens include sections devoted to roses (her mother's favorite flower) and camellias (the writer's preferred bloom). To take a virtual tour of the Welty house and gardens, visit *www.mdah.state.ms.us/welty.*

Welty House. "Visitors often comment that the home seems as if Eudora had just stepped out and will return at any time."

Welty's oeuvre includes the story collection *A Curtain of Green*, her first published book, and the Pulitzer Prize–winning novel *The Optimist's Daughter*. She crafted her unique brand of southern fiction at a desk in her bedroom overlooking a leafy, landscaped yard. On display in this spacious abode are cherished possessions, like a piano presented to nine-year-old Eudora by her parents; an antique comb, brush, and mirror set; a whimsical lamp featuring a dancing bear (made from a Venetian vase she brought back from her travels); and a 24-volume set of Charles Dickens's works that her mother once braved a burning house to rescue.

WILLIAM FAULKNER'S ROWAN OAK

Oxford, MS • Old Taylor Road • Tel: 662-234-3284 • *www.rowanoak.com* • Open daily, June and July; closed Mondays, August through May

An elegant residence graced by an oak-lined pathway, William Faulkner's Rowan Oak estate was in shambles when the writer purchased it in 1930. He completed much of the restoration himself, wielding hammer and saw to create a sanctuary where he lived for more than three decades.

FAULKNER COUNTRY: Faulkner was born in New Albany, Mississippi, on September 25, 1897, and his family moved to Oxford the day before his fifth birthday. Oxford and its environs serve as models for Faulkner's fictional landscape of Yoknapatawpha County, first evoked in *Sartoris* and later in *The Sound and the Fury* and other tales. "I discovered that my own little postage stamp of native soil was worth writing about," he said. To explore sites associated with Faulkner and his fiction, the brochure **"Faulkner Country"** is available at Visit Oxford (1013 Jackson Avenue East; *www.visitoxfordms.com*). On Oxford's main square, a **Faulkner statue** sits on a bench outside City Hall and **Square Books** (160 Courthouse Square; *www.squarebooks.com*) has an expansive section devoted to the writer. Faulkner's grave is located in **Saint Peter's Cemetery** (Jefferson Avenue and North 16th Street).

The moniker Faulkner bestowed on the house comes from a Celtic legend about the rowan tree, which is believed to harbor powers of safety and protection.

Rowan Oak was sold by Faulkner's daughter to the University of Mississippi in 1972, with the understanding that it was not to become a commercialized property. "Rowan Oak is hard to find, no signs, but worth the trouble," says curator William Griffith. Once visitors cross the house's threshold, they enter the intensely private author's personal and professional domains. Scrawled on the wall in Faulkner's office is the plot outline for his novel *A Fable,* which garnered a Pulitzer Prize in 1954. In the library, where the writer employed his carpentry skills to create built-in bookshelves, rests a wooden bust of Don Quixote. The rendering of Miguel Cervantes's fictional explorer was a gift from the president of Venezuela after Faulkner visited the country on a goodwill mission at the request of the U.S. State Department. A pair of boots is on display in Faulkner's bedroom, where the slumbering scribe's "alarm clock" was a mockingbird that imitated the sound of traffic on nearby roads. In 1962, the author's funeral was held in Rowan Oak's parlor.

IVY GREEN, HELEN KELLER'S BIRTHPLACE

Tuscumbia, AL • 300 West North Commons • Tel: 256-383-4066
• *www.helenkellerbirthplace.org* • Open Monday through Saturday

Playwright William Gibson's dramatization of the young Helen Keller's life, *The Miracle Worker*, is staged at Ivy Green on weekends in June and July. The **Helen Keller Festival** takes place annually in June with music, art exhibits, historical activities, and more at various venues in Tuscumbia.

On a verdant estate in northwestern Alabama, Helen Keller saw none of the beauty that graced the land—magnolia trees, roses, honeysuckle, and the English ivy that inspired the plantation's name. Born at Ivy Green, the home of her grandparents, Keller was stricken at 19 months with an illness that left her blind and deaf. She remained in a dark world until teacher Anne Sullivan entered her life. At a pump still standing at Ivy Green, the "miracle worker" poured water over one of seven-year-old Keller's hands while on the other she tapped out an alphabetic code that spelled the corresponding five-letter word. By day's end, Keller had learned 30 words and soon mastered writing and reading in Braille. In 1904, she graduated from Radcliffe College, one year after the publication of her autobiography, *The Story of My Life*. Keller devoted herself to improving conditions for the blind and the deaf-blind, lecturing in more than 25 countries.

On Ivy Green's grounds is the two-room cottage that was transformed into a bridal suite for Keller's parents and where she was born on June 27, 1880. The plantation's main house—built in 1820, the second house in Tuscumbia—contains family furnishings, china and silver, and other items such as a sugar chest, where the rare commodity was kept under lock and key. Personal mementos that belonged to Keller are on display, including her library of Braille books and original Braille typewriter. Situated between the main house and the cottage is the well-pump where Keller first learned to communicate under Sullivan's inspired tutelage.

THOMAS WOLFE MEMORIAL

Asheville, NC • 52 North Market Street • Tel: 828-253-8304 •
www.wolfememorial.com • Open Tuesday through Saturday

"I don't know yet what I am capable of doing," 23-year-old Thomas Wolfe wrote to his mother, "but, by God, I have genius—I know it too well to blush behind it." The young writer proved his boldly confident assertion six years later with the publication of *Look Homeward, Angel*, a fictionalized account of his boyhood in Asheville, which angered some of the town's residents. In his debut novel and its sequel, *Of Time and the River*, Wolfe immortalized his mother's Old Kentucky Home boardinghouse, where he lived as a boy. Renamed Dixieland in the novels, the 29-room mansion with its "rambling, unplanned, gabular appearance" is now part of the Thomas Wolfe Memorial.

A foray into Wolfe's days in this Blue Ridge Mountain town begins in the Visitors Center adjacent to the Old Kentucky

Wolfe is buried in Asheville's **Riverside Cemetery** (*www.cr.nps.gov*), beneath a tombstone with a line from *Look Homeward, Angel*: "The last voyage, the longest, the best." Also buried in this cemetery is William Sydney Porter (aka O. Henry). See pages 56–57 for more on Porter.

Home, where a film about his life is shown and an exhibit showcases personal effects, including his Harvard University diploma. Guided tours visit the boardinghouse, which has been restored to its appearance in 1916, the year Wolfe left Asheville to attend college. Chambers include the elegantly appointed dining room where Wolfe's mother served meals to boarders; the glass-paned sun parlor, a gathering place for dancing and listening to music; and the bedroom where the author stayed during a 1937 visit to Asheville. The visit turned out to be his last. Wolfe died from tubercular meningitis in Baltimore on September 15, 1938, less than three weeks short of his 38th birthday. A self-guided tour around Asheville, "From Cradle to Grave: Walking in Thomas Wolfe's Shoes," can be downloaded on the Memorial's website.

ON TENNESSEE WILLIAMS'S TRAIL, NEW ORLEANS, LOUISIANA

"If I can be said to have a home," declared Tennessee Williams, "it is New Orleans, which has provided me with more material than any other part of the country." The playwright lived in the city's picturesque French Quarter (see photo), and visiting the haunts he once frequented is still possible today.

Dine at **Galatoire's** (*www.galatoires.com*), where Williams could often be found at his preferred corner table and where Stella takes Blanche in *A Streetcar Named Desire*. Check into the **Maison de Ville**'s Tennessee Williams Suite, the same room in which the writer slept. He often worked in the adjoining courtyard and even recorded a television interview in the scenic space (*www.maisondeville.com*). Wind down your evening by toasting the writer at **Lafitte's Blacksmith Shop** (*www.lafittesblacksmithshop.com*) on Bourbon Street. This candlelit tavern was one of his favorite watering holes.

COLUMBUS, MISSISSIPPI

Tennessee Williams once described his first home, the rectory of St. Paul's Episcopal Church, where his grandfather served as reverend, as "very southern Gothic." The multicolored Victorian abode with twin gables and gingerbread trim was moved to its present location at 300 Main Street and given new life as the town's **Tennessee Williams Welcome Center**, where information about the writer is available. Each year in September, Columbus honors the writer with the **Tennessee Williams Tribute**, a multiday series of events, exhibits, and plays (*www.visitcolumbusms.org*).

CLARKSDALE, MISSISSIPPI

In 1916, Williams and his family moved to Clarksdale, where his grandfather served as pastor at St. George's Episcopal Church. The Coahoma County Tourism Commission offers a map of the historic district marked with sites related to Williams and his plays. The town stages the **Mississippi Delta Tennessee Williams Festival** annually in October with front porch readings of Williams's plays, along with a "Stella Calling Contest" (in commemoration of the well-known scene in *A Streetcar Named Desire*), and other events (*www.visitclarksdale.com*).

POETIC JUSTICE

ROBERT BURNS COUNTRY

ROBERT BURNS BIRTHPLACE MUSEUM

Ayrshire, Scotland • Murdoch's Lone, Alloway • Tel: (44) 129 244 3700
• www.burnsmuseum.org.uk • Open daily year-round

William Wordsworth and John Keats were among the first literary tourists who came to Alloway to drink in the lush landscapes that inspired the poems and songs of Robert Burns. All of the attractions below are within easy walking distance of Burns Cottage.

BURNS COTTAGE AND BURNS MUSEUM

The son of a poor tenant farmer who spent much of his youth engaged in manual labor, Robert Burns found relief from his physical toils in the exercise of putting pen to paper.

See page 144 for information on **Burns Night Suppers**, which take place annually on the date of the poet's birth.

From humble beginnings in a thatch-roofed cottage on January 25, 1759, Burns went on to achieve international celebrity by the time of his death 37 years later. During his short life, he wrote more than 600 popular poems and songs in the Scottish vernacular, including the world's universal anthem of parting, "Auld Lang Syne." In the tiny, well-preserved cottage of his youth, a single room functioned as both the family's kitchen and living quarters, while a small adjoining room housed the livestock.

A short walk from Burns Cottage, a modernized museum houses hundreds of Burns artifacts. Its treasures include the manuscript of the famous "Auld Lang Syne," journals the poet kept during his travels around Scotland, and a windowpane from an old inn that Burns inscribed with a stanza of poetry.

AULD KIRK ALLOWAY

"Kirk Alloway was drawing nigh, / Where ghaists and houlets nightly cry."
—**"Tam o' Shanter"**

Surrounded by moss-covered headstones, the crumbling, roof-less 16th-century ruins of "Alloway's auld haunted kirk"(old church) inspired many a ghost tale during Burns's time. These stories, imparted to the poet as a youngster, became fodder for his comical and cautionary epic poem, "Tam o' Shanter." Riding his trusty steed past the church after a late night of over-indulging in drink, errant farmer Tam sees firelight flickering and draws in for a closer look. An incredulous scene plays out before him—a wild party hosted by the devil himself, who plays the bagpipes in accompaniment to the frenzied dancing of warlocks and witches. When Tam cries out, the otherworldly creatures give chase, and the heroic Tam races to save his life by escaping over the River Doon—the "running stream they dare na cross." In addition to providing ghoulish inspiration for the poet, the Auld Kirk was a sacred place for Burns as well; his father was laid to rest here in 1784.

In nearby Ayr, the 18th-century thatch-roofed pub **Tam o'Shanter** (230 High Street) is where the poet's hero, Tam, knocked back a few rounds before setting off for home.

BRIG O' DOON
This 13th-century humpbacked bridge spanning the River Doon was the only crossing in the village when Burns lived in Alloway, and the poet immortalized it in the scene where Tam's mare jumps to safety in the terrifying climax of "Tam o' Shanter."

BURNS MONUMENT AND GARDENS
In the early 19th century, fans of the poet raised funds to erect this enormous circular Corinthian-columned temple, the country's first monument to the Scottish bard. The viewing platform on the 70-foot-high structure offers spectacular views of the lush surrounding countryside, including Burns Cottage, Auld Kirk Alloway, and the Brig o' Doon.

W. B. Yeats Country, County Sligo, Ireland

Although born in Dublin, Nobel Prize–winning poet William Butler Yeats spent many childhood summers in Ireland's northwest countryside surrounding Sligo, where his grandparents lived. His verse immortalized the iconic landscapes of the region, which were also captured on canvas by his brother Jack, an illustrator and painter.

See pages 10–11 for more on Yeats's Abbey Theatre in Dublin.

THE LAKE ISLE OF INNISFREE, LOUGH GILL
Innisfree, one of 22 islands situated in the jewel-toned Lough (lake) Gill, inspired one of Yeats's first great poems, written in London after the poet heard a tinkling fountain that reminded him of his beloved lake. Boat tours (*www.roseofinnisfree.com*) with onboard recitals of Yeats's poetry cruise Lough Gill to Innisfree during summer months; alternately, opt for the roadside circuit around the lake on the 26-mile Lough Gill Drive.

DRUMCLIFFE

In an emerald valley underneath the majestic mountain Ben Bulben lies the picturesque village of Drumcliffe, where Yeats's great-
grandfather served as rector in the early 19th century. At the poet's
request, he was laid to rest in the town's tiny churchyard, marked by
a gravestone with a haunting epitaph taken from the final lines of
"Under Ben Bulben," one of his last poems.

GLENCAR LAKE AND WATERFALL

This enchanting waterfall eight miles north of Sligo, reachable via a
peaceful wooded walk, inspired one of Yeats's early works.

KNOCKNAREA (SACRED HILL)

A 45-minute walk up a stony path leads to the top of humpbacked
Knocknarea and the 200-foot-long burial cairn of Queen Maeve,
a mythological Iron Age warrior. Sweeping panoramas of County
Sligo await.

LISSADELL HOUSE AND GARDENS

Set on Drumcliffe Bay with views of Ben Bulben and Knocknarea
mountains in the distance, this 19th-century Greek Revival–style
manor house was the childhood home of Countess Constance
Markievicz—"the countess of Irish freedom"—and her sister, Eva
Gore-Booth, an activist and poet. Yeats was friends with the sisters
and stayed at Lissadell House in 1894. The manse (*www.lissadell
house.com*) is open to the public seasonally.

THOOR BALLYLEE

County Galway, Ireland • Located 4 miles northeast of the
town of Gort: 0.6 mile off N18 (Galway-Limerick road) and
0.6 mile off N66 (Gort-Limerick road) • Tel: (353) 91 63 14
36 or (353) 91 53 77 00 • www.yeatsthoorballylee.org
• Open daily, mid-June through September

"I came here to take over my Tower, Ballylee
Castle," wrote Yeats in a 1917 letter to his father

shortly after his purchase of the crumbling Norman structure in the Irish countryside. "I shall make it habitable . . . It is certainly a beautiful place." Yeats lovingly restored the four-story tower, which he called by its Gaelic name, Thoor, and spent many idyllic summers there with his wife and two children. For him, it was "a place full of history and romance" that inspired some of his later masterful works, including "The Tower" and "The Winding Stair." He often wrote in the tower's "great ground floor" with its "wide window opening over the river and a round arched door leading to the thatched hall" where a spiral stone staircase led to a roof platform with sweeping views. Although he wrote in 1922 that "to go anywhere else is to leave beauty behind," his busy life after winning the Nobel Prize and gaining election to the new Irish Senate rendered his visits to Thoor Ballylee increasingly infrequent. After 1928, he never again returned and the tower sank back into its former ruinous state until it was rescued by The Kiltartan Society several decades later. Today the place the poet called "a permanent symbol of my work, plainly visible to the passer-by" remains exactly that.

"An ancient bridge, and a more ancient tower, A farmhouse that is sheltered by its wall, An acre of stony ground, Where the symbolic rose can break in flower" —"MEDITATIONS IN A TIME OF CIVIL WAR"

BRITISH POETS

JOHN MILTON'S COTTAGE

Chalfont St. Giles, England • 21 Deanway • Tel: (44) 149 487 2313 • *www.miltonscottage.org* • Open Wednesday through Saturday afternoons, April through October

The great English poet, civil servant, and champion of liberty John Milton came to this timber-frame cottage outside of London in 1665 to escape the Great Plague, which was then ravaging the city. While here, the blind poet completed his masterpiece epic poem, *Paradise Lost*, which—amazingly—was composed entirely in his head and dictated to his secretary. (John Milton's failing eyesight as a result of glaucoma had culminated in

Mary Shelley's *Frankenstein* draws heavily on the mythical themes of creation and expulsion from Eden in *Paradise Lost*. Upon reading the poem, Victor Frankenstein's intelligent, sensitive monster comes to view his deformed visage as the polar opposite of Adam, who had "come forth from the hands of God a perfect creature."

full-fledged blindness some 13 years earlier.) The complex blank-verse poem, which was originally published in ten volumes, is thought to have taken him approximately a decade to complete.

In Milton's ancient, simply furnished cottage, visitors can view rare first editions of his poetry, including one book dating back to 1649 that was the poet's own copy. Surrounding the rustic cottage is a colorful and fragrant garden planted with many of the same varieties of flowers, fruit trees, and herbs referred to in Milton's poems.

KEATS HOUSE

Keats Grove, London, England • Tel: (44) 207 332 3868 • *www.cityoflondon.gov.uk* • Open Wednesday through Sunday, March through October; Friday through Sunday, November through February

Underappreciated during his lifetime, John Keats became one of the most revered English Romantic poets in the decades following his tragically premature death. Keats lived in a Regency-style semidetached house on the edge of London's leafy Hampstead Heath with his friend Charles Brown for two of his most productive years; in that time he composed "Ode to a Nightingale" and other intensely moving poems. "In the spring of 1819, a nightingale had built her nest near my house," Brown later recalled of the poet's muse. "Keats felt a tranquil and continual joy in her song and one morning he took his chair from the breakfast table to a grass plot under a plum-tree, where he sat for two or three hours." In honor of the moment when inspiration struck, a plum tree (see photo foreground) has been replanted.

The house proved to be propitious for romance as well as writing: While living there, Keats met neighbor Fanny Brawne, with whom he fell passionately in love. On display is the garnet engagement ring he presented to her (the poet's tuberculosis prevented the star-crossed lovers from ever wedding) along with a gold mourning brooch in the form of a Greek lyre with strands woven from Keats's hair.

See page 204 for more information on the nearby tavern, the **Spaniards Inn**, where Keats sometimes wrote.

Keats House has undergone extensive restoration, and its collection now includes a famed love letter Keats wrote to Fanny Brawne, in which he despairs that he is unable to kiss her because of his contagious illness.

KEATS-SHELLEY HOUSE

Rome, Italy • 26 Piazza di Spagna • Tel: (39) 0 66 78 42 35 • *www.keats-shelley -house.org* • Open Monday through Saturday; closed during lunch

"There is no doubt that an English winter would put an end to me, and do so in a lingering hateful manner, therefore I must either voyage or journey to Italy as a soldier marches up to a battery," Keats wrote to fellow Romantic poet Percy Shelley in August 1820.

For information on Keats's and Shelley's final resting places in the **Non-Catholic Cemetery in Rome**, see page 100. To lodge at the **Keats-Shelley House**, see page 183.

At the urging of his doctor, Keats traveled to the warmer climes of Rome in 1820 to spend what were to be the last months of his life in a vain attempt to remedy his tuberculosis. The 26-year-old died on February 23, 1821, in an 18th-century *pallazzetto* at the base of the Spanish Steps.

The house was rescued from demolition at the turn of the 19th century by Anglo-American philanthropists who lovingly restored it

LORD BYRON'S ROMAN HOLIDAY: Lord Byron also lived in Italy during the Romantic era, and in the spring of 1817, the poet journeyed from Venice to Rome. There he stayed at 66 Piazza di Spagna, opposite where Keats would reside three years later. Byron loved the city, writing to his publisher, "As a whole, ancient and modern, it beats Greece, Constantinople, everything—at least that I have ever seen." While Byron and Shelley were friends, Byron and Keats never met and shared little mutual appreciation. The Keats-Shelley House contains numerous items relating to Byron, including a Carnival mask that the poet purchased in Venice.

A year before Byron's Roman holiday, he departed England in the wake of scandal surrounding his sexual escapades. He never returned, leaving behind the centuries-old English estate he inherited at age ten. **Newstead Abbey** (*www.newsteadabbey.org.uk*) had been gifted to the Byron family by King Henry VIII.

as a museum honoring Keats and Shelley, who met his own untimely demise in Italy a mere year after Keats. A month shy of his 30th birthday, Shelley mysteriously drowned off the Tuscan coast with a volume of Keats's poetry thrust in his pocket.

Today the short but brilliant careers of the tragically fated poets are celebrated in a collection of paintings, manuscripts, and letters displayed at the museum, also home to otherworldly artifacts like Keats's death mask, Shelley's bone fragments, and locks of hair from fellow poets John Milton and Elizabeth Barrett Browning. Literary luminaries such as Rudyard Kipling and Sinclair Lewis are among those who have paid their respects to Keats in the small room where the poet drew his dying breath.

SANDBURG SITES

CARL SANDBURG STATE HISTORIC SITE

Galesburg, IL • 313 East Third Street • Tel: 309-342-2361 • *www.sandburg.org*
• Open Thursday through Sunday

The prairie sings to me . . . In the night I rest easy in the prairie arms, on the prairie heart. —Carl Sandburg, "Prairie," 1918

From humble beginnings in a three-room cottage in southern Illinois, the man the *New York Post* called "the poet of the American dream and the American reality" went on to become a quintessential American success story. Born in 1878 to poor Swedish immigrants, the poet, biographer, and folklorist won two Pulitzer Prizes during his lifetime despite having never attended high school or obtained a college degree. Instead, Carl Sandburg's education came from working odd jobs and seeing the countryside by way of freight trains: At the age of 19 he restlessly took to the road, spending four months as a hobo before enlisting in the Army during the Spanish-American War. These formative experiences went on to influence both his populist politics and his late blooming career as a writer, where he found acclaim championing the working class and portraying both rural and city life in exuberant, unvarnished verse.

Upon his death in 1967, Sandburg's ashes were returned to his Galesburg birthplace as he had requested and buried beneath a boulder known as Remembrance Rock, named after the title of his first and only novel.

CARL SANDBURG'S CONNEMARA FARM

Flat Rock, NC • 81 Carl Sandburg Lane

• Tel: 828-693-4178 • *www.nps.gov/carl* • Open daily

Although his literary career is most often associated with the bustling Windy City and the prairies of the Midwest, Carl Sandburg moved from the shores of Lake Michigan to a 248-acre antebellum estate outside of Asheville, North Carolina, in 1945. The last 22 years of his life were spent on the secluded property with his daughters, grandchildren, and wife, Lilian, who had sought the benefit of the South's greener pastures and longer grazing seasons for her goat-breeding operation.

Despite being of retirement age by the time he moved to Connemara Farm, Sandburg's productivity never waned; he produced much work, including portions of his six-volume Pulitzer Prize–winning biography of Abraham Lincoln, in the peaceful surroundings. The three-story house and its possessions were donated to the National Park Service by Mrs. Sandburg after his death in 1967.

"It is necessary . . . for a man to go away by himself . . . to sit on a rock . . . and ask, 'Who am I, where have I been, and where am I going?'" Sandburg wrote. A rock behind his home provided the poet just such a place.

Goats of the same breeds formerly raised on the farm are still bred on the property today. In addition to touring the house, visitors can take in the dairy goat barn as well as hike the five miles of trails that the Sandburg family once enjoyed. (A trail map can be downloaded off the Connemara website.)

MID-ATLANTIC POETS

EDNA ST. VINCENT MILLAY'S STEEPLETOP

Austerlitz, NY • 440 East Hill Road • Tel: 518-392-3362 • *www.millay.org*

• Open Friday through Monday, May through October; off-season tours available by appointment

Two years after winning the Pulitzer Prize for poetry in 1923 (the first woman ever to do so), bohemian wordsmith Edna St. Vincent Millay and her husband, Eugen Boissevain, bought a former blueberry farm they named Steepletop in rural eastern New York.

Steepletop—which includes a white clapboard farmhouse, a writing cabin, ice house, tennis courts, a swimming pool and outdoor bar, and extensive sunken gardens landscaped by Millay—remains much as the poet left it upon her death at the house in 1950. Along with touring the house and gardens, visitors can watch a film about life at Steepletop during the poet's day and take a quarter-mile walk to her grave site on the wooded Millay Poetry Trail, signposted with her nature poems.

WALT WHITMAN BIRTHPLACE STATE HISTORIC SITE AND INTERPRETIVE CENTER

West Hills, NY • 246 Old Walt Whitman Road
• Tel: 631-427-5240 • *www.waltwhitman.org*
• Open daily mid-June through Labor Day; winter hours: Wednesday through Friday

Walt Whitman's father, a Quaker carpenter, handcrafted the two-story, cedar-shingled farmhouse in rural Long Island where the "good gray poet" was born on May 31, 1819. Although the family moved to Brooklyn just four years later, Whitman returned to the area as an itinerant schoolteacher in his teens before briefly establishing and running a weekly local newspaper, *The Long-Islander* (still in existence today). He left during his early 20s prior to penning his liberating free verse poems such as "Song of Myself" and "I Sing the Body Electric," celebrating the human spirit. Years later, he remembered the place he had spent his formative years, writing that he had "incorporated" it. Before his death, he made a trip to the area and "rode around all the old familiar spots, viewing and pondering and dwelling long upon them, everything coming back to me from fifty years."

His family's restored farmhouse, rescued from surrounding urban sprawl in the 20th century by the Walt Whitman Birthplace Association, houses 19th-century period furniture such as an old schoolmaster's desk like the one Whitman would have used. "The birthplace and grounds quietly evoke the time and spirit of Walt Whitman, widely recognized as America's greatest poet," says Cynthia Shor, executive director of the Walt Whitman Birthplace. An interpretive center showcases portraits, letters, and manuscripts and offers the rare opportunity to hear Whitman's voice on tape reading four lines of his poem "America," which were extracted from an original Edison wax cylinder. Observant visitors will notice other moving details throughout the property. Notes Shor, "The lilacs which inspired Walt's poem, 'When Lilacs Last in the Dooryard Bloom'd,' still bloom in the farmhouse dooryard today."

WALT WHITMAN HOUSE

Camden, NJ • 330 Mickle Boulevard • Tel: 856-964-5383 • *www.state.nj.us/dep/ parksandforests/historic/whitman* • Open Wednesday through Sunday; phone in advance to confirm hours

"Camden was originally an accident," Whitman once explained of his decision to settle in the working-class southern New Jersey town where his brother lived, "but I shall never be sorry . . . It has brought me blessed returns." In the last decade of his life, Whitman's belated international celebrity as the author of *Leaves of Grass* (originally self-published and selling only a handful of its 795-copy print run) enabled the 64-year-old poet to purchase "a little old shanty" in 1884. The simple wood-frame Greek Revival–style row house was the only home he ever owned, and his final years were spent there further refining *Leaves of Grass* (resulting in the definitive "deathbed edition") as well as preparing a collection of

During a yearlong trip to America in 1882, Oscar Wilde visited Whitman in Camden, where the two drank elderberry wine and the playwright told the poet that his Oxford friends carried *Leaves of Grass* with them on their strolls. "There is no one in this great wide world of America whom I love and honor so much," Wilde wrote later that year to Whitman.

essays and articles for his anthology *November Boughs.* Four years after a debilitating stroke in 1888, the bearded, silver-haired poet died in the house at age 72. Today, the six-room dwelling contains the death notice that was taped to his door along with many of the poet's letters, personal effects, and furnishings, including the bed on which he died. Whitman is buried in nearby **Harleigh Cemetery** in a granite-and-marble mausoleum of his own design.

NEW ENGLAND POETS

ROBERT FROST FARM

Derry, NH • 122 Rockingham Road • Tel: 603-432-3091 • *www.robertfrostfarm.org* • Grounds open year-round; farmhouse and barn open Wednesday through Sunday, May, June, September, and October; daily in July and August

"To a large extent, the terrain of my poetry is the Derry landscape," Robert Frost once admitted to his friend and biographer, Louis Mertins. "There was something about the experience at Derry which stayed in my mind, and was tapped for poetry in the years that came after." The white clapboard farmhouse where Frost found early inspiration was purchased by his grandfather as a gift for the poet and his young bride at the turn of the 19th century. Frost

A DAUGHTER'S LEGACY: Incongruously, the Derry farm became home to an auto graveyard in the 1940s, its once-bucolic pastures littered with spare parts and wreckage. A year after the poet's death in 1963, the property was purchased by the state of New Hampshire and restored to its earlier condition with the help of Frost's eldest daughter, Leslie Frost Ballantine. "Because of her involvement, visitors to the property can experience what has today become a living memorial to her famous father," says Laura Burnham, a trustee of the Robert Frost Farm. "People from all over the world come to honor a sense of poetry and place that defines so much of our connections to each other, the land and indeed, to 'the gift outright.' "

raised poultry during the day while penning poetry late into the evening, but neither endeavor proved successful. His farming business failed to earn a sizable income while a stinging rejection from the *Atlantic Monthly* informed him: "We regret that *The Atlantic* has no place for your vigorous verse."

In order to support his family, Frost returned to his earlier career of teaching while continuing to draft verse that would later make its way into his early collections. Increasingly frustrated by his lack of literary success, the struggling 38-year-old made a radical move with his wife and four small children. Selling the farm, the family set sail for England in 1912, determined to start fresh and make Frost's name as a poet.

Today, "most visitors to Frost Farm stop along the property's stone wall boundaries, framed by graceful birches, to understand the inspiration for Frost's poem 'Mending Wall,'" says Laura Burnham, a trustee of the Robert Frost Farm. Another treat for visitors: "Experiencing firsthand the hush of Hyla Brook," says Burnham of the burbling brook that the poet immortalized in verse while residing in Derry. An interpretive brochure for the **Hyla Brook Nature and Poetry Trail** can be downloaded from the farm's website.

FROST PLACE

Franconia, NH • 158 Ridge Road • Tel: 603-823–5510 • *www.frostplace.org*
• Open Thursday through Sunday afternoons from Memorial Day through late June; every afternoon except Tuesday from early July through mid-October

At the outbreak of World War I, the Frosts decided to leave England and return to the United States, where the now-established poet sought a farm in New Hampshire where he could "live cheap and get Yankier and Yankier." The family bought the Franconia farmhouse with its sweeping views of the White Mountains in 1915 and lived there for five years while launching Robert Frost's stateside career as a writer and teacher.

Today the Frost Place, which hosts a poet-in-residence program, is a gathering place for contemporary poets. Its house museum, open during summer months, contains Frost memorabilia and signed first editions of his works while a half-mile nature trail displays poems written during his time in Franconia.

ROBERT FROST STONE HOUSE MUSEUM

Shaftsbury, VT • 121 Historic Route 7A • Tel: 802-447-6200 • www.frostfriends.org
• Open Wednesday through Sunday, May through November

"I have moved a good part of the way to a stone cottage on a hill at South Shaftsbury in southern Vermont," Robert Frost wrote in a 1920 letter to a friend. "I mean to plant a new Garden of Eden with a thousand apple trees of some unforbidden variety." Frost lived in the 250-year-old granite and timber farmhouse for nearly a decade, tending to his beloved orchard and co-founding the prestigious Bread Loaf School and Conference of English at nearby Middlebury College.

In nearby Ripton, Vermont, visitors can hike the **Robert Frost Interpretive Trail** *(www.fs.fed.us)* in the Green Mountain National Forest off of Route 125. The one-mile hiking loop is annotated with Frost's poems and set amid pine, birch, and fir trees.

While living at Stone House, Frost wrote two volumes of poetry, including his ironically entitled *New Hampshire,* which won him a Pulitzer Prize. Contained in it was one of Frost's most famous poems, "Stopping by Woods on a Snowy Evening," incongruously written on a summer morning after a marathon all-night writing session at his kitchen table. Today, rooms in the house have been turned into miniature galleries with permanent and rotating exhibits highlighting aspects of Frost's distinguished career. A newly planted display orchard showcases the apple varieties that Frost once grew on the property.

The poet, who died in Boston in 1963, is buried in Bennington, Vermont, behind the **Old First Congregational Church,** where he had laid his wife and son to rest decades earlier. His epitaph reads: "I had a lover's quarrel with the world."

EMILY DICKINSON MUSEUM

The Homestead and The Evergreens, Amherst, MA • 280 Main Street • Tel: 413-542-8161 • *www.emily dickinsonmuseum.org* • Open Wednesday through Sunday, March through December; also open Monday from June through August

No doubt the famously reclusive poet—who lived much of her life confined to her bedroom in the 200-year-old brick manse known as The Homestead—would have been chagrined at the prospect of curious onlookers traipsing through her former sanctuary. But today the national historic landmark where she was born into a prosperous New England family draws inquisitive literary pilgrims from around the globe, many searching for insight into Dickinson's obsessively private inner world. Born at The Homestead on December 10, 1830, Dickinson never married and went on to spend all but 15 of her 55 years at the house, secretly penning verse that she sewed together in hand-bound volumes discovered by her sister posthumously. For unknown reasons, Dickinson chose to publish only seven works from her large oeuvre of some 1,800 untitled poems during her lifetime.

Connected to The Homestead by a path Dickinson described as "just wide enough for two who love" is The Evergreens, an Italianate-style house built for her beloved brother and his wife in 1856. Unlike The Homestead, which passed into new hands in the early 20th century, The Evergreens was occupied by Dickinson family heirs for a century and remains largely unchanged from the house the poet herself knew. The two historic dwellings merged in 2003 to form the Emily Dickinson Museum, which offers two different guided house tours daily.

During Dickinson's time, the family owned 14 acres surrounding the properties and the flower-loving poet could often be spotted tending the gardens attired in her signature white dress. (A replica is on display at The Homestead.) The reclusive poet often sent flowers to accompany her missives and at least a third of her poems feature floral references. Today, visitors can stroll the grounds surrounding the museum with an accompanying audio tour that integrates Dickinson's poetry with the landscape that inspired her.

Directly across the street from The Homestead is **The Amherst Inn** (*www.allenhouse.com*), built around the same time that Dickinson's brother was building The Evergreens. Dickinson's poem, "There's been a Death, in the Opposite House" may have been written about the dwelling, which once belonged to a family who lost several children to typhoid fever. Request "Emily's Room" for the best views of Dickinson's home. The poet, who died of a kidney ailment on May 15, 1886, is buried in nearby **West Cemetery** on Triangle Street.

Dickinson's birthday is celebrated every December at the museum with an open house featuring coconut cake made from the avid baker's own recipe. If poetic inspiration struck while she was in the kitchen, she drafted verse on handy scraps of paper, like the back of a wrapper for Parisian baking chocolate.

LONGFELLOW HOUSE– WASHINGTON'S HEADQUARTERS NATIONAL HISTORIC SITE

Cambridge, MA • 105 Brattle Street • Tel: 617-876-4491 • www.nps.gov/long • Open Wednesday through Friday, late May through October; grounds accessible year-round

Every house may have a story to tell, but the tales emanating from the yellow brick manse at 105 Brattle Street in Cambridge,

---

A LITERARY GATHERING: "To enliven the winter, I have formed the Dante Club, consisting of Lowell, Norton, and myself, meeting every Wednesday evening, with a good deal of talk and a little supper," Longfellow wrote to his son Ernest in 1865. The poet was a gifted linguist and the first American to translate *The Divine Comedy*, thus introducing Dante's 14th-century masterpiece to the New World upon the publication of his 1867 translation. Assisted by scholars such as Oliver Wendell Holmes, Charles Eliot Norton, and James Russell Lowell, Longfellow took up the project (begun earlier but set aside) as a way of coping after the death of his wife, Fanny, in a tragic fire. The group gathered in their host's study, which is seen during tours of the Longfellow House–Washington's Headquarters National Historic Site. Longfellow adorned the room with statuettes of various poets, including one of Dante. Among his other mementos were fragments from the Italian writer's coffin.

Longfellow's literary inner circle is re-created in Matthew Pearl's best-selling historical novel *The Dante Club*. When a cunning killer terrorizes Boston and Cambridge by executing murders modeled on punishments meted out in Dante's *Inferno*, the poet and his colleagues must use their knowledge of the work to find out who is behind the slayings.

Massachusetts, are enough to fill an entire bookshelf. Home to American poet Henry Wadsworth Longfellow for 40 years during the 19th century, the historic abode was also the headquarters for General George Washington during the Siege of Boston in 1775–76.

In the cozy study, where Washington once received a committee headed by Ben Franklin and decided that the American colonies should declare independence, Longfellow, too, made history. He penned dozens of his popular narrative poems, such as "Paul Revere's Ride" and "The Song of Hiawatha," and held his Wednesday night Dante Club meetings here (see shaded box, opposite).

"Longfellow and [his wife] Fanny were early preservationists and they were very concerned about maintaining the house," says Nancy Jones, a former supervisory park ranger at the Longfellow House. Fanny's father purchased the historic home for the couple as a wedding present in 1843, prompting Fanny to write, "How noble an inheritance this is where Washington dwelt in every room." When strangers knocked, asking to see "Washington's headquarters," Longfellow played the consummate host to the curiosity-seekers.

Many modern-day visitors to the house are surprised to learn of Longfellow's multidimensionality. "There were so many areas of the time that he had an interest in," explains Jones. The poet was a true polymath who traveled extensively and had a gift for foreign languages (he spoke eight, read twelve, and was a professor of languages at Harvard). He also took an active role in politics, advocating for abolitionism and the protection of Native American interests.

"He was a magnet who drew people from all walks of life, from the most humble to the most famous," Jones says of Longfellow, whose house was a lively gathering place for artists, politicians, and writers. Emerson, Hawthorne, and Dickens were but a few of the literary luminaries who graced the doorstep of his stately Georgian manse, which was preserved by members of the poet's family for more than a century. Today managed by the National Park Service, the house and its antiques remain largely unchanged since Longfellow's death in 1882. The poet is buried in Cambridge's **Mount Auburn Cemetery**.

See page 177 for Longfellow's Wayside Inn in Sudbury, Massachusetts.

WADSWORTH–LONGFELLOW HOUSE

Portland, ME • 489 Congress Street • Tel: 207-774-1822 • *www.hwlongfellow.org*
• Open daily May through October

Within the first wholly brick dwelling in the seaport town of Portland, Maine, lived three generations of Wadsworths and Longfellows, including the family's most famous member, Henry, who spent 14 years there shortly after his birth in 1807. The aspiring poet published his first poem in the *Portland Gazette* at age 13, the year before passing the entrance exam for Bowdoin College in nearby Brunswick.

Dating from 1786, the long, narrow, neoclassical-style dwelling where Longfellow grew up is the oldest standing structure on the Portland peninsula. Anne Longfellow Pierce, the poet's sister, lived in the house—which the family referred to as the "Old Original"—for nearly all of her 90 years, leaving it to the Maine Historical Society upon her death in 1901. In her bequest she designated that its rooms be "kept with appropriate articles for a memorial of the Home of Longfellow," with certain items to be left where they had been during the time of Henry's residence (such as the portrait of Washington "to hang where it has always hung over the mantle piece"). The house opened as a museum a year after her passing and today contains antique furnishings such as a graffiti-covered pine desk used by the Longfellow children, the four-poster bed with an oak-leaf cornice made for the poet's parents, and the leather traveling trunk Longfellow took with him during his European grand tour in the late 1820s.

Literary Houses on the Prairie

SINCLAIR LEWIS BOYHOOD HOME

Sauk Centre, MN • 812 Sinclair Lewis Avenue • Tel: 320-352-5201
• *www.sinclairlewisfoundation.com* • Open Tuesday through Saturday, May through September; other times by appointment

"We were a little put out when *Main Street* came out, but we soon forgot it. We soon saw the humor of his writings and were happy we were a part of them," declared the mayor of Sauk Centre on news of Sinclair Lewis's death in 1951. Sauk Centre served as the model for Gopher Prairie in Lewis's novel *Main Street,* a satire on small-town life and a 1920 best seller.

During a visit to Sauk Centre, novelist Pearl S. Buck mused about Lewis's boyhood abode, "Why should the fiery, honest, impatient spirit have come of such a house?" The two-story, wood-frame dwelling in which the future Nobel Prize–winning writer spent his youth stands on a street now bearing his name. The restored Sinclair Lewis Boyhood Home displays furniture and other items owned by the author and his family (among them Lewis's small wooden bed and a pewter vase he later purchased in Stockholm while attending the Nobel Prize ceremony). In a backyard carriage house, Lewis acted out dramas using house keys for the main players. Legend has it that by the time he left for college, he had read every book in the town's library. When the Lewises took up residence here, they didn't have far to move. The national historic landmark is located across the street from the house where Lewis was born on February 7, 1885.

After leaving Sauk Centre, Lewis attended Yale University and lived in Washington, D.C., New York, and Vermont. On one of his overseas voyages, he met with Edith Wharton at her home in France and later dedicated his novel *Babbitt* to her. (The honor made her "a little dizzy," she reported.) Lewis died in Rome, and his ashes were shipped to Sauk Centre for burial in his family's plot at **Greenwood Cemetery**. His tombstone bears the words "Author of *Main Street.*"

A teenage Lewis worked as a night clerk at the **Palmer House Hotel** (*www.thepalmer househotel.com*) and is believed to have immortalized it as the Minniemashie House in *Main Street*. The "tall lean shabby structure" he depicted is today an elegant lodging place listed on the National Register of Historic Places. Vintage photos, including snaps of Lewis, adorn the lobby.

WILLA CATHER CHILDHOOD HOME

Red Cloud, NE • Willa Cather Foundation • A Nebraska State Historical Society Site • 413 North Webster Street • Tel: 866-731-7304 • *www.willacather.org* • Open daily, April through September; closed Sundays, October through March

As a child Willa Cather moved west from Virginia with her pioneering

The **Cather Second Home** was the writer's parents' residence and the setting for the short story "The Best Years." Now it's a guest house with rooms named after towns in Cather's novels, including the Frankfort (*One of Ours*), where she once slept (*www.willacather.org*).

"By the end of the first autumn, that shaggy grass country had gripped me with a passion I have never been able to shake. It has been the happiness and the curse of my life."

—WILLA CATHER

family, who settled in the Nebraska prairie town of Red Cloud. She later resided in New York City and traveled to various locales in the United States and Europe, but it's with the Great Plains that Cather is most readily identified. Buildings and landmarks associated with her life and fiction, among them the novels *O Pioneers!*, *My Ántonia*, and the Pulitzer Prize–winner *One of Ours*, are preserved as the **Willa Cather Thematic Group**, which comprises the largest number of national historic–designated sites pertaining to an author in the United States.

The Willa Cather Foundation conducts tours of seven restored buildings in Red Cloud, among them the author's childhood home where she lived from 1884 to 1890. A highlight of the house is the small attic bedroom Cather—and Thea Kronborg in *The Song of the Lark*—decorated with wallpaper featuring "small red and brown roses on a yellowish background." Tours originate from the **National Willa Cather Center** located next door to the Foundation's restored 1885 Red Cloud Opera House. A bookstore features a voluminous selection of works by and about the author, and maps of self-guided driving and walking tours are available.

For those who would like a more expansive view of the region that inspired the author, the Willa Cather Foundation offers a Country Tour that highlights 20 historic sites across 50 miles of countryside.

O. HENRY MUSEUM

Austin, TX • 409 East Fifth Street • Tel: 512-472-1903 • *www.austintexas.gov/ department/o-henry-museum* • Open Wednesday through Sunday afternoons William Sydney Porter was accused of embezzling money from an Austin bank where he worked as a teller, went on the lam to Honduras, and returned to face charges after receiving the news that his young wife was dying. Convicted of the crime, Porter spent three years in an Ohio prison, where he occupied his time writing and adopted the pseudonym O. Henry.

The writer's Lone Star State legacy is preserved at the O. Henry Museum in Austin, where Porter lived with his wife and daughter from 1893 to 1895. "Most visitors relate O. Henry to New York, and here they learn about his years in Austin as a young man, a fledgling writer, a husband, and a father," says former curator Valerie Bennett. Guided tours reveal facts such as the scribe's favorite book (*The Arabian Nights*) and favorite food (chocolate cake).

On display in this Queen Anne–style cottage are the family's bedroom furniture and china, a writing desk, and a pair of chairs purchased by Porter's wife with money he gave her to attend the 1893 World's Columbian Exposition in Chicago—an act that is said to have inspired his most famous story, "The Gift of the Magi."

"The Gift of the Magi" was penned at **Pete's Tavern** in New York City. For more about O. Henry's haunt and other Big Apple bars for bibliophiles, see pages 199–201.

Porter held a number of jobs during his decade in Austin, including bookkeeper, pharmacist, journalist, and draftsman at the General Land Office. The Land Office building is now the **Capitol Visitors Center** (*www.tspb.state.tx.us*), and in the **O. Henry Room** guests can listen (via old-fashioned-style phones) to a biography of the writer as well as readings of two tales set in the structure he described as looking like a "medieval castle." Guests can traverse the spiral staircase featured in "Béxar Scrip #2692 (Murder at the Land Office)" and use a drafting table in the same area where Porter once drew maps.

Trail Porter around town with the **O. Henry in Austin Interactive Map** at *www.austinlibrary.com/ahc/ohmap.htm*, including a stop at **Scholz Garten** (1607 San Jacinto Boulevard), a bar and restaurant where he sang with the Hill City Quartet.

KATHERINE ANNE PORTER LITERARY CENTER

Kyle, TX • 508 Center Street • Tel: 512-268-6637 • *www.kapliterarycenter.com*

• Advance booking required

"I happen to be the first native of Texas in its whole history to be a professional writer. That is to say, one who had the vocation and practiced only that and lived by and for it all my life," Katherine Anne Porter declared. Successful and glamorous, Porter was at the epicenter of artistic and cultural life in the 20th century. She garnered a Pulitzer Prize in 1966 for *Collected Stories* and was acquainted with such figures as author Ford Madox Ford and artist Diego Rivera. She lived in Mexico, Denver, New York, and other locales in the United States and abroad, and once made her living as a reporter and an actress, but her rags-to-riches story begins in her home state of Texas.

Two-year-old Porter, her widowed father, and three siblings lived with her paternal grandmother in the railroad town of Kyle from 1892 to 1902, and her childhood was marked by strained financial circumstances and the cloud of her father's grief. These hardscrabble formative years provided substantial fodder for her short stories "Old Mortality" and "The Fig Tree," as well as the novella *Noon Wine*.

The family's Kyle home is part of the Katherine Anne Porter Literary Center and is occupied by a writer-in-residence from Texas State University's graduate writing program. The restored house (which then had three rooms) is decorated with early 20th-century furnishings and is open to visitors by appointment. A separate building, where photos of the author hang on the walls, is the site of readings and other literary events that are free and open to the public.

PORTER'S PORTFOLIO: Katherine Anne Porter's literary output included one full-length novel, *Ship of Fools,* and a collection of three novellas, *Pale Horse, Pale Rider.* The latter's titular story of the relationship between a Denver newspaper reporter and a soldier during the influenza epidemic of 1918 draws on Porter's own experiences. While living in a Denver boarding house at **1510 York Street** and working for the *Rocky Mountain News,* she was stricken with influenza and near death. The paper readied her obituary and her family began making burial arrangements, until she was given an experimental shot of the toxin strychnine and recovered.

LAURA INGALLS WILDER
HISTORIC HOME & MUSEUM

Mansfield, MO • 3068 Highway A
• Tel: 877-924-7126 • *www.lauraingallswilder home.com* • Open daily, March 1 through November 15

Missouri is simply glorious . . . Every turn of the wheels changes our view of the woods and the hills. The sky seems lower here, and it is the softest blue . . . It is a drowsy country that makes you feel wide awake and alive but somehow contented.
—Laura Ingalls Wilder, *On the Way Home*

In 1894, Laura Ingalls Wilder, her husband, Almanzo, and their daughter, Rose, undertook a wagon journey from the Dakota Territory to the Missouri Ozarks. It was here, on the homestead she named Rocky Ridge Farm, that Wilder transformed her childhood memories into a series of autobiographical novels. The publication of the 65-year-old author's *Little House in the Big Woods* in 1932 launched the "Little House" series and earned its creator a worldwide fan base.

The town of Mansfield honors Laura Ingalls Wilder with two annual events: the play *Laura's Memories*, staged on weekends July through September, and the **Wilder Days** festival in September (*www.mans fieldmissourichamber.weebly.com*).

The author's primary residence for more than six decades, Rocky Ridge Farm is now the Laura Ingalls Wilder Historic Home & Museum. The house is preserved much as Wilder left it at the time of her death in 1957, and Little House aficionados will take pleasure in seeing items like an ornate walnut clock Almanzo presented to Laura as a Christmas gift in 1886. Pa Ingalls's fiddle and other memorabilia are on display in a separate museum, which also highlights the accomplishments of Rose Wilder Lane, a noted author in her own right. A festive special event, "Christmas with Laura," takes place in December.

For other places associated with Laura Ingalls Wilder, visit *www .littlehouseontheprairie.com/historic-locations-and-museum-sites.*

CONTEMPLATIVE PLACES

THE ANNE FRANK HOUSE

Amsterdam, The Netherlands • Prinsengracht 263-267 • Tel: (31) 20 556 7100 • www.annefrank.org • Open daily

One day this terrible war will be over . . . The time will come when we'll be people again and not just Jews.
—Anne Frank, *The Diary of a Young Girl*

On August 4, 1944, an anonymous phone call led the German Security Police to a building in Nazi-occupied Amsterdam where Anne Frank and her family had lived in hiding for more than two years. Their makeshift home was a secret annex located in the rear of a canal-side warehouse that served as headquarters for her father's business. In this attic-like space, reached through a doorway hidden behind a bookcase (see photo), the aspiring teenage journalist penned what became *The Diary of a Young Girl*.

The Anne Frank House illuminates the experiences of the Frank family, the four others they invited to share the small space, and the friends who risked their safety to help keep them hidden. Passages from Anne's diary provide context about life in the annex, the isolation, and the fear of discovery. Along with the original diary, items in the house include a map of Normandy on which Anne's father optimistically charted the progress of Allied forces. In the small room she shared with another annex resident, Anne pasted postcards and magazine clippings of celebrities on the bare walls, making the space look "much more cheerful."

The museum also celebrates the legacy of the diary, first published in 1947 and translated into more than 65 languages. Foreign editions are on display, along with letters written by Anne's father, Otto Frank, after the war and video commentary by a friend who recalls speaking with Anne at the Bergen-Belsen concentration camp.

Otto Frank was the only one of those living in the annex to survive the war years. Anne and her sister, Margot, died of typhus at Bergen-Belsen in March 1945, a month before the camp was liberated.

The self-guided walking tour **Persecution and Resistance in Amsterdam: Memories of World War Two** points out pertinent landmarks as it leads from the Anne Frank House to the **Dutch Resistance Museum** (*www.verzetsmuseum.org*), where the atmosphere of the war years is re-created. The brochure detailing the walk is available for purchase at the Anne Frank House and the Dutch Resistance Museum.

VOLTAIRE'S CHÂTEAU DE CIREY

Cirey-sur-Blaise, France • 33 rue Emilie du Châtelet • Tel: (33) 3 25 55 43 04
• *www.chateaudecirey.com* • Open afternoons daily in July and August; Sunday afternoons and bank holidays in May and June; Sunday afternoons in September

Philosopher Voltaire was born François-Marie Arouet in Paris in 1694 and later adopted his one-name moniker. Due to the nature of his writing, in which he criticized both church and monarchy, Voltaire remained in constant danger of being jailed. When a warrant was issued for his arrest following the publication of his politically charged *Philosophic Letters* in 1734, the controversial scribe left Paris and took refuge at the Château de Cirey southeast of the city. The château was located near the border with Lorraine, at the time an independent province, which meant he could make an easy escape if pursued by authorities.

The outspoken Voltaire used his writing, including the satirical novel *Candide,* to crusade against social injustice, religious intolerance, cruelty, and war. Censorship laws frequently forced him to write anonymously, and the sale of most of his work was forbidden—and in great demand from the reading public. The absence of copyright laws in the 18th century made it difficult for writers to profit from sales of their books; instead Voltaire amassed a fortune by investing in foreign trade and other business ventures.

Voltaire lived at the Château de Cirey for 15 years. The estate was the ancestral home of the husband of Voltaire's mistress, Emilie de Breteuil, Marquise du Châtelet, who had a loveless and open marriage. While in residence at the château, Voltaire oversaw extensive renovations of the dilapidated manse. Among its notable chambers is the library, where the couple housed books from their astonishing 21,000-volume collection.

Voltaire had the Little Theater (one of the oldest stages in France) constructed in the attic of the château, and several of his plays were presented there before being staged in Paris. His other ambitious undertaking was the creation of a long, light-filled gallery, where he and Emilie, who continued their romantic and intellectual relationship until her death in 1749, entertained guests.

Voltaire spent his last years in exile in Switzerland (*www.pays devoltaire.com*). He returned to Paris in 1778 amid great fanfare after a change in political regimes, only to pass away three months later. In 1791, his remains were moved from an abbey in the Champagne region to the Panthéon in Paris.

RALPH WALDO EMERSON MEMORIAL HOUSE

Concord, MA • 28 Cambridge Turnpike

• Tel: 978-369-2236 • *www.facebook.com/emerson houseconcord* • Open late April through late October

The day after Ralph Waldo Emerson's wedding to his second wife, Lidian, on September 14, 1835, the newlyweds began married life in a house the writer had purchased in Concord. He was well acquainted with the pastoral town, the long-time home of his grandparents, and he preferred it to nearby Boston, where he had spent his youth.

The white, square-frame house (which is still owned by the family) served as Emerson's residence for more than 40 years and remains much as it did in the writer's day. "Our guided tours provide a portrait of Emerson's place in his family home and the world beyond," says director Marie Gordinier. Tours begin in the study, where the philosopher, poet, and lecturer penned thought-provoking works like the essays "The American Scholar" and "Self-Reliance." On display in the dining room are the writer's red rocking chair and a steel engraving of "School of Philosophy," a fresco by Raphael that Emerson saw at the Vatican Museum. A bay window in the master bedroom, decorated in Lidian's favorite hues (blues and grays), overlooks the gardens.

Emerson's move to Concord in 1834 and marriage to Lidian represented a new chapter for the philosopher, who had lost his first wife to tuberculosis in 1831 and resigned his position as a Unitarian minister the following year. His presence in Concord helped turn the town into an epicenter of American arts and letters, and he regularly entertained notable guests like fellow Concord residents Bronson Alcott and his daughter, Louisa, and Henry David Thoreau (who lived with the Emersons for a time).

In July 1872, Emerson's home was severely damaged by fire, although neighbors were able to salvage many of the family's possessions. They also took up a collection to pay for repairs, as well as send the writer on a European sojourn while renovations were being made. Upon his return home in 1873, Emerson was greeted with a festive celebration.

The original furnishings from Emerson's study are housed in the **Concord Museum** (*www.concordmuseum.org*) across the street from the author's abode. Emerson passed away in 1882 and is interred in **Sleepy Hollow Cemetery**. For more about the Concord burial place, see page 100.

OLD MANSE

Concord, MA • Home of Ralph Waldo Emerson and Nathaniel Hawthorne

• 269 Monument Street • Tel: 978-369-3909 • *www.thetrustees.org* • Open mid-March through December; grounds open daily

Built in 1770 for Ralph Waldo Emerson's reverend grandfather, the Old Manse has been home to more than one celebrated writer. A young Emerson lived there, and Nathaniel Hawthorne, too, once found shelter at the Old Manse. The house is situated along the Concord River and not far from the North Bridge, where the Revolutionary War began in 1775 with what Emerson later coined "the shot heard round the world" in his poem "Concord Hymn."

The Old Manse and its idyllic setting was a source of literary inspiration for Emerson, who drafted his essay "Nature" while living there. Some eight years later, Hawthorne penned stories in the collection *Mosses from an Old Manse* while living in the house after

To tour Hawthorne's hometown, Salem, Massachusetts, see pages 306–16.

marrying Sophia Peabody in 1842. A re-creation of the vegetable garden Henry David Thoreau created for the newlyweds flourishes in its original location and can be viewed during a self-guided tour of the grounds. Footpaths connect the house to the North Bridge and a reconstructed 19th-century boathouse by the Concord River.

The Old Manse is filled with Emerson family furnishings, including a Steinway cross-strung grand piano and 18th-century Canton-ware. Hawthorne's writing is on display in the study, where he and his bride used Sophia's diamond engagement ring to scratch still-visible missives on the windows.

"Walden is blue at one time and green at another, even from the same point of view. Lying between the earth and the heavens, it partakes of the color of both."

—WALDEN

HENRY DAVID THOREAU'S CABIN

Walden Pond State Reservation, Concord, MA • 915 Walden Street. • Tel: 978-369-3254 • *www.mass.gov* • Hours vary seasonally

Henry David Thoreau spent two years and two months living near Walden Pond in Concord, Massachusetts, in a one-room cabin he constructed on a plot of land owned by his friend Ralph Waldo Emerson. The philosopher and naturalist embarked on a quest in simple living, and his experiences at this wooded retreat became the basis of his treatise on self-reliance,

THOREAU REMEMBERED: The **Concord Museum** (*www.concordmuseum.org*) houses more than 250 artifacts related to Thoreau, including furniture from his cottage at Walden Pond, books, photos, and a flute that he often took with him on his sojourns through the woods and fields of Concord. After Thoreau's death on May 6, 1862, Concord resident Louisa May Alcott wrote a poem in tribute, "Thoreau's Flute," which was printed in *The Atlantic Monthly*. For more about *Little Women* author Louisa May Alcott, see pages 294-305.

Guided tours of **Thoreau Farm** (*www.thoreaufarm.org*), the author's birthplace in Concord, are given on Saturdays from May through October and other times by appointment.

Walden. "I went to the woods because I wished to live deliberately," wrote Thoreau, "to front only the essential facts of life."

A replica of Thoreau's small abode stands on the 462-acre Walden Pond State Reservation, and a bronze statue of the writer overlooks the home (see photo opposite). Visitors can trek to the cabin's original location near the pond, where granite posts designate its spot. Thoreau's domicile, which was moved and later demolished, was re-created using the author's detailed descriptions in *Walden.* Thoreau began planning and building the house in March 1845 and took up residence on July 4, still suffering from the loss of his brother three years earlier. While living at Walden Pond, he wrote his first book, *A Week on the Concord and Merrimack Rivers,* an account of a voyage the siblings had taken in 1839.

In the early 1800s, Thoreau's grandfather, a Boston merchant, purchased a building that is now part of the **Colonial Inn** (*www .concordscolonialinn.com*). Thoreau's family lived in the dwelling, located on Concord's Monument Square, from 1835 to 1837.

Walden Pond State Reservation is a popular recreation area for fishing, swimming, and walking. To preserve its natural resources, the number of visitors is limited to no more than a thousand at any given time. It's advisable to call the park in advance and check on availability, as well as to inquire about interpretive programs and guided walks. Trail maps are available at the visitor center, and can also be downloaded at *www.mass.gov/eea/docs/dcr/parks/trails/walden.pdf.*

HARRIET BEECHER STOWE CENTER

Hartford, CT • 77 Forest Street • Tel: 860-522-9258 • *www.harrietbeecherstowe.org*
• Open daily except Tuesdays January through March

During a meeting with Abraham Lincoln in 1862, as the Civil War raged, the President reportedly remarked to Harriet Beecher Stowe, "So you're the little woman who wrote the book that made this great war!" Published a decade before her encounter with the Commander in Chief, Stowe's best-selling novel *Uncle Tom's Cabin* is credited with galvanizing public opinion against slavery.

Born and raised in Connecticut, 21-year-old Stowe moved with her family to Cincinnati, Ohio, where she met her future husband.

For nearly 20 years Stowe lived in Cincinnati, first with her family and then with her husband, Calvin Stowe. The **Harriet Beecher Stowe House** (*www.stowehousecincy.org*) in Cincinnati commemorates the author and the Beecher family.

After leaving Ohio, Stowe settled in Brunswick, Maine, in 1850, where she lived at **63 Federal Street** and largely penned *Uncle Tom's Cabin*. The house is now owned by Bowdoin College.

After settling in Cincinnati, the Beechers aided fugitives from the neighboring slave-holding state of Kentucky, and were active in the abolitionist and women's rights movements.

A teacher, wife of a theology professor, and mother of seven children, Stowe once described herself as "retired and domestic." She was inspired in part to pen *Uncle Tom's Cabin* after the passage of the 1850 Fugitive Slave Act, which made it a crime to assist runaway slaves. During a literary career that spanned half a century, Stowe wrote novels, biographies, poetry, hymns, children's stories, and nonfiction tomes on domestic topics, but it was her humanizing portrayal of a woman fleeing slavery to protect her infant son that proved to be her most enduring work.

The New England native's last residence, where she lived for more than two decades, was a Gothic Revival–style house in Hartford's Nook Farm neighborhood, an enclave of writers and intellectuals that included Mark Twain. Adorning the 14-room house are Stowe's furnishings and artwork she created, along with pieces brought back from her European travels. In an 1851 letter, Stowe's daughter described a parlor table, now on display in this house, as the place where her mother was "working on her story"—*Uncle Tom's Cabin*.

The Center offers interactive tours where visitors discover the international impact of *Uncle Tom's Cabin* and discuss 19th-century issues connecting to today's headlines.

CABIN FEVER: The Reverend Josiah Henson served as inspiration for the title character in *Uncle Tom's Cabin*. He escaped from slavery on the Underground Railroad in 1830 and eventually settled in Dresden, Ontario, the location of the **Uncle Tom's Cabin Historic Site** (*www.uncletomscabin.org*).

FREDERICK DOUGLASS NATIONAL HISTORIC SITE

Washington, D.C. • 1411 W Street SE
• Tel: 202-426-5961 • *www.nps.gov/frdo*
• Open daily; reservations recommended

Frederick Douglass spent the last years of his life living on an elegant estate in the nation's capital. His home, Cedar Hill, was less than a hundred miles from where he was born into slavery on a farm on Maryland's Eastern Shore. He escaped slavery at age 20 and went on to become the leading voice of the abolitionist movement, an adviser to U.S. presidents, and author of the autobiography *Narrative of the Life of Frederick Douglass.*

Douglass moved to Washington, D.C., in 1872, after residing in Massachusetts and New York. He purchased Cedar Hill several years later and lived there until his death in 1895. Douglass more than doubled the size of the house, which remains much as it was during the author-orator's tenure and is furnished with his paintings and other objects. In the library, where he penned his last autobiography, *Life and Times of Frederick Douglass,* a Victorian Renaissance carved oak armchair originally made for the U.S. House of Representatives sits next to his rolltop desk. The house is shown during guided tours at specified times. On the grounds is a reconstructed "Growlery," a term coined in Dickens's *Bleak House* and the name of a tiny cabin where Douglass retreated to work and "growl" when the mood struck.

Frederick Douglass is buried in **Mount Hope Cemetery** (*www.fomh.org*) in Rochester, New York, his longtime home. Laid to rest near Douglass are his first wife, Anna Murray, who helped him escape from slavery, and his second wife, Helen Pitts, a white feminist 20 years his junior.

PEARL S. BUCK BIRTHPLACE MUSEUM

Hillsboro, WV • U.S. Route 219 • Tel: 304-653-4430 • *www.pearlsbuck
birthplace.com* • Open Friday through Monday, Memorial Day weekend
through October

"Had I been given the choice of place for my birth, I would have chosen exactly where I was born, my grandfather's large white house

The Good Earth won a Pulitzer Prize in 1932, and in 1938 Buck became the first American woman awarded the Nobel Prize for literature. Upon receiving the news that she had won a Nobel Prize, she responded in Chinese, "I don't believe it." The modest author then added in English, "That's ridiculous. It should have gone to [Theodore] Dreiser."

with its pillared double portico, set in a beautiful landscape of rich green plains and with the Allegheny Mountains as a background," Pearl S. Buck wrote in her autobiography, *My Several Worlds.*

Buck was born on June 26, 1892, in her mother's ancestral home in West Virginia. Three months later, she recalls in her autobiography, "I was transported across the seas to live and grow up in China." She journeyed with her missionary parents to the Far East, where she was raised in a small port city on the Yangtze River. Fluent in both English and Chinese, Buck was educated at Randolph-Macon Woman's College in Virginia, and after returning to China she married agricultural economist John Lossing Buck. Wed in 1917, the couple spent the first five years of their married life in a rural, impoverished farming province where she garnered material for her novel *The Good Earth.*

The writer's beginnings are immortalized at the Pearl S. Buck Birthplace Museum in the scenic Allegheny Mountains. The historic house museum contains some of her family's furnishings, among them the cradle in which she slept as an infant, objects brought by her parents from China, and jewelry and other items owned by Buck in later years. Also on the grounds are a restored barn displaying 1890s-era farm implements and the birthplace home of Buck's father, which was moved to the site from its original location 40 miles away.

THE PEARL S. BUCK HOUSE

Green Hills Farm, Perkasie, PA • 520 Dublin Road • Tel: 215-249-0100 • *www.pearlsbuck .org* • Open daily; guided tours given at specified times

After four decades living in China, Pearl S. Buck settled stateside on a 68-acre estate in Bucks County, Pennsylvania. At Green Hills Farm, she and her second husband, publisher Richard Walsh, raised seven adopted and many foster children. She was a leading voice in promoting cross-cultural understanding and an outspoken advocate for human rights. In 1949, Buck founded Welcome House, the first international adoption agency for biracial children.

The Pearl S. Buck House regularly hosts events, such as the **Taste of the World** food festival, book discussions, a fashion show, and the holiday-time **Festival of Trees** with a specially decorated tree in each room of the house. Attending the spring tea and garden party? Don your pearls.

Today Green Hills Farm serves as the headquarters of Pearl S. Buck International, which continues the author's global humanitarian efforts. The National Historic Landmark site has gardens, greenhouses, a renovated barn, and a 19th-century stone farmhouse that contains Buck's personal furnishings and belongings intact as she left them. The house where she resided for more than 40 years reflects her cultural duality, with Pennsylvania country furniture sitting alongside items like Chinese decorative screens, Chen Chi paintings, and a silk wall hanging presented by the Dalai Lama of Tibet. Buck died of lung cancer in 1973 and is buried at Green Hills Farm, where her gravestone spells out her name in Chinese characters.

LITERARY ADVENTURERS

MAISON JULES VERNE

Amiens, France • 2 rue Charles Dubois • Tel: (33) 3 22 45 45 75 • *www.amiens .fr/maisonjulesverne* • Open daily mid-April through mid-October; closed Tuesdays, mid-October through mid-April

"At my wife's wishes I settled in Amiens, a sober, civilized town whose society is cordial and cultured. We are close enough to Paris to see its reflection without the unbearable noise and the futile bustle," wrote Jules Verne. He had initially intended to stay in Amiens for only two days to attend a friend's wedding, but, smitten by the bride's sister, he extended his visit. He married the young widow in 1857, and they eventually made their home in this town in northern France. For nearly two decades, the writer's domain

Jules Verne is interred in Amiens's **Cimetière de la Madeleine,** where a dramatic stone sculpture depicts him rising from the grave with arm outstretched. Another tribute to the writer exists in a distant place he imagined in *From the Earth to the Moon* and *Around the Moon.* A crater on the far side of the celestial body is named for the French novelist.

was a three-story redbrick mansion with a circular tower.

Verne had already published *Around the World in Eighty Days, Journey to the Center of the Earth,* and other tales by the time he moved into what is now the Maison Jules Verne in 1882. This striking abode is decorated with period furnishings and various items, including a coffee service, which were owned by the writer and his wife. In the opulent cream-and-gold salon, the couple once hosted a costume ball, which they dubbed the "Inn of Around the World." Verne used the smallest room in the house (which adjoined a more spacious library) as his study, and it has been re-created with an iron bed for resting, an armchair, and a desk holding a globe that once belonged to the writer.

The first floor of the expansive house contains rooms memorializing Verne's longtime editor, Pierre-Jules Hetzel. On display is a couch owned by the editor where some famous guests once sat—among them Victor Hugo, Alexandre Dumas, and George Sand. The latter helped inspire Verne's adventure novel *Twenty Thousand Leagues Under the Sea* by suggesting to the writer that the only

THE ADVENTURER'S BIRTHPLACE: "I was lucky enough to be born in Nantes," declared Jules Verne of the town on the Loire River in western France where he spent his youth. He's remembered in Nantes at the **Musée Jules Verne** (3 rue de l'Hermitage; *www.julesverne.nantes.fr*), which is filled with items related to him and his fantastical works. The **"In the Steps of Jules Verne"** brochure highlights sites in and around Nantes associated with the writer, from residences he occupied to the shipyards that evoked a lifelong love of the sea. Rumor has it that a young Verne once stowed away on a ship bound for the West Indies but was discovered before the vessel set sail (*www.nantes-tourisme.com*).

territory to which he had yet to apply his "knowledge and imagination" was the sea.

ALEXANDRE DUMAS'S CHÂTEAU DE MONTE-CRISTO

Le Port-Marly, France • 1 avenue Kennedy
• Tel: (33) 1 39 16 49 49 • *www.chateau-monte
-cristo.com* • Open April 1 through November 1,
closed Mondays and every day for lunch; limited
hours November 2 through March 31

"I have created here a miniature paradise on earth," declared Alexandre Dumas of his Château de Monte-Cristo. The writer employed as much imagination designing his distinctive countryside retreat outside Paris as he did crafting the plot of the petite castle's literary namesake, *The Count of Monte Cristo.*

A wooded path, man-made grottoes, and a waterfall greet visitors on the walk to the château, where Dumas lavishly entertained guests such as Victor Hugo and George Sand. Dumas also had a smaller structure (which he called a "Gothic pavilion") erected opposite the main house for his workspace, and the exterior of the turreted edifice—named Château d'If for the prison in *The Count of Monte Cristo*—is engraved with the titles of Dumas's works. When informed by the architect he employed that it would cost several hundred thousand francs to transform his vision of an elaborate

THE ADVENTURER'S BIRTHPLACE: Alexandre Dumas was born in 1802 in Villers-Cotterêts, France, a village north of Paris. His mother regaled him with stories about the battlefield bravery of his father, a general in Napoleon I's army who died when Dumas was three. The **Musée Alexandre Dumas** (*www.picardietourisme.com*) houses items related to three generations of Dumas men: the writer, his father, and his namesake son. The younger Alexandre Dumas inherited his father's literary talent, penning the novel *The Lady with the Camellias* and other works.

English-style park into reality, the high-living writer replied, "I certainly hope so!"

Dumas lived life with gusto. From an impoverished childhood he went on to become a celebrated playwright, journalist, and author of such swashbuckling tales as *The Three Musketeers* and *The Man in the Iron Mask*. He owned a theater, indulged in frequent amorous adventures, and was a gourmet chef. "I want to finish the 500 volumes of my literary work with a cookery book," he declared, and the prolific wordsmith added the *Great Dictionary of Cuisine* to his oeuvre. Each room in the château explores a different facet of the writer's varied personal and professional interests.

For instance, when Dumas journeyed to Tunisia in 1846, he returned to France with two craftsmen who adorned a salon at the château in the style of the governor's palace in Tunis. Named the Moorish Room, it features intricately carved stucco walls, stained-glass windows, and colorful mosaic tiles.

Eventually Dumas's sumptuous lifestyle led him into debt and he was forced to sell the estate in 1849, only two years after throwing a housewarming party with 600 guests (most of whom showed up uninvited). The château fell into disrepair and was due for demolition before being rescued and restored to its storied grandeur. Dumas's days came to an end in 1870, and the writer is interred in the Panthéon in Paris.

BATEMAN'S, RUDYARD KIPLING'S ESTATE

East Sussex, England • Bateman's Lane, Burwash TN19 7DS • Tel: (44) 143 588 2302 • www.nationaltrust.org.uk/batemans • Open year-round, hours vary seasonally

"We have loved it ever since our first sight of it," said Rudyard Kipling of Bateman's, his English country estate. The centerpiece is a 17th-century stone mansion, surrounded by flowers, fruit trees, and fields and bordered by the River Dudwell.

Kipling was born in Bombay, India, to British parents, attended school in England, and returned to India, where he began a career as a journalist. He used the country as the backdrop for such stories as *The Jungle Book* and *Kim*, and the decor of his English abode reflects his associations with the East. Oriental rugs and artifacts adorn the house, from a terracotta statue of Ganesha, the elephant-headed god, to the Indian red lacquer bridal chest in the author's study. In the kitchen, an iPad plays a newsreel with the only known footage of Kipling speaking.

Visitors to the estate can view a restored water mill and meander through a rose garden planned by Kipling (the design hangs in his study), which was financed with the award money that came with winning the Nobel Prize for literature in 1907. A pioneer motorist, Kipling owned several "horseless carriages," and his Phantom I Rolls-Royce is on view in the garage.

Kipling lived in Vermont for four years until a public falling out with his American brother-in-law brought him negative attention in the press. He returned to England in 1896, giving up **Naulakha**, the house he had built in Dummerston. Available for holiday rentals (minimum stay three nights), this fully restored abode is decorated with furnishings owned by the writer, including his desk and pool table (*www.landmarktrustusa.org*).

The writer resided at Bateman's for more than three decades until his death in 1936. Three years later the house was bequeathed to the National Trust by his wife, who wanted the estate preserved as a memorial to her husband.

HERMAN MELVILLE'S ARROWHEAD

Pittsfield, MA • 780 Holmes Road • Tel: 413-442-1793 • *www.mobydick.org*
• Open daily Memorial Day through Columbus Day; grounds open year-round

"I have a sort of sea-feeling here in the country, now that the ground is all covered with snow . . . My room seems a ship's cabin; and at nights when I wake up and hear the wind shrieking, I almost fancy

MORE ON MELVILLE: The **Herman Melville Memorial Room** at the Berkshire Athenaeum houses the world's largest collection of Melville memorabilia. Items include the desk where he wrote his last prose work, *Billy Budd*, his customs house badge, and his passport—signed by both Melville and Nathaniel Hawthorne, Melville's overseas sponsor while serving as U.S. Consul in Liverpool, England (*www.pittsfieldlibrary.org*). For more about Hawthorne, see pages 306–18.

there is too much sail on the house, and I had better go on the roof and rig in the chimney." Herman Melville's vivid description was of the landlocked abode in western Massachusetts where he wrote his seafaring epic *Moby-Dick* and three more novels. A rambling 18th-century farmhouse set amid acres of fields in the scenic Berkshires, Arrowhead (named for artifacts Melville found on the property) was home to the writer for 13 years beginning in 1850.

Melville's time on whaling ships in the South Seas and other adventures served as the basis for *Typee, Omoo,* and other novels written before he resided at Arrowhead. He voyaged with *Moby-Dick*'s imaginary Captain Ahab and crew in a second-floor study, restored —as is the rest of the house—to its Melville-era appearance. A window in the room offered him expansive views of the highest point in the state, Mount Greylock, whose outline is said to resemble the shape of a whale.

The writer immortalized Arrowhead in the short story "I and My Chimney," and his brother, who succeeded him at the farm, was so taken with the tale he had lines from the text (which are still visible) inscribed above and on the fireplace. A porch Melville had built—and featured in "The Piazza Tales"—has been added back on to the house after being removed by a subsequent owner, and it offers the same view the writer once admired from a rocking chair.

Penning tales afforded Melville some critical acclaim but not financial success. Mounting debts forced him to leave Arrowhead and return with his wife and children to New York City, where he worked as an inspector at the New York Customs House for the next two decades.

FENIMORE ART MUSEUM

Cooperstown, NY • 5798 State Highway 80 • Tel: 607-547-1400 or 888-547-1450
• *www.fenimoreartmuseum.org* • Open April through December, hours vary seasonally

Growing up in the frontier lands of central New York State, commonly referred to as the Leatherstocking region, provided James Fenimore Cooper with fodder for his famous five-volume collection, *Leatherstocking Tales*. The Fenimore Art Museum, located on land that once belonged to the writer, houses a collection of paintings and artifacts celebrating the state's fascinating heritage, from North American Indian art and Hudson River School landscapes to eclectic folk-art pieces such as weather vanes and ship figureheads. Changing exhibits by celebrated artists are presented seasonally. A room dedicated to Cooper and his family contains author-related memorabilia, books, and paintings, among them a scene from the Leatherstocking novel *The Last of the Mohicans*. The Fenimore Café offers panoramic views of Otsego Lake, known as Glimmerglass in Cooper's tales.

A statue of a seated James Fenimore Cooper can be found in **Cooper Park** on Fair Street, while a monument depicting Natty Bumppo of the *Leatherstocking Tales* was erected in **Lakewood Cemetery** in 1860. The storyteller's final resting place is at **Christ Episcopal Church** (46 River Street).

ROBERT LOUIS STEVENSON MUSEUM

St. Helena, CA • 1490 Library Lane • Tel: 707-963-3757 • *www.stevensonmuseum .org* • Open Tuesday through Saturday from 12 to 4 p.m.; other times by appointment

Robert Louis Stevenson first set foot in California in 1879. He traveled from his native Scotland to marry American Fanny Osbourne, whom he had met three years earlier at an artists' colony in France. When the San Francisco fog proved damaging to Stevenson's sensitive lungs, the newlyweds headed north to the upper

THE ADVENTURER'S BIRTHPLACE: James Fenimore Cooper began his adventure-filled life on September 15, 1789. The 11th of 12 children, he was born in a house in Burlington, New Jersey, where he lived for a year before his family moved to the central New York State region he immortalized in print. His birthplace, the **James Fenimore Cooper House,** was built in 1781 and is part of the Burlington County Historical Society complex. Before turning to farming and eventually writing, Cooper (who was expelled from Yale for perpetrating pranks) had a seafaring career and once served under the command of his friend, James Lawrence, whose home is also under the historical society's auspices. The **Capt. James Lawrence House** is located next door to the Cooper dwelling (*www.tourburlington.org*).

Follow in the writer's footsteps with the listing of locales on *www.stevensonmuseum.org* in the section "RLS in Napa Valley." Visit the same vineyards he did or hike to the site where the newlyweds' cabin once stood, now part of **Robert Louis Stevenson State Park** (*www.parks.ca.gov*), where a marker identifies its location.

Napa Valley. Strained finances soon led the couple from the hotel cottage they had rented to Silverado, an abandoned mining town, where for two months they lived in a ramshackle bunkhouse on the slopes of Mount St. Helena. Stevenson recorded their experiences in his travel memoir, *The Silverado Squatters*.

The Robert Louis Stevenson Museum houses thousands of objects representing the writer's life from childhood to his last years. Highlights include an ornate mahogany writing desk Stevenson owned at the time he penned *Treasure Island*, a box he made while learning carpentry as a boy, his toy soldiers, rare first editions of his works, portraits of the writer, and his wedding ring.

STEVENSON HOUSE

Monterey, CA • 530 Houston Street • Tel: 831-649-7109 • *www.parks.ca.gov* • Open Thursday through Sunday, May through September

While waiting for his future bride to obtain a divorce from her husband, Stevenson lived for a time in the seaside town of Monterey,

THE ADVENTURER'S BIRTHPLACE: Stevenson was born in Edinburgh, Scotland, on November 13, 1850, and when he was seven his family moved to a residence at 17 Heriot Row in the city's New Town section. The author's childhood home, the **Robert Louis Stevenson House** (*www.stevenson-house.co.uk*), is privately owned and occasionally accepts overnight lodgers. For those who would like to sample Scottish cooking with a literary twist, there are also opportunities to dine, lunch, or have tea at the home. For more information email *mail@stevenson-house.co.uk*.

On display in the **Writers' Museum** (*www.edinburghmuseums.org.uk*) in Edinburgh is an array of items that belonged to Stevenson, among them a tortoiseshell ring given to him by a Samoan chief and inscribed with the name Tusitala ("Teller of Tales"). For more about exploring literary Edinburgh, see page 169.

California. The French Hotel, formerly a boardinghouse where the writer lodged, is now the Stevenson House. Among the intriguing objects on display are furniture from his childhood home, the travel trunk he inherited from his father, his mother's scrapbook, his dark green velvet smoking jacket and chessboard, and a telegram he sent to Fanny preceding his 1879 arrival in America. His missive? "Hold tight. I'll be right there."

ROBERT LOUIS STEVENSON MEMORIAL COTTAGE

Saranac Lake, NY • 44 Stevenson Lane • Tel: 518-891-1462

• Open July through Columbus Day, closed Mondays; other times by appointment

During the winter of 1887–88, Robert Louis Stevenson lived in the Adirondack Mountains in northern New York State, where he worked on *Master of Ballantrae*—when he could. Temperatures sometimes plummeted so low that the writer's ink froze in its pot.

The visit was Stevenson's second to America, and he was drawn to Saranac Lake for its proximity to a specialist pioneering an open-air cure for tuberculosis. He found the sharply cold climate bracing, a boon to both his health and his imagination. He was working, he told a friend, "with much vivacity." At the time, famous for tales like *Treasure Island, Kidnapped,* and *The Strange Case of Dr. Jekyll and Mr. Hyde,* he reveled in the solitude of the cottage's remote location.

Opened as a museum in 1915, the cottage contains the original furniture from Stevenson's stay, bagpipes that belonged to the Scottish scribe's family, the ice skates he wore to take a turn on a nearby pond, a lock of his hair, original letters, a signed portrait he presented as a Christmas gift to friend and writer Henry James, and other personal mementos. The modest desk where the writer toiled is preserved in the study, while the mantelpiece above the fireplace bears a reminder of Stevenson's stay: burns in the wood from the chain-smoker's cigarettes.

Stevenson spent the last years of his life in the South Pacific where he built a mansion in Apia, Samoa, preserved as the **Robert Louis Stevenson Museum** (*www.rls museum.org*). When the writer died in 1894 from a cerebral hemorrhage at age 44, Samoan natives carried his body to a hilltop grave site overlooking the sea. Twenty years later Fanny's ashes were buried alongside her husband.

After leaving Saranac Lake, Stevenson had no need for the full-length buffalo-skin coat, hat, and boots he wore to ward off the chill. He was headed for balmier climes: a sojourn aboard a yacht in the South Pacific.

MUSEO CASA NATAL DE CERVANTES (CERVANTES BIRTHPLACE MUSEUM)

Alcalá de Henares, Spain

• 48 Calle Mayor • Tel: (34) 918 899 654
• *www.museocasanataldecervantes.org*
• Open Tuesday through Sunday

Down in a village of La Mancha, the name of which I have no desire to recollect, there lived, not long ago, one of those gentlemen who usually keep a lance upon a rack, an old buckler, a lean stallion, and a coursing greyhound.
—Miguel de Cervantes, *Don Quixote*

Although few details exist about the life of 16th-century Spanish novelist Miguel de Cervantes, he is believed to have been born just north of Madrid in the small university town of Alcalá de Henares. A reconstruction of his birthplace home features wood-beamed rooms arranged around an open-air courtyard (see photo) and heavy walnut furnishings that evoke the traditional domestic atmosphere of Spain's golden age. A Castilian kitchen displays iron saucepans and earthenware jars while the *estrado*—an Arabian-style room where women read, played music, and prayed—is blanketed in carpets and pillows. In the re-created study of Cervantes's father are the remains of a 16th-century mural that may have graced the family's original home.

Upstairs rooms display editions of *Don Quixote* in more than 60 languages, including a 1605 first edition. Achieving instant popularity upon its publication,

In his memoir *Travels with Charley*, John Steinbeck recalls traversing the United States in a pickup truck camper he named Rocinante after Don Quixote's horse. The moniker was painted on the side of the truck in 16th-century Spanish script. See pages 344-58 for more about Steinbeck.

Don Quixote is considered the first modern novel as well as one of the greatest works in Western literature. More than 400 years after they traveled the Spanish countryside "redressing all manner of wrongs," the chivalry-obsessed knight errant and his faithful squire, Sancho Panza, continue to entertain audiences with the tale of their comic misadventures.

William Shakespeare, a Cervantes contemporary, is believed to have read *Don Quixote* and co-written a play based on a story from the novel, although no copies survive today. The two groundbreaking wordsmiths coincidentally died on the same date—April 23, 1616—honored by UNESCO each year as World Book Day. See pages 4–8 for more on Shakespeare's England.

In the building adjacent to the Museo Casa Natal de Cervantes, open the heavy wooden doors to peer into the courtyard of the historic **Antezana Misericordia** hospital, where Cervantes's itinerant father worked as a bloodletter. Then head for a literary lunch at the 500-year-old parador **Hosteria del Estudiante** (Calle Colegios 3; 34 918 880 330) and sample Quixotic dishes such as *duelos y quebrantos* (sorrow and sadness), a curious Cervantine term for a delicious mixture of eggs, potatoes, ham, and chorizo.

The hosteria adjoins one of Europe's best preserved Renaissance universities, the **University de Alcalá,** where daily tours conducted in Spanish allow access to the chapel where Cervantes was baptized.

CASA DE MEDRANO

Argamasilla de Alba, Castilla–La Mancha, Spain • Follow sign postings upon arrival into town • *www.turismocastillalamancha.es* (Spanish only) • Open Tuesday through Saturday, plus Sundays in summer

You may suppose it the Child of Disturbance, engendered in some dismal prison . . . —Don Quixote

Cervantes had the misfortune of being imprisoned at least twice for irregularities in his accounts while working as a tax collector. During one of those stints, he was confined in the atmospheric stone cave underneath the Casa de Medrano. Based on comments the author made in the book's prologue, it is widely believed that he began *Don Quixote* while imprisoned, likely at this location.

CAMPO DE CRIPTANA

Castilla-La Mancha, Spain • 62 miles north
of Argamasilla de Alba

On a hillside in nearby Campo de Criptana, one can still witness the spectacles put on by the famous windmills that Quixote valiantly battled after mistaking them for giants.

LA CASA DE DULCINEA (DULCINEA'S HOUSE)

El Toboso, Castilla-La Mancha, Spain • Follow sign postings upon arrival into
town • *www.eltoboso.es* • Open Tuesday through Sunday

Don Quixote and Sancho Panza pilgrimaged to El Toboso on a quest to find the knight's idealized princess, the beautiful Dulcinea. Today the traditional 16th-century Manchegan house of Doña Ana Martínez Zarco de Morales (the real personage on whom Cervantes is thought to have modeled his fictional Dulcinea) has been restored and opened as La Casa de Dulcinea. Nearby is the small **Museo Cervantino** with many editions of *Don Quixote* on display.

Vampires, Ghosts, and Ravens

POE MUSEUM

Richmond, VA • 1914-16 East Main Street • Tel: 804-648-5523
• *www.poemuseum.org* • Open year-round; closed Mondays

Although he spent much of his short, tempestuous life roaming the eastern seaboard, Boston-born Edgar Allan Poe—who became known as "the father of the mystery story"—identified himself as a Virginian. Orphaned in 1811 at just two years of age, young Poe was taken in by a wealthy Richmond tobacco merchant, John Allan, and his wife, Frances. While later enrolled at the University of Virginia, Poe ran up $2,000 in gambling debts, prompting his departure from Richmond after a bitter dispute with his foster father, who later disinherited him.

Prior to achieving literary fame, Poe returned to the city in August 1835 to work as a contributor and editor at the *Southern Literary*

Messenger, a position he lost a month later due to erratic behavior and drunkenness. (The magazine's sympathetic publisher later gave Poe his job back.) By year's end, Poe had made temporary peace with his demons, writing, "My health is better than for years past, my mind is fully occupied, my pecuniary difficulties have vanished . . . in a word, all is right." Contributing to his happiness was his impending marriage to his 13-year-old cousin, Virginia Clemm.

Although the Richmond homes in which Poe resided have since disappeared, the city boasts one of the largest existing collections of Poe memorabilia. The Poe Museum's four buildings include one of Richmond's oldest structures, the Old Stone House. Exhibits reveal the fascinating story of the writer's life in Richmond, from his acrimonious relations with his foster father to his tenure as a magazine writer-editor. A scale model shows the city as it existed during Poe's day, while other rooms showcase items such as an 1845 first edition of *The Raven and Other Poems* and the engraved walking stick the writer accidentally left behind in Richmond in the days prior to his mysterious death.

EDGAR ALLAN POE HOUSE & MUSEUM

Baltimore, MD • 203 Amity Street • Tel: 410-462-1763 • *www.poeinbaltimore.org*
• Open seasonally Friday through Sunday

"I am very anxious to remain and settle myself in Balto [Baltimore] as . . . I no longer look upon Richmond as my place of residence," Poe wrote in an 1831 letter to the *Baltimore Gazette and Daily Advertiser,* in hopes of obtaining employment. After a brief stint in the Army and a self-orchestrated expulsion from West Point, the budding writer took up residence in a five-room Baltimore duplex with his grandmother, aunt, and Virginia Clemm, the cousin whom he later married. Poe worked odd jobs to support himself while publishing his second volume of poetry and turning his pen to short stories. Although the itinerant scribe abandoned Baltimore just four years after his arrival, his legacy lives on in the Amity Street house, rescued from demolition several decades ago by the Poe Society.

In October 1839, Poe wrote to fellow gothic raconteur Washington Irving, asking him for "a word or two" of praise to include with his book *Tales of the Grotesque and Arabesque*. "I am deliberately convinced that your *good* opinion . . . would ensure me that public attention which would carry me on to fortune hereafter." For more on Washington Irving, see pages 84–86.

Visitors to the house museum—whose tiny, sparse rooms evoke the writer's hardscrabble years there—can view Poe's traveling writing desk, his telescope and office chair, and Allan family plates, while informative plaques put Poe's life in Baltimore and beyond in context. Up a winding narrow staircase is the atmospheric attic garret believed to have been Poe's bedroom and the location where he penned his earliest stories, including "MS. Found in a Bottle," which won him a $50 literary prize, and "Berenice," the tale that marked his foray into horror.

EDGAR ALLAN POE NATIONAL HISTORIC SITE

Philadelphia, PA • 532 North Seventh Street • Tel: 215-597-8780
• *www.nps.gov/edal* • Open Friday through Sunday, closed for lunch

Seeking a fresh start, Poe moved with his wife and mother-in-law to Philadelphia, where he published more than 30 stories during his six productive years there beginning in 1838. While working as a magazine editor, Poe achieved notoriety with his creepy tale of a cursed abode in "The Fall of the House of Usher," his genre-defining detective story "The Murders in the Rue Morgue," and other fantastic fictions like "The Tell-Tale Heart."

As his literary star rose, Poe experienced a profound personal crisis. In January 1842, his beloved wife, Virginia, was stricken with tuberculosis and her long, emotional illness drove Poe into a downward spiral. "I became insane, with long intervals of horrible sanity," he later explained of the time period. "During these fits of absolute unconsciousness I drank, God only knows how often or how much."

The year following Virginia's diagnosis, the couple moved into a redbrick house on Seventh Street, the last of their Philadelphia residences. The minimalist house-museum—maintained by the National Park Service—contains no furnishings but plenty of atmosphere. After watching a short video on Poe's life, visitors embark on a self-guided or ranger-led tour through the abode. Bare walls, peeling paint, and creaking floors provide the perfect back-drop to contemplate Poe's spine-chilling tales. Don't miss the dimly lit cobwebbed basement thought to have inspired a similar setting in the short story "The Black Cat."

Though it is not known for certain, many biographers believe Poe's poetic masterpiece, "The Raven," was started on Seventh Street prior to his subsequent move to New York.

POE COTTAGE

Bronx, NY • Poe Park, Grand Concourse at Kingsbridge Road • Tel: 718-881-8900 • *www.bronxhistoricalsociety.org* • Open Thursday through Sunday

"I feel in excellent spirits and haven't drank a drop—I hope so to get out of trouble," Poe wrote shortly after his and Virginia's departure for New York in 1844, possessing little more than a few dollars to their name. While working at the *Daily Mirror,* he soon became famous with the dramatic success of his poem "The Raven," although he earned little from its publication and continued to be "ground into the very dust with poverty." In 1846, Poe moved with his wife and mother-in-law into a cramped wood-frame bungalow in a then rural

A GRAVE EVENT: In an incident that could come straight from one of his eerie tales, Poe's death at age 40 is a mystery that will forever remain unsolved. After visiting Richmond to give a lecture, he was found roaming the streets of Baltimore, unkempt and wearing clothes that were not his own. Barely conscious, he was taken to a hospital and four days later, on October 7, 1849, uttered the final words, "Lord, help my poor soul."

No autopsy was performed and no death certificate filed, giving rise to a swirl of unsubstantiated theories surrounding Poe's demise. Possible causes of death that have been hypothesized range from drunkenness and rabies to epilepsy and a violent beating. At the **Poe Museum** in Richmond is a key found in his pocket that opened his "wandering trunk," missing in the days following his delirium. It was later recovered and also is on display at the museum. Poe is buried in the yard of **Westminster Presbyterian Church** (509 West Fayette Street) in Baltimore.

enclave of the Bronx, writing cheerily, "We are in a snug little cottage keeping house." But Virginia's health continued to decline and in January 1847, she succumbed to her long illness at the age of 25.

Poe's own physical and mental health—already precarious—took a turn for the worse and rumors of his insanity circulated. Fervently, he struggled against his demons, writing poignantly to his mother-in-law shortly before his death, "I was never really insane, except on occasions when my heart was touched." The missive was written from Richmond, where he had gone to deliver a lecture before meeting his tragic demise in Baltimore in October 1849.

Today, the cottage where he spent the last three years of his life is an emotional reminder of those sad times. Among the items on display are Poe's wicker rocking chair and the bed where Virginia died, its posts shorn to fit under the low-slung ceiling of the couple's tiny attic bedroom.

"The whole neighborhood abounds with local tales, haunted spots, and twilight superstitions."
—"THE LEGEND OF SLEEPY HOLLOW"

WASHINGTON IRVING'S SUNNYSIDE

Tarrytown, NY • 150 White Plains Road • Tel: 914-366-6900 • *www.hudsonvalley.org/ historic-sites* • Open Wednesday through Sunday, May through mid-November; admission by timed tour

"It is a beautiful spot," Washington Irving wrote of the land he purchased on the banks of the Hudson River in 1835, "capable of being made a little paradise." Located on the property was a 17th-century Dutch stone farmhouse that had formerly been occupied by members of the Van Tassel family, whom the writer had immortalized in his popular ghost tale "The Legend of Sleepy Hollow" 15 years earlier. "I have had an architect here and shall build a mansion upon the place this summer," he effused, setting out to turn the house he had christened Sunnyside into a pastiche of architectural styles from both the Old World and the New. The result was a charming wisteria-draped cottage featuring Dutch gables, English chimneys, and a Spanish tower—elements influenced by Irving's 17 years abroad serving as a statesman and historian.

The writer had initially spied the cottage while hiking through the Hudson River valley as a teen, when he was sent to bucolic Tarrytown from Manhattan to escape a yellow fever epidemic. His rambles around the area's old Dutch settlements and his forays into "the haunted regions of the Kaatskill Mountains" inspired the settings for Ichabod Crane's flight from the Headless Horseman and Rip Van Winkle's long snooze after too many "visits to the flagon."

Irving had a lifelong fascination with Spanish culture, spoke fluent Spanish, and served for several years in diplomatic posts in the country. His 1829 stay in Granada's Moorish palace, the **Alhambra**, inspired his travelogue, *Tales of the Alhambra*, which weaves history with folklore about buried treasure, enchanted caves, and imprisoned princesses. The room in the Alhambra where Irving stayed is commemorated with a plaque, and literary pilgrims can retrace the footsteps of his Andalusian travels from Seville to Granada with the interactive route map at *www.spain.info/en*.

Although Irving had already led an extraordinary life by the time he settled down to enjoy his twilight years in his "little nest," he forged ahead with "the crowning effort" of his literary career—an ambitious five-volume history of his namesake, George Washington. Within weeks of its completion, Irving died at age 76 in his Sunnyside bedroom on November 28, 1859.

SPOOKY SITE: October is a spine-tingling time to visit Washington Irving territory. Taking place throughout the month at historic locales in and around Sleepy Hollow are special events such as a haunted trail walk and a jack o' lantern blaze with thousands of hand-carved, illuminated pumpkins (*www.hudsonvalley .org/events*).

Sleepy Hollow's **Old Dutch Church** and the adjacent **Old Dutch burying ground** are the memorable locales where Ichabod Crane had his fateful encounter with the Headless Horseman. The church hosts dramatic readings of Irving's ghostly tale in October while the cemetery—where the Headless Horseman tethered his steed—still has ghoulish tombstones dating from the 17th century. Nearby is the **Sleepy Hollow Cemetery** (540 North Broadway; *www.sleepyhollowcemetery.org*), where Irving was laid to rest.

Irving's relatives continued to inhabit the cottage for nearly a century, after which it was purchased by John D. Rockefeller, Jr., who wanted to ensure Sunnyside's preservation. Today, visitors are immersed in the writer's world during guided tours of his enchanting home. Rooms are decorated with Irving's eclectic blend of antique furnishings, from a curvaceous Voltaire armchair and a rosewood pianoforte (which Irving often played) to an oak writing desk given to him by his publisher.

DRACULA'S LAIR: ENGLAND AND ROMANIA

WHITBY, ENGLAND

Masses of sea fog came drifting inland . . . so dank and damp and cold that it needed but little effort of imagination to think that the spirits of those lost at sea were touching their living brethren with the clammy hands of death. —Bram Stoker, *Dracula*

Bram Stoker may have journeyed to the mist-shrouded English seaport of Whitby in 1890 seeking a relaxing summer vacation, but he returned home to London invigorated by more than fresh sea air. Whitby's unpredictable North Sea climes, rugged cliffs, and dramatic location in the shadow of a ruined abbey made it an ideally ominous backdrop for chapters of Stoker's novel in progress, *Dracula*. Fueling Stoker's imagination was the story told to him by a Whitby Coast Guardsman about a ship that had run aground in the town's harbor five years earlier.

From these fertile seeds came Dracula's memorable entrée onto English shores via the shipwrecked vessel *Demeter*, which runs aground at Whitby bearing 50 wooden boxes of Transylvanian soil. In the guise of an immense dog, Dracula sprang ashore, making for the 199 steps leading up to **St. Mary's Church** and disappearing into the night. The spot where Stoker is said to have

Take the **In Search of Dracula** tour with the Man in Black, Whitby native Harry Collett (*www.whitbywalks.com*), who dons Victorian attire and top hat to lead an evening walk to places where the vampire stalked.

peered out to sea crafting this ghoulish scene is commemorated with the **Bram Stoker Memorial Bench**. From this vantage point are views of the harbor and the menacing Gothic skeleton of **Whitby Abbey**, "a most noble ruin, of immense size, and full of beautiful and romantic bits." As Stoker noted, "Between it and the town there is another church, the parish one, round which is a big graveyard, all full of tombstones." Stoker would pause during his walks to watch the bats circling over the 12th-century church, known as St. Mary's. In its ancient graveyard strewn with tilted, crumbling tombstones, Dracula claimed his first English victim, Lucy Westenra.

TRANSYLVANIA AND ENVIRONS, ROMANIA
BRAN CASTLE

Traian Mosoiu Street, number 489, Bran (105 miles north of Bucharest) • Tel: (40) 268 237 700 • *www.bran-castle.com* • Open daily; hours vary seasonally

"A vast ruined castle, from whose tall black windows came no ray of light, and whose broken battlements showed a jagged line against the moonlit sky" was the ominous Transylvanian abode of the fictional Count Dracula, thought to be inspired in part by an actual figure from Romanian history. Prince Vlad Dracula, the 15th ruler of Wallachia (today part of Romania), earned his fierce reputation warring with the Turks and meting out cruel punishments that garnered him the nickname Vlad the Impaler.

A GHOSTLY GATHERING: Before there was *Dracula*, there was *The Vampyre*, published 70 years earlier by Lord Byron's personal physician, John Polidori. The story was conceived during a wet, uncongenial summer in 1816 at Byron's Villa Diodati on Lake Geneva. To while away the hours stuck indoors, the poet proposed that he and his guests—Polidori, Percy Bysshe Shelley, and Shelley's 18-year-old wife, Mary, create horror stories. Polidori later turned the fragment of a tale started by Byron into *The Vampyre*, while Mary Shelley's monstrous creation became *Frankenstein*. Villa Diodati (Chemin de Ruth 9, Cologny, Switzerland) is a private residence and can only be viewed from the outside.

Although Stoker never set foot in Romania and the Castle Dracula of his book is a fictional creation, Transylvania's Bran Castle—where Vlad Dracula may have briefly stayed—is a fitting doppelgänger. Perched high on a 200-foot precipice in the densely forested Carpathian Mountains, the turreted medieval castle attracts more than a half million visitors a year by virtue of its slender connection to the Prince of Darkness.

Underneath the castle's distinctive profile of soaring, red-tiled turrets are labyrinthine layers of rooms, towers, and secret passageways surrounding a central courtyard. Worthy of a visit for its stunning architecture alone, the castle doubles as a museum of history and feudal art.

POENARI FORTRESS

Located near the town of Curtea de Arges (138 miles northwest of Bucharest)
• www.romaniatourism.com/bucharest.html

Only the crumbling walls and towers of this remote stone fortification—reached by 1,462 steps—still remain, but locals consider it the authentic Dracula Castle due to its history as Vlad Dracula's hideout during a bloody Turkish invasion. Legend has it that Vlad's wife jumped to her death from one of the towers to avoid being taken captive by bloodthirsty Turks.

SIGHISOARA

Mureş County (180 miles northeast of Bucharest)
• www.romaniatourism.com/medieval.html

The almost perfectly preserved medieval village of Sighisoara, a UNESCO World Heritage site, was the place of Vlad Dracula's birth in 1431. Said to be one of Romania's most beautiful towns, the former citadel boasts thick defensive walls that embrace its narrow cobblestone streets. Vlad's house—now a restaurant and small museum of medieval weaponry—is identified with a plaque.

SNAGOV MONASTERY

Snagov (29 miles north of Bucharest) • www.snagov.ro/en

Situated on a small island in the middle of Snagov Lake, a rustic

14th-century cloister is the reputed burial place of Vlad Dracula, who died under mysterious circumstances in 1476. Modern-day archaeological excavations of the grave site found no human remains.

Russian Raconteurs

Tip: Book with a tour group or hire an English-speaking guide to get the most out of your visit to these museums.

TOLSTOY ESTATE-MUSEUM

Moscow • Ulitsa Lva Tolstovo 21 • Tel: (8 499) 246 9444 • *www.tolstoy museum.ru* • Open Tuesday through Sunday, closed last Friday of the month

"My dream of stunning you with a remodeled house will not come true," Leo Tolstoy wrote in a September 1882 letter to his wife, Sofya. "I am afraid you will be disagreeably surprised by the disorder you will find when you arrive." At his wife's urging, the city-averse Tolstoy moved from the country to a 20-room, two-story wooden house that he purchased and renovated for his family on the outskirts of Moscow. The move was made for the benefit of their children's education, and the family remained in the house during long Russian winters for two decades. They spent summers in the countryside at the Tolstoy ancestral estate, Yasnaya Polyana (see pages 90–92).

By the time of the move at age 54, Tolstoy had already found fame with the publication of his epic masterpieces, *War and Peace* and *Anna Karenina*. But despite his extraordinary success, after completing the latter, he experienced a profound existential crisis that led him to sideline fiction writing in favor of penning philosophical and ideological treatises. Increasingly, he renounced bourgeois society while extolling the virtues of poverty, vegetarianism, and sexual abstinence. His extremist views frequently led to tempestuous battles with his wife during their later Moscow years.

Russian leader Vladimir Lenin, who called Tolstoy "the mirror of the Russian revolution," opened the family's home as a memorial museum in 1921, 11 years after the author's death. Nearly all of the Tolstoys' possessions have been preserved in rooms such as the salon where the writer played chess with writer Maxim Gorky and hosted composers Rachmaninoff and Rimsky-Korsakov. Tolstoy's spacious study contains the austere black leather chair and heavy desk at which he penned one of his final fictional works, *The Death of Ivan Ilyich*, while his children's rooms reflect their distinct personalities. Paintings and sketches adorn the walls of the bedroom belonging to his artist daughter, Tatyana, while the sparsely furnished room of his favorite daughter, Masha, reflects her adherence to Tolstoy's renouncement of material possessions. A high chair and rocking horse in another small bedroom are sad reminders of the Tolstoys' son, Ivan, who died of scarlet fever.

TOLSTOY ESTATE MUSEUM, YASNAYA POLYANA

Tula Province • Shchekino District

• Tel: (7 487) 517 6073 • www.ypmuseum.ru

• Open Tuesday through Sunday, closed last Tuesday of the month

RUSSIAN ROULETTE: The short-tempered Tolstoy notoriously kept his distance from most of his writerly contemporaries, barring one notable exception. A perceived insult from his onetime friend Ivan Turgenev incited Tolstoy to challenge the writer to a pistol duel in 1861, and although apologies were eventually extended on both sides, the two did not speak again for 17 years.

Perhaps fortunately for Dostoyevsky, his path never crossed Tolstoy's, and the two shared few commonalities. Although the former wrote admiringly that "*Anna Karenina* was a perfect work of art," Tolstoy once remarked that he couldn't stick it out to the end of Dostoyevsky's *The Brothers Karamazov*. Nonetheless, he was reading the second volume of the book at the time of his death.

"I could hardly imagine Russia, or my relationship with her, without my Yasnaya Polyana," Leo Tolstoy wrote in 1858, referring to his family's sprawling ancestral estate in the countryside south of Moscow. The author had been born there 30 years earlier into a distinguished line of Russian nobility (the aristocratic poet Pushkin was a fourth cousin) on a black couch that is still on view today. He lived at Yasnaya for much of his life, including later years when he was joined by his wife and children. Both *War and Peace* and *Anna Karenina* were penned in the study, where he could often be found writing at his desk in a billowing peasant blouse. While at Yasnaya, his sympathies for peasants blossomed—for him, they were the "real" people while nobility were the usurpers. Among his many grand gestures of generosity, he founded a school for peasant children, today the site of a small literary museum on the property.

In addition to hosting friends such as Turgenev, Gorky, and the young playwright Anton Chekhov, the bearded writer later welcomed dozens of Tolstoyan "disciples" who made pilgrimages to bask in his sage presence. Despite his failing health, Tolstoy left his beloved estate in the fall of 1910 to live as a wandering ascetic. Tragically, he

COUNTRY RETREAT: Located 112 miles south of Moscow, Yasnaya Polyana is an easy day trip from the city and tours in English are offered daily. Allow several hours to visit the estate, situated on hundreds of acres containing numerous buildings, ponds, an orchard, two parks, and a greenhouse built by Tolstoy himself. Yasnaya owes much of its well-preserved existence to efforts made by the writer's widow. Later, during a civil war in which estates were burned, peasants at Yasnaya Polyana protected it from destruction in gratitude to Tolstoy, who had treated them well.

Among the rooms on view are Tolstoy's study, bedroom, and 22,000-volume library as well as the vaulted pantry where he often sought solitude. In the property's lush fir tree grove is a charming birch bench on which Tolstoy found respite during his long strolls.

died of pneumonia only ten days later at a remote railway junction (now a museum; *www.tolstoymuseum.ru*). Per his request, his body was returned to Yasnaya and buried in an unmarked grave at the edge of the forest.

Thousands of peasants followed behind his coffin in the funeral procession, bearing a mournful banner: "Dear Lev Nikolayevich, the memory of your goodness will not die among us, the orphaned peasants of Yasnaya Polyana."

CHEKHOV HOUSE MUSEUM

Moscow • Ulitsa Sadovaya-Kudrinskaya 6 • Tel: (8 495) 691 6154 • *www.goslitmuz* *.ru* • Open Tuesday through Sunday, hours vary; closed last day of the month

"Medicine is my lawful wife, and literature is my mistress," playwright Anton Chekhov wrote to his editor in 1888. "When I get fed up with one, I spend the night with the other." Born into a family of former serfs, he originally began writing to supplement his physician's income in order to support his father, mother, and siblings. By the time he moved with them into this small house in the fall of 1886, the bespectacled 26-year-old writer-physician had already published more than 400 witty short stories

YALTA YEARS: Best known for his humor-infused tragedies depicting the provincial Russian middle class, Chekhov's career as a playwright blossomed only in the last decade of his short life. His friend Leo Tolstoy once told him, "Shakespeare's plays are bad enough, but yours are even worse!" and urged him to concentrate on his short stories instead.

Fortunately, Chekhov persevered and went on to pen such masterpieces as *The Three Sisters* and *The Cherry Orchard*. The plays were written in Yalta, a town on the Black Sea that was his home from 1898 until tuberculosis felled him six years later at age 44. His White Dacha and surrounding gardens are preserved as the **Yalta Chekhov Estate-Museum** (*www.chekhov-yalta.org/en*), which contains turn-of-the-20th-century furnishings belonging to the dramatist, including a piano that composer Rachmaninoff once played during a visit.

and comedy sketches as well as two books. During the four years he spent here, he went on to launch his career as a dramatist by penning his first play, *Ivanov,* and several one-act comedies all while running a busy medical practice.

Chekhov and writer Nikolai Gogol are buried just south of Moscow in the cemetery at the beautiful fortified **Novodevichy Convent** (Novodevichy proezd 1), whose buildings date from the 16th and 17th centuries.

Today the house—refurbished in consultation with the playwright's widow—is a modest museum marked by a nameplate that reads "Dr. AP Chekhov." On view are Chekhov's study and consulting room with his doctor's bag, his simply furnished bedroom, and the family's surprisingly lavish living room. In the dining area are original playbills, manuscripts, and first editions of Chekhov's works.

PASTERNAK DACHA (COUNTRY HOUSE) MUSEUM

Peredelkino village • Ulitsa Pavlenko 3 • Tel: (7 495) 934 5175 • *www.pasternak museum.ru* • Open Tuesday through Sunday; closed last Tuesday of the month

"Leaving the motherland will equal death for me," implored poet and novelist Boris Pasternak in a letter to Soviet Premier Nikita Khrushchev, pleading his case against deportation amid the furor caused by his novel *Doctor Zhivago.* "I am tied to Russia by birth, by life, and work." Although a supporter of the Russian government, Pasternak was harshly condemned for his epic tale of a love triangle set during the aftermath of the Russian Revolution, and the book was banned for its supposed "non-acceptance of the socialist revolution."

Vilified in his home country, Pasternak was lauded abroad where *Doctor Zhivago* became a best seller in 24 languages and won the 1958 Nobel Prize for literature. Sadly, the author was forced to decline the honor under threat of exile and further political persecution. His controversial masterpiece, which had taken him nearly ten years to complete, was written at his wood-framed Tyrolean-style dacha

The best way to visit Peredelkino is by booking an organized tour or English-speaking guide with transport through your hotel. Alternatively, the town is a 20-minute journey by *elektrichka* suburban train from Moscow's Kievskaya Metro Station.

nestled in the pine forests of the Peredelkino writer's colony outside Moscow. Pasternak and his wife had settled there in 1939 as a place of refuge during Stalin's purge and he wrote to his father that the "gentle, eloquent, colorful setting" of Peredelkino was "what one might have dreamed all one's life." The author remained there in seclusion until his death from lung cancer in 1960.

Pasternak's family, desiring to preserve the dacha as a museum, continued to reside there for two decades until they were evicted in a contentious court battle. With the advent of glasnost, belated acceptance finally came for the long-suffering writer and on the centenary of his birth, his dacha was opened as a memorial.

On display is the couch upon which Pasternak died, paintings and sketches by his father (a talented artist who illustrated Tolstoy's *War and Peace*), and the author's sparsely furnished, window-lined study. At the room's heavy oak table, Pasternak penned *Doctor Zhivago*, which finally graced Russian bookshelves more than three decades after it was written.

DOSTOYEVSKY HOUSE MUSEUM

Moscow • Ulitsa Dostoevskovo 2 • Tel: (8 495) 681 1085 • *www.goslitmuz.ru*
• Open Tuesday through Sunday; closed last day of the month

A grim, unheated ground-floor apartment—then situated in one of the worst slums of Moscow—was the inauspicious locale where Fyodor Dostoyevsky, one of Russia's most profound and prolific writers, spent most of his first 16 years. His despotic father, who would later exert a strong influence on the writer's work, earned a small salary as a surgeon in the adjacent Mariinski Hospital for the Poor, and the family lived in humble, isolated lodgings on its grounds. As a teenager, Dostoyevsky witnessed the tragic death of his beloved mother from tuberculosis in the apartment in 1837, after which he was sent to the Military Engineering Academy in St. Petersburg. Two years later, his father died mysteriously, a shock that triggered the first of many epileptic seizures that were to plague Dostoyevsky throughout his life.

His less than idyllic childhood is commemorated at the Dostoyevsky House Museum, which re-creates his boyhood home based on descriptions in his diaries. Its cramped quarters include the tiny, windowless bedroom that the writer shared with his older brother, the living room where they played, and the makeshift "bedroom" of his parents, who slept in a narrow bed behind a partition. Among the items on display are the family's small library of books (the writer's mother read voraciously, a habit she encouraged in her children) and the parish ledger recording Dostoyevsky's birth in 1821.

DOSTOYEVSKY MEMORIAL APARTMENT
St. Petersburg • Kuznechny Pereulok 5/2 • Tel: (7 812) 571 4031 • *eng.md.spb.ru*
• Open Tuesday through Sunday; closed last Wednesday of the month

"Our apartment consisted of six rooms, an enormous storeroom for books, an entry hall, and a kitchen," wrote Anna Grigoryevna, Dostoyevsky's wife, describing their St. Petersburg home. (The couple met when he hired her to work as a stenographer on his novel *The Gambler.*) Of the more than 20 apartments the writer is said to have rented in the city throughout his life, the Kuznechny apartment was to be his last and the place in which he died on January 28, 1881. During his brief time there, he completed his epic novel of patricide, *The Brothers Karamazov,* a year before passing away at age 59.

Owing largely to the contributions of manuscripts, letters, and memorabilia owned by the writer's grandson, the apartment has been restored as it was during the Dostoyevsky family's time. In addition to rooms such as the writer's study and the office of Anna Grigoryevna, who conducted her husband's business affairs, other rooms showcase a surprising domestic side of the writer's personality

A map of Dostoyevsky's 19th-century St. Petersburg, highlighting the many locations in the city associated with the writer, is displayed in the Kuznechny apartment. See pages 158–59 for information on the Dostoyevsky St. Petersburg walking tour.

that belie the bleak worlds portrayed in his novels. Dostoyevsky's wife and two surviving children were the center of his universe, and he always made time for them by insisting the family gather for the evening meal each night promptly at six o'clock in the dining room. His children's rooms display books he read aloud to them and sweet notes they penned, such as "Dear Papa, I love you, from Luba."

Other rooms are devoted to an exhibition illuminating the writer's fascinating life, from his lifelong struggle with epilepsy and his radical political activities (which resulted in a commuted death sentence and a four-year Siberian imprisonment) to the gambling addiction that brought him to the brink of ruin.

Upon Dostoyevsky's death, thousands followed his coffin through the streets of St. Petersburg to his final resting place in the Tikhvin Cemetery at the **Alexander Nevsky Monastery** (1 Pl. Alexandra Nevskovo), where his funeral was attended by 30,000 mourners.

PUSHKIN APARTMENT MUSEUM

St. Petersburg • Naberezhnaya Reki Moyki 12 • Tel: (7 812) 571 3531
• www.museumpushkin.ru • Open Wednesday through Monday; closed last Friday of the month

Although he lived there just four months, the opulent 11-room apartment where celebrated poet Aleksandr Pushkin dramatically bled to death on February 10, 1837, is today one of the most revered museums in all of Russia. Stealing a page from his most famous work, the verse novel *Eugene Onegin,* Pushkin met his untimely demise in defending the honor of his coquettish wife, Natalya. After receiving a satirical certificate electing him into "The Most Serene Order of Cuckolds," Pushkin flew into a jealous rage over Natalya's shameless pursuer, the dashing Frenchman Georges d'Anthès. On a wintry January morning, the two faced off to duel in a snowy field where Pushkin fell victim to his adversary's sharp shooting, sustaining a fatal wound. Two agonizing days later, the delirious 37-year-old poet died on the couch in his study while imagining he was scaling his vast collection of books.

The leather couch—and Pushkin's soaring bookshelves containing more than 4,000 tomes—still remain. Among the otherworldly relics in the ghostly shrine are the waistcoat Pushkin was wearing at the time of his shooting, his death mask, and one of his dark locks of hair. The study where the poet expired looks just as it did at the time of his death, by virtue of sketches drawn by the poet's friend Vasily Zhukovsky, who held vigil during his final hours.

Other airy, light-filled rooms contain luxurious Empire-style furnishings, plush red carpets, and walls hung with portraits showcasing Natalya's duel-worthy visage, the couple's four children, and the last known rendering of Pushkin during his lifetime.

Near the apartment, Pushkin is said to have had his last meal at **The Literary Café** (formerly the 19th-century Beranger café; Nevsky Prospekt 18; 7 812 312 6057) on February 8, 1837, before setting off to meet his tragic end. Today the elegant second-floor restaurant pays homage to its doomed former patron with a wax effigy in the entryway and a menu containing several of Pushkin's favorite dishes.

REMEMBERING PUSHKIN: A bronze statue of the poet, located in Moscow's **Pushkin Square**, was unveiled in 1880 in the presence of two other literary luminaries, Ivan Turgenev and Fyodor Dostoyevsky, the latter of whom delivered a moving memorial speech.

Also in Moscow, the city of the poet's birth, is **The Pushkin Memorial Apartment** (53 Arbat Street; *www.pushkinmuseum.ru*) where the poet lived in 1831 after his marriage to the exquisite young beauty Natalya Goncharova. The pastel-blue Empire-style mansion contains ornate period furnishings and Pushkin memorabilia such as his writing desk and Natalya's embroidery table.

LITERARY RESTING PLACES

PÈRE-LACHAISE CEMETERY

Paris, France • *www.pere-lachaise.com*

Among those buried at what has been called "the grandest address in Paris" are Proust, Colette, and Oscar Wilde, whose tomb (at left) bore lipstick marks left by zealous mourners until it was cleaned and a barrier erected around it. Père-Lachaise "is a solemn city of winding streets and miniature marble temples and mansions of the dead gleaming white from a wilderness of foliage and fresh flowers," noted Mark Twain during an 1867 visit. "Not every city is so well peopled as this."

PANTHÉON

Paris, France • *www.pantheonparis.com*

Victor Hugo, Voltaire, and Émile Zola are buried in this domed, neoclassical mausoleum where many other great French men and women are also laid to rest. More recently interred here was Alexandre Dumas, whose remains were moved from his hometown to the Panthéon under the edict of French president Jacques Chirac in 2002.

THE MONTPARNASSE CEMETERY

Paris, France • *www.pariscemeteries.com*

"The communication of the dead is tongued with fire beyond the language of the living."
—T. S. ELIOT, "LITTLE GIDDING"

If, as Jean-Paul Sartre once wrote, "Hell is other people," the famed existentialist is no doubt rolling in his grave at this cemetery, which he shares with thousands of others. In death, as at the café table, he rests next to his lifelong love, Simone de Beauvoir. Poet Charles Baudelaire and Irish expatriate playwright Samuel Beckett are also buried in this cemetery in Paris's bohemian Montparnasse quarter.

WESTMINSTER ABBEY

London, England • www.westminster-abbey.org

Many of England's most distinguished literary luminaries, including Robert Browning, Geoffrey Chaucer, Charles Dickens, Thomas Hardy, Rudyard Kipling, and Alfred Tennyson, are buried in the abbey's south transept, known as Poets' Corner. Other writers, including John Milton, William Wordsworth, John Keats, Percy Bysshe Shelley, Robert Burns, William Blake, Jane Austen, and the Brontë sisters, are commemorated with memorials.

Henry James attended Robert Browning's 1889 funeral at Westminster Abbey, where he marveled at "the magnificent old cathedral" and its "dim sublime vastness." James, an American who lived most of his life in England, is also commemorated in Poets' Corner.

ST. PAUL'S CATHEDRAL

London, England • www.stpauls.co.uk

In St. Paul's Cathedral, scorch marks from the Great Fire of London in 1666 can still be seen on a memorial statue dedicated to 16th-century poet and preacher John Donne. The statue, executed from a sketch the poet had made on his deathbed, was one of the few monuments from "old St. Paul's" to survive the fire's devastation.

HIGHGATE CEMETERY

London, England • www.highgate-cemetery.org

Author George Eliot (aka Mary Ann Evans Cross) and German socialist Karl Marx, who spent the last three decades of his life in London, are buried in this Victorian Gothic cemetery. Emblazoned on Marx's tombstone is a command from the grave—"Workers of All Lands, Unite"—taken from the final line of his famed treatise, *The Communist Manifesto*.

HOLY TRINITY CHURCH

Stratford-upon-Avon, England • www.stratford-upon-avon.org

William Shakespeare was baptized and buried in this church on the banks of the River Avon in his beloved Stratford. Buried with him is his wife, Anne Hathaway.

"The stroke of death is as a lover's pinch, which hurts and is desired."
—SHAKESPEARE, ANTONY AND CLEOPATRA

THE NON-CATHOLIC CEMETERY IN ROME

Rome, Italy • *www.cemeteryrome.it*

English Romantic poets John Keats and Percy Bysshe Shelley died tragically young a mere year apart while living in Italy, and they are both buried in this Roman cemetery. Henry James visited their graves in 1873, describing the cemetery as "a mixture of tears and smiles, of stones and flowers, of mourning cypresses and radiant sky" and Keats's grave as "buried in roses—a happy grave every way for a poet who was personally poetic."

TOMBA DI DANTE

Ravenna, Italy • *www.turismo.ra.it*

BASILICA DE SANTA CROCE

Florence, Italy • *www.visitflorence.com*

Although Dante is buried in the northern Italian town of Ravenna where he had taken up residence after being exiled from Florence, the Florentines came to regret their harsh treatment of the poet and later demanded the return of his remains. Monks hid them away for safekeeping, and they remained undiscovered in Ravenna's **Church of San Francesco** for nearly two centuries until construction workers happened on them by accident in 1865. A tomb and funerary monument erected in Florence's **Basilica de Santa Croce** to this day remains empty.

A museum illustrating the life and times of Dante Alighieri, the **Casa di Dante** (39 055 219 416; *www.museocasadidante.it*), is located in a section of Florence, Italy, where the medieval-era poet is believed to have been born. Nearby is the **Church of Santa Margherita**, where Dante married Gemma Donati and first met Beatrice Portinari, the muse who inspired some of his work.

SLEEPY HOLLOW CEMETERY

Concord, MA • *www.concordchamberofcommerce.org*

Acquainted in life, Ralph Waldo Emerson, Henry David Thoreau, Nathaniel Hawthorne, and Louisa May Alcott are all laid to rest in a section of the cemetery known as Authors Ridge. In contrast to the modest tombstones marking the graves of Thoreau, Hawthorne, and Alcott, the monument to Emerson is a large rose quartz boulder.

VICARIOUS THRILLS FOR MYSTERY READERS:

Murder and Mayhem

SLEUTHING LIKE SAM SPADE

"A glorious golden falcon encrusted from head to foot with the finest jewels" is the coveted object that leads to murder in Dashiell Hammett's *The Maltese Falcon*. Sam Spade, the enigmatic private eye who unravels the mystery in the hard-boiled tale, plies his trade on the same San Francisco streets where Hammett once worked as an operative for the Pinkerton National Detective Agency.

John's Grill was a favorite haunt of Hammett, as well as the fictional Spade. For more about the Union Square eatery, see page 193. For information on slumbering in the Dashiell Hammett Suite at the Hotel Union Square, see page 175.

Don Herron leads amateur sleuths in the footsteps of Hammett and his characters on the **Dashiell Hammett Walking Tour** (*www.donherron.com/the-tour*). Sites include the apartment building where Hammett wrote *The Maltese Falcon*, as well as the novels *Red Harvest* and *The Dain Curse* featuring San Francisco–based secret agent the Continental Op, and the alley where Spade's sidekick, Miles Archer, meets his maker at the hands of a dangerous dame.

Those who can't make a scheduled tour can go it alone by purchasing a copy of Herron's *The Dashiell Hammett Tour: Thirtieth Anniversary Guidebook*, which includes maps and self-guided tours.

CASING SHERLOCK'S HOME

Sherlock Holmes Museum • 221b Baker Street • London NW1 6XE • Tel: (44) 207 224 3688 • *www.sherlock-holmes.co.uk* • Open daily

221b
SHERLOCK HOLMES
CONSULTING DETECTIVE
1881-1904

"I have my eye on a suite on Baker Street," confided Sir Arthur Conan Doyle's fictional detective Sherlock Holmes to the new acquaintance who was to become his roommate and unwitting partner in detection, Dr. Watson. Despite the renowned deductive powers of the masterful sleuth, there's one thing even Holmes couldn't have divined at the start of his adventures: That his unassuming flat would become one of the world's most famous addresses.

Although it's been more than a hundred years since the detective left his lodgings at 221b Baker Street—now the Sherlock Holmes Museum—visitors can be forgiven in thinking that he might reappear at any moment. The Victorian-era rooms have been vividly re-created just as they're described in *A Study in Scarlet* and other tales.

Awaiting Holmes's return are his most prized possessions: his tweed deerstalker cap and magnifying glass haphazardly tossed down after a long day's detecting, the Persian slipper where he eccentrically chose to store his tobacco, and the Stradivarius violin upon which he often gratingly scraped. While Watson gamely tolerated Holmes's eccentricities as a roommate, he rightfully considered him to be "the worst tenant in London." The detective forever tried the patience of their landlady, Mrs. Hudson, with his strange habits such as affixing correspondence to the mantelpiece with a jackknife and carrying out bizarre chemical experiments in the study.

To enter the fictional duo's quarters—the starting point of so many remarkable adventures—is to become, much like Watson himself, an accomplice in Holmes's exhilarating world. Posing for a picture on the armchair where inspiration often struck in front of the crackling fireplace, you can't help but pause, awaiting the dramatic moment when "a ring comes at the bell; a step is heard upon the stair." Then, without further ado, you are summoned: "Come, Watson, come, the game is afoot!"

UNCOVERING HOLMES'S LONDON

"What do you say to a ramble through London?" Holmes once proposed to Watson. Don your deerstalker hat and take him up on his offer by following **In the Footsteps of Sherlock Holmes** (*www.walks .com*). The walking tour imparts the same vicarious thrills that Holmes and Watson experienced in "watching the ever changing kaleidoscope of life as it ebbs and flows through Fleet Street and the

Strand." Among the sights you'll sniff out are Charing Cross Station, where the fictional duo often dashed to hop a train in hot pursuit of a clue, and Covent Garden's Royal Opera, where Holmes and Watson hurried to catch a Richard Wagner performance in *The Adventure of the Red Circle*.

"When we have finished at the police station, I think that something nutritious at Simpson's would not be out of place," Holmes said to Watson in the final line of *The Adventure of the Dying Detective*. Dating back to 1828, **Simpson's-in-the-Strand** (100 Strand; *www.simpsonsinthestrand.co.uk*) is a venerable London institution. With its rich wood paneling, crystal chandeliers, and beef carved tableside from antique serving ware, it's no wonder that Holmes and Watson mulled over clues and celebrated the end of successful cases in the restaurant's luxurious surroundings. Real-life literary luminaries like Charles Dickens dined here as well.

See pages 205–206 for the **Museum Tavern**, where Sir Arthur Conan Doyle once imbibed.

After dinner, savor a pint of Sherlock Holmes Ale at **The Sherlock Holmes** pub (10 Northumberland Street; *www.sherlockholmes -stjames.co.uk*), which featured as the Northumberland Hotel where Sir Henry Baskerville slumbered in *The Hound of the Baskervilles*. The hound's stuffed and mounted head is just one of the many Holmesian items on show, including period scientific equipment like Holmes used and illustrations that accompanied his adventures in the *Strand Magazine*. In the upstairs restaurant, dishes named after characters are served up adjacent to a room that re-creates the detective's Baker Street study.

Slumber at the grand Victorian-era **Langham Hotel** (*www.lang hamhotels.com*), where Holmes's creator, Sir Arthur Conan Doyle, dined in 1889 with an editor from *Lippincott's Monthly Magazine,* who commissioned his second novel, *The Sign of Four.* (Oscar Wilde was also at the dinner and later wrote *The Picture of Dorian Gray* for the magazine.) Captain Morstan, Watson's future father-in-law, stayed at the Langham in *The Sign of Four,* as did the King of Bohemia in *A Scandal in Bohemia*.

ON THE CASE IN OXFORD

English poet Matthew Arnold described Oxford as "that sweet city with her dreaming spires" in his verse "Thyrsis," but the collegiate town northwest of London has no shortage of intrigue and mayhem—at least on the page.

Dorothy L. Sayers's tenure at the University of Oxford's Somerville College served as inspiration for her pageturner *Gaudy Night*. Like her creator once did, the novel's Harriet Vane attends a gaudy (reunion feast) at her Oxford alma mater, Shrewsbury College. She's later called upon to find the perpetrator behind a series of malicious acts at the fictional academic institution.

DOROTHY L. SAYERS
Writer and Scholar
was born here
13th June 1893

After wrapping up the case, mystery writer Harriet accepts a marriage proposal from intrepid sleuth Lord Peter Wimsey near the **Magdalen Bridge** in *Gaudy Night*. The duo returns to Oxford to exchange vows at **St. Cross Church** in *Busman's Honeymoon*. In both books, Lord Peter slumbers at the **Mitre** (17 High Street), one of Oxford's oldest establishments, now operated by the Beefeater Restaurant chain.

Sayers was born at **1 Brewer Street,** where a plaque notes the occasion. (Oxford is also the birthplace of mystery novelist P. D. James.) In 1916, a year after graduating from Somerville, Sayers worked for the publishing division of Blackwell's in Oxford. The company's flagship store, **Blackwell's Bookshop** (48-51 Broad Street; *www.blackwells.co.uk*), has been an Oxford institution since 1879. "Mr. Blackwell's little shop" began as a 12-square-foot space and now comprises several storefronts. The cavernous 10,000-square-foot Norrington Room houses more than 250,000 tomes on about three miles of shelving. Blackwell's offers a **Literary Tour** (typically mid-April through October), a walking jaunt that illustrates Oxford's literary heritage. Along with sites related to Sayers are those connected to Percy Bysshe Shelley, C. S. Lewis, Lewis Carroll, and other classic authors.

Oxford resident Colin Dexter used the city as the milieu in 13 novels featuring Inspector Morse, who made his debut in *Last Bus to Wood-*

stock and subsequently leaped from page to screen as the star of a phenomenally popular television series. The sleuth was a regular patron at Oxford's drinking establishments, among them the **Eagle and Child** (49 St Giles), where Morse and his sidekick, Inspector Lewis, theorize over pints; the **White Horse** (52 Broad Street), situated next to Blackwell's Bookshop; the bar at the **Randolph Hotel** (Beaumont Street), now named Morse for the inspector; the **Bear Inn** (6 Alfred Street), where "a drinking house has been on the site since 1242" (*Death Is Now My Neighbor*); and the **Turf Tavern** (4 Bath Place), with its "rough-stoned, black-beamed rooms" reached "via a narrow, irregularly cobbled lane of medieval aspect" (*The Daughters of Cain*).

See page 203 for more on the **Eagle and Child** and its literary history.

The Oxford Information Centre (*www.visitoxfordandoxfordshire .com*) offers the **Inspector Morse Walking Tour** and more, including literary-themed excursions related to *Alice in Wonderland* and to *Lord of the Rings* creator J.R.R. Tolkien.

INVESTIGATING THE SCENE OF THE CRIME (CAPER)

Soak up the atmosphere in southwest Scotland, where Dorothy Sayers and her husband often vacationed and where Lord Peter Wimsey solves a murder in *The Five Red Herrings,* a colorful crime caper set in nearby towns Kirkcudbright and Gatehouse of Fleet.

Sayers penned the book while staying in Kirkcudbright, an artists' colony and fishing village, at **No. 14a High Street** near the atmospheric ruins of a 16th-century castle. When a widely disliked painter is murdered in the tale, Wimsey deduces the killer from among six artist suspects. Top off a day of sleuthing at the **Selkirk Arms** (129 High Street; *www.selkirkarmshotel.co.uk*), a dining and lodging establishment used as the model for the McClellan Arms in *The Five Red Herrings.* The mystery scribe herself stayed at the Anwoth Hotel in Gatehouse of Fleet. Now named the **Ship Inn** (*www.theshipinngate house.com*), it's where Wimsey dined and a suspect stayed.

See page 185 for more about the **Selkirk Arms**, which has connections to Scottish bard Robert Burns.

On the Trail of Agatha Christie

O N THE GENTEEL ENGLISH RIVIERA that went on to provide the perfect foil for evil under the sun, Agatha Christie was born on September 15, 1890. Although the Queen of Crime lived out many of her 85 years near the seaside town of her birth in Torquay, Devon, her travels to exotic locales provided further inspiration for her large oeuvre.

◉ Say a prayer at Torquay's **All Saint's Church** (Bampfylde Road), where the author was baptized and later attended Sunday services.

◉ Walk the **Agatha Christie Mile,** which takes in Christie landmarks along Torquay's palm tree-lined harbor, including the Princess Pier, where the author would often roller-skate as a young girl. Pick up the scent with a leaflet at the visitor information center (5 Vaughan Parade).

◉ Go behind the scenes of Christie's works at the **Torquay Museum** (529 Babbacombe Road; *www.torquaymuseum.org*). In the Christie Gallery, visitors can step inside Poirot's study and lounge, a recreation of the London art deco apartment that featured in the TV adaptations of *Agatha Christie's Poirot*. Also on display are some of Poirot's dapper three-piece suits and his walking stick, donated by actor David Suchet.

◉ Have an *Endless Night* at one of Devon's three elegant seaside hotels boasting Christie connections:

• Agatha and Archie Christie honeymooned at **The Grand Hotel** (*www.grandtorquay.co.uk*) overlooking Torquay Bay following their Christmas Eve wedding in 1914.

• The **Imperial Hotel** (*www.thehotelcollection .co.uk*) was the thinly disguised Majestic Hotel in *Peril at End House, The Body in the Library,* and Christie's final novel, *Sleeping Murder.*

• Christie wrote *And Then There Were None* and *Evil Under the Sun* in a specially commissioned beach hut (see photo) at the art deco **Burgh Island Hotel** (*www.burghisland.com*), dramatically set on a private isle off the Devon coast.

◉ Make yourself comfortable at **Greenway** (Galmpton; *www.nationaltrust.org .uk/greenway*), the Devonshire retreat that Christie called "the loveliest place in the world." For Christie, the gracious Georgian mansion was a place for relaxation. While at Greenway, she read, worked on her notebooks, and enjoyed time with family but did not write. After Christie's death, the house was donated to the National Trust by her descendants and remains much as the author would have known it, with its contents intact. Among its highlights are Christie's Remington typewriter and Steinway piano, which she was too shy to play in public.

◉ Disappear at the **Old Swan Hotel** (*www .classiclodges.co.uk*), a former 18th-century stage-coach inn located in the northern English spa town of Harrogate. When Christie mysteriously vanished in 1926, an 11-day nationwide manhunt ended at the Old Swan, where the Queen of Crime had checked in under an alias using the surname of her husband's mistress, Nancy Neele.

Mystery writers Sir Arthur Conan Doyle and Dorothy L. Sayers were among those enlisted to consult on the case of Agatha Christie's 11-day disappearance in 1926.

◉ Make tracks on the decadent **Venice Simplon Orient Express** (*www.orient-express.com*). While not the original train used as the setting for Christie's *Murder on the Orient Express,* the vintage carriages of its modern-day doppelgänger so closely evoke the novel's feel that scenes from the Oscar-winning big-screen adaptation were filmed on board. At the train's

"All my life I had wanted to go on the Orient Express," Agatha Christie wrote in *An Autobiography.* Her 1931 journey on the train, during which passengers were stranded onboard in rural Greece due to flooding, inspired her novel *Murder on the Orient Express.*

southern terminus in Istanbul, Christie stayed at the **Pera Palace Hotel** (*www.jumeirah.com*) after her own journeys on the Orient Express. Guests can check into room 411, where the author once slumbered and reportedly hid a mysterious key that was found under the floorboards.

◉ Walk like an Egyptian at Aswan's **Old Cataract Hotel** (*www.sofitel.com*). Christie stayed at these exotic Moorish-style lodgings overlooking the Nile with her second husband, archaeologist Max Mallowan, during their trips to Egypt. The author was fascinated with the subject of Egyptology and found inspiration for her novels *Death on the Nile* and *Death Comes in the End* while traveling in the country.

◉ Take in a production of Christie's dramatic thriller, **The Mousetrap**—the world's longest running play—at London's St. Martin's Theatre.

"I'd like to go up the Nile, wouldn't you?"
—DEATH ON THE NILE

Novel Dispatches:

WRITERS AT HOME AND ABROAD

In this chapter . . .
CHRONICLER OF THE JAZZ AGE: F. SCOTT FITZGERALD
RUGGED ADVENTURER: ERNEST HEMINGWAY
AN INNOCENT ABROAD: MARK TWAIN
FAMED FRANCOPHILE: EDITH WHARTON
MORE AND MORE, NEVER APART: HENRY JAMES AND EDITH WHARTON

These five nomadic writers plied their craft on both sides of the Atlantic, occasionally returning to the familiar comforts of home, but more often than not seeking out adventure and inspiration around the globe. Although their writings varied in content and style, these authors shared a wanderlust that shaped their lives and defined their work. Evoked in the novels of Ernest Hemingway, F. Scott Fitzgerald, and Henry James, as well as the travel narratives of Mark Twain and Edith Wharton, are timeless renderings of their sublime and remarkable journeys. From a cave on the banks of the Mississippi River to the glamorous beaches of the French Riviera, many of the places they immortalized still echo with the sound of their footsteps.

F. Scott Fitzgerald

F. Scott Fitzgerald is synonymous with the Jazz Age (a phrase he coined), capturing in his novels and short stories the glamour and excess that epitomized the 1920s. From his days at Princeton University to the expatriate life in France and his tempestuous marriage to southern belle Zelda Sayre, Fitzgerald mirrored many of his own experiences in his fiction. He also used the landscapes with which he was familiar to create a vivid sense of place in his literary works—Princeton in *This Side of Paradise*, New York City and its environs in *The Beautiful and Damned* and *The Great Gatsby*, the French Riviera, Paris, and Switzerland in *Tender Is the Night*, and Hollywood in his final novel, *The Love of the Last Tycoon*, left unfinished at the time of his death from a heart attack at age 44.

St. Paul, Minnesota

FITZGERALD'S BIRTHPLACE

481 Laurel Avenue

Francis Scott Key Fitzgerald was born in a second-floor apartment in this St. Paul building on September 24, 1896, and lived here with his family for two years. The future scribe was named for the composer of "The Star-Spangled Banner," a distant relative. (The building is privately occupied and can only be viewed from the outside.)

FITZGERALD HOUSE

599 Summit Avenue

After a postcollege stint in the Army and a poverty-stricken turn as an advertising copywriter in New York City, Fitzgerald returned to St. Paul. During the summer of 1919, he sequestered himself in a top-floor room in his parents' home and revised his first novel. In September, Fitzgerald

Nobel Prize winner Sinclair Lewis once rented a house at **516 Summit Avenue** in late 1917. He intended to write about robber baron and railway magnate James J. Hill (referenced by Fitzgerald in *The Great Gatsby*), whose red sandstone mansion at 240 Summit gave the street the epithet "Avenue of the Barons." For more about Sinclair Lewis, see pages 54–55.

received word that the novel had been accepted by the renowned Manhattan publisher Scribner's, and he promptly gave up the job he had taken as a railroad laborer. "That day I quit work and ran along the streets," he recalled, "stopping automobiles to tell friends and acquaintances about it—my novel, *This Side of Paradise,* was accepted for publication." (The building is privately occupied and can only be viewed from the outside.)

F. SCOTT FITZGERALD WALKING TOUR

The St. Paul Public Library's **F. Scott Fitzgerald in St. Paul: Homes and Haunts** self-guided walking tour highlights landmarks in the city associated with the writer and his works, among them *The Great Gatsby* and the short stories "The Ice Palace" and "The Scandal Detectives." A free copy of the walking tour can be downloaded at *www.sppl .org/research/special-collections/f-scott-fitzgerald-reading-alcove.* On display in the **F. Scott Fitzgerald Reading Alcove** at the Central Library branch (90 West Fourth Street) is a small collection of items related to the writer. Located in nearby **Rice Park** is a statue of Fitzgerald.

MONTGOMERY, ALABAMA

Fitzgerald met his future wife, Zelda Sayre, in July 1918 at a country club dance in her hometown of Montgomery. During his senior year at Princeton, Fitzgerald had enrolled in the Army and was stationed at Camp Sheridan near Montgomery, where nearly 18-year-old Zelda was famous for wild behavior like smoking in public.

THE SCOTT AND ZELDA FITZGERALD MUSEUM

919 Felder Avenue • Tel: 334-264-4222
• *www.thefitzgeraldmuseum.org* • Closed Mondays

After their return from Europe in 1931, the Fitzgeralds resided in this house for several months with their nine-year-old daughter, Scottie. Here Fitzgerald worked on *Tender Is the Night* and Zelda on her semi-autobiographical novel, *Save Me the*

Waltz. The museum's broad array of artifacts, heirlooms, and memorabilia spans the couple's lives, marriage, and careers and includes personal letters, Zelda's original artwork, accessories like her flapper-era, feather-adorned headband, all of Scott's short stories published in the *Saturday Evening Post* and *Esquire,* and their record collection. Located in the Old Cloverdale Historic District, this is the only museum dedicated to the Jazz Age pair.

New York, New York

Young newlyweds Scott and Zelda lived in New York City, basking in the author's overnight celebrity after the publication of *This Side of Paradise* in 1920. They were regularly written up in gossip columns for their outrageous escapades, such as Zelda jumping into the Washington Square Park fountain and Scott undressing at a theater. Their manic lifestyle provided fodder for Fitzgerald's second novel, *The Beautiful and Damned.*

ST. PATRICK'S CATHEDRAL

Fifth Avenue between 50th and 51st Streets • www.saintpatrickscathedral.org
• Open daily

The Fitzgeralds were married in the rectory of St. Patrick's Cathedral on April 3, 1920. This Fifth Avenue church is the largest Gothic-style Catholic cathedral in the United States. Zelda had previously broken off her engagement to Scott, refusing to marry the struggling writer until he had achieved a measure of success.

PLAZA HOTEL

Fifth Avenue and Central Park South • Tel: 212-759-3000 • www.theplazany.com

Scott and Zelda lodged, drank, and dined at this posh Manhattan hotel located steps from Central Park. While living nearby in an apartment at 38 West 59th Street, they ordered their meals from the Plaza. Fitzgerald used this national historic landmark as a setting in *The Beautiful and Damned,* as well as for the backdrop of a pivotal scene in *The Great Gatsby.* In a suite at the Plaza, Jay Gatsby, Daisy

Buchanan, and their friends convene to drink mint juleps on a hot summer day. Before Daisy can mix the drinks, though, Gatsby has a confrontation with her husband, Tom, over his feelings for her.

The *Gatsby* group motored to the Plaza from Long Island. Fitzgerald modeled the town of West Egg, the site of Gatsby's mansion, on upscale **Great Neck**, where he and Zelda lived for 19 months and often hosted soirees (which sometimes lasted for days) reminiscent of the nouveau riche title character's lavish parties.

BALTIMORE AND ROCKVILLE, MARYLAND

After a fire at their rented house in Towson, Maryland, the Fitzgeralds moved to **1307 Park Avenue** in Baltimore, the last place they lived together as a family. (A commemorative plaque adorns the building, a private residence.)

Forty miles outside Baltimore, Scott and Zelda are interred in the cemetery at **St. Mary's Church** in Rockville, where their tombstone is etched with the concluding line of *The Great Gatsby*: "So we beat on, boats against the current, borne back ceaselessly into the past."

PARIS, FRANCE

"We were going to the Old World to find a new rhythm for our lives, with a true conviction that we had left our old selves behind forever," Fitzgerald penned in an essay for the *Saturday Evening Post* in 1924, shortly after he and Zelda arrived in France for their first extended stay. A favorable exchange rate meant they could live a more lavish lifestyle abroad than they could in the United States. Once there, Fitzgerald became part of the famed circle of 1920s expatriate writers known as the lost generation.

AUBERGE DE VENISE
(FORMERLY THE DINGO AMERICAN BAR)

10 rue Delambre, 14e • Tel: (33) 1 43 35 43 09 • www.aubergedevenise.fr

This Montparnasse location used to be the site of the Dingo American Bar where Fitzgerald first made Hemingway's acquaintance two

Fitzgerald Slept Here (AND YOU CAN TOO!)

CAPRI TIBERIO PALACE RESORT, CAPRI, ITALY

www.capritiberiopalace.it

Fitzgerald spent two months on the Italian isle of Capri in 1925, lodging in this Mediterranean-style hotel overlooking the Gulf of Naples. While on the island, he anxiously awaited *The Great Gatsby*'s publication on April 10th of that year.

GRAND HÔTEL DE LA PAIX, LAUSANNE, SWITZERLAND

www.hoteldelapaix.net

Fitzgerald spent time in Switzerland in the early 1930s to be near Zelda while she received psychiatric treatment at a sanitarium. One of the places he lodged is this luxury hotel on the shores of Lake Geneva in the Alps, where he had an affair with an eccentric and titled Englishwoman who became the model for a character in the short story "The Hotel Child."

GROVE PARK INN, ASHEVILLE, NORTH CAROLINA

www.groveparkinn.com

Fitzgerald stayed at this Blue Ridge Mountain resort in the 1930s while seeking treatment for tuberculosis, and he later returned for rest and relaxation while Zelda convalesced in a nearby mental hospital. The writer is lauded with a birthday salute annually in late September, and the three-day fest includes musical tributes, lectures, tours of the room he occupied (number 441), and a poetry contest.

LOEWS DON CESAR HOTEL, ST. PETE BEACH, FLORIDA

www.loewshotels.com/don-cesar

Dubbed "Florida's Pink Castle" when it opened in 1928, this brightly hued hotel—featuring Mediterranean and Moorish architectural accents—sits on an island in the Gulf of Mexico. The grandiose surroundings were far from idyllic for Scott and Zelda, who suffered a mental breakdown during the couple's visit in January 1932.

weeks after the publication of *The Great Gatsby* in 1925. Today the once rowdy bar is a cozy Italian restaurant.

RITZ PARIS
15 place Vendôme, 1e • Tel: (33) 1 43 16 30 30
• *www.ritzparis.com*

The Bar Hemingway (now named for Fitzgerald's friend and fellow scribe Ernest Hemingway) was a favorite destination for the writer when he had the cash to live the high life. *Tender Is the Night*'s Abe North drinks solo at the Ritz Paris, where a guest suite bears Fitzgerald's name.

PARIS ADDRESSES
In 1925, Scott and Zelda rented a furnished apartment at **14 rue de Tilsitt** on the city's Right Bank. Hemingway, then a fledgling novelist, later described the space as gloomy in *A Moveable Feast*, but the address—near the fashionable Champs d'Élysée and the Arc de Triomphe—was far more posh than his own on the cheaper, bohemian Left Bank. Other

IN FITZGERALD'S FOOTSTEPS: On their first trip abroad, a two-month sojourn in 1921, Scott and Zelda visited London and Paris before heading to Rome, Florence, and Venice. They took in sites like **Buckingham Palace** in London, the palace of **Versailles** near Paris, and Venice's picturesque canals. "We had fun in a gondola," the couple recalled of their Venetian jaunt, "feeling like a soft Italian song."

In London, Fitzgerald's friend, the writer Shane Leslie, escorted Scott and Zelda on a nighttime excursion to places where the notorious Jack the Ripper had slain his victims. The trio donned caps and work clothes, with Zelda disguised as a man. Those who would like to do something similar (disguise optional) can take the evening **Jack the Ripper Tour** given by **London Walks** (*www.walks.com*).

Fitzgerald had an emotional response while visiting the Rome residence where his favorite poet, John Keats, had died from consumption at the age of 26. For more about the **Keats-Shelley House**, see pages 43-44.

Parisian pads the couple rented were at **58 rue Vaugirard** by the Luxembourg Gardens in 1928, and **10 rue Pergolèse** the next year. (All are private buildings.)

Côte d'Azur, France

The French Riviera beckoned to Scott and Zelda time and again, spurring their frequent return to the fashionable seaside towns dotting this stretch of Mediterranean coastline in southeastern France. Here they experienced both pleasant and sad times, escalated by Fitzgerald's drinking and Zelda's affair with a French pilot. The author used the sun-drenched backdrop of the Riviera as the glamorous setting for the tragic unraveling of Dick and Nicole Diver's dysfunctional marriage in *Tender Is the Night,* published after Fitzgerald's return to America.

Fitzgerald once described his Paris days as a time of "1,000 parties and no work." Along with the Ritz, he could frequently be found carousing at **Harry's New York Bar** (5 rue Daunou; *www.harrysbar.fr*) and other establishments on his own or with a group of expatriate writers. For more places to drink and dine in the City of Light, see Parisian Cafés of the Literati on pages 201–203.

ANTIBES
Scott and Zelda were introduced to the Riviera by their wealthy friends Gerald and Sara Murphy, who owned a villa in Antibes and served unwittingly as the models for socialites Dick and Nicole Diver. In this chic resort town, the Fitzgeralds spent tranquil days at **La Garoupe Beach** with the Murphys, and Scott later immortalized the neighboring ultra-exclusive **Hôtel du Cap-Eden Roc** (*www.edenroc-hotel.fr*) as the "large, proud" Hôtel des Étrangers in *Tender Is the Night.*

JUAN-LES-PINS
"Our big house is right on the sea," Fitzgerald wrote of the elegant Villa Saint-Louis, which he and Zelda rented in 1926. "We are looking forward to a splendid summer." Fitzgerald entertained a then unknown Hemingway while living here, even critiquing a version of his breakthrough novel, *The Sun Also Rises.* Today the villa is the

picturesque **Hôtel Belles Rives** (*www.bellesrives.com*), where visitors can toast both writers with a cocktail at the Bar Fitzgerald.

ST.-PAUL-DE-VENCE

In this walled medieval hill town, Scott and Zelda dined at the **Colombe d'Or** hotel-restaurant (*www.la-colombe-dor.com*) with the Murphys, whose circle of acquaintances included the painter Pablo Picasso. (The Colombe d'Or boasts a magnificent collection of art, donated by Picasso and other artists as payment for food and lodging.) When Scott flirted with dancer Isadora Duncan, who was seated at a nearby table, Zelda threw herself down a set of stairs to recapture her husband's attention.

CITY OF WRITE: On the Left Bank of Paris, the English-language bookshop Shakespeare and Company at 12 rue de l'Odéon was a popular gathering place and lending library for expatriate writers in the 1920s and 1930s. Proprietor Sylvia Beach—an expat herself—fostered literary talent, floated the occasional loan, and in 1922 published James Joyce's controversial novel *Ulysses* at her own expense. Another customer and friend, Ernest Hemingway, aided Beach in having the book smuggled into the United States, where it was banned. The bookshop proprietor shares her story, and those of her famous patrons, in the memoir *Shakespeare and Company*.

Beach closed up shop in 1941 during the Nazi occupation of Paris, but the Shakespeare and Company legacy lives on. Partly to pay homage to Beach, American expat George Whitman changed the name of his Parisian bookstore from Le Mistral to Shakespeare and Company. Since opening in 1951, the shop has literally housed amid the stacks thousands of writers and artists (dubbed Tumbleweeds) in need of a place to stay. Author readings and events are regularly held at the store, which Henry Miller once described as "a wonderland of books." Shakespeare and Company is located at **37 rue de la Bûcherie** in an enviable spot along the Seine. A café next door has indoor and outdoor seating with views of Notre-Dame Cathedral. On offer is a lemon pie made George's way (*www.shakespeareandcompany.com*).

RUGGED ADVENTURER:

ERNEST HEMINGWAY

Hemingway's larger-than-life persona lingers in destinations spanning the globe, from Cuban watering holes and Parisian cafés to Spanish bullrings and the plains of Africa. Both in reality and on the page, he boldly celebrated the places that captured his imagination.

Wanderlust first overtook the budding writer in 1918, when the 19-year-old abandoned his job as a cub reporter at the *Kansas City Star* to enlist in the war effort. His myopic eyesight prevented him from passing the Army physical so he instead signed on as a Red Cross ambulance driver on the Italian front lines. This first taste of life abroad whetted Hemingway's insatiable appetite for adventure, and he was destined to live out the next 40 years in search of new thrills in distant lands.

OAK PARK, ILLINOIS

Ernest Hemingway was born in the middle-class Chicago suburb of Oak Park in 1899 and remained in the area with his parents and five siblings for the first 18 years of his life.

ERNEST HEMINGWAY BIRTHPLACE HOME AND MUSEUM

339 North Oak Park Avenue • *www.ehfop.org*

• Open Wednesday through Sunday

The writer's early childhood years were spent in a grand turreted Queen Anne–style, six-bedroom home owned by his wealthy maternal grandfather, Ernest Hall. Young Ernest was delivered by his father, Dr. Clarence Hemingway, who afterward stepped out on the porch and blew his cornet to herald the birth of his first son.

After grandfather Hall's passing, the Hemingways built a new home nearby at 600 Kenilworth Avenue (today a private residence) where they moved when the author was six years old. In 1992, the birthplace home was acquired by the Ernest Hemingway Foundation of Oak Park, which restored the dwelling to its original condition with period furnishings and items originally owned by the Hemingways.

Operated in conjunction with the birthplace home, the nearby **Ernest Hemingway Museum** displays rare photos and artifacts from the author's life, including childhood drawings and a report card. Also on display is the famous rejection letter he received from his first love, nurse Agnes von Kurowsky, who tended the shrapnel wounds he sustained on the European front lines. Hemingway later portrayed their relationship in his novel about a doomed World War I romance, *A Farewell to Arms*.

KEY WEST, FLORIDA

Hemingway resided on the isle from 1928 to 1939—one of the most prolific periods of his life—and it provided the backdrop for his only novel set in the United States, *To Have and Have Not*.

ERNEST HEMINGWAY HOME AND MUSEUM

907 Whitehead Street • Tel: 305-294-1136 • *www.hemingwayhome.com*
• Open daily

Hemingway's first home on U.S. soil after nearly a decade of life abroad was a two-story Spanish-colonial stone mansion purchased for $8,000 in 1931. See pages 319–33 for more on Key West.

SUN VALLEY AND KETCHUM, IDAHO

Hemingway came to this region in central Idaho on a publicity junket for glamorous Sun Valley Lodge in 1939, using the opportunity to rendezvous with the woman who became his third wife, Martha Gellhorn. The author relished the chance to hunt big game and feathered prey in the area's wooded terrain, and he returned on several occasions before settling in Ketchum for the final two years of his life.

The writer loved Sun Valley, but the region featured in only one of his stories, "The Shot," which describes a hunting excursion in which he felled a buck from 275 yards.

HEMINGWAY HOME

www.nature.org

"This place . . . was a wonderful buy," Hemingway wrote to a friend about his April 1959 purchase of the two-story chalet overlooking Big Wood River just west of Ketchum. "My health and Mary's [his fourth wife] needs a change of climate from the subtropics for part of each year." Unfortunately, Hemingway's brief time at his Ketchum home was overshadowed by his failing mental and physical health. Depressed by the prospect of losing his ability to write, Hemingway died of a self-inflicted gunshot wound in the house's front foyer during the early morning hours of July 2, 1961. He was 61 years old. During his final months in his Ketchum home, Hemingway finished work on his Paris memoir, *A Moveable Feast.*

Sun Valley was a popular resort with the Hollywood set, and Hemingway often socialized with stars such as Ingrid Bergman and Gary Cooper, who starred in the film version of his novel *For Whom the Bell Tolls.*

Upon Mary Hemingway's death 25 years later, the house was bequeathed to the Nature Conservancy, which has maintained it as it was during the writer's time there. The house, located approximately one mile north of Ketchum, is not open to the public.

KETCHUM CEMETERY

Located off Highway 75 between Knob Hill Park and the Bigwood Golf Course

Ernest and Mary Hemingway are buried beneath three spruce trees in side-by-side graves marked by plain granite slabs. Nearby is the grave of Hemingway's granddaughter Margaux, who also took her own life.

HEMINGWAY MEMORIAL

Trail Creek Road

Northeast of Ketchum near Sun Valley Lodge is a memorial to the author. The bronze bust of Hemingway is inscribed with his words, originally penned for a friend who died in a 1939 hunting accident: "Best of all he loved the fall / The leaves yellow on the cottonwoods / Leaves floating on the trout streams / And above the hills / The high blue windless skies / Now he will be a part of them forever."

MICHEL'S CHRISTIANIA RESTAURANT AND OLYMPIC BAR

Sun Valley Road • Tel: 208-726-3388 • *www.michelschristiania.com*

This elegant French restaurant was one of Hemingway's favorite local eating establishments and the place where he dined with Mary the night before his death.

TRAIL CREEK CABIN

1.5 miles east of Sun Valley on Trail Creek Road • Tel: 208-622-2135

The Hemingways dined at this cozy log cabin on New Year's Eve 1947 with a star-studded crowd that included Ingrid Bergman and Gary Cooper. A decade later, the Hemingways threw a dinner party for 40 here on December 26, 1958. Today, diners are whisked by romantic sleigh ride to the restaurant, which serves up hearty fare such as steak and prime rib.

PARIS, FRANCE

At the urging of writer Sherwood Anderson, newlyweds Ernest and Hadley Hemingway pulled up stakes from Chicago in 1921 and moved to Paris, where the cost of living was cheap and inspiration from the bohemian artistic scene was as free flowing as the wine. The aspiring writer quickly fell in with other American expat scribes including T. S. Eliot, Ezra Pound, John Dos Passos, and Gertrude Stein, who famously coined the phrase "lost generation" in reference to their motley group.

"If you are lucky enough to have lived in Paris as a young man, then wherever you go for the rest of your life it stays with you, for Paris is a moveable feast."

—A MOVEABLE FEAST

The expression resonated with Hemingway, who popularized it in the epigraph of his roman à clef *The Sun Also Rises*, which follows a dissolute band of expats from the cafés of Paris to the *corridas* of Pamplona.

74 RUE DU CARDINAL LEMOINE, 5E

"Home in the Rue Cardinal Lemoine was a two-room flat that had no hot water and no inside toilet facilities except an antiseptic container, not uncomfortable to anyone who was used to a Michigan outhouse," Hemingway reminisced in *A Moveable Feast*, recalling the Paris apartment that he and Hadley rented shortly after their arrival.

"With a fine view and a good mattress and springs for a comfortable bed on the floor, and pictures we liked on the walls, it was a cheerful, gay flat," he recollected.

Explore the writer's Latin Quarter haunts on the **Hemingway's Paris walking tour**. See pages 157–58 for details.

The couple rented the furnished fourth-floor walk-up, located in the Latin Quarter, for 250 francs a month (about $18 at the time). (This building is privately occupied and can only be viewed from the outside.)

39 RUE DESCARTES, 5E

"I had a room on the top floor where I worked. It was either six or eight flights up to the top floor and it was very cold," Hemingway recalled of the space he rented to write around the corner from his small apartment. Formerly a hotel, it is also the location where French poet Paul Verlaine died in 1896. (This building is privately occupied and can only be viewed from the outside.)

6 RUE FÉROU, 6E

Hemingway moved into an apartment at this address with his second wife, Pauline Pfeiffer, in 1927. It was here where the author began work on his World War I novel, *A Farewell to Arms,* which he would later finish in Key West. Two weeks prior to his departure, Hemingway had an unfortunate run-in with a glass skylight during a late-night bathroom break. After mistakenly yanking what he thought was the toilet chain, the overhead skylight came crashing down, resulting in a head wound that required nine stitches and left a permanent scar. (This building is privately occupied and can only be viewed from the outside.)

"It is the conversation of Paris that I always miss so. That and the Luxembourg Gardens and the wine and the newspapers."
—ERNEST HEMINGWAY IN A 1925 LETTER

JARDIN DU LUXEMBOURG, 6E

During the seven years Hemingway lived in Paris, his favorite refuge was this 60-acre park bridging the Latin Quarter with Montparnasse. Hemingway once claimed to have been

Hemingway Slept Here (AND YOU CAN TOO!)

HOTEL D'ANGLETERRE, PARIS, FRANCE

www.hotel-dangleterre.com

Upon arrival in Paris on December 21, 1921, Ernest and Hadley Hemingway checked into room 14 at this hotel in the city's chic St.-Germain-des-Prés area. Sherwood Anderson, who had urged the Hemingways to move to Paris, had stayed here the previous fall.

HOTEL AMBOS MUNDOS, HAVANA, CUBA

www.hotelambosmundos-cuba.com

"I have a wonderful place to work in Cuba with no telephone, nobody can possibly bother you," Hemingway wrote to his editor from the Ambos Mundos in March 1939. The manuscript he was hard at work on was *For Whom the Bell Tolls*, and the room in which he stayed, number 511, has been maintained as a veritable shrine. (Hotel guests can view it free of charge; nonguests pay a small fee.)

HOTEL LA PERLA, PAMPLONA, SPAIN

www.granhotellaperla.com

Hemingway stayed at this hotel in the Plaza del Castillo occasionally during his trips to Pamplona for the Festival of San Fermín, although he usually preferred the less expensive La Quintana, which no longer exists. While Hemingway's room can be requested, don't hold out hope for booking it during the festival—it's been reserved through 2040 by a zealous Swedish fan.

SUN VALLEY LODGE, SUN VALLEY, IDAHO

www.sunvalley.com

Hemingway first came to Sun Valley Lodge in December 1939 at the invitation of the resort's owner. The writer was given Parlor Suite number 206, which he dubbed "Glamour House" and returned to several times. The final chapters of *For Whom the Bell Tolls* were written in this room, where Hemingway posed at his typewriter for the dust jacket photo.

so poor during his early Paris years that he resorted to snatching pigeons from the park for his wife to cook for dinner.

HAVANA, CUBA

ERNEST HEMINGWAY MUSEUM (LA FINCA VIGÍA)

San Francisco de Paula, Cuba • Tel: (53) 7 91 08 09 • *www.hemingwaycuba.com* • Open daily; call to confirm opening times

This 13-acre estate overlooking Havana was home to Hemingway for nearly two decades. Known as La Finca Vigía (Spanish for "lookout farm"), the hundred-year-old colonial-style property became a refuge for the author in 1939, and he went on to live there for nearly two decades. At La Finca, he wrote arguably the two most important works of his career: his Spanish Civil War novel, *For Whom the Bell Tolls,* and his 1952 Pulitzer Prize–winning tale of man versus marlin, *The Old Man and the Sea.*

Remarkably, most of his personal possessions have remained at La Finca nearly as they were at the time of his 1960 departure—from the daily record of his weight and blood pressure penciled on the bathroom wall (he suffered from several ailments in later years and continually worried about his health), to fishing rods and marlin lures, his library of 9,000 books (including several on a strategically located bookcase in the bathroom), and his favorite armchair. (Note that rooms are only viewable from outside of La Finca's large open windows. English-speaking guides posted outside each room share stories of Hemingway's time at the home.)

In addition to surveying La Finca's rooms, visitors can take in the lush surrounding grounds to see the pool where Ava Gardner famously swam naked and the place where Papa's presence is most palpable: his beloved fishing yacht, *Pilar.*

Lack of funding for upkeep, heat and humidity, and the ravages of time took a toll on the home. The American nonprofit Finca Vigía Foundation (*www.fincafoundation.org*), in association with the Cuban government, is spearheading ongoing restoration efforts to preserve the house and its treasures.

AN INNOCENT ABROAD:

Mark Twain

"Travel is fatal to prejudice."
—THE INNOCENTS ABROAD

Before Mark Twain penned *The Adventures of Tom Sawyer* and other novels, he earned his living as a newspaper correspondent and travel writer. In his first full-length book, *The Innocents Abroad,* he wittily chronicled an 1867 voyage to Europe and the Holy Land. One reviewer deemed Twain's travelogue "instructive, humorous, racy, full of quaint expressions that make you laugh unexpectedly."

During an era when travel was no easy feat, the man whom William Faulkner credited as "the first truly American writer" managed to cover a lot of ground. Throughout his lifetime, Twain crisscrossed the United States and navigated the globe, visiting such far-flung locales as England, Italy, Scotland, Australia, India, and South Africa. Even his nom de plume reflected his love of travel: "Mark Twain" is a nautical term meaning 12 feet—water deep enough for a riverboat to pass through safely.

FLORIDA, MISSOURI

MARK TWAIN BIRTHPLACE STATE HISTORIC SITE

37352 Shrine Road • Tel: 573-565-3449 • *www.mostateparks.com* • Open daily April through October; Friday through Sunday, November through March

CRUISING THE MISSISSIPPI: Make like Mark Twain, who was once a riverboat pilot, and cruise the Mighty Mississippi. From May through October, the Hannibal-based **Mark Twain Riverboat** (*www.marktwainriverboat.com*) offers one-hour sightseeing cruises and two-hour dinner excursions, along with weekend music cruises during the summer months. For lengthier Mississippi River outings, the **American Queen Steamboat Company** (*www.americanqueensteamboat company.com*) offers five- to 23-day vacations aboard a paddle-wheel steamboat with Victorian-style decor.

Mark Twain was born Samuel Langhorne Clemens in 1835 in a two-room cabin in small-town Florida, Missouri. The cabin is now preserved inside a museum at the Mark Twain Birthplace State Historic Site, which is adjacent to the 2,775-acre Mark Twain State Park. A monument marks the spot of the cabin's original location. "The village contained a hundred people and I increased the population by one per cent," wrote humorist Twain in his autobiography. "It is more than the best man in history ever did for any other town."

HANNIBAL, MISSOURI

Hannibal is immortalized as the fictional St. Petersburg in Mark Twain's *The Adventures of Tom Sawyer* and *The Adventures of Huckleberry Finn*. He drew on his rich memories of growing up in this Mississippi River town in the 1840s to create many of the characters and events in the stories. Twain lived in Hannibal, which he described as "a boy's paradise," from 1839 to 1853, when he boarded a boat heading down the Mississippi bound for St. Louis.

MARK TWAIN BOYHOOD HOME AND MUSEUM

120 North Main • Tel: 573-221-9010
• *www.marktwainmuseum.org* • Open daily; hours vary seasonally

The **Mark Twain Boyhood Home** was saved from demolition by a generous benefactor and presented to the city in 1912. Among the **Museum Gallery's** treasures are Twain's typewriter and one of the signature white suit coats he took to wearing later in life. Fifteen original Norman Rockwell paintings depict scenes from *The Adventures of Tom Sawyer* and *The Adventures of Huckleberry Finn*.

The **National Tom Sawyer Days** festival is held annually in Hannibal in early July. Activities include frog jumping and fence-painting contests (*www.hannibaljaycees.org*).

Museum properties also include an **Interpretive Center** with an exhibit highlighting Twain's experiences in Hannibal, as well as several historic buildings related to the legendary raconteur—including the **Becky Thatcher House,** the childhood home of Laura Hawkins, the inspiration for the character in *The Adventures of Tom Sawyer;* and the **Huckleberry Finn House,** a reconstruction of the home of Tom Blankenship, the boy Twain declared to be the model for Huck Finn.

"By-and-by somebody shouted: 'Who's ready for the cave?' Everybody was."

—THE ADVENTURES OF TOM SAWYER

MARK TWAIN CAVE

300 Cave Hollow Road • Tel: 800-527-0304 • *www.marktwaincave.com* • Open daily; hours vary seasonally

Known as McDougal's cave in *The Adventures of Tom Sawyer* and now named after the writer, this "vast labyrinth of crooked aisles" is where Tom and Becky become lost during a picnic—and where Tom and Huck later return to collect a fortune. An hour-long tour through the peculiar rock formations and passageways in the cave (where young Twain ventured time and again) highlights points of interest mentioned in his writings.

ELMIRA, NEW YORK

While sailing on board the steamship *Quaker City* on his first European voyage in 1867, Twain was intrigued by a miniature portrait shown to him by fellow passenger Charley Langdon. The face belonged to Charley's sister, Olivia, whom Twain later married. The couple wed in the parlor of the Langdon home in Elmira and often returned to this town in northern New York State to spend summers at Quarry Farm, the home of Olivia's sister. For information on the area, visit *www.marktwaincountry.com.*

MARK TWAIN STUDY AND MARK TWAIN EXHIBIT

The Center for Mark Twain Studies • Elmira College • One Park Place • Tel: 607-735-1941 • *www.elmira.edu* • Study: May through mid-October; Exhibit: May through Labor Day; other times by appointment

Twain's sister-in-law presented him with an octagonal gazebo on the property of Quarry Farm to use as a study, and it has since been moved to the Elmira College campus. An accompanying exhibit in Cowles Hall presents photos and mementos related to Twain. A bronze Mark Twain statue, a gift from the college, measures 12 feet—or, in the vernacular used by riverboat pilots, "mark twain."

In Elmira in 1889, Twain entertained then unknown Rudyard Kipling, who sought him out while journeying through America en route from India to England. It wasn't until a year later, when Twain was given a copy of *Plain Tales from the Hills* and a newspaper clipping about the writer, that he realized exactly who his visitor was. For more about Rudyard Kipling, see pages 72–73.

MARK TWAIN'S GRAVE SITE

Woodlawn Cemetery • 1200 Walnut Street

This cemetery is the final resting place of Mark Twain, his wife, and their four children. "I came in with Halley's comet," Twain wrote in 1909, referring to the celestial wonder visible in the skies the year he was born. "It is coming again next year, and I expect to go out with it. It will be the great disappointment of my life if I don't." His wish was granted. Twain died on April 21, 1910, at the age of 74.

CHEMUNG VALLEY HISTORY MUSEUM

415 East Water Street • Tel: 607-734-4167 • *www.chemungvalleymuseum.org* • Open year-round; closed Sundays

The museum's collection includes Twain's laptop writing desk and photographs of him at various locations in Elmira. A cell phone audio tour leads to sites around town associated with the writer.

HARTFORD, CONNECTICUT

MARK TWAIN HOUSE AND MUSEUM

351 Farmington Avenue • Tel: 860-247-0998 • *www.marktwainhouse.org* • Open daily; closed Tuesdays, January and February

"We could not enter it unmoved," Twain said of the 25-room Victorian Gothic manse where he put down roots for 17 years. Gables,

For more about Twain's famous Hartford neighbor, *Uncle Tom's Cabin* author Harriet Beecher Stowe, see pages 65–66.

chimneys, porches, and a colorful palette of painted brick come together to form an architecturally whimsical abode that a Hartford newspaper called "one of the oddest looking buildings in the state ever designed for a dwelling, if not the whole country." Twain commissioned construction of the house, which has design elements by Louis C. Tiffany & Co. and contains grandiose souvenirs the writer brought back from his travels. A mantelpiece above the library fireplace was purchased from Ayton Castle in Scotland, and in the master bedroom stands an elaborately carved wooden bed bought in Venice. Twain and his wife slept at the foot of the bed so they could admire the angels that decorate the headboard.

A museum center on the property features an exhibit on Twain's life and legacy, a Ken Burns documentary about the writer, and a gallery with changing exhibits.

THE BIG ISLAND, HAWAII

HAWAI'I VOLCANOES NATIONAL PARK

www.nps.gov/havo

Under cover of darkness, Mark Twain witnessed "a scene of wild beauty. There was a heavy fog over the crater and it was splendidly illuminated by the glare from the fires below," he recalled in *Roughing It*. One of the most active volcanoes on earth, Kilauea has erupted more than 60 times since 1823. Twain saw the "crimson cauldron," now part of **Hawai'i Volcanoes National Park**, while touring the Pacific islands (then known as the Cook Islands) on assignment for the *Sacramento Union* in 1866. He lodged at the **Volcano House Hotel** (*www.hawaiivolcanohouse.com*) near the geologic wonder, declaring in one of his newspaper dispatches that "the surprise of finding a good hotel in such an outlandish spot startled me considerably more than the volcano did." The four-bedroom wooden frame structure where Twain stayed, now the Volcano Art Center, has been replaced with a newer hotel.

Twain Slept Here (AND YOU CAN TOO!)

HOTEL NORMANDY, PARIS, FRANCE

www.hotel-normandy.com

Twain spent three months at this Parisian hotel in 1879, where street noise kept him awake at night. After he moved his bed to a quieter part of his rooms, he reported, "I sleep like a lamb and write like a lion." Shut-eye helped him produce the travel narrative *A Tramp Abroad*.

LANGHAM HOTEL, LONDON, ENGLAND

london.langhamhotels.com

This Victorian landmark had been open less than a decade when Twain stayed here in 1872, and he returned the next year accompanied by his wife and infant daughter. In his suite at the luxurious hotel, Twain received such callers as British poet Robert Browning and Russian novelist Ivan Turgenev.

HOTEL AMBASSADOR, VIENNA, AUSTRIA

www.ambassador.at

Twain and his family stayed at this opulent hotel (then called the Hotel Krantz) from October 1898 to May 1899. A month before his stay, Twain ventured to Vienna from the Austrian countryside, where from a vantage point at the hotel, he witnessed the funeral procession of the Empress Elisabeth (assassinated by an Italian anarchist) to the burial vault in the nearby imperial palace.

GARTH WOODSIDE MANSION, HANNIBAL, MISSOURI

www.garthmansion.com

Stay in the garden-view room that Mark Twain used while a guest in what he described as a "spacious, beautiful house," the home of his childhood friends John Garth and Helen Kercheval, who later married. Regardless of which chamber you choose, enjoy a nightcap of Mark Twain Bourbon.

Paris, France

169 RUE DE L'UNIVERSITÉ, 7E

Twain had fond memories of this "large, rambling, quaint" house built by a French artist, where the writer and his wife hosted dinner parties while living there in 1894 and 1895. "It goes without saying," Twain confided to an acquaintance, "that in these circumstances my defects had a large chance for display." Olivia devised a series of signals to correct her husband's faux pas when company was present. (This building is privately occupied and can only be viewed from the outside.)

London, England

23 TEDWORTH SQUARE

Twain lived in London's Chelsea neighborhood in quiet seclusion with his family after the death of his eldest daughter, Susy, from meningitis in 1896. When a cousin of Twain's fell seriously ill while visiting the house, it sparked a rumor that it was the writer who was near death. (This building is privately occupied and can only be viewed from the outside.)

RITZ HOTEL

www.theritzlondon.com

A welcome fit for a king greeted Mark Twain on his 1907 arrival in England, where he received an honorary degree from Oxford University. A London paper reportedly compared the excitement surrounding his visit to the attendant fanfare of Voltaire's triumphant 1778 return from exile to Paris. Twain mingled with luminaries like Bram Stoker and George Bernard Shaw and was feted nearly nonstop, including a lunch held in his honor at the Ritz.

Twain's Travels

T HE *INNOCENTS ABROAD* was Mark Twain's best-selling book during his lifetime, and he followed the lively and humorous travelogue with several other volumes chronicling his colorful adventures.

ROUGHING IT (1872)

Twain recounts his youthful years exploring the untamed American West and the Hawaiian Islands, including a writing stint in a booming Nevada mining town where he began using his famous pseudonym. (The Territorial Enterprise building in Virginia City, Nevada, houses the **Mark Twain Museum**; 775-847-0525.)

A TRAMP ABROAD (1880)

This unofficial sequel to *The Innocents Abroad* follows Twain as he treks through Germany, Switzerland, Italy, and France—meandering through the Black Forest, traversing the Alps, rafting on the Neckar River, and other ambitious and cleverly rendered escapades.

LIFE ON THE MISSISSIPPI (1883)

Twain recalls his tenure as a riverboat pilot, a profession he once claimed to love "far better than any I have followed since." He was forced to abandon ship when Civil War embargoes halted transport along the Mississippi River.

FOLLOWING THE EQUATOR:
A JOURNEY AROUND THE WORLD (1897)

After declaring bankruptcy due mainly to bad investments, Twain returned to the lecture circuit. In *Following the Equator*, he describes the tour he undertook in 1895–96—from riding the rails in India, "a land of dreams and romance, of fabulous wealth and fabulous poverty, of splendor and rags, of palaces and hovels," to sailing into Sydney Harbor, "the darling of Sydney and the wonder of the world," to exploring South Africa, where he toured a diamond mine and took in Cape Town's Table Mountain, a 3,000-foot-high "majestic pile."

EDITH WHARTON

···

Best known for her novels chronicling New York's Gilded Age, Wharton was an avid traveler who crossed the Atlantic more than 60 times. She penned 48 books and traveled throughout France, Italy, England, Spain, Greece, and North Africa. Wharton was awarded the Pulitzer Prize in Fiction for *The Age of Innocence* in 1921, and was the first woman to receive an honorary doctorate from Yale University.

NEW YORK, NEW YORK

14 WEST 23RD STREET

Edith Wharton (née Edith Newbold Jones) was born on January 24, 1862, into one of New York's wealthiest and most patrician families, who were often associated with the phrase "Keeping up with the Joneses" due to their lavish lifestyle. Young Edith lived at a brownstone at this address for the first three years of her life, although the building (which is privately occupied and can only be viewed from the outside) has been significantly altered since her time.

GRACE CHURCH, 802 BROADWAY AT 10TH STREET

This beautiful 150-year-old Gothic Revival cathedral in Greenwich Village is where all of New York high society held their baptisms, and Wharton was no exception; she was christened here on April 20, 1862. She later used the church as the setting for Newland Archer's wedding to debutante May Welland in *The Age of Innocence*.

NEWPORT, RHODE ISLAND

LAND'S END MANSION

Like much of old New York, Wharton's family summered in Newport, an opulent Gilded Age playground. A few years after the writer's marriage to Teddy Wharton, a blue-blooded Bostonian 11 years her senior, the couple purchased a seaside manse known as Land's End. "The outside of the house was incurably ugly," Wharton recalled in her memoirs, and she immediately embarked on a bold interior decoration and landscape design project. The couple lived at Land's End intermittently from 1893 to 1902, dividing their time between a Park Avenue brownstone in New York and travels in Europe.

Though today a private residence, Land's End—located on the southeast end of Ledge Road—is viewable at the southern tip of Newport's legendary **Cliff Walk**, a three-mile path along the rocky bluffs of the Atlantic coast lined with sumptuous 19th-century mansions.

LENOX, MASSACHUSETTS

THE MOUNT ESTATE AND GARDENS

2 Plunkett Street • Tel: 413-551-5111 • *www.edithwharton.org*
• Open daily May through October

"The Mount was my first real home . . . its blessed influence still lives in me," Edith Wharton once wrote of the three-story, 42-room mansion in the Berkshire Mountains that she designed and built from the ground up in 1902. "No one," said close friend and regular houseguest Henry James, "fully knows our Edith who hasn't seen her in the act of creating a habitation for herself." Long before she became known as the chronicler of the Gilded Age, Wharton penned influential works such as *The Decoration of Houses* and *Italian Villas and Their Gardens,* establishing herself as a tastemaker in interior and landscape design.

"Decidedly, I'm a better landscape gardener than a novelist," she once modestly wrote, "and this place, every line of which is my own work, far surpasses *The House of Mirth.*" It was in her upstairs bedroom suite overlooking the gardens that she penned the best-selling novel, which launched her into literary superstardom in 1905.

She had finished writing it the previous year while a visiting Henry James was drafting essays for *The American Scene* in a guest room down the hall. The pair spent mornings working and afternoons motoring through the countryside, where Wharton was greatly moved by the hardship she witnessed in the communities they visited. "For years I had wanted to draw life as it really was in the derelict mountain villages of New England," she later wrote of the impetus behind her austere novel *Ethan Frome*, which was written after she had moved to Paris.

During her final years at The Mount, Wharton's unhappy marriage began to unravel along with her husband's mental and physical health. Unable to manage the burden of such a large home by herself, the "Lady of Lenox," as James fondly called her, sold the manse in 1911.

Today The Mount is one of the 5 percent of national historic landmarks dedicated to women. Among its highlights is the writer's 2,700-volume library, which includes a copy of Henry James's *The Golden Bowl* inscribed to Wharton and an 1866 American first edition of *Alice's Adventures in Wonderland* (one of a thousand copies printed), a book Wharton once knew "by heart."

The Mount has become an important cultural destination reflecting Wharton's own love of culture and the arts. Year-round programming includes live storytelling events, writing workshops, theatrical and musical performances, and a popular lecture series. In July and August, weekly readings of Wharton's works take place on The Mount's wraparound terrace.

PARIS, FRANCE, AND ENVIRONS

In 1907 at age 45, Wharton and her husband began wintering in Paris, where they hoped the milder climate would benefit Teddy Wharton's failing health. Gradually, life in France overtook life at The Mount as Wharton quickly became re-enamored with the city where she had spent part of her childhood. "*Je l'ai dans mon sang!*" ("It is in my blood!"), she wrote to a friend a few days after their arrival.

53 RUE DE VARENNE, 7E
Wharton once said that the decade 1910–20, which she spent living in a rented apartment in the wealthy Faubourg St.-Germain district, was full of "rich years, crowded and happy years." It was also a

decade of sadness and disruption: she ended her marriage in 1913, wrote dispatches from villages and hospitals during World War I, and suffered the loss of her friend Henry James in 1916.

While living on Rue de Varenne, Wharton published nearly two dozen novels, essays, short stories, and poems, including her critically acclaimed novel *Ethan Frome* (its first draft was penned in French to help Wharton hone her language skills). In between writing and traveling, Wharton hosted many visitors, including Theodore Roosevelt, who came to tea in April 1910.

The building (today located next to the French prime minister's office) is privately occupied and can only be viewed from the outside, which is graced by a commemorative plaque.

3/5 RUE EDITH WHARTON, ST.-BRICE-SOUS-FORET

"I saw the house and fell in love with it in spite of its dirt and squalor . . . the little house has never failed me since," Wharton wrote of the derelict 18th-century estate ten miles north of Paris purchased in March 1918 and named Pavillon Colombe. She set about renovating her first country home since The Mount, taking delight in the tranquility of her surroundings after her hectic years in Paris. "As soon as I was settled . . . peace and order came back into my life. At last I had leisure for the two pursuits which never palled; writing and gardening," she wrote in her memoir.

She continued to frequently entertain, and one social occasion was particularly memorable. In July 1925, she extended an invitation to F. Scott Fitzgerald, who arrived fortified on cocktails and told an off-color story about a brothel. Wharton described their meeting in her diary as "horrible" while the editors of her letters referred to it as "one of the better-known failed encounters in the American literary annals." (The residence is privately occupied and can only be viewed from the outside, which features a commemorative plaque.)

VERSAILLES, FRANCE

Wharton died of a stroke on August 11, 1937, at Pavillon Colombe and was buried in Versailles at the **Cimetière des Gonards** next to her lifelong friend and literary advisor, Walter Berry. Although their friendship was platonic, she once called him "the love of all my life" in a diary entry, and their closeness engendered much speculation.

HYÈRES, FRANCE

SAINTE-CLAIRE CHÂTEAU AND LE PARC SAINTE-CLAIRE

Chemin de Sainte-Claire and Avenue Edith Wharton • Tel: (33) 4 94 12 82 30

While wintering in the south of France, Wharton became enamored with a curious château—a former convent built into the ruins of a medieval fortress above the town of Hyères. The château, with its expansive gardens and sweeping views of the Mediterranean, became Wharton's winter home for the last two decades of her life. "I feel as if I were going to get married—to the right man at last!" she wrote to a friend. In 1920 she penned portions of *The Age of Innocence* here. Sainte-Claire Château is not open to the public, but visitors can stroll the gardens at Le Parc Sainte-Claire.

Many literary notables graced Hyères—the most southerly town in Provence—including Joseph Conrad, who visited Wharton in 1921; Rudyard Kipling, who wintered there in the 1920s; and Robert Louis Stevenson, who rented a tiny hillside chalet in 1883. Stevenson later wrote, "I was only happy once; that was at Hyères." See pages 72–73 for more on Kipling and pages 75–78 for more on Stevenson.

NOHANT, FRANCE

LA MAISON DE GEORGE SAND

Tel: (33) 2 54 31 06 04 • *www.maison-george-sand.monuments-nationaux.fr/en*

• Open daily; hours vary seasonally

A pilgrimage to the 18th-century château of feminist writer George Sand was the highlight of a chauffeured "motor-flight" that Wharton took with her husband and Henry James through northern France in the spring of 1907. Both James and Wharton were longtime admirers of Sand and had humorously christened Wharton's car "George" in the author's honor. During their visit, they vividly reimagined Sand's time in Nohant, where she had conducted passionate affairs and entertained many of Europe's literati, including Flaubert, Balzac, Delacroix, Liszt, and Chopin. Sand died in 1876 and was buried in Nohant. The château is still viewable today via guided tours in French (English speakers are provided printed text).

MORE AND MORE, NEVER APART:

Henry James and Edith Wharton

"The great thing is that we always tumble together—more and more, never apart," Henry James wrote to Edith Wharton in February 1910. The two peripatetic expatriate writers, who first met at a Parisian dinner party in 1887, went on to form one of the most famed friendships in literary history. At the time of their meeting, James was already renowned as an astute chronicler of the cultural differences between New World Americans and Old World Europeans, having penned best sellers like *Portrait of a Lady*, while Wharton had only self-published a slim volume of poetry. Despite the differing stages of their literary careers and a nearly 20-year age gap, the author noted, "Perhaps it was our common sense of fun that first brought out our understanding." Likely as well, their shared passion for travel and similar backgrounds (both were progeny of wealthy old New York families and spent their childhoods abroad) were further factors in solidifying their unique bond.

Much as Wharton adopted France as her home country, James did so with England, settling there in 1876 and declaring a decade later, "I am getting to know English life better than American."

34 DE VERE GARDENS, LONDON, ENGLAND

In March of 1886, the 43-year-old James settled into his first long-term residence, a spacious three-bedroom apartment in the city's

James Slept Here (AND YOU CAN TOO!)

HOTEL D'INGHILTERRA, ROME, ITALY

www.hoteldinghilterra.com

"At last—for the first time—I live!" Henry James enthused during his first visit to the Eternal City in a letter written from this hotel in October 1869. Situated in a 17th-century palazzo, these lodgings were one of the many luxurious places James stayed during his visits to Rome, where he set portions of both *Portrait of a Lady* and *Daisy Miller*.

PENSIONE WILDNER, VENICE, ITALY

www.hotelwildner.com

"I had rooms on Riva Schiavoni, at the top of a house near the passage leading off to San Zaccaria," he recalled of the simple Venetian lodgings where he completed *Portrait of a Lady* in the spring of 1881. James occupied a fourth-floor room where "the waterside life, the wondrous lagoon spread before me and the ceaseless human chatter of Venice came in at my windows."

Wharton Slept Here (AND YOU CAN TOO!)

AMBA HOTEL CHARING CROSS, LONDON, ENGLAND

www.amba-hotel.com

Wharton had a tryst in room 92 at this hotel on June 4, 1909, with her lover Morton Fullerton, an American journalist who wrote for the *London Times*. Afterward, she penned the poem "Terminus" about the torrid encounter, recalling "the long secret night you gave me, my lover . . . lying there hushed in your arms, as the waves of rapture receded."

HÔTEL DE CRILLON, PARIS, FRANCE

www.crillon.com

From 1920 on, Wharton spent several weeks each year living at this sumptuous hotel (originally commissioned by Louis XV in 1758) while her staff closed one home and opened another each season. She used the Crillon as a backdrop in her World War I–set novel *A Son at the Front*.

tranquil Kensington neighborhood close to Hyde Park. "My flat is perfection," he wrote to his brother, William, "and ministers, more than I can say, to my health, my spirits, and my work." During his time there, he hosted Joseph Conrad for lunch and befriended his famed literary neighbor, the widower Robert Browning, who resided at **29 De Vere Gardens**. (These buildings are privately occupied and can only be viewed from the outside.)

LAMB HOUSE, RYE, SUSSEX, ENGLAND

West Street • Tel: (44) 158 076 2334 • *www.nationaltrust.org.uk/lamb-house*
• Open Tuesdays, Fridays, and Saturdays, late March through October

"It is exactly what I want and secretly and hopelessly coveted (since knowing it) without dreaming it would ever fall," wrote James in 1897 upon hearing that the country house he had set his sights on had become available. He went on to purchase and occupy the three-story redbrick Georgian home for the majority of the last two decades of his life, entertaining many literati, some of whom slumbered in the historic guest room where King George I had overnighted a century earlier. Among James's guests were H. G. Wells, Ford Madox Ford, Rudyard Kipling, and, of course, Edith Wharton, who first visited Lamb House in May 1904 and came regularly thereafter. "Some of my richest hours were spent under his roof," she recalled. Today the house remains little altered, and rooms display some of the writer's furnishings and tomes from his library.

21 CARLYLE MANSIONS ON CHEYNE WALK
LONDON, ENGLAND

Depressed and in poor health, James sought a change of scenery and leased a five-bedroom flat at this exclusive Chelsea address along the Thames in 1912. He spent the last few years of his life there working on the second volume of his autobiography, which was never completed. He suffered a stroke and died at the apartment on February 28, 1916. (This building is privately occupied and can only be viewed from the outside.)

Jamesian Journeys

HENRY JAMES ONCE WROTE THAT "the ideally arranged existence would be five months of London, five months of Italy (mainly Rome), a month for Paris and a month for the imprévu [spontaneous excursions]." Readers can get a taste of that ideal existence in his travel writings.

A LITTLE TOUR IN FRANCE (1884)

In the fall of 1882, James visited the French countryside on a six-week tour for a *Harper's Magazine* serial, traveling first through the Touraine château region, then downward to Provence "where the silver-gray earth is impregnated with the light of the sky" before ending his sojourn in Burgundy. "I have seen more of France than I had ever seen before, and on the whole liked it better," he concluded.

ENGLISH HOURS (1905)

James's lifelong Anglophilic affection for the English—a "decent and dauntless people"—is celebrated in this collection of essays about London and the southern English countryside, written during his first three decades of residence in his adopted country.

THE AMERICAN SCENE (1907)

During the author's 1904 trip back to America—his first in 20 years—his journey down the eastern seaboard provided meditative fodder on the myriad changes that had been wrought in the country during the two decades of his absence. As James once noted, "It's a complex fate, being an American."

ITALIAN HOURS (1909)

"I am very happy indeed to feel that—as I grow older—many things come and go, but Italy remains," James wrote in an 1892 letter. His adoration of that "disheveled nymph" of Italy was second only to his love for England and it provided the setting for many of his works of fiction as well as for this book of essays drawing on his 40 years of Italian travels.

Wharton's Wanderings

IN ADDITION TO HER WELL-KNOWN NOVELS, Edith Wharton's "incurable passion for the road" led her to pen several nonfiction books documenting three decades of travel. Many of these titles, published individually in her time, have been abridged and collected into one volume, *Edith Wharton Abroad: Selected Travel Writings, 1888-1920.*

THE CRUISE OF THE VANADIS (2004)
In the winter of 1888, 26-year-old Wharton set sail with her husband on a chartered yacht, the *Vanadis,* on a four-month tour of the Mediterranean. She later called the cruise—which took them to exotic locales such as Algiers, Tunis, and Malta—"a taste of heaven." The book was published in 2004 after the belated discovery of the manuscript.

ITALIAN BACKGROUNDS (1905)
Edith and Teddy Wharton traveled to Italy nearly every year for two decades, traversing the length of the country from Sicily to the Italian Alps. Wharton's observations of the country's art, history, and culture are woven into these compelling essays that were originally serialized.

A MOTOR-FLIGHT THROUGH FRANCE (1908)
Wharton once declared that the automobile had "restored the romance of travel," and in 1906, she and her husband motored to virtually every corner of France. Among the highlights of their travels was a pilgrimage to Nohant with Henry James to tour the ancestral home of the writers' heroine, George Sand.

IN MOROCCO (1920)
Wharton was given an unusual opportunity to tour French-controlled Morocco in 1917. Traveling by motorcar through exotic cities such as Rabat, Fez, and Marrakech, Wharton gives her unique impressions—both as a woman and a Westerner—of the markets, palaces, harems, and mosques that she encountered along the way.

Literary Festivals, Tours, and More

The true charm of pedestrianism does not lie in the walking, or in the scenery, but in the talking," claimed Mark Twain. Sometimes the charm lies in being able to do all three. From rural Wales to the Windy City there are ample opportunities to ramble, remark, and remember famous scribes in picturesque locations. Pay homage to a favorite author, attend a literary festival, uncover a locale's literary history on a walking tour, or take a vacation with an itinerary that includes discussions with other bibliophiles. The only time when perhaps you shouldn't talk? While checking out the offerings at a few legendary libraries.

WORD UP:

TOASTING FAVORITE AUTHORS

ZORA! THE ZORA NEALE HURSTON FESTIVAL OF THE ARTS AND HUMANITIES

Eatonville, FL • Annually in late January/early February • www.zorafestival.org

Writer, folklorist, and anthropologist Zora Neale Hurston may have been the dominant female voice of the 1920s Harlem Renaissance, but she grew up a far cry from the Big Apple in tiny Eatonville, Florida, a town of just 2,000 people. Established in 1887, Eatonville is America's oldest incorporated black municipality and the setting for Hurston's novel *Their Eyes Were Watching God*. For nine days each January, this suburb of Orlando swells to nearly 50,000 as Hurston fans gather for what festival director N. Y. Nathiri calls "a multicultural, multidisciplinary celebration of the arts."

Novelist Alice Walker was instrumental in establishing the first event in 1989, and which has grown to include celebrations of literature, art, music, and film. On the itinerary is HAT-itude, a fashion show and brunch celebrating Hurston's penchant for hats; the multiday Outdoor Festival of the Arts featuring musical performances, craft artists like basket weavers, doll makers, and

Zora Neale Hurston was all but forgotten at the time of her death in 1960, buried in an unmarked grave in the **Garden of Heavenly Rest** cemetery (North 17th Street and Avenue S) in Fort Pierce, Florida. Hurston languished in obscurity until the 1970s when Alice Walker ignited a resurgence of interest in her works. The novelist also commemorated Hurston's final resting place with a headstone inscribed: "A Genius of the South."

MORE ZORA: The **Zora Neale Hurston National Museum of Fine Arts** in Eatonville, open year-round, showcases rotating exhibits celebrating artists of African descent (227 East Kennedy Boulevard). In Fort Pierce, farther south on the Florida coast, follow the **Zora Neale Hurston Dust Tracks Heritage Trail** through the city where the writer, whose works include the autobiography *Dust Tracks on a Road*, spent her last years (*www.cityoffortpierce.com*).

sculptors; and much more. Some events are free, and others require tickets and/or paid admission.

BURNS NIGHT SUPPERS

Scotland • Annually on January 25 • *www.robertburns.org*

Lovers of Scottish culture the world over gather this eve to celebrate the birth of the country's national bard, Robert Burns, in 1759. The first recorded Burns Night Supper honoring the "ploughman poet" took place in 1801 in his birthplace village of Alloway, and the evening's lineup has varied little ever since. A traditional meal of haggis (sheep organ meats blended with oatmeal and spices), neeps (turnips), and tatties (potatoes) is served, washed down with drams of whisky. The haggis is brought to the table accompanied by a bagpiper and is traditionally sliced open with a dirk (a sharp knife worn as part of Highland dress) during a recital of Burns's poem "Address to a Haggis." Many toasts, poems, and speeches follow, including the Toast to the Lassies and Their Reply. The evening is capped off with the singing of the bard's great song of parting, "Auld Lang Syne."

The **Burns an' a' that! Festival**, held each May in County Ayrshire (the bard's birthplace), is a rousing celebration of Scottish dance, drama, art, poetry, and, of course, whisky tasting (*www.burnsfestival.com*).

SHAKESPEARE'S BIRTHDAY CELEBRATIONS

Stratford-upon-Avon, England • Annually in April
• *www.shakespearescelebrations.com*

The exact day of William Shakespeare's birth remains unknown but is widely thought to be April 23, the same auspicious date on which he passed away 52 years later in 1616. Although more than four centuries have elapsed since his death, Stratford preserves the memory of its hometown bard with an annual festival and lively street procession to Holy Trinity Church, the site of the playwright's baptism and burial. The procession forms the centerpiece of the weekend-long celebration and features brass bands, drummer corps, costumed actors, dignitaries,

For more on Shakespeare's England, see pages 4–8.

Morris dancers (whose members perform an ancient folk dance ritual), and students from Shakespeare's grammar school (still in existence today).

Kicking off with the unfurling of flags and banners displaying the titles of Shakespeare's works, the parade wends its way along a three-mile route through the picturesque Tudor-style town. It culminates with the laying of floral tributes on the dramatist's grave. Throughout the weekend, Stratford takes on the atmosphere of a lively Elizabethan carnival as musicians and actors stroll the streets performing scenes from the Bard's repertoire.

TENNESSEE WILLIAMS/NEW ORLEANS LITERARY FESTIVAL

New Orleans, LA • Annually in March

• *www.tennesseewilliams.net*

"Stellaaaa!" Echoes of the famous utterance from *A Streetcar Named Desire* can be heard in New Orleans' Jackson Square during the **Stanley and Stella Shouting Contest** (see photo), part of the annual Tennessee Williams/New Orleans Literary Festival. Along with celebrating

THE FRENCH QUARTER BY THE BOOK: Tennessee Williams wasn't the only writer who succumbed to the lure of the Big Easy. Truman Capote, F. Scott Fitzgerald, Eudora Welty, and William Faulkner also spent time in New Orleans. Faulkner lived at 624 Pirate's Alley, where he wrote his first novel, *Soldier's Pay*, and today the building is the site of **Faulkner House Books** (*www.faulknerhousebooks.com*). It's also home to the Pirate's Alley Faulkner Society, which stages an annual festival, **Words & Music: A Literary Feast in New Orleans** (*www.wordsandmusic.org*).

Also in the French Quarter is the **Beauregard-Keyes House and Garden Museum**, once home to Frances Parkinson Keyes, who penned New Orleans–set novels and other works (*www.bkhouse.org*). See page 36 for more on **Tennessee Williams's haunts**, pages 174–75 for the **Hotel Monteleone**, and page 154 for the **French Quarter Literary History Tour**.

the city's rich cultural heritage, this five-day fete honors the creative genius of the playwright in the place he called his "spiritual home."

The festival draws famous figures from page, stage, and screen, from Margaret Atwood, Rick Bragg, and other award-winning writers to Hollywood heavyweights such as actor Alec Baldwin and director John Waters. Events take place in landmark locales throughout the French Quarter. The festival's executive director, Paul Willis, notes that a range of experiences is available to attendees, from scholarly discussions and theatrical performances to food and wine soirees, a breakfast book club, and literary walking tours.

A paid Festival Panel Pass is required to attend panel discussions; special events also require payment. Both panel passes and event tickets can be purchased through the festival's website.

STEINBECK FESTIVAL

Salinas, CA • Every other year in May • www.steinbeck.org

"I think that I would like to write the story of all the little towns and all the farms and the ranches in the wilder hills," Steinbeck mused to a friend in 1933, referring to the novel that would later become the semi-autobiographical *East of Eden*. "I can see how I would like to do it so that it would be the valley of the world." Steinbeck drew much inspiration from the fertile lands of his birthplace in Salinas, and although his sympathies for the plight of farmworkers often made him unpopular with the locals, who once burned copies of *The Grapes of Wrath*, today he's venerated by them. The author's legacy is celebrated with a biennial festival hosted by the National Steinbeck Center and featuring a dynamic lineup of activities.

DON'T MISS: The **Open House** at **Ed Ricketts's lab** at 800 Cannery Row in Monterey: Have a rare glimpse inside the lab of marine biologist and Steinbeck friend Ed Ricketts, on whom the character of Doc in *Cannery Row* was based. Steinbeck's interest in marine biology led him to accompany Ricketts on a historical voyage documented in *Sea of Cortez*, which blends science and philosophical musings.

The three-day festival offers fans a unique opportunity to be immersed in all things Steinbeck: the man, his writing, and the landscape that inspired him. For more on Steinbeck's California, see pages 344–58. Events such as lectures, walks, wine and beer tastings, archive tours, and films are on the agenda, along with bus trips to Steinbeck-related sites in the area; past outings have included the Red Pony ranch and the historic town of Spreckels, where Steinbeck and his father both worked in a sugar beet plant. Each festival is centered around a different theme that illuminates a particular aspect of his life and work, like his stint as a war correspondent or the numerous artistic adaptations of his novels.

FOWEY FESTIVAL OF WORDS AND MUSIC

Fowey, England • Annually in May • www.foweyfestival.com

Best known for her haunting novel *Rebecca,* the first major gothic romance of the 20th century, Daphne du Maurier found inspiration in the dramatic seascapes and quaint fishing villages of the windswept Cornish Riviera in southwest England. Though born in London, she spent much of her life in her beloved Cornwall, where her family often vacationed and where she returned as an adult to live and work. The author is the inspiration for the Fowey Festival of Words and Music, a weeklong celebration of literature and the arts that includes walks, talks, and other programming related to du Maurier.

HEMINGWAY DAYS

Key West, FL • Annually in July

• www.fla-keys.com/hemingwaymedia

After falling in love with the laid-back island lifestyle during a brief Key West stopover en route from Paris to the U.S. mainland, Hemingway settled permanently in this tropical paradise from 1928 to 1939. In addition to drinking, socializing, and pursuing his newfound hobby of deep-sea fishing, he found time during his decade in the Conch

ReJoyce!

BLOOMSDAY

Dublin, Ireland • Annually on June 16 • *www.bloomsdayfestival.ie*

All of Dublin provides the backdrop for this unusual celebration, which marks the date in 1904 on which Leopold Bloom made his epic journey through the city streets in James Joyce's *Ulysses*. Festivities traditionally begin just outside Dublin at an imposing stone tower immortalized in the first chapter of Joyce's masterpiece.

"There is no other celebration of a book or writer quite like Bloomsday," says Robert Nicholson, curator of the James Joyce Museum at the Joyce Tower and author of *The Ulysses Guide: Tours Through Joyce's Dublin*. Here, he shares his take on Bloomsday.

"Celebrations originated in 1954, when a small band of Dublin writers set out in horse-drawn cabs from the tower with the intention of visiting all the locations of the novel. Their odyssey met shipwreck in a series of city pubs long before its completion, but it set a pattern for future celebrations. Today, wandering Joyceans go to the places where *Ulysses* is set, to reconstruct the events of the novel through readings, dramatizations, and chance encounters. Like their predecessors and many of the characters of *Ulysses,* they find much feasting and singing along the way and are likely to end up in good company.

"As an occasion rather than a festival, Bloomsday has no official program and events are organized by various bodies. **The James Joyce Centre** runs a program of lectures, readings, and walking tours that traditionally follow episodes of *Ulysses*. Other favorite activities include the **Bloomsday Breakfast** (inner organs of beasts and fowl with entertainment) held in various locations, a visit to the **James Joyce Museum** at the tower where readings are held on the open-air gun platform, refreshments at **Davy Byrnes** pub (featured in *Ulysses*), and meeting up with **The Balloonatics** theater company here, there, and everywhere as it presents the novel live on street corners, in pubs, restaurants, and other venues throughout the day."

For more about James Joyce's Dublin, see pages 272-82.

Republic to pen several works, including a Depression-era novel of Key West, *To Have and Have Not*. The macho legend of Papa

For more on Hemingway's Key West, see pages 118 and 319–33.

was born on the isle, and his larger-than-life presence lives on. In July, one can even be forgiven for thinking he still roams the streets when stocky, gray-bearded participants gather for the **Papa Hemingway Look-Alike Contest** (see photo, page 147). The contest is the centerpiece of the writer's lively annual birthday celebrations, which also feature literary events, a nationally acclaimed marlin fishing tournament, and even an unusual take on one of Hemingway's favorite activities, the running of the bulls.

JANE AUSTEN FESTIVAL

Bath, England • Annually in September
• *www.janeaustenfestivalbath.co.uk*

Austenian landmarks abound in the fashionable Georgian city the author called home from 1801 to 1806 and used as a backdrop in her novels *Northanger Abbey* and *Persuasion*. During ten Austen-themed days, visitors can revel in the unique atmosphere of Bath as a spectator or by taking part in events such as a costumed promenade and a masked ball at the elegant Pump Room, preceded by a reception at the Roman Baths. Festivalgoers can also sample the delights of an 18th-century breakfast. Plum cake, anyone? No aspect of Regency life is left uncovered by the ambitious program of workshops, plays, walks, and talks, many of which have fanciful names

DON'T MISS: Don your best Jane Austen-era attire for the spectacular **Grand Regency Costumed Promenade**, which holds the Guinness world record for "the largest gathering of people dressed in Regency costume." More than 600 Austen fans take part each year, bringing traffic to a halt in the center of Bath on the first Saturday of the Festival.

See pages 215–27 for more on Jane Austen's Bath.

like "Austen Undone!," "Rummaging through the Reticule," and "Hands on Harps." (Specific offerings vary annually; check the website in advance for the program schedule and ticketing information.)

"The Jane Austen Festival attracts visitors from places as distant as Australia and Russia," says festival director Jackie Herring. "Everyone is made welcome whether they dress in costume or not, and many make good friends and return year after year." Indeed, the chance to indulge your inner Austen by mingling with fellow Jane-ites is perhaps the most rewarding opportunity of all.

INTERNATIONAL AGATHA CHRISTIE FESTIVAL

Torquay, Devon • Annually in September • *www.agathachristiefestival.com*

Head to the English Riviera, Agatha Christie's favored holiday spot, for a multiday celebration that combines crime writing with vintage glamour. A packed agenda includes discussions of Christie's life and literary works, theatrical performances, guest author talks, garden parties, tea times, tours of Christie's home, **Greenway**, and events for kids. At host venue Torre Abbey, a historic site and museum, there is a tribute befitting the Queen of Crime. The **Agatha Christie Garden** displays beautiful, deadly foxglove and other potent plants featured in her books. More than half of her fictional victims met their end by poisoning. For more Christie capers, see pages 106–107.

ERNEST HEMINGWAY FESTIVAL

Ketchum, Idaho • Annually in September • *www.comlib.org*

Ernest Hemingway first came to Sun Valley in 1939 and returned to the area many times before buying a house in Ketchum in 1959. The Ernest Hemingway Festival honors the heritage of his strong bond to this Idaho valley with scholarly presentations, book discussions, and special events that vary annually. In addition, the **Sun Valley Museum of History** (First and Washington in the Forest Service Park) has an exhibit about the writer.

Literary Walks and Tours

United States

THE HUB OF LITERARY AMERICA

Boston By Foot • Boston, MA • *www.bostonbyfoot.com* • Saturdays, May through October; offered year-round by private booking

This 90-minute tour highlights locations associated with the writers, poets, and intellectuals who made Boston an epicenter of American letters in the 1800s. One notable place is the former site of the Old Corner Bookstore, a designated landmark on the city's historic Freedom Trail. Not only was the bookstore a gathering place for literati, it was the original location of the publishing house Ticknor & Fields, whose distinguished roster of authors included Henry Wadsworth Longfellow, Ralph Waldo Emerson, Harriet Beecher Stowe, Mark Twain, Nathaniel Hawthorne, and Henry David Thoreau.

A stroll through the city's Beacon Hill neighborhood, known for its Federal-style row houses and cobblestone streets, highlights the residences of Hawthorne, Thoreau, and *Little Women* author Louisa May Alcott. Other stops on the tour include the Boston Athenaeum, a library and museum built in 1807 and frequented by Hawthorne, and the Omni Parker House, a hotel that served as the gathering place for the Saturday Club founded by Emerson.

> *"Methinks that the moment my legs begin to move, my thoughts begin to flow."*
> —HENRY DAVID THOREAU

IN A LONELY PLACE: RAYMOND CHANDLER'S LOS ANGELES

Esotouric • Los Angeles, CA • *www.esotouric.com* • Offered four times per year

"Raymond Chandler made nothing up, and his fiction is filled with references to real people, real places, real crimes," says Kim Cooper, co-founder of Esotouric, an L.A.-based company that conducts local true crime-, culture-, and literature-themed tours. Amateur gumshoes can delve into the city Chandler knew and portrayed in his hard-boiled detective fiction, beginning with the introduction of private eye Philip Marlowe in 1939's *The Big Sleep*.

"We have crafted the tour to highlight the time capsule locations that still evoke the city that inspired Chandler, and where his presence can be felt," notes Cooper. Among the stops on the bus tour are the grand lobby of the 1896 Barclay Hotel, formerly the Van Nuys Hotel, where a murder-by-ice-pick occurs in *The Little Sister*, the locale where a likely model for Marlowe worked as a beat cop, Larry Edmunds Bookshop (the last bookstore on Hollywood's Booksellers' Row), and the eatery Scoops for noir-themed gelato created in homage to Chandler.

Can't make a scheduled tour? Sleuth on your own with Cooper's *The Raymond Chandler Map of Los Angeles* as a guide. She is also the author of *The Kept Girl*, a novel starring a young Raymond Chandler.

CHICAGO GREETER LITERATURE TOUR
Chicago, IL • *www.chicagogreeter.com* • Year-round on request

Explore Chicago's literary legacy with a local bibliophile as your guide. Tours are uniquely customized and may encompass such sites as the Chicago Cultural Center, a Beaux Arts–style building completed in 1897 and dedicated as the city's original Chicago Public Library, and the Printers Row neighborhood, once home

CALLING ALL BIBLIOPHILES: At long last, book-loving museumgoers have a space to call their own at the first and only museum in the United States dedicated to the written word. The **American Writers Museum** (*www.americanwritersmuseum.org*), located on Chicago's famed Michigan Avenue, presents permanent and temporary exhibits exploring the influence of American writers on the nation's history, identity, and culture. Virtually visit famous literary landmarks and explore books associated with different parts of the country via an interactive map. A "surprise bookshelf" reveals facts about legendary works through entertaining features like audio, video, and hidden windows. The dynamic museum's other offerings include a children's literature gallery and special exhibits showcasing artifacts on loan from author house museums.

to a 24-hour-a-day printing industry. Some of the famous writers with local connections are Carl Sandburg, Upton Sinclair, and Theodore Dreiser. Sinclair's novel *The Jungle* exposed the dreadful conditions of the Chicago meatpacking district, while Dreiser once worked as a young journalist in the city and later returned to cover the 1893 Chicago World's Fair for a St. Louis newspaper.

Chicago Greeter is a free service of Choose Chicago that uses local volunteer guides who conduct two- to four-hour highlight tours of the city on foot and via public transportation. Requests can be made by filling out a form on the website; a minimum of ten business days advance notice is required.

GREENWICH VILLAGE LITERARY PUB CRAWL

New York, NY • www.literarypubcrawl.com • Saturday afternoons

Legendary New York City neighborhood Greenwich Village has seen its share of literary triumphs and tragedies. During a lively, three-hour walking tour, hear about Edgar Allan Poe, Jack Kerouac, O. Henry, and other writers who lived, wrote, drank, and sometimes brawled in Greenwich Village. Along the way, quench your thirst in bars where famous scribes once did the same. Tours begin at the White Horse Tavern, where liquor-loving Dylan Thomas would shout out his own verse while standing on a table. Poet and actress Edna St. Vincent Millay occupied the narrowest house (9.5 feet across) in Greenwich Village. Several streets away, Henry Miller once ran a speakeasy from his abode. This entertaining outing is led by highly knowledgeable guides who are passionate about the topic, sharing colorful tales, offering fascinating historical tidbits about the area, and even reciting poetry in between tipples.

"One belongs to New York instantly, one belongs to it as much in five minutes as in five years."
—THOMAS WOLFE

ALGONQUIN ROUND TABLE WALKING TOURS

Dorothy Parker Society • www.dorothyparker.com • Tours offered once a month March through November; private tours on request

Short-story scribe Dorothy Parker and members of the Round Table are best remembered for trading witticisms during daily lunches at the Algonquin Hotel in the 1920s. Kevin Fitzpatrick, founder of the

Dorothy Parker Society and author of *The Algonquin Round Table New York: A Historical Guide*, leads a two-hour tour that encompasses more than 40 destinations—former speakeasies, theaters, homes, and hangouts—of Parker and the Vicious Circle (the Round Table's original name). For more Jazz Age glamour, the Dorothy Parker Society co-sponsors a monthly vintage dance party with jazz bands and classic cocktails.

FRENCH QUARTER LITERARY HISTORY TOUR

G L-f de Villiers Tours • New Orleans, LA • *www.glfdevilliers.com* • Mondays and Saturdays at 10 a.m. or by private booking

On an 1882 foray through the French Quarter, Mark Twain had a companion who was familiar with the terrain: novelist and New Orleans native George Washington Cable. "With Mr. Cable along to . . . describe and explain and illuminate, a jog through that old quarter is a vivid pleasure," declared Twain in *Life on the Mississippi*. Present-day bibliophiles can follow suit by taking the French Quarter Literary History Tour, led by writer and historian Glenn De Villier, also a native New Orleanian and longtime French Quarter resident.

During the two-hour trek, meander past notable literary landmarks and hear entertaining tales about the endeavors and exploits of the wordsmiths who passed through the city's oldest neighborhood. ("Y'all have the real history and the best gossip," declared a tourgoer.) Walk along colorful Pirate's Alley, where William Faulkner produced his first novel, *Soldier's Pay*. His second novel, the satire *Mosquitoes*, was inspired by the time he spent in New Orleans in the 1920s, palling around with Sherwood Anderson (who once showed Gertrude Stein and Alice B. Toklas the French Quarter) and other writers and artists. See Anderson's apartment building, along with the abodes of Truman Capote and Tennessee Williams. The tour concludes at Antoine's restaurant, where Twain, Faulkner, and other literati have enjoyed the renowned Creole cuisine.

No Ordinary Happy Hour

DUBLIN LITERARY PUB CRAWL

Dublin, Ireland • *www.dublinpubcrawl.com* • April through October: 7:30 p.m. nightly
• November through March: 7:30 p.m. Thursday through Sunday

Leopold Bloom mused in *Ulysses* that it would be a "good puzzle [to] cross Dublin without passing a pub." With the rich literary associations of many of these establishments, the bigger challenge for a visiting bibliophile is which one to sample first.

Dublin's public houses are intrinsically woven into the city's literary fabric, and its very notoriety stems from the illustrious writers who fashioned high art out of the lives of ordinary Dubliners. Since much of daily life took place in the convivial confines of a pub, it's no surprise that these colorful settings fermented an inextricable link between subject, author, and audience.

How better, then, to pay homage to the stories that Irish raconteurs brought to life on the page than by lifting a "frothy freshener" at the same bygone watering holes where they sipped for inspiration? Luckily, by grazing the bookish smorgasbord offered on the popular **Dublin Literary Pub Crawl**, one can do just that.

Led by two actors who perform famed passages from Irish literature in prose, drama, and song, bibliophiles can follow in the echoing footsteps of Joyce, Beckett, Wilde, and a host of contemporary Irish writers to centuries-old haunts where men of letters argued, conversed, daydreamed, and, of course, drank.

Trivia buffs will drink in the anecdotes revealed about the writers and the pubs they called home, sometimes quite literally. (For instance, playwright Samuel Beckett reputedly lived above famed "moral pub" Davy Byrnes, where Joyce's Bloom lunched on a Gorgonzola and mustard sandwich accompanied by a glass of Burgundy on June 16, 1904.) More than a hundred years may have passed since Bloom's fictional visit, but Davy Byrnes on Duke Street still stands, as do many of Dublin's other pubs with literary associations. So don't linger at the door; come on in and experience some traditional Irish *craic* (good times) for yourself.

EUROPE

THE LONDON OF OSCAR WILDE

London Walks • *www.walks.com*

• 11 a.m. on Saturdays

Famed for his command of language, witty Irish playwright Oscar Wilde met with both enormous success and dramatic downfall in London, where his bisexuality and flamboyant style clashed with the conservative mores of Victorian society. While some of Wilde's haunts no longer remain, this entertaining walk through London's posh Mayfair and St. James's districts brings his remarkable story to life. Among the locales visited are the site of the former St. James's Theatre, where *The Importance of Being Earnest* and other Wilde plays were first performed; a street featured in *Lady Windermere's Fan*; the tobacconist where Wilde fueled his 80-cigarettes-a-day habit; and the Royal Arcade (see photo), once home to the florist who created the dyed green carnations he often wore on his lapel. Also in the area is **Hatchards**, the oldest surviving bookstore in London, where Wilde was a much-loved regular.

SHAKESPEARE'S LONDON

London, England • Self-guided walking tour • *wwww.cityoflondon.gov.uk/things-to-do/visit-the-city/walks*

Chart a course through the City of London neighborhood, taking in the sites of former playhouses and pubs associated with Shakespeare,

MORE LITERARY LONDON STROLLS: London Walks has a vast offering of regularly scheduled tours, along with literary-themed and other excursions given occasionally during the year. Follow in the footsteps of Shakespeare and Sherlock Holmes, Dickens and 007, or stroll through legendary Bloomsbury, once home to a bohemian circle of writers and artists that included Virginia Woolf (*www.walks.com*).

a memorial for two actors instrumental in publishing the First Folio edition of his plays after his demise, and other Bard-related landmarks.

Then cross the Thames via London Bridge into Southwark to see Shakespeare's Globe Theatre, a reconstruction of the octagonal, open-air Elizabethan playhouse. Nearby, a plaque pinpoints where the original stood before its thatched roof caught fire, burning it to the ground. The area was once home to other Elizabethan playhouses as well, including the Swan, Hope, and Rose, which in addition to theater had another popular—and bloodthirsty—use at the time: bear- and bull-baiting. Also along the walk is Southwark Cathedral, where Shakespeare's brother Edmund is interred; the George Inn, London's only remaining galleried stagecoach inn; and cobbled Clink Street, the site of Clink Prison (now a museum).

LONDON LITERARY PUB CRAWL

London, England • www.londonliterarypubcrawl.com • Thursdays and Saturdays

Charles Dickens is back from the beyond to join revelers on a three-hour excursion visiting watering holes from Fitzrovia to Soho that are steeped in literary history. More performance than traditional guided tour, professional actors play the parts of famed writers like Dylan Thomas, who first locked eyes with his future wife in a Fitzrovia tavern; T. S. Eliot, who renounced his U.S. citizenship to become a Brit; Virginia Woolf, who lived in a house once occupied by George Bernard Shaw; and George Orwell, who found inspiration for *1984* in the area.

"Work is the curse of the drinking classes."
—OSCAR WILDE

HEMINGWAY'S PARIS

Paris Walks • Paris, France • www.paris-walks.com • 10:30 a.m. on Fridays, March through December; private tours offered year-round

There is never any ending to Paris and the memory of each person who has lived in it differs from that of any other.
—Ernest Hemingway, *A Moveable Feast*

Explore the colorful Latin Quarter, where Ernest Hemingway lived when he moved to the City of Light as a journalist in 1921. The celebrated scribe paints a vivid picture of the neighborhood and his early Parisian days in the memoir *A Moveable Feast*. Whether strolling along the Rue Mouffetard, "that wonderful narrow crowded market street" or passing through the "windswept" Place du Panthéon, walkers will find the vibrant area still very much alive with his presence. Hemingway receives top billing on the tour, but highlighted too are James Joyce, George Orwell, French poet Paul Verlaine (who died in the same building where Hemingway later rented a room to write), and others with ties to the Quartier Latin.

THE DOSTOYEVSKY WALK

Peter's Walking Tours • St. Petersburg, Russia • *www.peterswalk.com*
• Offered year-round by private booking

Though born in Moscow, Dostoyevsky spent most of his life in the baroque northern Russian city of St. Petersburg, where he wrote and set many of his novels, including his masterpiece, *Crime and Punishment*. This three-hour tour, led by energetic English-speaking guides (often by the eponymous Peter himself), visits places associated with the writer's life as well as sites from his works. Among the stops is the location of the writer's mock execution at Semenovsky Square prior to his stint in

ON THE ROAD: Embark on travel adventures for the mind with **Classical Pursuits**, which offers trips themed around books, art, and music. "This is nothing like most escorted tours," says Ann Kirkland, the company's founder. "We opt for depth over breadth. We prefer discovery of the big ideas embodied in great works of literature and art through informal discussion, not lecture. And we look for opportunities to hear from local people in their own words."

Whether in Flannery O'Connor's Savannah, Dante's Florence, or elsewhere, the hallmark of a Classical Pursuits sojourn is book discussions with fellow travelers guided by an expert. These nomadic literary salons are part of a rich itinerary of cultural and recreational activities, along with time to explore on your own. Small group sizes, ranging between 12 and 18 participants, encourage camaraderie and conversation. Itineraries vary each year, from discovering Cuba's literary side to recreating the spirit of 1920s Paris. The only prerequisites: Read before you go and come with an open mind (*www.classicalpursuits.com*).

a Siberian penal colony for socialist activities. Dostoyevsky based many of the locations in his novels on actual places, and another highlight of the walk is retracing Raskolnikov's infamous murder route between his house and the pawnbroker's shop in *Crime and Punishment.*

Peter's Walking Tours also runs an evening **Dostoyevsky Pub Crawl** biweekly during summer months, in homage to the fact that much of *Crime and Punishment's* action takes place in the city's taverns. "While there are no historic taverns left dating from Dostoyevsky times, we improvise by selecting places which may have a similar atmosphere—old-style vodka bars, the kind with 'sticky little tables in a dark and dirty corner,' in the area of the Hay Market," says Peter Kozyrev. "The Dostoyevsky Pub Crawl actually follows the murder route; during the tour, the guide points out the details mentioned in the novel, as well as generally helping the walkers get into the atmosphere of *Crime and Punishment.*"

See pages 94–96 for more on Dostoyevsky's Russia, including the St. Petersburg apartment (now a museum) where he lived the final years of his life and where he penned *The Brothers Karamazov.*

Email *info@peterswalk.com* to inquire about scheduling and pricing for either of the above walks. In the past, Peter has also customized Tolstoy and Gogol walks for interested bibliophiles.

IN THE STACKS:

LIBRARIES WORTH CHECKING OUT

TRINITY COLLEGE

Old Library • Dublin, Ireland • *www.tcd.ie/visitors*

One of the most revered literary treasures to have survived the Middle Ages—the *Book of Kells*—rests here in Ireland's largest library. Produced by Celtic monks around A.D. 800, the illuminated manuscript contains the four Gospels of the Bible written in a vividly

Library Offerings

While the books in the world's great libraries aren't for the taking, their gift shops offer a trove of literary treasures for bibliophiles—no library card required.

◉ "All the wizardry of letter, initial, and word swept over me," recalled Eudora Welty of viewing the *Book of Kells* at Dublin's Trinity College. For an up close and personal look at the ornately illustrated medieval tome, *The Book of Kells* by Bernard Meehan, the Keeper of Manuscripts at Trinity College, reproduces important pages and illuminates their meaning through accompanying text. An iPhone app presenting every page in high resolution is also available (*www.tcd.ie/library/shop*).

◉ Help preserve literary history by adopting *Jane Eyre*, *The Wind in the Willows*, or another page-turner at the British Library. Accompanying perks, such as a book-jacket card to keep or send to a gift recipient, vary according to donation level (*adoptabook.bl.uk*).

◉ Patience and Fortitude, the marble lion statues flanking the entrance of the New York Public Library's main branch at Fifth Avenue and 42nd Street, aren't for sale, but replica bookends can reside on your shelves (*www.libraryshop.org*). The grand guardians' monikers were bestowed on them in the 1930s by the city's mayor, for two qualities he felt were essential to surviving the economic depression.

◉ "I cannot live without books." Thomas Jefferson's dramatic (and understandable) statement adorns the Library of Congress's signature café mug, while the other side is emblazoned with the organization's logo. Browse the library's online shop for bookish home decor and more (*library-of-congress-shop.myshopify.com*).

colored decorative script interspersed with ornate illustrations. An accompanying display highlights the story of the book's origins and the consummate skill of the artists who produced it under primitive conditions. Included in the cost of admission is access to the awe-inspiring 300-year-old, barrel-vaulted Long Room of the Old Library. A central aisle spanning 70 yards is flanked by row upon row of towering two-story bookcases. The 200,000 leather-bound volumes nestled on the shelves are among the oldest in the library's collection. Lined with busts of great writers and thinkers from Milton to Socrates, the room also displays two objects representative of Ireland's history: a copy of the 1916 Proclamation of the Irish Republic and a 15th-century harp—the oldest in Ireland and the country's national symbol.

> *"The student has his Rome, his Florence, his whole glowing Italy, within the four walls of his library. He has in his books the ruins of an antique world and the glories of a modern one."*
> —HENRY WADSWORTH LONGFELLOW

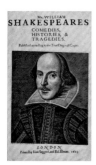

BRITISH LIBRARY

Sir John Ritblat Gallery • London, England • *www.bl.uk*

To enter this public gallery—home to more than 200 millennia-spanning treasures—is to step inside a bibliophile's Louvre. But instead of works of art taking center stage, it's the humble word that stars in documents like the 800-year-old Magna Carta, the Gutenberg Bible, and Shakespeare's First Folio (see photo).

While most libraries keep prized items locked away from the public eye, the British Library's literary gems are on permanent display.

TURNING THE PAGES: At *www.bl.uk/onlinegallery/ttp/ttpbooks.html*, readers can virtually turn the pages of library treasures such as these:
- Lewis Carroll's illustrated manuscript of *Alice's Adventures Under Ground*, the original version of *Alice's Adventures in Wonderland*
- Jane Austen's draft of *The History of England* "by a partial, prejudiced, and ignorant historian," a youthful parody of her childhood history book
- Poet and painter William Blake's writing-and-sketch-filled notebook, accompanied by expert commentary about what appears in its pages

For Kristian Jensen, head of collections and curation, this accessibility is what sets the institution apart. "It's designed to be a friendly, open place," he says of the library, located in northwest London. "People use it as a public living room, and to have a public living room next to [a gallery] that is of serious historic and intellectual importance is wonderful. It allows people to engage with something meaningful to them."

Must-see items include the original manuscript and accompanying illustrations for *Alice's Adventures in Wonderland,* Leonardo da Vinci's notebooks on technological innovations (penned in his famous mirror handwriting), and the final two manuscript chapters of Jane Austen's *Persuasion* (sitting atop her writing desk).

Bibliophiles also can take a monthly behind-the-scenes tour of the adjoining Centre for Conservation, where experts employ a mix of cutting-edge technology and traditional skills to ensure the library's literary riches are preserved for generations to come.

NEW YORK PUBLIC LIBRARY
Stephen A. Schwarzman Building • New York, NY
• *www.nypl.org*

Two marble lions nicknamed Patience and Fortitude guard the immense Beaux-Arts facade fronting the largest marble structure to be attempted in the United States at the turn of the 20th century. Known to locals as "the main library," from early days this opulent building was not just a place for scholars but a democratic institution that has welcomed all comers. While not a lending library, the bulk of its noncirculating items can be requested and perused within the grand Rose Main Reading Room. Soaring 52 feet high and spanning the length of a football field, the room is well worth a visit even if you aren't requesting a book. Literati such as Norman Mailer and E. L. Doctorow have sat at the long oak tables, which are illuminated by original hundred-year-old bronze reading lamps. Overhead, immense chandeliers dangle like earrings, accenting Tintoretto-style ceiling murals depicting cerulean skies and cotton candy clouds. Free guided tours take place six days a week.

In residence at the library is the famous stuffed bear that Christopher Robin Milne received on his first birthday. Keeping Winnie the Pooh company are his four best friends—Eeyore, Piglet, Kanga, and Tigger—subsequent gifts to young Christopher, whose father, A. A. Milne, made the menagerie storybook stars. They're displayed in the children's room on the ground floor.

The two blocks leading up to the library, known as **Library Way** (41st Street between Fifth and Park Avenues), are embedded with bronze sidewalk plaques sporting quotes by the likes of Langston Hughes, Ernest Hemingway, and Emily Dickinson.

LIBRARY OF CONGRESS

Thomas Jefferson Building • Washington, D.C.

• *www.loc.gov*

"I cannot live without books," declared Thomas Jefferson. Nonetheless, the avid bibliophile sold his collection of 6,487 books to the Library of Congress in 1815 as a replacement for the library's original contents, which burned when British troops invaded the capital the year before.

As both the country's oldest federal cultural institution (founded in 1800) and the world's largest library (containing more than 162 million items on 838 miles of shelves—and counting), the Library of Congress is the undisputed grand dame of the stacks. The crown jewel of its three Capitol Hill edifices, the palatial Thomas Jefferson Building, befits its stature with murals, mosaics, and sculpture galore and a Great Hall rising 75 feet from marble floor to stained glass ceiling. It's well worth the time to take a free, docent-led tour (offered multiple times daily, six days a week) for insights on the library's creation and collection, as well as its impressive architecture, some of which draws on the Italian Renaissance style. Among its eye-catching adornments are themes of literature, music, philosophy, and education, along with references to the zodiac and mythology. Displayed in the Great Hall are two Bibles, a handwritten Mainz and a printed Gutenberg, and themed exhibits are on view throughout the library.

CELEBRATING THE PRINTED WORD

*"The really impor-
tant thing in books is
the words in them—
words, the wine of
life—not their bind-
ings or their print,
not their edition
value or their bib-
liomaniac value, or
their uncuttability."*

—E. M. FORSTER

Literary festivals are a book lover's paradise. These lively annual events, ranging from one to several days, are open to the public and feature author appearances, readings, book signings, panel discussions, cooking demonstrations, and other activities, and often have special programming for young readers.

UNITED STATES

Dozens of literary festivals take place across the United States each year, and while some of the biggest are spotlighted here, it's worth checking with your state arts and humanities council to find out about smaller ones in your area. Ticketing requirements and entry fees vary, so visit event websites for details and rosters of author appearances.

VIRGINIA FESTIVAL OF THE BOOK
Charlottesville, VA • Annually in March • *www.vabook.org*
Situated at the foot of the Blue Ridge Mountains, historic Charlottesville plays host to a five-day literary extravaganza that draws more than 20,000

DON'T MISS: Edgar Allan Poe attended the **University of Virginia in Charlottesville** for ten months in 1826. Short on funds for tuition, he turned to gambling but proved unlucky at cards. Upon finding out, his disapproving stepfather forbade him to return to the university. Visitors to the UVA campus (which is open to the public) can view Poe's room re-created with period furniture; a recording provides a brief history on his days as a student there. In the university's Rotunda is a pane of glass taken from a window in the room, on which Poe reportedly etched a verse. Poe's experiences in Charlottesville are evoked in the poems "Tamerlane" and "A Tale of the Ragged Mountains" (*www.uvaravensociety .com*; 434-924-3239). For more about Edgar Allan Poe, see pages 80–84.

visitors. Along with 300 authors and illustrators, publishing industry professionals provide an inside look at the book business. Festival director Jane Kulow notes that in addition to presenting a wide variety of programs featuring debut to internationally recognized authors, the festival offers a chance for attendees to meet them in personal settings.

Events take place at various locations in Charlottesville and Albemarle County, among them the University of Virginia campus, notable for being the first U.S. university centered around a library rather than a church. The school's founder was an author himself—Thomas Jefferson, U.S. President and chief architect of the Declaration of Independence. His **Monticello** estate, located in Charlottesville, is a great side trip for festivalgoers.

Festival events are free of charge with the exception of a few that require payment. On *www.vabook.org,* you can sign up for advance notice of events and customize a festival schedule.

LOS ANGELES TIMES FESTIVAL OF BOOKS
Los Angeles, CA • Annually in April • *events.latimes.com/festivalofbooks*

Touted as "rousing and fun," this two-day book festival held on the UCLA campus tops 150,000 visitors every year and boasts a robust event roster of nearly 450 authors and Hollywood celebrities. No bibliophile will go home empty-handed after browsing the goods of some 300 exhibitors, including booksellers, publishers, and literacy and cultural organizations. General admission to the festival is free, including all outdoor programming; tickets are required for indoor events. Paid passes entitle festivalgoers to special perks.

CHICAGO TRIBUNE PRINTERS ROW LIT FEST
Chicago, IL • Annually in June • *www.printersrowlitfest.org*

The Midwest's largest free outdoor literary event takes place in Chicago's historic Printers Row neighborhood. Once the city's book-making hub, Printers Row celebrates its roots each year in a two-day showcase spanning five city blocks and drawing 150,000 ardent readers. More than 200 authors make an appearance with entertainment

"It is hopeless for the occasional visitor to try to keep up with Chicago."
—MARK TWAIN

taking place on multiple stages, while booksellers from across the country offer new, used, and antiquarian books. Some events require tickets. A paid Fest Pass is available and so is TribBooks, an app with Lit Fest information.

NATIONAL BOOK FESTIVAL

Washington, D.C. • Sponsored by the Library of Congress
• Annually in September/early October • *www.loc.gov/bookfest*

Page turners trump politics during the one-day National Book Festival in Washington, D.C., when 100,000 book lovers gather to meet some 175 authors, illustrators, and poets and to browse pavilions devoted to genres such as fiction, food, history, biography and memoir, contemporary life, and teen and children's titles.

In the popular Pavilion of the States, learn about literary traditions across the country and pick up a map and reading list, "52 Great Reads About Great Places," with state-by-state recommendations for kids. Multimedia exhibits in the Library of Congress Pavilion offer the chance to virtually explore the cultural treasures housed in the library's vast collections. The National Book Festival app is available for planning out your day in advance, and a Children's Guide has tips for turning the festival into an adventure for young readers. All events are free and take place at the Walter E. Washington Convention Center.

BROOKLYN BOOK FESTIVAL

Brooklyn, NY • Annually in September • *www.brooklynbookfestival.org*

More than 300 literary stars and emerging authors, hailing from Brooklyn and beyond, take part in panels, discussions, and readings on multiple stages during the free, one-day book festival in this vibrant New York City borough. Plus there is plenty more excitement in the days before and after the main draw. Bookend Events such as parties, film screenings, literary-themed games, and author appearances take place in clubs, parks, bookstores, theaters, and libraries throughout NYC. For young readers, a Children's Day spotlights writers and illustrators of kids' books.

TEXAS BOOK FESTIVAL

Austin, TX • Annually in late October/early November
• *www.texasbookfestival.org*

The State Capitol in Austin provides a striking backdrop for the Texas Book Festival, a weekend fiesta attended by 40,000 literary enthusiasts. Numerous events take place in the national historic landmark building, including author presentations and panels in the House and Senate chambers, and on the surrounding grounds. More than 250 writers from the Lone Star State and across the nation participate in events ranging from a black-tie gala to Spanish-language programs to a street festival with 80+ exhibitors, live music, food trucks, and family activities. Events are free with the exception of the First Edition Literary Gala. For after-hours entertainment, **Lit Crawl Austin** takes place on Saturday evening during the festival weekend with author performances, storytelling sessions, trivia matches, and more at various venues (*www.litcrawl.org*).

"Texas is a state of mind. Texas is an obsession."
—JOHN STEINBECK, TRAVELS WITH CHARLEY

MIAMI BOOK FAIR

Miami, FL • Annually in November
• *www.miamibookfair.com*

South Florida's sun and surf pale in comparison to the festivities at this literary celebration, held on Miami Dade College's Wolfson campus. Eight days of happenings include a "comic con" with creator panels and workshops; a pop-up lounge showcasing Florida writers, musicians, and artists; the Ibero-American Authors Program (in Spanish); an evening conversation series spotlighting noted U.S. and international wordsmiths; and extensive offerings for teens and kids. A street fair presents hundreds of book-related vendors, along with more than 450 authors discussing their work. Program guides are available in English and Spanish. Admission is charged on two of three days the street fair is held; otherwise events are free. In Miami another time? The festival offers year-round programming.

EUROPE

THE INDEPENDENT BATH LITERATURE FESTIVAL

Bath, England • Annually in late February/early March

• *bathfestivals.org.uk/literature*

Immortalized in the pages of onetime resident Jane Austen's novels *Persuasion* and *Northanger Abbey,* this elegant former spa town (whose origins date to Roman times) is the site of a ten-day literary fest that draws 15,000 visitors. More than 150 authors take part in over a hundred events, among them discussions on everything from classic writers to current affairs, creative writing workshops, poetry salons, musical acts, and walking tours. Says Viv Groskop, artistic director of the Bath Literature Festival, "I want the festival to involve readers as much as writers. Books are a blissful part of all our lives, regardless of whether we create them or simply devour them." There is a fee for all events at the Bath Literature Festival.

HAY FESTIVAL

Hay on Wye, Wales • Annually in late May

• *www.hayfestival.com/wales*

Hay on Wye's 1,800 well-read residents are rich in choices: The town supports about 15 bookstores, many of which sell secondhand and antiquarian books and specialize in specific genres like mysteries and thrillers, poetry, cinema, and even Charles Dickens. With such a high book-to-bibliophile ratio, this tiny market town in southeastern Wales is the ideal locale for an internationally renowned literary festival. For ten days beginning the last week in May, 80,000 visitors usher in summer by partaking in what previous attendee Bill Clinton called "the Woodstock of the mind."

Festival co-founder Peter Florence notes that regulars often cite three things they enjoy about the event: "the informal, hanging-out atmosphere, discovering new voices, and hooking up with each other every year." The festival includes a mix of both free and paid events. Advance bookings can be made through the festival's website.

EDINBURGH INTERNATIONAL BOOK FESTIVAL
Edinburgh, Scotland • Annually in August • www.edbookfest.co.uk

Robert Louis Stevenson, Sir Arthur Conan Doyle, and the Encyclopaedia Britannica all hail from Edinburgh, so it's no surprise that the city's 17-day International Book Festival has become the world's premier literary event since its inception in 1983. Each year, 250,000 visitors flock to Charlotte Square Gardens—nestled under magisterial Edinburgh Castle—to rub elbows with blockbuster authors and discover new ones. With about 800 authors from more than 45 countries taking part in over 750 events, choosing among the offerings can be more difficult than thinning out overflowing bookshelves. Entry to Charlotte Square Gardens is free, as are some events. The festival program schedule is released in early June, and tickets go on sale soon after.

EDINBURGH BY THE BOOK: A spirited way to bask in the bookish pleasures of the world's first designated UNESCO City of Literature is to take the **Edinburgh Literary Pub Tour**, led by professional actors who deliver a lively performance in and out of atmospheric Old Town's famed taverns. The tour departs from **The Beehive**, a 16th-century stagecoach inn once frequented by classic Scottish scribes (*www.edinburghliterarypubtour.co.uk*). Or embark on the **Edinburgh Book Lovers' Tour** (*www.edinburghbooktour.com*) with in-the-know guide Allan Foster, author of *The Literary Traveller in Edinburgh*.

Both *www.cityofliterature.com* and *www.visitscotland.com* have an abundance of information on literary Edinburgh, including self-guided walking tour itineraries and apps related to classic and contemporary writers. But if you only have time for one site, make it Lady Stair's Close, a 17th-century building housing the **Writers' Museum** (*www.cac.org.uk*). It's packed with memorabilia related to the Scottish literary trifecta: Robert Burns, Robert Louis Stevenson, and Sir Walter Scott.

From Page to Screen

The next best thing to following in the footsteps of beloved authors is to visit the locales where their books were brought to life on film.

PRIDE AND PREJUDICE BY JANE AUSTEN

Elizabeth was distressed. She felt that she had no business at Pemberley, and was obliged to assume a disinclination for seeing it. She must own that she was tired of seeing great houses; after going over so many, she really had no pleasure in fine carpets or satin curtains.

England's splendidly regal **Chatsworth House** (*www.chatsworth.org*; open daily mid-March through December)—home to the Duke and Duchess of Devonshire—has been called the country's greatest private palace and served as a stand-in for Mr. Darcy's house, Pemberley, in the 2005 film starring Keira Knightley and Matthew Macfadyen. In the BBC adaptation a decade earlier, Pemberley's interior scenes were shot a short distance away at **Sudbury Hall** (*www.nationaltrust.org.uk*; open Wednesday through Sunday, mid-February through October) while the infamous scene where Darcy emerges from a lake was filmed at the Italianate-style **Lyme Park** estate in Cheshire (*www.nationaltrust.org.uk*; open Friday through Tuesday, mid-February through October, grounds year-round).

SENSE AND SENSIBILITY BY JANE AUSTEN

The Dashwoods were now settled at Barton with tolerable comfort to themselves. The house and the garden, with all the objects surrounding them, were now become familiar.

Efford House on the **Flete Estate** (*www.flete.co.uk*) in southern Devon was the setting used for the exterior shots of Barton Cottage, where the Dashwood ladies take up residence after the death of Henry

Dashwood in the 1995 movie. The house is a seven-bedroom holiday home available for rent.

A ROOM WITH A VIEW BY E. M. FORSTER

It was pleasant to wake up in Florence . . . to fling wide the windows, pinching with fingers in unfamiliar fastenings, to lean out into sunshine with beautiful hills and trees and marble churches opposite, and close below, the Arno, gurgling against the embankment of the road.

Situated along the Arno River in Florence, Italy, the **Hotel Degli Orafi** (*www.hoteldegliorafi.it*) is where Lucy Honeychurch checks in and finds herself in a room *without* a view in the 1986 film. Lucy later scores a room overlooking the Arno, although for guests who aren't as lucky, panoramic vistas can also be had from the rooftop bar. The hotel boasts a prime location near the Uffizi Gallery and the Piazza Signoria, where Lucy witnesses a murder.

HAMLET BY SHAKESPEARE

"But what is your affaire in Elsenour? Wee'l teach you to drinke deepe, ere you depart."

Located on a rocky promontory on Scotland's east coast, the crumbling ruins of eerie **Dunnottar Castle** (*www.dunnottar castle.co.uk*; open daily) were partially used as the exterior model for Shakespeare's Elsinore Castle in the 1990 film starring Mel Gibson. **Blackness Castle** near Edinburgh was also used for several scenes, including that of Ophelia's first appearance, which takes place in the large hall in the Stern tower (*www.historic-scotland.gov.uk*; open year-round except Thursday and Friday during winter).

The setting for Shakespeare's *Hamlet* is widely believed to be Denmark's **Kronborg Castle** (*www.kronborg.dk*), built in the mid-16th century and located in the town of Elsinore. On his first European sojourn, John Steinbeck visited the castle and took in a production of *Hamlet* cut short by rain. See pages 344–58 for more on Steinbeck.

Booked Up:

LITERARY PLACES TO DRINK, DINE, AND DOZE

ONE CANNOT THINK WELL, love well, sleep well, if one has not dined well," proclaimed Virginia Woolf, who knew a good meal was a key ingredient for stimulating both inspiration and conversation. Writers (and mere mortals, too) have always needed more than words alone to sustain them. Some, like Dashiell Hammett, fueled their creative fires with hearty fare like lamb chops. Others, like F. Scott Fitzgerald, found sustenance in liquid form.

After eating and imbibing, these peripatetic scribes sought the comforts of a warm bed to sleep off their indulgences. In the anonymity of the hotel rooms that so often welcomed them, masterpieces were created, writerly love affairs were ignited, and sometimes life came to an ignominious end.

Modern-day travelers, having heeded Woolf's advice to dine well, can stay in such places as the Venetian palazzo where Hemingway recuperated after a plane crash, the ivy-clad English inn where Agatha Christie resurfaced after her mysterious disappearance, or the Paris hotel where the story concluded for Oscar Wilde.

Literary Lodgings in the U.S.

ALGONQUIN HOTEL

New York, NY • 59 West 44th Street • Tel: 212-840-6800 • *www.algonquinhotel.com*

Jazz Age novelist F. Scott Fitzgerald lodged at this elegant midtown Manhattan hotel, William Faulkner worked on his 1950 Nobel Prize acceptance speech in an Algonquin suite, and, most famously, Dorothy Parker and a group of literati regularly gathered here to trade witticisms in the 1920s. The site of their famous lunches, now dubbed the **Round Table Restaurant** (they referred to themselves as the Vicious Circle), is open for dining, and the **Blue Bar** serves a gin-based Dorothy Parker cocktail. Guests who need reading material can download free ebooks during their stay, while animals lovers can meet the feline-in-residence—males are always named Hamlet, females Matilda—a tradition since the 1930s when a stray was given shelter.

HOTEL ELYSÉE

New York, NY • 60 East 54th Street • Tel: 212-753-1066 • *www.elyseehotel.com*

A disgruntled guest at this midtown Manhattan hotel called the front desk to complain about the sound of late-night typing coming from another room. Rather than disturb hard-at-work playwright

PARKER'S RESTING PLACE: "Excuse my dust" was the reply given by Dorothy Parker when asked about an epitaph for her tombstone. The scribe's ashes are interred at the **Dorothy Parker Memorial Garden** at the Baltimore headquarters of the National Association for the Advancement of Colored People (NAACP). An admirer of Martin Luther King, Jr., the writer (who had no heirs) willed her estate to the civil rights leader, whom she had never met, and following his death a year later it passed on to the NAACP (*www.naacp.org*). Parker's ashes remained unclaimed for 21 years until 1988, when the NAACP created a shrine for them. A brick emblem in the shape of a circle at the site honors Parker's association with the Algonquin Round Table.

Tennessee Williams, staffers moved the unhappy lodger elsewhere. Williams lived at the Elysée on and off for the last fifteen years of his life and passed away there in February 1983 at age 71. Hanging in the Presidential Suite named for him is a framed letter he wrote asking a friend to visit him at the hotel, while volumes of his works can be found in the Library Lounge. Stop by the ground-level **Monkey Bar**, opened in the waning days of Prohibition, where one of the figures depicted in a mural by illustrator and caricaturist Ed Sorel is cigarette-smoking, bowtie-wearing Williams.

THE PLAZA HOTEL

New York, NY • Fifth Avenue and Central Park South • Tel: 212-759-3000 • www.theplazany.com

This Manhattan grande dame was the site of Truman Capote's legendary extravaganza, the Black and White Ball, on November 28, 1966. The Plaza's illustrious guest roster also includes Dashiell Hammett, F. Scott and Zelda Fitzgerald, and Carson McCullers, who booked herself a stay at the hotel to celebrate her 50th (and final) birthday. Famed New Yorker Dorothy Parker (who was annoyed to be left off the guest list for Capote's gala) once stayed here, and was fired from her job at *Vanity Fair* magazine over tea at the Plaza. Built in 1907 and located on fashionable Fifth Avenue near Central Park, this château-style hotel is also home to spirited children's book character Eloise.

HOTEL MONTELEONE

New Orleans, LA • Royal Street • Tel: 504-523-3341 • www.hotelmonteleone.com

Southern scribes Eudora Welty, Truman Capote, Tennessee Williams, and William Faulkner all lodged at this sumptuous French Quarter hotel, where suites now bear their names. Ernest Hemingway's moniker graces the penthouse. The hotel is immortalized in print with mentions in Faulkner's novel *Mosquitoes*, Williams's play *The Rose Tattoo*, and Hemingway's short story "Night Before Battle." Although Capote often claimed he was born at the Monteleone, where his parents had taken a suite, he actually made his arrival at a nearby infirmary. The hotel is at the heart of the Big Easy literary scene,

For the **Tennessee Williams/New Orleans Literary Festival**, see pages 145–46.

including serving as a host venue for the annual Tennessee Williams/ New Orleans Literary Festival. One of the Monteleone's distinctive landmarks is the whimsical **Carousel Bar & Lounge**, which has a circus motif and revolving bar.

HOTEL UNION SQUARE

San Francisco, CA • 114 Powell Street

• Tel: 415-397-3000 • *www.hotelunionsquare.com*

Slumbering in the Hotel Union Square's Dashiell Hammett Suite is akin to entering the pages of the crime writer's fictional world. The atmospheric corner guest room (see photo) features a desk with an old-fashioned typewriter; an antique suitcase with copies of Hammett's books; "Spade and Archer," the name of the detective agency in *The Maltese Falcon,* stenciled on the window; and a statue of the black bird. Hammett booked his bride-to-be in a suite at this hotel (then known as the Golden West) before their 1921 wedding. Around the corner is **John's Grill**, a favored haunt of both Hammett and Sam Spade.

See page 193 for more about **John's Grill** and page 101 for a walking tour of Dashiell Hammett's San Francisco.

WILLARD INTERCONTINENTAL

Washington, D.C. • 1401 Pennsylvania Avenue NW • Tel: 202-628-9100

• *washington.intercontinental.com*

Located two blocks from the White House, the Willard has played host to such notables as Mark Twain, Walt Whitman, and Nathaniel Hawthorne, who journeyed to Washington, D.C., in 1862 to report on the Civil War for the *Atlantic Monthly* magazine. "This hotel," he wrote, "may be much more justly called the center of Washington and the Union than . . . the Capitol, the White House, or the State

Department . . . It is the meeting-place of the true representatives of the country."

Whitman gave the hotel a nod in his essay "Battle of Bull Run, July, 1861," noting its "sumptuous parlors and barrooms." Julia Ward Howe penned "The Battle Hymn of the Republic" while staying at the hotel in 1861, and Martin Luther King, Jr. found similar political fervor there in 1963. He worked on his "I Have a Dream" speech at the Willard on the eve before he delivered the famous address on the steps of the Lincoln Memorial.

The **Round Robin Bar's** signature drink is the mint julep, introduced here to the capital city in the early 19th century by Kentucky senator Henry Clay. "You adopt the universal habit of the place, and call for a mint-julep, a whiskey-skin, a gin-cocktail, a brandy-smash, or a glass of pure Old Rye, for the conviviality of Washington sets in at an early hour," declared Hawthorne in the *Atlantic Monthly*, "and, so far as I had an opportunity of observing, never terminates at any hour, and all these drinks are continually in request."

THE JEFFERSON

Richmond, VA • 101 West Franklin Street • Tel: 804-649-4750
• www.jeffersonhotel.com

Opened in 1895 and located in Richmond's historic district, the Jefferson's southern hospitality has beckoned famous figures from presidents to movie stars. Among the writers who luxuriated in its splendor are Thomas Wolfe, F. Scott and Zelda Fitzgerald, and companions Gertrude Stein and Alice B. Toklas. The sumptuous hotel—"where the haute Monde are most comfortable," a friend told Stein in a 1935 letter—features two-story faux-marble columns, chandeliers, oil paintings, and a sweeping staircase that would make Scarlett O'Hara proud. Afternoon tea (open to the public) is served several days a week in the Jefferson's Palm Court lobby beneath a 70-foot ceiling adorned with a Tiffany-designed stained-glass skylight.

During a 1935 U.S. lecture tour, Gertrude Stein visited Edgar Allan Poe's former room, a shrine to the writer, at the University of Virginia in Charlottesville. For more about Poe, see pages 80–84 and 164.

OMNI PARKER HOUSE

Boston, MA • 60 School Street • Tel: 617-227-8600 • www.omnihotels.com

On the last Saturday of the month, Ralph Waldo Emerson, Henry Wadsworth Longfellow, and other members of the 19th-century Saturday Club convened at the Omni Parker House for festive roundtable discussions. The illustrious group hosted a dinner in honor of Shakespeare's 300th birthday and feted Charles Dickens during his 1867–68 American lecture tour. Dickens is said to have given a private reading of *A Christmas Carol* to Saturday Club members before presenting it to the public. The British writer's presence in Boston caused a furor, and zealous fans would try to catch a glimpse of the scribe in his room at the hotel. The Omni Parker House, which opened in 1855 and was replaced with a new building in 1927, is located along Boston's historic Freedom Trail.

LONGFELLOW'S WAYSIDE INN

Sudbury, MA • 72 Wayside Inn Road • Tel: 978-443-1776 • www.wayside.org

A visit to this colonial-era landmark inspired Henry Wadsworth Longfellow to use it a backdrop in his 1863 book of poems, *Tales of a Wayside Inn,* in which a group of people share stories, including a vivid account of Paul Revere's midnight ride. The Wayside's roots extend back to 1716, when it opened as the Howe Tavern, offering travelers sustenance and lodging. The dining room is open to the public, as is the Old Bar Room, one of the Wayside's two original rooms. Patrons can sit at a rustic wooden table and sip a Coow Woow, billed as America's first cocktail, by firelight. Along with ten charming guest rooms, this "place of slumber and of dreams" offers guests the tranquility of its sprawling acreage with oak trees, historic buildings such as a gristmill, and the Longfellow Rose Garden. A walking tour brochure of the grounds is available on the Wayside's website. Once a stagecoach stop, Sudbury is located about 20 miles from Longfellow's historic home in Cambridge, Massachusetts. For more on the poet, see pages 52–54.

"As ancient is this hostelry As any in the land may be, Built in the old Colonial day."
—TALES OF A WAYSIDE INN

INN OF THE TURQUOISE BEAR

Santa Fe, NM • 342 East Buena Vista Street • Tel: 505-983-0798 • *www.turquoisebear.com*

The adobe villa that once belonged to poet, translator, and essayist Witter Bynner is steeped in architectural and literary history. The original rooms in the Spanish pueblo revival–style dwelling date to the mid-1800s, and it became a hub of Santa Fe's cultural scene in the first half of the 20th century. Bynner (once engaged to fellow poet Edna St. Vincent Millay) entertained the likes of controversial English writer D. H. Lawrence, Willa Cather, and Robert Frost, over whose head the host reportedly poured a mug of beer after being on the receiving end of a joke. The back-to-nature surroundings at the inn include a rock terrace, ponderosa pines, and gardens filled with lilacs, wild roses, and other blooms.

Willa Cather's 1927 saga *Death Comes for the Archbishop*, set partly in Santa Fe, was named by *Time* magazine as one of the 100 best English-language novels published after 1923. For more on Cather, see pages 55–56.

LITERARY AMBIANCE IN ABUNDANCE

AKWAABA DC

Washington, D.C. • 1708 16th St. NW • Tel: 866-466-3855 • *www.akwaaba.com*

This bed-and-breakfast is located in an 1890s town house in the heart of the U.S. capital. Akwaaba means "welcome" in the language of Ghana, West Africa, and a gracious greeting awaits guests at this haven owned by Monique Greenwood, former editor-in-chief of *Essence* magazine. Four of the Akwaaba's seven guest rooms are devoted to specific writers—Zora Neale Hurston, Langston Hughes, Toni Morrison, and Walter Mosley—complete with a selection of reads by the person for whom the chamber is named. Also available is the two-bedroom Writer's Retreat Apartment. Scheduled author readings take place in the Akwaaba's parlor, as does an evening happy hour.

ALEXANDER HOUSE BOOKLOVERS' BED & BREAKFAST

Princess Anne, MD • 30535 Linden Ave • Tel: 410-651-5195 • *www.bookloversbnb.com*

At this colorful and whimsical B&B, literary travelers can check into one of three rooms devoted to different time periods—the Harlem Renaissance of Langston Hughes, the 19th-century high seas of adventure writer Robert Louis Stevenson, and the Regency-era England of Jane Austen—or the floral-bedecked *Secret Garden* chamber. The Mark Twain Library and Parlor has a fireplace and a variety of reading selections on hand. In the Café Colette (named for the French novelist), guests can partake of afternoon tea and evening liqueurs, and test their literary prowess with a selection of entertainments such as Trivial Pursuit Book Lovers Edition, Pride & Prejudice: The Game, and the Author's Card Game.

Nicknamed "the poet laureate of Harlem," Langston Hughes lived his last two decades in the northern Manhattan neighborhood that inspired his writing. He resided in a brownstone at **20 E. 127th Street**, now a city landmark, where he wrote the jazz-influenced *Montage of a Dream Deferred* and other works.

INN BOONSBORO

Boonsboro, MD • 1 N. Main Street • Tel: 301-432-1188

• *www.innboonsboro.com*

Romance is always in the air at the Inn Boons-Boro. Each room at this elegant boutique hotel—housed in a restored historic building—is named for a pair of literary lovers. Slumber in the art deco elegance of the Nick and Nora Charles room, which pays homage to the husband-and-wife sleuths in Dashiell Hammett's *The Thin Man*, or revel in the ethereal ambiance of the chamber honoring Titania and Oberon from Shakespeare's *A Midsummer Night's Dream*. Each room is not only individually decorated but also stocked with custom-scented bath amenities, like English lavender for *Pride and Prejudice* duo Elizabeth and Darcy.

The inn is owned by best-selling author Nora Roberts, whose own Eve and Roarke from the "In Death" series (written as J. D. Robb) lend their monikers to a room. In addition, art imitates life in the author's Inn BoonsBoro trilogy, which features three brothers as they restore and run a bed-and-breakfast and find love in a small Maryland town.

LIBRARY HOTEL

New York, NY • 299 Madison Avenue
• Tel: 212-983-4500 • www.libraryhotel.com

One block from the New York Public Library, this midtown Manhattan hotel houses more than 6,000 volumes organized according to the Dewey decimal system. Tomes can be found from the lobby, lined with floor-to-ceiling bookcases, to the 14th-floor rooftop, which features a glass-enclosed Poetry Garden and terrace, a mahogany-paneled Writer's Den, and the after-hours Bookmarks Lounge with literary-inspired drinks. Each of the hotel's ten floors of guest rooms is devoted to a different category, among them history, philosophy, and the arts. For literature buffs, the choices range from classics and poetry to fairy tales and mysteries, and chambers feature a collection of books relating to each room's theme. Guests can enjoy a complimentary evening wine and cheese reception in the Reading Room, and turn-down service includes a treat: chocolates with wrappers featuring a literary quote.

The hotel is located on a thoroughfare known as **Library Way**. Extending along 41st Street between Fifth and Park Avenues, the sidewalk is dotted with plaques containing poetry and quotes from literary figures. For more about the **New York Public Library**, see pages 162–63.

SPENCER HOTEL & SPA

Chautauqua, NY • 25 Palestine Avenue • Tel: 800-398-1306 • www.thespencer.com

Even the bedtime snacks are literary at this hotel in western New York State: homemade cookies in shapes that correspond to bookish room themes. Individually decorated guest rooms bear the monikers of famous writers, among them Agatha Christie and C. S. Lewis, with décor evoking each scribe's era and works. The Jules Verne Room features a fanciful painted sky and hot-air balloon motif in homage to the author's adventurous first novel, *Five Weeks in a Balloon*. A mural in the Shakespeare Room recreates the balcony scene in *Romeo and Juliet,* and the Dorothy Parker Room is adorned in the art deco style of the 1920s. Along with in-room music selections representative of each author's time period, works of featured writers are available for perusing and purchase. The hotel is located on the grounds of the Chautauqua Institution, a resort and educational center with an emphasis on the arts.

THE HEATHMAN HOTEL

Portland, OR • 1001 SW Broadway • Tel: 800-551-0011 • *www.heathmanhotel.com*

There's no need to bring your own reading material when you lodge at this luxurious downtown Portland hotel. Guests can borrow books from a cataloged lending library, which is stocked with more than 2,700 volumes—most of which are first editions signed by the hotel's author guests. The library is open for reading and relaxing to those checked in at the Heathman, and receptions are held among the stacks. For more of a literary fix, take a short stroll to **Powell's City of Books** (*www .powells.com*), a vast space housing approximately one million tomes. Color-coded maps help shoppers find their way around.

SYLVIA BEACH HOTEL

Newport, OR • 267 N.W. Cliff • Tel: 541-265-5428 • *www.sylviabeachhotel.com*

Book lovers seeking solitude will find it at this Oregon retreat situated on Nye Beach on a bluff overlooking the Pacific. The hotel features three room categories—classics, novels, and best sellers—and individually decorated chambers are named after literary figures ranging from Emily Dickinson to Dr. Seuss. While there are no televisions, radios, phones, or computers to be found here, there is a reading room boasting a plethora of page-turners, a fireplace, and a spectacular ocean view. The Tables of Content restaurant is open to the public for dining nightly at set times, and community-style seating provides the perfect arrangement for bibliophiles to share reading suggestions.

For more on the hotel's namesake, Sylvia Beach, onetime proprietor of Parisian bookshop **Shakespeare and Company**, see page 116.

INNSBRUCKER INN

Leavenworth, WA • 703 Highway 2 • Tel: 509-548-5401 • *www.innsbruckerinn.com*

Once a hub of the Great Northern Railroad, Leavenworth has been transformed into a Bavarian-themed village. The Innsbrucker Inn is situated above A Book For All Seasons, an independent bookstore, and features six rooms that include nods to Shakespeare and *Charlie and the Chocolate Factory*'s Willy Wonka. Emblazoned on the wall in a chamber devoted to Sherlock Holmes is a quote uttered by the detective in the short story "A Case of Mistaken Identity": "Life is infinitely stranger than anything which the mind of man could invent." Guests check in at the bookstore, where they receive an enticing perk— 10 percent off purchases during their stay at the inn.

Literary Lodgings Abroad

CASA GUIDI

Florence, Italy • Piazza San Felice 8 • Tel: (44) 162 882 5925
• www.landmarktrust.org.uk/search-and-book

I heard last night a little child so singing / 'Neath Casa Guidi windows, by the church, / O bella libertà, O bella!—stringing / The same words still on notes he went in search.
—Elizabeth Barrett Browning, "Casa Guidi Windows"

After a whirlwind 20-month courtship (during which 574 love letters were exchanged) and a clandestine wedding, poetic powerhouses Robert and Elizabeth Barrett Browning abandoned England in 1846 to escape the reproach of Elizabeth's tyrannical father. The couple settled into a grand Florentine apartment in a 15th-century palazzo. "In fact we have really done it magnificently," Elizabeth wrote in an 1847 letter. "We have six beautiful rooms and a kitchen, three of them quite palace rooms and opening on a terrace." Through the 14 years of happily married life that followed, the legendary romantics lived, loved, and wrote primarily at Casa Guidi, where the green drawing room was the center of activity. Their only child was born in Casa Guidi, and Elizabeth died there in Robert's arms on June 30, 1861.

Four of Casa Guidi's high-ceilinged rooms have been restored to close

In the town of Asolo in the Venetian countryside, check into the intimate 16th-century **Hotel Villa Cipriani** (*www.villa ciprianiasolo.com*); Robert Browning was negotiating to purchase the villa at the time of his death in 1889. He called the area "the most beautiful spot I ever was privileged to see."

approximations of how they were furnished and painted during the Brownings' time while a modern kitchen and bathrooms were installed in the former servants' quarters. Some of Casa Guidi's chambers are available as a holiday rental most weeks during the year, while the main rooms are open for public viewing on select afternoons.

Elizabeth Barrett Browning is buried in Florence's **Protestant Cemetery**, while Robert Browning, who died 28 years after his wife, is buried in the Poets' Corner of **Westminster Abbey**. For more on the London cathedral, see page 99.

KEATS-SHELLEY HOUSE

Rome, Italy • Piazza di Spagna 26 • Tel: (44) 162 882 5925
• *www.landmarktrust.org.uk/search-and-book*

English Romantic poet John Keats spent the last months of his short life in an 18th-century pallazzetto overlooking the Spanish Steps, hoping in vain that Rome's temperate climes would stave off his worsening tuberculosis. But his condition continued to deteriorate, and he died here at the age of 26 on February 23, 1821. Today, his rooms have been preserved as a museum dedicated to him and his English contemporary, Percy Bysshe Shelley.

"Rome is yet the capital of the world. It is a city of palaces and temples, more glorious than those which any other city contains, and of ruins more glorious than they."
—PERCY BYSSHE SHELLEY LETTER, MARCH 23, 1819

On the floor above, visitors can awaken to the same soothing sounds of Bernini's burbling fountain that Keats once enjoyed by renting the Keats-Shelley House apartment (see photo), managed by the U.K.'s Landmark Trust. (Sleeps up to four; three-night minimum stay required.) Along with comfortable period-style furnishings and a modernized kitchen and bath, the spacious apartment boasts tall shuttered windows, tiled floors, and soaring wood-beam rosette ceilings restored to their 1800s appearance. For more about **Keats-Shelley House**, see pages 43–44.

HOTEL DE RUSSIE

Rome, Italy • Via del Babuino 9 • Tel: (39) 06 32 88 81 • *www.roccofortehotels .com/hotels-and-resorts/hotel-de-russie*

Housed in a 19th-century palazzo, this five-star hotel with a charming terraced *giardino segreto* (secret garden) was where Henry James opted to stay during his 1907 visit to the Eternal City. Charles Dickens had checked into the Russie six decades earlier while attending Carnival—"a very remarkable and beautiful sight"—with his wife. He returned to the hotel in 1853, renting the grand top-floor suite, which boasted a "large back dining room, a handsome front drawing-room looking into the Piazza del Popolo, and three front bedrooms." During World War II, the elegant building was usurped by the Germans for their headquarters, and it later stood vacant until reopened as a luxury hotel at the turn of the millennium.

HOTEL GRITTI PALACE

Venice, Italy • Campo Santa Maria del Giglio
• Tel: (39) 041 794 611 • *www.thegrittipalace.com*

A 16th-century former doge's palace on the Grand Canal was Hemingway's Venetian pied-à-terre during trips he took to the water-bound Italian city in the late 1940s and early 1950s. After his 1948 stay there, he tattled to his publisher that his archenemy Sinclair Lewis, a fellow guest at the Gritti, "would go down to the bar and have three or four double whiskies in the evening and then write." Hemingway's time in Venice inspired his critically dismissed novel, *Across the River and into the Trees,* whose doomed protagonist checks into his familiar room at the Gritti, feeling at last "really home, if a hotel room can be so described." In early 1954, Hemingway spent several weeks recuperating at the Gritti after surviving two near-fatal plane crashes during an African safari. With typical bravado, he relished sitting on the hotel's canal-side terrace each morning with a glass of cold champagne while reading his obituaries, which had erroneously appeared in newspapers around the world after his second plane crash. Today, guests can book the luxurious suite (see photo) where Hemingway nursed himself back to health.

HOTEL DANIELI

Venice, Italy • Castello, Riva degli Schiavoni, 4196 • Tel: (39) 041 522 6480
• *www.danielihotelvenice.com*

During an 1834 sojourn to Venice, French scribe George Sand checked into room 10 of the opulent Hotel Danieli with her lover, poet Alfred Musset (an inscription above the room's door commemorates their stay here). Despite the splendor of their surroundings and their enviable location near St. Mark's Square and the Bridge of Sighs, the couple's time at the Danieli was far from idyllic; financial troubles and illness hovered over them like a black cloud. First, Sand was stricken with dysentery, after which Musset came down with a mysterious illness, likely caused by his sexual indiscretions while Sand was bedridden. Sand nursed him around the clock, afraid to leave his side lest his hallucinations and symptoms of madness worsen. Soon after Musset was on the mend, the authoress began an affair with his handsome Italian doctor and the spurned poet eventually returned to France alone. Later guests at the Danieli included Marcel Proust, Theodore Dreiser (who found it "a delicious old palace"), and Mark Twain, who spent ten days here with his family in 1892.

SELKIRK ARMS

Kirkcudbright, Scotland • High Street • Tel: (44) 155 733 0402
• *www.selkirkarmshotel.co.uk*

The artists' enclave and fishing village of Kirkcudbright was a favored vacation destination of mystery writer Dorothy L. Sayers. The novelist used the Selkirk Arms as the model for the popular watering hole the McClellan Arms in the Lord Peter Wimsey tale *The Five Red Herrings*. Well before Sayers's time, in 1794, Scottish bard Robert Burns dined at the Selkirk, then known as the Heid Inn, and reportedly first delivered the now famous "Selkirk Grace," a blessing that is a staple of Burns Night Suppers each January. Elsewhere in the area, the annual **Big Burns Supper** (*www.bigburns supper.com*) is a contemporary performing arts festival that pays tribute to the bard.

See page 144 for more about **Burns Night Suppers**.

BROWN'S HOTEL

London, England • Albemarle Street • Tel: (44) 207 493 6020 • *www.brownshotel.com*
Founded in 1837 by Lord Byron's valet and comprising 11 conjoined

See page 73 for information on checking into Rudyard Kipling's Vermont home, Naulakha. For Christie-related lodgings on the English Riviera, see pages 106-107.

Georgian town houses, this luxurious hotel is where Rudyard Kipling reportedly made himself comfortable while penning portions of *The Jungle Book*. On a later visit in the winter of 1936, Kipling and his wife were lodging at Brown's when the writer suffered a hemorrhage and was rushed to the hospital. He died of a perforated ulcer six days later on January 18, the day of his 44th wedding anniversary. Agatha Christie was also a frequent guest at Brown's and based her 1965 Miss Marple mystery *At Bertram's Hotel* on the genteel locale. "If this was the first time you had visited Bertram's, you felt, almost with alarm, that you had re-entered a vanished world," Christie wrote in the tale. "Time had gone back. You were in Edwardian England once more."

SAVOY HOTEL

London, England • The Strand • Tel: (44) 207 836 4343 • www.fairmont.com/savoy

"When I went to the window of my room I noticed the mist parting," recalled French novelist Émile Zola of his 1893 visit to London's Savoy, "one mass of vapor ascending skyward, while the other still hovered over the river." The same year Zola stayed at the glitzy art deco hotel on the Thames, Oscar Wilde scandalously took a room there with a young Scottish aristocrat, Lord Alfred Douglas, an event that led to the playwright's downfall. Two years later,

To explore Oscar Wilde's London on a walking tour, see page 156.

Savoy chambermaids provided damaging testimony against Wilde when he faced trial on charges of "gross indecency." During the Blitz, the Savoy—considered safe because of its iron and concrete construction—provided refuge for another playwright, Noël Coward, who hunkered down there in early 1941. One evening while he was at the hotel, bombs fell nearby. "Wall bulged a bit and door blew in. Orchestra went on playing, no one stopped eating or talking. Blitz continued," recalled Coward, whose plays were often performed at the adjacent Savoy Theatre. The playwright's lighter and cigarette case are among the memorabilia in the Savoy Museum.

BELMOND CADOGAN HOTEL

London, England • 75 Sloane Street • *www.belmond*
.com/cadogan-hotel-london

On April 5, 1895, Oscar Wilde was arrested in room 118 (now part of Enhanced Suite 101) of this upscale Edwardian hotel on a charge of "gross indecency" stemming from his homosexual relationship with Lord Alfred Douglas. Friends had urged Wilde to flee the country once word of his impending arrest leaked out, but Wilde was resolute, saying, "I shall stay and do my sentence, whatever it is." The poet-dramatist was sentenced to two years imprisonment with hard labor, a cruel punishment that was to signal the beginning of the end for Wilde's brightly shining star. The arrest was immortalized by British poet laureate John Betjeman in his poem "The Arrest of Oscar Wilde at the Cadogan Hotel."

FARRINGFORD

Isle of Wight, England • Bedbury Lane, Freshwater Bay • Tel: (44) 198 375 2500
• *www.farringford.co.uk*

(Take it and come) to the Isle of Wight; / Where, far from noise and smoke of town, / I watch the twilight falling brown / All around a careless ordered garden, / Close to the ridge of a noble down. / You'll have no scandal while you dine, / But honest talk and wholesome wine.
—Lord Alfred Tennyson, "To the Rev. F. D. Maurice"

Seeking refuge "far from noise and smoke of town," Lord Alfred Tennyson settled on this peaceful English Channel resort isle in 1853 and remained there happily for the last 40 years of his life. Stables and other buildings on the scenic estate where the poet resided have been converted into self-catering cottages. Tennyson's "house half hid in the gleaming wood," where he composed his famed poems "Maud" and "The Charge of the Light Brigade," is a **museum** restored to how it looked during his day. In a wing added at the end of the 19th century are two vacation apartment rentals. Accessible from Farringford, the island's **Tennyson Trail** (download a trail map at *www.islandbreaks.co.uk*), a 15-mile route running through forests and along cliff tops, commemorates the poet's daily ritual of taking long morning walks.

In addition to Tennyson, the Isle of Wight has long attracted other literati in search of peace and inspiration, including Henry Wadsworth Longfellow and Lewis Carroll, who called on Tennyson at Farringford; Charles Darwin, who is thought to have begun *Origin of Species* during his stay on the isle; John Keats, who cut short his initial visit after becoming overwhelmed by solitude; and Charles Dickens, who summered on the island in 1849 and worked on *David Copperfield*.

After "hard Copperfieldian mornings" in his study, Dickens walked, swam, and picnicked on the Isle of Wight.

HÔTEL DU QUAI-VOLTAIRE

Paris, France • 19 quai Voltaire • Tel: (33) 1 42 61 50 91 • *www.quaivoltaire.fr*

Years before his rise to fame and scandalous downfall, Oscar Wilde stayed in a suite of second-floor rooms overlooking the Seine and the Louvre in this hotel, which started out as a 17th-century abbey. When a friend came to visit and remarked on the magnificent view, Wilde responded with characteristic wit, "Oh, that is altogether immaterial, except of course to the innkeeper, who of course charges it in the bill." During the months Wilde spent here between February and April 1883, he wrote *The Duchess of Padua,* one of his early plays. American novelist Willa Cather stayed at the Quai-Voltaire twice in 1920. In between she toured battlefields and the war-torn countryside, researching for her Pulitzer Prize–winning novel *One of Ours,* which is partly set in France during World War I.

L'HÔTEL

Paris, France • 13 rue des Beaux-Arts • Tel: (33) 1 44 41 99 00 • *www.l-hotel.com*

A prison stint and derailed writing career behind him, Oscar Wilde took up residence at these intimate lodgings (formerly known as the Hotel d'Alsace) in August 1899 after running up bills he couldn't pay at another

Paris establishment. By fall of the following year, he was largely bed-ridden but never lost his infamous wit, remarking to a friend on one of his last outings, "My wallpaper and I are fighting a duel to the death. One or the other of us has to go." The wallpaper was victorious, and Wilde died in room 16 (see photo) on November 30, 1900, at the age of 46. A plaque at the boutique hotel's entrance marks his time there.

HÔTEL PONT ROYAL

Paris, France • 5-7 rue de Montalembert • Tel: (33) 1 42 84 70 00

• www.hotel-pont-royal.com

Once known as Paris's literary hotel, these elegant Left Bank lodgings were a favorite haunt of Arthur Miller, Jean-Paul Sartre, Albert Camus, and Truman Capote, who stayed there multiple times during his European sojourns. During one stay, the bon vivant wandered into the secluded basement bar where Sartre and Simone de Beauvoir liked to sit and write undisturbed. No love was lost between the threesome during their encounter. De Beauvoir snarkily recalled that Capote—who was dressed in powder blue velvet pants and an oversize white sweater—looked like a "white mushroom," while he later wrote scathingly of the couple in his unfinished novel, *Answered Prayers*: "At the time the Pont Royal had a leathery little basement bar that was the favored swill bucket of haute Boheme's fatbacks. Walleyed, pipe-sucking, pasty-hued Sartre and his spinsterish moll, de Beauvoir, were usually propped in a corner like an abandoned pair of ventriloquist's dolls."

"Tell them that I have got them a reservation at the Pont-Royal for July 10th. It is a wonderful place to stay and I'm sure they will like it."

—TRUMAN CAPOTE LETTER, JUNE 15, 1948

HÔTEL D'EUROPE

Avignon, France • 14 Place Crillon • Tel: (33) 4 90 14 76 76 • www.heurope.com

During his 1891 river-rafting trip down the Rhône, Mark Twain stopped in the Provençal town of Avignon and slumbered at the Hôtel d'Europe, built in 1580 as the home of a marquis. Nomadic fellow scribe F. Scott Fitzgerald later checked in with his wife, Zelda, in the early 1920s, noting the wisteria-draped courtyard and the nearby Palace of the Popes rising "chimerically through the gold end of day over the broad still Rhône, while we did nothing, assiduously, under the plane trees on the opposite bank."

BEAU-RIVAGE PALACE

Lausanne, Switzerland • 17-19 Place du Port • Tel: (41) 21 613 33 33 • *www.brp.ch*

Lausanne is a block of picturesque houses, spilling over two or three gorges . . . crowned by a cathedral like a tiara. —Victor Hugo

While Zelda was being treated in a nearby sanatorium, F. Scott Fitzgerald briefly checked into the Beau-Rivage Palace overlooking Lake Geneva in 1930, but the dazzling marble-drenched interiors of the Belle Époque hotel had welcomed other literati years before the arrival of the Jazz Age scribe. In the 19th century, guests included Victor Hugo, who is thought to have stayed there while delivering the opening address at the 1869 Lausanne Peace Congress, and Mark Twain, who ensconced his family in the hotel before embarking on his rafting voyage down the Rhône River in 1891. Twain sent daily missives to his wife, reporting, "We glide noiseless and swift—as fast as a London cab-horse rips along—eight miles an hour . . . It's too delicious, floating with the swift current under the awning [of] these superb sunshiny days in deep peace and quietness."

GOLDENEYE RESORT

Oracabessa, Jamaica • St. Mary Parish • Tel: 876-622-9007 • *www.goldeneye.com*

"James Bond was delighted. He had had many assignments in Jamaica and many adventures on the island."

—THE MAN WITH THE GOLDEN GUN

While working as a naval intelligence officer during World War II, 007 creator Ian Fleming visited Jamaica and fell in love with the lush tropical isle, deciding to create an Edenic retreat there to escape the drab English winters. In the late 1940s, he designed and built Goldeneye (named in part for the Carson McCullers novel *Reflections in a Golden Eye*) from the ground up. Located on a cliff overlooking the aquamarine waters of Jamaica's north coast, the villa was the locale where Fleming penned all 14 of his Bond novels. Portions of three of them—*Dr. No, Live and Let Die,* and *The Man with the Golden Gun*—are set in Jamaica. Among the lodging options at this sprawling resort is the Fleming Villa, which includes the writer's three-bedroom bungalow and a private beach.

BLUE HARBOUR
Oracabessa, Jamaica • St. Mary Parish • Tel: 876-401-9332 • www.blueharb.com

After a three-month stay at Ian Fleming's Goldeneye in 1948, British actor-playwright Noël Coward began searching for Jamaican land on which to build "an idyllic bolt-hole to return to when life became too frustrating." Just a few miles down the road from Fleming, he found a peaceful cove that became home to his own island retreat, Blue Harbour. Today, Coward's two-story villa and adjacent guest cottages—which still contain some of the dramatist's original furnishings, such as his four-poster pineapple bed—are available to rent separately or as an entire property.

In the late 1950s, the playwright—overwhelmed with the continual onslaught of visitors to Blue Harbour, including A-listers such as Marlene Dietrich and Katharine Hepburn—began to seek out an additional island refuge. On a lush hillside one thousand feet above Blue Harbour, he built his second Jamaican home, **Firefly** (*www.firefly-jamaica.com*), now a museum and the location where Coward is buried. "The Noël evening was typical," Ian Fleming wrote to his wife after he and Truman Capote paid a visit to Coward's new home. "His firefly house is a near-disaster and anyway the rain pours into it from every angle and even through the stone walls so that the rooms are running with damp."

FAIRMONT HAMILTON PRINCESS
Hamilton, Bermuda • 76 Pitts Bay Road • Tel: 441-295-3000
• www.fairmont.com/hamilton-bermuda

The pink sands of Bermuda beckoned to Mark Twain again and again: The writer made eight trips to the isle via steamship during his lifetime, returning from his last sojourn just days before his death in April 1910. He could often be spotted at the island's "Pink Palace," the elegant Hamilton Princess hotel, which opened to great fanfare in 1885. A life-size bronze statue of Twain commemorates his time at the hotel.

"Life continues here the same as usual. There isn't a flaw in it. Good times, good home, tranquil contentment all day and every day . . . I shouldn't know how to go about bettering my situation."
—MARK TWAIN, LETTER FROM BERMUDA, JANUARY 1910

Three decades after Twain's Bermuda travels, Ian Fleming—then a naval intelligence officer—lodged at the Princess during World War II, when it became a British counterintelligence outpost. Fleming later set portions of *For Your Eyes Only* on the isle and was said to have taken inspiration from the enormous fish tanks that once graced the hotel's bar for the predator-filled aquarium in Dr. No's headquarters. In 1974, a controversial biography penned by Fleming's friend and former assistant, John Pearson, claimed the real James Bond was one Sir William Stephenson. Code-named "Intrepid," Stephenson oversaw British intelligence operations in the Western Hemisphere, including Bermuda, where he occupied the Bond-like penthouse suite at the Princess.

EL MINZAH

Tangier, Morocco • 85 rue de la Liberté • Tel: (212) 539 333 444 • *www.leroyal.com*

"Gertrude Stein's habitual hotel, the Villa de France, was filled with vacationists; our cabdriver took us to Minzah, a new hotel built at the end of the twenties," author Paul Bowles (*The Sheltering Sky*) recalled of his 1931 arrival in the exotic Moroccan port town of Tangier. Then, as now, the Minzah was one of the city's most elegant places to slumber. The once itinerant composer and writer settled permanently in Tangier in 1947, the first of many American expatriate writers—including Truman Capote and Tennessee Williams—drawn to the "anything goes" lifestyle of the North African outpost.

EL MUNIRIA

Tangier, Morocco • 1 rue Magellan • Tel: (212) 539 935 337

William Burroughs lived in Tangier in the 1950s, befriending Paul Bowles and spending drug-fueled days at El Muniria, a budget pension he christened Villa Delirium. While staying at the Muniria, he was joined by fellow beats Jack Kerouac and Allen Ginsberg, who journeyed to Tangier in 1957 (the threesome had first met in New York a decade earlier). Burroughs's writer pals traveled to North Africa to lend him a hand, assisting with the editing and typing of his work in progress, *Naked Lunch*, whose title Kerouac suggested.

Literary Places to Sip and Sup

JOHN'S GRILL

San Francisco, CA • 63 Ellis Street • Tel: 415-986-3274
• www.johnsgrill.com

He went to John's Grill, asked the waiter to hurry his order of chops, baked potato, and sliced toma-toes, ate hurriedly, and was smoking a cigarette with his coffee when a thick-set youngish man with a plaid cap set askew above pale eyes and a tough cheery face came into the Grill and to his table. —Dashiell Hammet, *The Maltese Falcon*

BLOODY BRIGID

2 oz Ketel One vodka

½ oz special mix*

Splash of sweet and sour

Fresh lime juice

Top with soda and a drop of grenadine

Serve on the rocks

*Equal parts Cointreau, St. Germain, and Pama liqueur

Dashiell Hammett frequented John's Grill while working as a Pinkerton opera-tive in a nearby building, and Sam Spade does the same in *The Maltese Falcon*. Opened in 1908, the restaurant's interior contains original period furnishings and exudes an elegant, welcoming ambiance. Dark oak-paneled walls are lined with photos of famous patrons, Hammett among them, and Sam Spade's lamb chops are on the menu. The establishment's signature drink is the Bloody Brigid (see recipe above), which is served in a souvenir glass. Sweet and strong, the red-hued concoction is named for *The Maltese Falcon*'s dangerous dame, Brigid O'Shaughnessy.

VESUVIO

San Francisco, CA • 255 Columbus Avenue • At Jack Kerouac Alley
• Tel: 415-362-3370 • www.vesuvio.com

Jack Kerouac was introduced to Vesuvio in 1955 by his friend Neal Cassady, the model for Dean Moriarty in Kerouac's classic *On the Road*. Little has changed in this North Beach saloon in the ensuing

The **Henry Miller Memorial Library** (*www .henrymiller.org*), a tribute to the controversial author of *Tropic of Cancer* and other works, is situated in a redwood grove on the California coast. "It was here in Big Sur," said Miller, "I first learned to say Amen!" Located in the former home of a longtime friend of Miller, the library hosts concerts, readings, and other events throughout the year.

decades since Kerouac, Allen Ginsberg, and other beatniks drank and discoursed in its eclectic environs. Low lighting, stained-glass pendant lamps, paintings, and vintage posters make for a cozy setting, and second-story seating with a balcony overlooks the bar and the main floor.

One evening Kerouac kept imbibing at Vesuvio and missed a dinner meeting with literary luminary Henry Miller in Big Sur, poet Lawrence Ferlinghetti once recalled. Repeated phone calls were made to assure Miller that Kerouac would soon be on his way. "He never did make it that night," remarked Ferlinghetti. The saloon's signature drinks are the rum- and tequila-fueled Jack Kerouac and Bohemian coffee with brandy and amaretto. Inscribed in the sidewalk along Kerouac Alley outside Vesuvio are quotes by Kerouac, Ferlinghetti, and others.

THE OWL BAR

Baltimore, MD • 1 East Chase Street • Tel: 410-347-0888 • *www.theowlbar.com*

Samuel Clemens (aka Mark Twain) is said to have visited this Baltimore establishment, which began serving patrons in the early 1900s. The Owl Bar's libations later proved a potent attraction for

THE BEATS' BEAT: Located next to Vesuvio is **City Lights Bookstore** (*www .citylights.com*), co-founded by Lawrence Ferlinghetti in 1953. The nearby **Beat Museum** (*www.thebeatmuseum.org*) provides an interesting look at the world of Kerouac and his contemporaries, including the impact of the landmark 1957 First Amendment trial that gave City Lights Press the right to publish Allen Ginsberg's controversial work *Howl & Other Poems* after it was declared obscene. The museum offers Beat Generation walking tours of North Beach. **Caffe Trieste**'s Vallejo Street location (*www.caffetrieste.com*) was another haunt of the beats and still counts writers and artists among its patrons.

novelist F. Scott Fitzgerald, who resided in the city for several years in the 1930s and frequented the pub with friend and journalist H. L. Mencken. Known as the Sage of Baltimore, Mencken was a noted literary critic, humorist, and reporter for the *Baltimore Morning Herald* and later the *Baltimore Sun*. He was married to a childhood friend of Zelda Fitzgerald, and the fellow literary influentials he counted as acquaintances included *Sister Carrie* author Theodore Dreiser.

Baltimore's literary roots run deep. Explore sites associated with F. Scott Fitzgerald, H. L. Mencken, Edgar Allan Poe, Gertrude Stein, Carl Sandburg, Dashiell Hammett, and other writers with the self-guided **Literary Heritage Tour** mapped out at *explore .baltimoreheritage.org*. For more about Fitzgerald, see pages 109–16.

Located in the former Belvedere Hotel (where Fitzgerald once threw a party for his teenage daughter in the ballroom), the Owl Bar operated as a speakeasy during Prohibition. Exposed brick, stained glass, an expansive wooden bar, and an owl motif make for a storied setting.

HARRY'S BAR

Venice, Italy • Calle Vallaresso 1323 • 30124 San Marco • Tel: (39) 041 5285777 • *www.harrysbarvenezia.com*

A Venice institution since 1931, Harry's Bar is not just home to the Bellini cocktail (white peach puree and prosecco) but also to a literary clientele that over the years has included Marcel Proust, Sinclair Lewis, and Somerset Maugham. No sign trumpets the bar's location (the name is discreetly etched on the door and windows) near the Piazza San Marco. Harry's decor of buttery yellow walls and round wooden tables enhance the elegant ambiance, while a second floor for dining has views of the Grand Canal. Ernest Hemingway was a regular at Harry's Bar, and he could often be found at his preferred corner table. Truman Capote (who was fond of the shrimp sandwiches) spent Christmas Eve 1953 at the establishment. On a "dark wintry Venetian night" Capote and a friend joined in the revelry and feasted on "a big Christmas dinner with martinis and cheese sandwiches." Declared Capote, "Harry's Bar was marvelous."

CAFFÈ FLORIAN

Venice, Italy • Piazza San Marco 57 • Tel: (39) 041 5205641 • *www.caffeflorian.com*

Caffè Florian's long and illustrious history began on December 29, 1720. In the ensuing centuries, famous figures have been drawn to its lushly decorated interior, which features hand-painted mirrors, frescoes, ornate woodwork, and plush red seating. Native Venetian and legendary lothario Giacomo Casanova went in search of female company at Florian's, which was then the only café to admit women. Other famous patrons have included Lord Byron, Goethe, Marcel Proust, Charles Dickens, and Henry James, who features the café in the short stories "The Aspern Papers" and "The Chaperon."

Florian's is located in the Piazza San Marco, which James described in *The Wings of the Dove* as "a great social saloon, a smooth-floored, blue-roofed chamber of amenity." A particular treat is to enjoy an evening on the piazza—as James once did—where live chamber music is played during warm-weather months. He reminisced in *Italian Hours* about enjoying "star-light gossip at Florian's, feeling the sea-breeze throb languidly between the two great pillars of the Piazzetta and over the low black domes of the church."

Casanova is best remembered for his amorous exploits, but his most daring adventure was his 1755 escape from a prison in the Doges Palace in the Piazza San Marco. In his autobiography *History of My Life*, the adventurer, spy, poet, and novelist recounts the story of his incarceration (for suspicion of espionage) and subsequent flight. On the **Doges Palace Secret Itinerary Tour**, visitors can see the cell where he was housed and trace his not-so-subtle escape route—through a hole cut in the ceiling above his cell, down the Golden Staircase, and through the palace's ceremonial entrance (*www.museicivicineveziani.it*).

GRANCAFFÈ QUADRI

Venice, Italy • Piazza San Marco 121 • Tel: (39) 041 5222105 • *www.alajmo.it*

Frequenting one café in the Piazza San Marco wasn't Henry James's style. He breakfasted at Florian's and then "wandered about, looking at pictures, street life, etc.," before heading to the Quadri for a noon meal. He recommended the dining establishment to a friend with the declaration that "in the Piazza: the best place is the Caffè Quadri."

The Quadri opened in 1775 and is situated beneath the 13th-century porticos of the Piazza San Marco. Visitors can opt to soak up the atmosphere outdoors on the piazza, in the ground-floor café, or in the dining room on an upper floor. As opulently furbished as the palazzi that line the Grand Canal, the Quadri also served Marcel Proust—who, like James, frequented Florian's as well. Lord Byron was a guest at the café, and half a century later so was John Ruskin, author of the historical tome *The Stones of Venice*, who lamented the fact that he would never meet his admired literary predecessor. "If he were only at Venice now," Ruskin declared of Byron, "I think we should have got on with each other."

ANTICO CAFFÈ GRECO

Rome, Italy • Via Condotti 86 • Tel: (39) 06 6791700 • www.anticocaffegreco.eu

Encompassing several rooms, the Antico Caffè Greco's rich interior boasts red and gold damask, paintings, mirrors, and marble-topped tables. Opened in 1760, it has hosted Charles Dickens, Mark Twain, and Hans Christian Andersen, who resided in the building beside the Greco and picked up his mail at the café. Greco patrons John Keats and Percy Shelley are immortalized at the nearby **Keats-Shelley House** (see page 183) located at the base of the Spanish Steps. Now a museum dedicated to the Romantic poets, it's where Keats died of tuberculosis at age 26.

The Roman residence in which *The Little Mermaid* and *The Ugly Duckling* author Hans Christian Andersen resided is now the luxurious **Inn at the Spanish Steps** (*www.atspanishsteps.com*).

CAFÉ DE LA PAIX

Paris, France • InterContinental Paris le Grand • 5 place de l'Opéra, 9e • Tel: (33) 1 40 07 36 36 • www.cafedelapaix.fr

Suave spy James Bond regularly "had luncheon at the Café de la Paix" when in Paris, Ian Fleming revealed in *For Your Eyes Only*. "The food was good enough and it amused him to watch the people."

Ernest Hemingway was once caught short on funds at the pricey café when he and his wife dined there during their first Christmas in Paris in 1921. The embarrassed writer had to jog back to their apartment for cash after they misinterpreted menu prices and came up lacking. Hemingway later used the Café de la Paix as a setting in the short story "My Old Man."

Patrons can sip and sup in the terrace café or in the gold-bedecked restaurant, as did Irish writers Oscar Wilde, James Joyce (in the company of bookshop proprietor Sylvia Beach), and Samuel Beckett (who feasted on cold chicken and champagne). In *Of Time and the River*, novelist Thomas Wolfe notes the café's desirable locale near the "great soaring masses" of the grandiose Opéra building.

LE PROCOPE

Paris, France • 13 rue de l'Ancienne-Comédie 6e • Tel: (33) 1 40 46 79 00 • *www.procope.com*

Opened in 1686 during the reign of Louis XIV, Le Procope is one of the oldest dining places in the world and is said to have introduced coffee to Parisians. In the 1700s the establishment attracted future U.S. president Thomas Jefferson and the first American ambassador to France, Benjamin Franklin, along with philosophers Jean-Jacques Rousseau and Voltaire (whose writing desk is on display). The latter particularly enjoyed the signature caffeinated beverage, quaffing some 40 cups of coffee a day. In the next century, Le Procope was the haunt of such French scribes as Victor Hugo, Honoré de Balzac, and George Sand. Visitors today can dine on three floors in ornately decorated rooms featuring dark red walls, chandeliers, gilt-edge mirrors, and busts and portraits of famous writers. It's advisable not to act like Oscar Wilde, who reportedly banged his walking stick on the table to attract a waiter's attention.

CAFÉ/BAR ODEON

Zurich, Switzerland • Limmatquai 2 • Tel: (41) 44 251 16 50 • *www.odeon.ch*

The art nouveau Odeon was James Joyce's second favorite café (after the Pfauen, which is gone) while living in Zurich for several years during World War I. Situated in the city's Old Town, the elegant, marble-walled café opened in 1911 and counted Einstein among its clientele.

Joyce and his family settled in Switzerland in 1915, after leaving their adopted home, Trieste, then part of Austria-Hungary (now Italy) and in a war zone. By day Joyce worked on *Ulysses* and the play *Exiles*, and by night he zealously imbibed white wine in Zurich's cafés.

For more on Joyce and his native Dublin, see pages 272–82.

Two decades later, Joyce's last call came in Zurich. He again sought refuge in the Swiss city when Paris, where he had moved, fell to the Nazis. Fifty-eight-year-old Joyce died several weeks later on January 13, 1941, following intestinal surgery. Near his grave in Zurich's **Fluntern Cemetery** is a statue of the bespectacled writer, seated and holding a book in one hand.

WHITE HART INN

Edinburgh, Scotland • 34 Grassmarket • Tel: (44) 131 226 2806
• *www.whitehart-edinburgh.co.uk*

Reputed to be Edinburgh's oldest pub (and haunted), the White Hart Inn hosted Robert Burns during his last visit to Edinburgh in 1791. It's where the Scottish poet is said to have composed the verse "Ae Fond Kiss." Less than a decade later, English bard William Wordsworth and his sister, Dorothy, lodged at the White Hart (an old-fashioned term for stag) on an 1803 visit at the recommendation of an acquaintance. They arrived "a little before sunset," recalled Dorothy in *Recollections of a Tour Made in Scotland,* and after taking tea she and her wordsmith sibling ambled to Edinburgh Castle a short distance away.

BIG APPLE BARS FOR BIBLIOPHILES

CHUMLEY'S

86 Bedford Street • www.chumleysnewyork.com

Located in a former blacksmith shop, Chumley's opened as a speakeasy during Prohibition. Despite no sign ever having marked the Bedford Street entryway, John Steinbeck, Theodore Dreiser, Willa Cather, Edna St. Vincent Millay, Eugene O'Neill, and plenty of

"There is nothing which has yet been contrived by man, by which so much happiness is produced as by a good tavern or inn."

—SAMUEL JOHNSON

other literary types found their way here to raise a glass (including French novelist and philosopher Simone de Beauvoir, who drank whiskey until 5 a.m.). Inside this clandestine haunt, today a plusher yet still cozy version of the original, photos of famous partiers Scott and Zelda Fitzgerald and other authors, as well as original book jackets, line the walls.

MCSORLEY'S OLD ALE HOUSE

15 East Seventh Street • Tel: 212-473-9148 • *www.mcsorleysoldalehouse.nyc*

Poet e. e. cummings immortalized this Irish alehouse in the 1925 verse "i was sitting in mcsorley's." The scribe would not have been joined by any female writerly counterparts while sipping pints here. One of the city's oldest saloons, McSorley's did not admit women until after a court ruling in 1970. More recent literary clientele included Frank McCourt, who bestowed on McSorley's a signed copy of his memoir, *Angela's Ashes*. All patrons need to adhere to the motto emblazoned behind the bar and above the fireplace in the back room, where the ale continued to flow during Prohibition: Be good or be gone.

PETE'S TAVERN

129 East 18th Street • Tel: 212-473-7676

• *www.petestavern.com*

Among the brews served at Pete's is the tavern's own creation, 1864 Ale, named for the year it opened. Sip a pint at the original 30-foot rosewood bar or imbibe at O. Henry's favorite table, where a sign marks it as the spot where the short story scribe penned "The Gift of the Magi" in 1905. The writer lived the last eight years of his life in New York and used the city as the backdrop for numerous works. Years after O. Henry's 1910 demise, Pete's Tavern remained open during Prohibition, disguised as a flower shop.

WHITE HORSE TAVERN

567 Hudson Street • Tel: 212-989-3956

Welsh poet Dylan Thomas was a White Horse regular during stateside visits and boasted of downing 18 whiskies in a single sitting in the days before his death. (The 39-year-old writer's carousing ended in November 1953 after he went into a coma and never recovered, likely from a combination of factors, including respiratory illness and bad medical care.) A portrait of Thomas hangs in one of three wood-paneled rooms, and other memorabilia related to him is scattered throughout the bar. Jack Kerouac also favored this Greenwich Village tavern and mentions it in his novel *Desolation Angels*.

PARISIAN CAFÉS OF THE LITERATI

LA ROTONDE

105 Bd. du Montparnasse, 6e • Tel: (33) 1 43 26 48 26

• *www.rotondemontparnasse.com*

"No matter what café in Montparnasse you ask a taxi-driver to bring you to . . . they always take you to the Rotonde," wrote Ernest Hemingway in *The Sun Also Rises*. Simone de Beauvoir was born in an apartment building above La Rotonde on Paris's Left Bank, and she and her sister were regular patrons there as teenagers. The feminist writer later edited Jean-Paul Sartre's works at the café. During a 1922 stay in Paris, American poet Edna St. Vincent Millay lived near La Rotonde and enjoyed the establishment's wines and liqueurs. Even Ian Fleming's James Bond liked to dine and people-watch in this Montparnasse haunt.

LE DÔME

108 Bd. du Montparnasse, 14e • Tel: (33) 1 43 35 25 81

Onetime café Le Dôme opened in 1897 and is now an upscale sea-food restaurant. Ernest Hemingway and his wife Hadley made a beeline for this Montparnasse locale soon after their 1921 arrival in Paris. They sat outdoors in the chilly December air, warmed by char-coal braziers and glasses of hot rum punch. Fellow American expats F. Scott Fitzgerald and Ezra Pound also sipped here in the 1920s. Another stateside writer, Sinclair Lewis, flush from the success of

Main Street and *Babbitt*, reportedly caused a scene by standing up and loudly comparing himself to French novelist Gustave Flaubert. A fellow diner shouted at him to sit down.

LA COUPOLE

102 Bd. du Montparnasse, 14e • Tel: (33) 1 43 20 14 20
• *www.lacoupole-paris.com*

This Montparnasse brasserie was opened in 1927 by two former employees of Le Dôme who had aspirations of making it bigger and better than their rival. Adorned in the then-brand-new art deco style, the Coupole was a favorite place of inseparable companions and existentialists Simone de Beauvoir and Jean-Paul Sartre. When de Beauvoir suffered a serious illness in 1937 and convalesced in a nearby hotel, Sartre brought her a meal from La Coupole each day. In later years it was the site of the duo's standing Sunday luncheon date.

CAFÉ DE FLORE

172 Bd. Saint-Germain, 6e • Tel: (33) 1 45 48 55 26 • *www.cafedeflore.fr*

Café de Flore opened its doors circa 1887 in St.-Germain-des-Prés, a section of Paris known as a hub for booksellers, publishers, and writers. The café attracted writers like Albert Camus, author of the existential novel *The Stranger* and other works. Simone de Beauvoir and Jean-Paul Sartre were regulars here as well, installing themselves on the quieter second floor at separate tables to avoid the temptation to talk while writing. They began frequenting the café partly to keep warm during the German occupation of Paris in the 1940s. Heat in private homes was scarce, and the café had a large woodstove fueled by black market coal.

LES DEUX MAGOTS

6 Place St.-Germain-des-Prés, 6e • Tel: (33) 1 45 48 55 25 • *www.lesdeuxmagots.com*

Formerly a novelty shop that went by the same name (which comes from two Chinese figurines still on display), this famed St.-Germain café has been in business since 1885. Les Deux Magots was frequented by a young Ernest Hemingway (who recalls drinking dry sherry with James Joyce here in *A Moveable Feast*) and other expatriate writers of the lost generation of the 1920s and 1930s. Edna St. Vincent Millay dropped in on occasion, and exiled Irish playwright Oscar Wilde lived nearby and frequented the café daily for breakfast and an evening glass of absinthe. In warm weather, preferred seating is at the marble-topped tables clustered on the sidewalk.

England's Best Literary Pubs

THE EAGLE AND CHILD

Oxford • 49 St Giles • Tel: (44) 186 530 2925
• www.nicholsonspubs.co.uk

Known locally as the Bird and Baby, this watering hole was once home to the famed literary group The Inklings, which included C. S. Lewis and J. R. R. Tolkien, both of whom taught at Oxford University. The group (whose name was suggested by Tolkien) met in the pub's cozy, wood-paneled Rabbit Room from the 1930s to the early 1960s, when renovations compelled them to convene at the Lamb and Flag instead. During meetings, they would passionately discuss books and share their own works in progress for critique.

"My happiest hours are spent with three or four old friends in old clothes tramping together and putting up in small pubs."

—C. S. LEWIS

THE LAMB AND FLAG

Oxford • 12 St. Giles • Tel: (44) 186 551 5787

Thomas Hardy is said to have written parts of his final novel, *Jude the Obscure,* in this 500-year-old pub and former stagecoach inn during a stay in Oxford. The novel, a tale of a poor boy whose dreams of academia are thwarted by lack of money, is set in Christminster, a thinly veiled Oxford. Passages in the novel are thought to be based on The Lamb and Flag, an "obscure and low-ceilinged tavern" where Jude's wife, Arabella, was a barmaid. The pub was also a meeting spot for The Inklings. Their last gathering was held here on November 18, 1963; C. S. Lewis died four days later.

See pages 104–105 for more on literary Oxford.

SPANIARDS INN

London • Spaniards Road • Tel: (44) 208 731 8406
• www.thespaniardshampstead.co.uk

A chalkboard in the garden at this 400-year-old pub near Hampstead Heath claims that poet John Keats, who lived nearby, was inspired to write "Ode to a Nightingale" after hearing birdsong in the leafy space. In addition to Keats, fellow English Romantic poets Byron and Shelley were among the literati who patronized the famed pub, which garners a mention in Bram Stoker's *Dracula* and features as the setting for the tea party scene in Charles Dickens's *The Pickwick Papers*. In winter months, curl up in the cozy upstairs Turpin Room (named after famed English rogue Dick Turpin, rumored to have been born at the pub in 1705), which boasts a roaring fireplace and plenty of board games to while away the hours. Rain or shine, a stop at Spaniards for a pint and some hearty pub grub is the perfect way to cap off a day of rambling on the heath.

"Well, Mr. Raddle," said Mrs. Bardell, "I'm sure you ought to feel very much honored at you and Tommy being the only gentlemen to escort so many ladies all the way to the Spaniard at Hampstead."

—THE PICKWICK PAPERS

FITZROY TAVERN

London • 16 Charlotte Street • Tel: (44) 207 580 3714

The Fitzroy Tavern boasts the distinction of being the only pub in London said to have given its name

---

ON THE TRAIL OF DYLAN THOMAS: "I walked on to the cliff path again, the town behind and below waking up now so very slowly," Dylan Thomas once wrote in his radio sketch "Quite Early One Morning." The Welsh town of New Quay, where Thomas moved in 1944, is said to be the "cliff-perched town at the far end of Wales" featured in the work. **The Dylan Thomas Trail** (*www.newquay -westwales.co.uk/trail.htm*) traces the writer's route along the coastal path above town as well as other local haunts in the city center, such as the restaurant and bar at the **Black Lion Hotel** (*www.blacklionnewquay.co.uk*).

In the Welsh town of Swansea, where Thomas was born, **The Dylan Thomas Centre** (*www.dylanthomas.com*) is home to a permanent exhibition on the writer and also hosts the annual Dylan Thomas Festival each October.

to the neighborhood of its location, Fitzrovia, located just west of its more celebrated neighbor, Bloomsbury. Situated on a street that was once an artists' quarter, the Fitzroy became a legendary bohemian meeting place in the 1930s. Welsh poet Dylan Thomas, famed as much for his heavy drinking as he was for his lyrical poetry and prose, was a regular during the years he lived in London. Said his wife, Caitlin, "To Dylan the pubs were sacred: they were like churches—places for declaiming and holding an audience."

THE WHEATSHEAF

London • 25 Rathbone Place • Tel: (44) 207 580 1585

Down the block from the Fitzroy, the unassuming Wheatsheaf is where Dylan Thomas met fiery-spirited dancer Caitlin Macnamara in April 1936. The two reportedly spent a passionate night together following their encounter at the bar and were married the next year. Journalist and novelist George Orwell, while not a heavy drinker, would sometimes stop for a half-pint at the Wheatsheaf's long, narrow bar, which was located a stone's throw from his offices at the BBC. (He probably needed a pint after T. S. Eliot, who worked in the area at the publisher Faber and Faber, rejected *Animal Farm*. Eliot likely followed suit after the book became a best seller.) Today, the Wheatsheaf hosts regular comedy and improv nights in an upstairs room.

"Holmes pushed open the door of the private bar and ordered two glasses of beer from the ruddy-faced, white-aproned landlord."

—"THE ADVENTURE OF THE BLUE CARBUNCLE"

MUSEUM TAVERN

London • 49 Great Russell Street • Tel: (44) 207 242 8987

• *www.taylor-walker. co.uk*

An alehouse has stood on this spot in Bloomsbury since the early 18th century, when the surrounding lands were a swampy hunting ground and the pub was known as the Dog and Duck. With the 1759 arrival of the British Museum—open to "all studious and curious Persons"—the neighborhood became an artistic and educational hub. The tavern, located opposite the sprawling museum complex, changed its name and has been serving thirsty culture vultures and academics ever since. Among its patrons were some of the regulars at the museum's domed, circular reading room (the former home of the British Library collections), including Karl Marx and Sir Arthur Conan Doyle. The latter is thought to have used the pub as the doppelgänger for the Alpha Inn where the Christmas Goose Club meets in *The Blue Carbuncle*. Redesigned in the Victorian era, the peaceful tavern remains chock-full of authentic period details like original stained glass and etched mirrors behind the bar.

YE OLDE CHESHIRE CHEESE

London • Wine Office Court • 145 Fleet Street • Tel: (44) 207 353 6170

Rebuilt in 1667 after the Great Fire of London and little changed since, this tavern truly merits its "Ye Olde" moniker with an unparalleled anachronistic ambiance and literary pedigree. Plunging into its dimly lit labyrinth of nooks and crannies—sprawling over three floors connected by narrow passages and rickety stairwells—is like entering an alternate

WORD COUNT: "Lexicographer: a writer of dictionaries; a harmless drudge, that busies himself in tracing the original, and detailing the signification of words." —*Samuel Johnson's Dictionary*

One of the first comprehensive English-language dictionaries—published in 1755 and containing 42,773 words as well as some 114,000 illustrative quotations—was composed in a 300-year-old brick Georgian town house that, like many of the witticisms from the dictionary itself, has stood the test of time. The house at **17 Gough Square** (*www.drjohnsonshouse.org*), located near London's former publishing hub on Fleet Street, was home to the dictionary's creator, Dr. Samuel Johnson, for nearly 11 years during the time he wrote the famed tome. Working tirelessly in his fourth-floor attic garret with six assistants, Johnson crafted one of the most influential books of the 18th century, which predated the *Oxford English Dictionary* by more than 100 years and was employed by such scribes as Jane Austen, Charles Dickens, William Wordsworth, and Oscar Wilde.

universe. Thought to be among the pub's earliest literary habitués was 18th-century essayist and lexicographer Dr. Samuel Johnson, who lived around the corner (see sidebar at left) and had authored a comprehensive, landmark English-language dictionary. (A reproduction copy of the enormous 22-pound tome—18 inches tall by 20 inches wide—resides in the Cheshire Cheese's tiny first-floor restaurant, the Chop Room.) Also housed in the Chop Room are the long oak "Johnson table" and a chair, bolted to the wall, claimed to be the writer's favorite. Settling into one of the room's intimate, high-backed wooden booths for a steak and kidney pudding, it's not difficult to imagine Johnson having done the same two and a half centuries earlier.

" 'I've seen all of England,' she said. 'I've seen Westminster Abbey and the Houses of Parliament and His Majesty's Theatre and the Savoy and the Cheshire Cheese.' "

—P. G. WODEHOUSE, PICCADILLY JIM

Among the pub's other charming rooms are the cozy, wood-paneled Gentleman's Bar (no longer just for gents) with a fireplace at which Dickens reputedly warmed himself (the pub is presumed to be the one he alluded to in *A Tale of Two Cities*), and the atmospheric stone vaulted cellar bars, formerly part of a 13th-century monastery. Many other scribes are said to have trod across the pub's sawdust floors, including P. G. Wodehouse, Thomas Carlyle, E. M. Forster, Joseph Conrad, Sinclair Lewis, and W. B. Yeats, who met there regularly in the 1890s with fellow members of his Rhymers' Club to discuss poetry.

GEORGE INN

London • 77 Borough High Street • Tel: (44) 207 407 2056
• www.nationaltrust.org.uk/george-inn

As London's last surviving galleried stagecoach inn, the George preserves a colorful and important slice of the city's history. Located south of the River Thames in the storied Southwark borough (in medieval times known as "the Stews" and home to all manner of entertainments from theater and prostitution to bull- and bear-baiting), the George would have beckoned to a vibrant cross-section of patrons. An inn has been operating on the spot since the reign of Henry VIII, although the current structure dates from shortly after a devastating fire swept the area in 1676. It is thought likely that

For a walking tour of Shakespeare's London that takes in sites around Southwark, see page 156–57.

Shakespeare would have drunk here—his Globe Theatre was just a few hundred yards away—and his plays may have been performed in the cobblestone courtyard, which doubled as a performance space.

The place from where Chaucer's pilgrims set off in *The Canterbury Tales*, the famed Tabard Inn, once stood adjacent to the George and would have looked much like its surviving neighbor. (The Tabard, like other stagecoach inns, fell victim to the advent of rail service; a blue plaque commemorates its former location.) The George itself narrowly escaped destruction, and two of its picturesque galleried fronts were demolished before it was preserved as a National Trust site. Today, the galleried upper tiers that remain house the pub's restaurant (formerly the bedchambers) while downstairs is a series of interconnecting bars with wood-beam ceilings and rough-hewn floors. The Old Bar was formerly the passenger waiting room, while the Middle Bar was the Coffee Room, a reputed haunt of Charles Dickens, who mentions the tavern in *Little Dorrit*.

THE ANCHOR

London • 34 Park Street • Tel: (44) 207 407 1577

In the Anchor pub on the south side of the Thames, famed diarist Samuel Pepys is thought to have taken refuge as he watched the destruction of London in the Great Fire of 1666. "So near the fire as we could for smoke and all over the Thames, with one's face in the wind, you were almost burned with a shower of fire-drops." Its riverside location once made it the haunt of thirsty sailors and dockworkers, particularly from the 19th-century tea clippers that plied the Thames. Although an alehouse has stood on this spot for nearly 800 years, the present-day Anchor has been rebuilt twice after devastating fires, as well as undergone refurbishment in modern times. Its prime waterfront location next to the new Globe Theatre and its sprawling beer garden with spectacular views of the City of London and the dome of St. Paul's, have made it a perennially popular watering hole for locals and tourists alike.

"When we could endure no more upon the water, we [went] to a little alehouse on the Bankside . . . And there staid till it was dark almost and saw the fire grow."

—THE DIARY OF SAMUEL PEPYS

Six Hemingway Watering Holes

LA CLOSERIE DES LILAS

Paris, France • 171 Bd. du Montparnasse, 6e

• Tel: (33) 1 40 51 34 50 • www.closeriedeslilas.fr

"The Closerie des Lilas was the nearest good café when we lived . . . at 113 Rue Notre-Dame des Champs, and it was one of the best cafés in Paris," reminisced Ernest Hemingway in *A Moveable Feast.*

While living in Paris, the writer could often be found hunkered over his blue-backed notebook at one of the "square, regular tables under the big awnings along the boulevard" at what he referred to as his "home café." The locale features in *The Sun Also Rises,* portions of which were likely written here. Hemingway enjoyed the solitude of the café, where he could work undisturbed since "people from the Dôme and the Rotonde never came to the Lilas." That was fine with him, since he cared little for the see-and-be-seen atmosphere of trendier literary establishments. Occasionally he would be joined by John Dos Passos, Ford Madox Ford, and at one point, a melancholy F. Scott Fitzgerald, who was upset that his new book, *The Great Gatsby,* wasn't selling well. The scribes sat on the terrace drinking whisky and soda while watching "people passing on the sidewalk and the grey light of the evening changing."

Today the 170-year-old café has evolved into an upscale, conservatory-set restaurant and brasserie. The Closerie's historic heart, its romantic, warmly lit piano bar with plush red leather banquettes and gold accents, provides the perfect setting for a pre-dinner aperitif. Mahogany tables and a bar bearing brass nameplates remind revelers of former habitués, such as poet Paul Verlaine, Gertrude Stein, Samuel Beckett, Jean-Paul Sartre, and, of course, Hemingway.

"You're an expatriate. You've lost touch with the soil. You get precious. Fake European standards have ruined you. You drink yourself to death."

—THE SUN ALSO RISES

BRASSERIE LIPP

Paris, France • 151 Bd. St-Germain, 6e • Tel: (33) 1 45 48 53 91 • www.brasserielipp.fr

Hemingway renewed his friendship with writer John Dos Passos (whom he had first met in Italy during World War I) over dinner at this Parisian brasserie in 1922. The writer had a weakness for Lipp's cold Alsatian beer and delicious potato salad and began frequenting the place after his first marriage crumbled. Two decades later, Hemingway famously "liberated" Lipp with his cronies at the end of World War II.

Before Hemingway's time, the brasserie was known for its Proustian connection. Although French novelist and intellectual Marcel Proust rarely drank, sometimes the fancy struck him for cold beer and he would send his assistant to the brasserie for carafes of its renowned brew. Later, Simone de Beauvoir's father took her there to celebrate passing her examinations at the Sorbonne (where she first met Jean-Paul Sartre, a fellow student). She, along with Sartre and Albert Camus, became Brasserie Lipp habitués.

A replica of Proust's unusual bedroom, which he had lined with cork to block out noise and pollutants, is on display with his brass bed, desk, chaise lounge, and other furnishings at Paris's **Musée Carnavalet** (*www.carnavalet.paris.fr*). The invalid writer rarely left the cork-lined room in his last decade, and it was there that he penned his masterpiece, *Remembrance of Things Past.*

Alsatian Léonard Lipp opened the establishment in 1880, and its tables have been coveted by writers, celebrities, politicians, and mere mortals ever since. Today the famed restaurant—which retains its magnificent art nouveau frescoed ceiling and ceramic murals in tropical motifs—has been designated a *lieux de mémoire* (historic place) by the French Ministry of Culture.

RITZ PARIS

Paris, France • 15 Place Vendôme, 1e • Tel: (33) 1 43 16 30 30 • *www.ritzparis.com*

"We entered Paris with very first troops. Liberated the Traveler's Club and the Ritz the first afternoon. Finest time [I] ever had in my life."

—ERNEST HEMINGWAY, OCTOBER 1944 LETTER

While serving as a foreign correspondent during World War II, Hemingway and his motley group of friends famously "liberated" the glamorous Parisian hotel after the end of the City of Light's occupation. Copious rounds of dry martinis and magnums of champagne were their weapons of choice, brandished at what was then known as Le Petit Bar. Today renamed the **Bar Hemingway**, the oak-paneled room with its comfy leather club chairs is just as its namesake would have known it. The writer had other fond associations with the Ritz Paris as well; while checked into room 612 following the liberation, he rendezvoused with fellow journalist Mary

Welsh, who became his fourth wife. On their many returns to the city, the couple would convene at the bar to imbibe the inimitable Bloody Marys concocted by the Ritz's famed bartender, Bertin.

During Hemingway's final trip to Paris in 1956, staff returned a long-forgotten trunk that had been stored in the Ritz Paris cellars for 30 years. In it were journals from his early Paris years, which he went on to repurpose for his colorful memoir *A Moveable Feast*.

In addition to Hemingway, other famous guests who have graced the hotel's luxe Louis XV interiors include F. Scott Fitzgerald, James Joyce, Graham Greene, Truman Capote, and its most loyal patron, Marcel Proust, who became known as "Proust of the Ritz."

RESTAURANTE BOTÍN

Madrid, Spain • Calle de los Cuchilleros 17 • Tel: (34) 91 366 42 17 • www.botin.es

This famed restaurant was a Hemingway favorite, and he used it as the setting in the final scene of *The Sun Also Rises*. Dating back to 1725, Casa Botín is one of the oldest restaurants in the world as well as one of the most atmospheric, with exposed brick walls, beamed ceilings, and dining enclaves that sprawl over four floors. Traditional Castilian-style food is prepared in centuries-old wood-burning ovens, which you'll likely pass on the way to your table; dine as Hemingway did, on the house specialty, *cochinillo asado* (roast suckling pig).

> "We lunched upstairs at Botín's. It is one of the best restaurants in the world. We had roast young suckling pig and drank rioja alta."
>
> —THE SUN ALSO RISES

CAFÉ IRUÑA

Pamplona, Spain • Plaza del Castillo 44 • Tel: (34) 948 222 064 • www.cafeiruna.com

Hemingway attended his first bullfight during Pamplona's legendary running of the bulls in July 1923, and he found the death-defying spectacle of man against beast so enthralling that he returned nearly every year for the rest of the decade. Bullfighting became an enduring passion and one that he immortalized in his novel *The Sun Also Rises* and a later nonfiction work, *Death in the Afternoon*. Much of the action of the former takes place during the Fiesta of San Fermín at Pamplona, where a dissolute band of expats spend their days drinking absinthe and brandy at Café Iruña. Written in the weeks during and immediately following Hemingway's 1925 trip to the fiesta, *The Sun Also Rises* is a roman à clef

> "After lunch we went over to the Iruña. It had filled up, and as the time for the bull-fight came it got fuller, and the tables were crowded closer."
>
> —THE SUN ALSO RISES

loosely based on real people, including Hemingway himself as the doppelgänger for protagonist Jake Barnes.

EL FLORIDITA

Havana, Cuba • Calle Obispo 557 • Tel: (53) 7 8 67 13 01 • *www.floridita-cuba.com*

Christened *la cuna del daiquiri* (the cradle of the daiquiri), Cuba's El Floridita was Hemingway's preferred watering hole from the 1930s through the 1950s—the place he called "the best bar in the world." While the rum-based cocktail is thought to have been invented by a visiting engineer working in Cuba's Daiquiri mine, it was El Floridita that popularized the well-known frozen version. Credit goes to El Floridita's bartender and proprietor, Constantino Ribalaigua Vert, whose daiquiris were immortalized in Hemingway's posthumous novel, *Islands in the Stream:* "The great ones that Constante made had no taste of alcohol and felt, as you drank them, the way downhill glacier skiing feels running through powder snow and, after the sixth and eighth, felt like downhill glacier skiing feels when you are running unroped."

"We drank seventeen double frozen daiquiris apiece in the course of the day without leaving the bar except for an occasional trip to the can. Each double had 4 ounces of rum in it. That makes 68 ounces of rum."

—ERNEST HEMINGWAY, 1952 LETTER

Papa is said to have first come across El Floridita during a 1932 trip to the island while staying down the street at the Ambos Mundos (see page 122). After sampling the bar's signature cocktail, he requested a more potent variation made with no sugar and double rum, to which Constantino added grapefruit juice, dubbing it the Hemingway Special (also known as the Papa Doble).

SIPPING MOJITOS AT THE SOURCE: Hemingway may have occasionally downed cocktails at another colorful Havana watering hole that started life as a grocery store, **La Bodeguita del Medio** (Calle Empedrado 207). Above the tiny, graffiti-bedecked bar is a sign scrawled on butcher paper in what is alleged to be Hemingway's script: "My mojito in La Bodeguita, my daiquiri in El Floridita. Ernest Hemingway." La Bodeguita, known for its potent mojitos, Cuban fare, and live music, was a popular 1950s hangout for artists and bohemians.

Part Two:

Journeys Between the Pages

The pages of literature come to life in the following eleven locales,

immortalized by famed novelists.

Unpersuaded:

JANE AUSTEN IN BATH, ENGLAND

WORKS BY JANE AUSTEN

Sense and Sensibility (1811)

Pride and Prejudice (1813)

Mansfield Park (1814)

Emma (1815)

Northanger Abbey (1818)

Persuasion (1818)

THE JANE AUSTEN CENTRE

In *Northanger Abbey* Catherine Morland gushed, "I really believe I shall always be talking of Bath when I am at home again—I do like it so very much." Unfortunately, this fond sentiment didn't rub off on her creator, who once wearily penned in correspondence, "Bath is still Bath." Having spent most of her youth in rural Hampshire, Jane Austen loved the simple pleasures of country life and was purportedly so upset that she fainted when her father decided to resettle the family in the fashionable spa town of Bath when she was 25.

She nonetheless resigned herself to the change, writing in January 1801, "I get more and more reconciled to the idea of our removal." Austen was fortunate to be moving to Bath in the early 1800s as opposed to a century earlier when it was a crumbling medieval market town. During the Middle Ages, Bath had become a shadow of the glorious place it had been in Roman times when thousands flocked there to visit its elaborate and awe-inspiring Roman Baths— an enormous spa and temple complex fed by sacred underground hot springs.

After the eventual exodus of the Romans, their great baths sank into ruin, and while newer ones continued to attract ailing visitors who came for curative soaks, the great 16th-century traveler and historian John Leland noted that the waters "rikketh like a seething potte" while the surrounding town itself was "sumwhat decayed."

And so Bath might have continued down its slide into decline, diminished to a mere footnote in England's history, if it weren't for the efforts of three pivotal figures: a visionary architect, a wealthy local businessman, and a charming opportunist.

The latter, black-wigged dandy and ladies' man Richard "Beau" Nash, was a particularly unlikely agent of change. An Oxford University dropout, he had turned his attention to gambling and socializing after abandoning careers in both the army and the law. But whatever he lacked in ambition in the traditional sense of the word, he made up for as an entrepreneur who could sniff out opportunity in the unlikeliest of situations. When Queen Anne's visits brought renewed attention to Bath at the turn of the 18th century, Nash saw just such an occasion avail itself. He was soon elected as Bath's master of ceremonies and quickly set about transforming the decaying cityscape into a fashionable arena where his gambling pursuits would prosper and his social skills could sparkle.

Nash enthusiastically raised funds for the repair of the town's ancient infrastructure, the paving of its streets, and the commissioning of grand new public buildings such as the Lower Assembly Rooms (for dancing and, of course, card playing) and the Pump Room (for taking in the curative spa waters). As Nash was establishing Bath's social prominence, architect John Wood was creating a fittingly elegant backdrop of neoclassic streetscapes designed to evoke the grandeur of ancient Rome. With the patronage of exalted businessman and eventual mayor Ralph Allen (whose quarries supplied the honey-hued Bath stone that gives the town its distinctive appearance), the architect ushered the city out of its tattered medieval frocks and into its golden age finery. Among his iconic creations was the three-tiered colonnaded Circus, modeled after the Roman Colosseum and completed in 1768 by his son, who also designed the nearby Royal Crescent.

England's well-to-do classes responded in droves to Bath's emergent social and architectural charms and the city's population multiplied 15 times over the course of the 18th century—rising to nearly 30,000 by the time of Austen's arrival. Just as when the Romans had flocked there at the dawn of the first millennium, Bath again became a thriving pleasure resort. Many an artist and writer visited Bath during this time, including Henry Fielding and Daniel Defoe, who described the city in 1724 as "the resort of the sound, rather than the sick" where the chief diversions were "raffling, gameing [sic], visiting, and in a word, all sorts of gallantry and levity."

Following in their footsteps some 80 years later, Austen seems to have been largely unswayed by any charms Fielding and Defoe found. Much like her fictional heroine Anne Elliot in *Persuasion,* who "disliked Bath, and did not think it agreed with her," Austen never felt at home in the bustling confines of this high society outpost and seemed to find many of its inhabitants and preoccupations tiresome. In one of her early letters from the city, she writes of "another stupid party . . . with six people to look on, and talk nonsense to each other."

Beyond its petty annoyances, Bath also brought with it larger misfortune for the author. While living there, Austen faced the acute social embarrassment of reneging on a marriage proposal and, more devastatingly, suffered the loss of her father. The death of George Austen was traumatic for Jane, her sister, and their mother while also greatly diminishing their financial circumstances. With these painful events and the distractions of city life, it's no wonder that Austen wrote little during her time there. When the Austen women departed Bath in 1806, it was with what the novelist later described as "happy feelings of escape."

Nonetheless, Austen chose the city as the setting for her novel *Northanger Abbey* as well as for the closing chapters of her final work, *Persuasion,* perhaps recognizing that Bath's status-conscious chattering classes and their playful preoccupations would provide fertile ground for her unique brand of social comedy. Modern-day Jane-ites entering the city can't help but feel as though they are stepping into the pages of the real-life and fictional milieus that merged in Austen's Bath novels. Nowhere is this sensation more powerful than at the illustrious **Pump Room,** where the tinkling sounds of glassware, the lively hum of voices, and the refined strains of classical music immediately transport readers into the world of *Northanger Abbey*'s Catherine Morland.

It was at this legendary institution—the social heart of Bath for nearly 200 years—where Catherine "paraded up and down" to see and be seen with friends during her regular morning visits. The Pump Room's hot spa waters drawn for drinking were revered for their therapeutic benefits, and everyone from Jane Austen and Charles Dickens to William Wordsworth and Queen Victoria purportedly took them in. Today the curious-tasting waters

"They all three set off in good time for the pump-room, where the ordinary course of events and conversation took place . . . the ladies walked about together, noticing every new face, and almost every new bonnet in the room." —*Northanger Abbey*

A Novel-Reader's Novelist

ALTHOUGH THE MOVE TO BATH GREATLY AFFECTED Jane Austen's life—the full extent of which will never be known since most of her Bath correspondence has not been preserved—an even more important influence was her love of reading.

During her time, novels were often undervalued, and reading them was thought to be a silly pastime that poet Samuel Taylor Coleridge decried for bringing about the "destruction of the powers of the mind." Similarly, early feminist writer Mary Wollstonecraft wrote derisively: "The best method, I believe, that can be adopted to correct a fondness for novels is to ridicule them." Austen thankfully did not share their viewpoints—she once wrote that she and her family were "great novel-readers, and not ashamed of being so."

Given this proclivity, it's no surprise that most of her heroines revered reading as well. Books offered women, whose roles and fortunes were largely circumscribed by the men in their lives, a way of independently seeking knowledge, entertainment, and connection.

More so than any of Austen's other works, *Northanger Abbey* is a novel about reading—both reading novels and reading people— a theme personified in the youthful illusions of voracious reader Catherine Morland. Unable to read between the lines of people's words and actions, her perceptions of reality are often colored by the fictional world of the imaginative novels she reads.

Although Austen satirizes the overwrought gothic plots that were so beloved by Catherine and were immensely popular at the time, she also offers up her famous "Defense of the Novel," which praised novels—particularly Fanny Burney's *Cecilia* and *Camilla*, as well as Irish novelist Maria Edgeworth's *Belinda*—for conveying "the most thorough knowledge of human nature," the selfsame characteristic for which Austen's own novels were later to become renowned.

can still be sampled from a burbling fountain or, alternatively, visitors can linger over lunch or tea while partaking in the Austenesque sport of people-watching.

Making an appearance at the Pump Room was not the only required activity for the town's fashionable set during the 18th and 19th centuries. During the height of the social season from October to June, everyone who was anyone attended a whirlwind of balls, dinners, and concerts. Austen herself loved dancing during her youth, writing exuberantly to her sister in 1798, "There were twenty dances, and I danced them all, and without any fatigue." She attended several of the public balls held at the city's **Upper** and **Lower Assembly Rooms**, and it's no surprise that they became the setting of pivotal scenes in *Northanger Abbey* and *Persuasion*—providing the perfect backdrop against which romances blossomed and rivalries were revealed. While the Lower Rooms were later destroyed by fire, the Upper Rooms (so named due to their location in the upper part of town and more commonly known today as the Bath Assembly Rooms) remain just as they were during Austen's day.

"The season was full, the room crowded, and the two ladies squeezed in as well as they could. As for Mr. Allen, he repaired directly to the card-room, and left them to enjoy a mob by themselves."
—*Northanger Abbey*

Still a hub for social events in the city, this gilded neoclassic entertainment complex was built in 1771 to host all manner of popular pursuits in Georgian society. Dances took place in the grand Ballroom, an immense room a hundred feet in length adorned with a decorative paneled ceiling and five glittering eight-foot crystal chandeliers, which are among the finest examples of their kind to have survived from the 18th century.

Between dances, guests could take refreshment in the ornately pillared Tea Room, also used for concerts on alternate evenings, while those feeling playful could try their luck in the Card Room.

Catherine Morland delighted in the number of balls and concerts there were to attend in Bath, where the Assembly Rooms alone hosted events at least twice a week that often attracted 800 to 1,200 guests at a time. It was during one such crowded affair that Catherine tried vainly to make her way through a throng of people so thick she could

Don't Miss

In July and August, follow in the writer's footsteps to the places she lived and wrote about on **Jane Austen's Bath Walking Tour.** Tours take place on weekends several times a day and depart from the Tourist Information Centre in Abbey Churchyard.

Alternately, view the exteriors of these Bath residences (all privately occupied) associated with the author at your own pace:

- 13 Queen Square: Former home of Jane's wealthy brother Edward, whom she visited in 1799.
- 1 Paragon: Former home of Austen's wealthy aunt and uncle, James and Jane Leigh-Perrot, whom she visited in 1797 and with whom the family stayed in 1801 while securing their own lodgings.
- 4 Sydney Place: The Austens' primary residence during their time in Bath, leased between 1801 and 1804. Arrive by walking up Great Pulteney Street, where Catherine Morland stayed with the Allens in *Northanger Abbey,* and note that some of the largest houses in Bath are located in the vicinity.
- 25 Gay Street: The Austen women had to give up their more spacious accommodations and take up lodgings here after the death of George Austen.

- **Walk to the Royal Crescent** where Jane and her characters would promenade in their finery on Sundays after church services.

- **Climb up Beechen Cliff**, where Catherine Morland walked with the Tilneys, describing it as "that noble hill, whose beautiful verdure and hanging coppice render it so striking an object from almost every opening in Bath."

See pages 149–50 for information on the Jane Austen Festival (*www.janeausten festivalbath.co.uk*), which takes place in Bath each September.

see "nothing of the dancers, but the high feathers of some of the ladies."

When the congested ballrooms got to be too much for even the most dedicated of social butterflies, Sundays provided a welcome reprieve and, literally, a breath of fresh air. "A fine Sunday in Bath empties every house of its inhabitants, and all the world appears on such an occasion to walk about and tell their acquaintance what a charming day it is," observed Catherine Morland on the morning she eagerly made her way to Crescent Fields in vain hope of spotting the dancing partner who had so enraptured her.

The Georgian custom of promenading was de rigueur in a fashionable town like Bath, and each week genteel society in their Sunday best jockeyed for position along the landscaped walkways in front of the **Royal Crescent**. This palatial street—one of the quintessential images representing Bath—takes its name from the regal row of town houses lining its crescent-shaped perimeter. The sloping fields in front of the arc, known as the Crescent Fields in Jane Austen's time, are today part of the Royal Victoria Park. They remain much as they were when Austen strolled their gravel paths on a Sunday evening in May 1801, finding it "too cold to stay long," as she wrote in a letter to her sister Cassandra.

No matter what the social activity of the time—taking curative libations at the Pump Room, dancing the night away at the

IF YOU GO: Bath has good bus and rail connections from London as well as most other U.K. cities and is an excellent town to explore on foot. From London, trains depart every half-hour from Paddington Station, and journey time is approximately 90 minutes. Upon exiting, follow the signs to the Jane Austen Centre, a ten-minute walk from the train station. A visit during the holidays is a special treat as the house gives itself over to Regency Christmas festivities, with exhibits and live demonstrations highlighting how Jane would have decorated and entertained. **The Jane Austen Centre** 40 Gay Street • Queen Square • Bath BA1 2NT • Tel: (44) 122 544 3000 • *www.janeausten.co.uk* • Open daily

Assembly Rooms, or promenading along the Royal Crescent—the most important consideration was that it be done fashionably. Fortunately, the shops in Bath were second only to those in London, providing every opportunity for ladies and gentlemen of means to indulge themselves in the latest styles displayed on **Milsom Street**. Just as Austen's characters flocked there, the street is still a hub for modern visitors seeking retail therapy. Fashionistas wanting to feast their eyes on the finery that Austen's characters would have set their sights on should alternatively make a beeline to the nearby **Fashion Museum**.

"Bath is a charming place, sir; there are so many good shops." —NORTHANGER ABBEY

Although fashion and frivolity may have been the primary preoccupations of life in Bath during Austen's time, the author nonetheless managed to seek out some of the town's simpler pleasures as well. Walking was one such activity, and her letters often made mention of lengthy walks around town and journeys to neighboring villages.

Given this predilection, there's no better way to follow in Austen's footsteps than by setting off on a promenade of one's own, starting down the block from one of her former residences. At number 40 Gay Street is the **Jane Austen Centre**, located in a handsome Georgian town house that has been reconstructed into a replica of the one occupied by the novelist. Focusing on the places Austen knew in Bath, as well as those her characters visited, the centre provides the perfect jumping-off point for any literary sojourn.

Through the aid of informative guides and an introductory video, visitors can obtain a broad perspective on Austen's life and work. Afterward, a wander through the centre's museum—which displays period costumes, household artifacts from Regency society, and copies of the author's extensive correspondence—sheds further light on what life was like during Austen's Bath years.

Whatever ill will Austen may have harbored toward the city, Bath left its mark on her, and she—like no other author before or since—left her mark on Bath. In an interesting twist of symmetry, both of her Bath novels, *Northanger Abbey* and *Persuasion,* were published together posthumously in 1818, despite being written nearly 15 years apart. The two books were also the author's first works to bear her name (Austen's four other novels had been published anonymously as per contemporary convention). With the simultaneous publication of Austen's two Bath novels and her emergence from anonymity, the link between the novelist and the city was firmly cemented.

DRINK, DINE, AND DOZE

THE PUMP ROOM

Roman Baths • Stall Street • Bath BA1 1LZ • Tel: (44) 122 544 4477

• *www.romanbaths.co.uk* • Advance bookings not available on weekends

Have lunch or afternoon tea while enjoying live music in this striking Corinthian-columned salon that was one of Catherine Morland's favorite spots in *Northanger Abbey*. Make sure to sample a glass of the distinctive-tasting hot spa water from the fountain, where it is often served by a professional "pumper" in period costume dating from 1795, the year the existing Pump Room opened. A marble statue of Beau Nash surveys the room from above the antique Tompion Clock.

REGENCY TEA ROOMS

40 Gay Street • Queens Square • Bath BA1 2NT • Tel: (44) 122 544 2187

Located on the second floor of the Jane Austen Centre, visitors can take a break from sightseeing and have "Tea with Mr. Darcy" or a slice of Mrs. Bennett's lemon drizzle cake.

ELSEWHERE IN THE AREA

THE ASSEMBLY ROOMS AND FASHION MUSEUM

Bennett Street • Bath BA1 2QH • Tel: (44) 122 547 7789

• *www.fashionmuseum.co.uk* • Museum of Costume: Open daily

• Assembly Rooms: Open to view when not booked for private functions

Take in the grandeur of the Assembly Rooms, which received a number of famous visitors in the 18th and 19th centuries, including both Austen and Charles Dickens, who mentions the Assembly Rooms in his fiction. Concerts were popular, and many well-known musicians played there, among them Joseph Haydn, Johann Strauss, and Franz Liszt.

Today the Assembly Rooms also house the Fashion Museum, which contains an excellent collection of Regency-era dress as worn during Jane Austen's time.

Farther Afield

JANE AUSTEN'S HOUSE MUSEUM

Chawton, Alton • Hampshire GU34 1SD

• Tel: (44) 014 208 3262 • *www.jane-austens*

-house-museum.org.uk

In July 1809, Jane's wealthy brother Edward offered his widowed mother and sisters a permanent home in this 17th-century cottage on his Chawton estate, and the Austen ladies were able to move back to their beloved Hampshire countryside not far from the writer's birthplace. Prior to living in Chawton, none of Austen's work had been published, and the period that she lived there was the most prolific and productive of her life. She revised *Sense and Sensibility* as well as *Pride and Prejudice,* both of which she had written some years earlier, and went on to write *Mansfield Park, Emma,* and *Persuasion.*

The museum houses a variety of items that once belonged to Austen, including her infamous three-legged writing table and a turquoise cabochon ring the museum purchased in 2013. The Old Bakehouse on the property displays the writer's donkey carriage, which she relied upon when illness overtook her.

WINCHESTER CATHEDRAL

1, The Close • Winchester, Hampshire SO23 9LS • Tel: (44) 196 285 7200

• *www.winchester-cathedral.org.uk*

This ancient Romanesque cathedral with origins dating to the seventh century is Jane Austen's final resting place. In addition to her tombstone, it contains a memorial brass engraving and stained-glass window.

During her years in Chawton, the author contracted Addison's disease, a tubercular disease of the kidneys, for which there was no cure at the time. By May 1817, she was so ill that she moved into rented rooms in Winchester to be near her physician. Jane Austen died in her beloved sister Cassandra's arms at the age of 41 on July 18, 1817.

STEVENTON ST. NICHOLAS CHURCH

Basingstoke • Hampshire RG25 3BE • www.nwsadhs.co.uk

The small Hampshire village of Steventon was Jane Austen's birthplace and the town where she resided until the time of her move to Bath in 1801. While the family house at the Steventon Rectory no longer exists, the simple 12th-century Norman stone church where Austen worshipped stands almost unchanged. The author was baptized here, and the church was an everyday part of her life because her father, the Reverend George Austen, was rector of the Steventon parish. Subsequently, her brothers James and then Henry assumed the role upon their father's retirement.

The grave of James Austen is located here, as is that of Jane's

THEY CAME TO BATH: Fanny Burney (1752–1840), hailed as "the mother of English fiction" by Virginia Woolf, was one of the most successful writers of her day and a significant influence on many of her contemporaries, particularly Jane Austen. Burney's three major novels center on the experiences of a young and naive girl's entrance into society, a theme that Austen took up with her early novel *Northanger Abbey*. After Burney's triumph with her best-selling work, *Evelina*, she came to Bath in 1780 as the guest of a wealthy couple and returned again in 1815 with her husband and son.

Subsequent to Burney and Austen, Charles Dickens traveled to Bath as a young journalist, and his first work, the comic novel *The Pickwick Papers*, features two chapters satirizing the town's social life. The novel's hero and founder of its eponymous club, Mr. Samuel Pickwick, is named after Moses Pickwick, the real-life proprietor of a Bath stagecoach inn. A grandfather clock from Pickwick's Bath office resides in the **Charles Dickens Museum** in London (see page 237).

maternal grandmother, along with a bronze plaque dedicated to Jane erected by one of her great-nieces. On the wall hangs one of the three prayers she wrote that were preserved by her sister Cassandra.

NATIONAL PORTRAIT GALLERY

St. Martin's Place • London WC2H 0HE • Tel: (44) 207 312 2463
• www.npg.org.uk

The only undisputed portrait of Jane Austen, a color sketch done by her sister Cassandra in approximately 1810, is on display here.

THE BRITISH LIBRARY

96 Euston Road • London NW1 2DB • (44) 207 412 7332 • www.bl.uk

The library's Sir John Ritblat Rare Treasures gallery displays Austen's portable writing desk, manuscript pages from *Persuasion,* and her notebook containing *The History of England,* "by a partial, prejudiced and ignorant historian." See pages 161–62 for more on the British Library.

LYME REGIS

Dorset, England • www.lymeregis.com

This fashionable seaside town and former bustling port on England's south coast is known as the "pearl of Dorset" and was the setting for the middle chapters of *Persuasion* prior to when Anne Elliot settled in Bath. Austen herself visited Lyme Regis with her family during the summer of 1804, writing to her sister about dancing in the Assembly Rooms and walking along the Cobb, a picturesque stone wall fronting the semicircular harbor. It was on the Cobb's steep stone steps known as Granny's Teeth where Austen set one of her most dramatic fictional incidents in *Persuasion.*

A Novel Character:

CHARLES DICKENS IN LONDON, ENGLAND

SELECTED WORKS BY CHARLES DICKENS

The Pickwick Papers (1836)

Oliver Twist (1837)

Nicholas Nickleby (1838)

The Old Curiosity Shop (1840)

Barnaby Rudge (1841)

A Christmas Carol (1843)

Martin Chuzzlewit (1843)

Dombey and Son (1846)

David Copperfield (1849)

Bleak House (1852)

Hard Times (1854)

Little Dorrit (1855)

A Tale of Two Cities (1859)

Great Expectations (1860)

Our Mutual Friend (1864)

THE CHARLES DICKENS MUSEUM

"I have in my heart of hearts a favorite child," Charles Dickens confided three years before his death in 1870. "And his name is David Copperfield." His fatherly bias toward this fictional offspring is understandable given that many elements of the semiautobiographical coming-of-age tale mirror Dickens's own life. Copperfield, much like his creator, was cast adrift to fend for himself as a child but triumphed over circumstances through sheer determination, strength of will, and headstrong ambition.

The Georgian brick dwelling at 48 Doughty Street in London was home to Dickens from 1837 to 1839 and the location where he penned his earliest novels.

Both the fictional protagonist and his real-life counterpart saw their childhoods abruptly yanked away when they were thrust into the workforce at an early age. Toiling laboriously for ten hours a day under grim conditions, Copperfield affixed labels to wine bottles, working in rooms "discolored with the dirt and smoke of a hundred years" while Dickens was removed from school and consigned to perform similar work at Warren's Blacking (shoe polish) Factory in "a crazy, tumbledown old house . . . literally overrun with rats." His six-shilling-a-week income was needed to help support his struggling family, a task that his spendthrift and improvident father, John Dickens, was constitutionally incapable of performing.

The family's prospects became even bleaker when the elder Dickens was arrested for debt in February 1824 and incarcerated for 14 weeks at **Marshalsea Debtors Prison,** where he was joined (as per the charitably minded custom) by his wife and youngest children. Twelve-year-old Charles was left to his own devices, shuttling back and forth between his despised job at the blacking factory, his solitary evenings in hardscrabble lodgings, and his visitations to the jailhouse. The humiliation and loneliness he suffered during this period would forever color his view of the world, and the oppressive symbol of prison became one he employed frequently in his work. *David Copperfield's* Mr. Micawber, who was eternally insolvent and hanging on "until something turns up," was modeled on John Dickens, while debt-ridden characters in other novels, including Samuel Pickwick and William Dorrit, were similarly incarcerated at Marshalsea.

When young Dickens was eventually released from his employment at the blacking factory, it was with "a relief so strange that it was like oppression." His forced tenure had scarred him so deeply that he kept it a lifelong secret from his children and all but one of his closest friends. As an adult, his thoughts would often "wander desolately back to that time of my life," and from this immense well of grief sprang his compassionate depictions of vulnerable people on society's fringes.

Dickens's own vulnerability and fear of ending up like his father, or worse, in the utterly hopeless position of the lower classes he had rubbed shoulders with at the blacking factory, instilled in him a ceaseless energy and perpetual restlessness. A lifelong workaholic, Dickens had a habit of working on two novels simultaneously, usually while editing one of the many literary journals he helmed during his career. The result of this feverish pace was that he was "never at rest, and never satisfied, and ever trying after something that is never reached."

Before finding fame as a writer, Dickens was employed as a legal clerk, learning shorthand in his spare time, and eventually leapfrogging to a coveted position as a parliamentary reporter. After ending his workday at the House of Commons, he would toil away into the wee hours on his stories and sketches (a career trajectory shared

MARSHALSEA DEBTORS PRISON, where John Dickens was incarcerated, is no longer extant, but a fragment of its arched brick entrance wall remains. Marked by a plaque, it can be found in the churchyard at **St. George the Martyr** (*www.stgeorge-themartyr .co.uk*) off London's Borough High Street south of the River Thames. Dickens's character Little Dorrit was born in Marshalsea and christened at St. George's.

by his fictional doppelgänger, David Copperfield). His comic first novel, *The Pickwick Papers,* published under the pen name Boz, was a runaway success soon after its first installment appeared in March 1836. "People … talked of nothing else," noted an early biographer, adding that *Pickwick*'s sales (which skyrocketed to 40,000 copies a month) outstripped those of all the most famous books of the century.

Portions of *The Pickwick Papers* are set in the spa town of Bath, where the novel's namesake resided and where Dickens had traveled as a young journalist. For more on Bath, see pages 215–27.

"If I were to live a hundred years, and write three novels in each, I should never be so proud of any of them as I am of Pickwick," Dickens wrote to his publisher. Flush from the financial gains reaped by this early triumph, the 24-year-old moved with his wife and newborn son (the first of the couple's ten children) from cramped quarters at **Furnival's Inn** to **48 Doughty Street,** a "frightfully first-class Family Mansion, involving awful responsibilities." Now a museum devoted to the writer, the four-story brick Georgian town home was a physical embodiment of Dickens's rising star. Within its gracious confines, he indulged his need to be surrounded by family and friends, frequently hosting dinner parties and entertaining in his richly decorated drawing room. Today the room has been restored to its Regency-style appearance, incorporating many of the Dickenses' furnishings. Among them are candelabras the writer purchased during his travels in Italy and a wine-colored leather armchair in which he is thought to have sat for his portrait by George Cruikshank, the famed illustrator of *Oliver Twist.*

In his second-floor study, Dickens—who fastidiously arranged his desk before beginning work each day—completed *The Pickwick Papers* and wrote *Oliver Twist.* (In the dining room, Pickwick fans should take note of the grandfather clock that belonged to Bath coach proprietor Moses Pickwick, the real-life namesake of Dickens's first novel.) Displayed in the study is a desk Dickens later owned and on which he penned *A Tale of Two Cities, Great Expectations,* and his unfinished final novel, *The Mystery of Edwin Drood.*

No Place Like Home

"THE SPOT AND THE VERY HOUSE ARE LITERALLY 'a dream of my childhood,' " Dickens wrote to a friend of **Gad's Hill Place**, which was his home for the last 14 years of his life. The long-coveted manse near the Kentish town of Rochester was one that he would gaze at longingly during childhood walks. "And my poor father used to bring me to look at it, and used to say that if I ever grew up to be a clever man perhaps I might own that house, or another such house," Dickens recalled. Amazingly, this prophesy came true when he purchased it in 1856.

His beloved house was steeped in literary history, coincidentally sited on the very locale where Shakespeare set the scene of Falstaff's highway robbery in *Henry IV*. As Dickens wrote to a friend, "The robbery was committed before the door . . . and Falstaff ran away from the identical spot of ground now covered by the room in which I write." It was during his early years at Gad's Hill—which he had immortalized in *A Christmas Carol* as "a mansion of dull red brick with a little weather-cock surmounted Cupola on the roof and a bell hanging in it"—that Dickens seemed at his happiest.

During his time there, he undertook many home improvements, including the addition of a conservatory (which he deemed "a brilliant success; but an expensive one!") and the incongruous installation of a tiny, gingerbread-trimmed Swiss chalet across the road. The chalet had been a Christmas gift from a friend and Dickens delighted in its whimsy, often choosing to work there in summer months. Several of his later works, including *A Tale of Two Cities, Great Expectations,* and his unfinished novel, *The Mystery of Edwin Drood* (which he was penning in the chalet just hours before his death), were written largely at Gad's Hill Place before he passed away in its dining room on June 9, 1870.

Today his "little Kentish freehold" houses a private school, but the writing chalet has been moved into Rochester town and can be viewed from the outside at **Eastgate House** (on High Street).

As a young journalist, Dickens once stayed at Rochester's **Royal Victoria and Bull Hotel** (16-18 High Street; *www.rvbhotel .com),* a former stagecoach inn that features in the opening scenes of *The Pickwick Papers* as a "good house" with "nice beds."

Another room in the house serves as a sad reminder of the tragedy that befell the Dickens family shortly after their move to Doughty Street. After suddenly taking ill in May 1837, Dickens's beloved sister-in-law, Mary Hogarth, died in the writer's arms in the bedroom that today bears her name. The untimely death of the 17-year-old, with whom Dickens had shared a close bond, affected him deeply. Uncharacteristically, he missed an installment of *The Pickwick Papers,* announcing to his disappointed fans that "its publication was interrupted by a severe domestic affliction of no ordinary kind."

Two years later in *The Old Curiosity Shop,* Dickens used Mary Hogarth as the basis for the character of "dear, gentle, patient, noble" Little Nell, whose fictional death caused a real-life public outcry. "All night I have been pursued by the child," Dickens wrote mournfully in a letter to a friend. "Nobody will miss her like I shall." The writer often viscerally inhabited the worlds of his memorable characters, and displayed in the study is a famed watercolor called "Dickens's Dream." The picture depicts the dozing author encircled by celebrated Dickensian creations, including Little Nell, who nestles in his lap.

In addition to drawing inspiration from those he knew personally, Dickens spent endless hours wandering the city observing "the stream of life that will not stop, pouring on, on, on," as he characterized it in the opening pages of *The Old Curiosity Shop*. His perambulations, often undertaken during the cover of night through "the most wretched and distressful streets" of London, provided bountiful fodder for his vividly realistic characters as well as his enduring depictions of the city itself.

Victorian London became a living, breathing entity in many of his novels, which were infused with the cacophony of sights, sounds, and smells emanating from its miasmic confines. Over the course of the writer's life, the city's population exploded, doubling to nearly two and a half million by the middle of the 19th

"The sky was dark and gloomy, the air was damp and raw, the streets were wet and sloppy. The smoke hung sluggishly above the chimney-tops as if it lacked the courage to rise, and the rain came slowly and doggedly down, as if it had not even the spirit to pour."

—*The Pickwick Papers*

century. The by-product of such rapid expansion in the newly industrialized society was rampant disease, an omnipotent coal-induced fog, overflowing sewers, and seething slums, where vast numbers of the poor lived in unspeakable conditions.

Dickens's own childhood experience skirting the edge of poverty made him a sympathetic and vocal advocate for the downtrodden lower classes, particularly orphaned and neglected children. In two of his early works, *Oliver Twist* and *Nicholas Nickleby,* he forged his reputation as one of the era's preeminent social novelists and reformers. Employing his trademark blend of humor and pathos, he took aim at the grim conditions of orphanages, workhouses, and "ragged schools" for destitute children, often gleaning material from firsthand research.

In 1838 while residing at Doughty Street, he traveled to Yorkshire in northern England under an assumed name to visit the area's notoriously ironfisted boarding schools. Dickens used the headmaster at one such school, who had been prosecuted for incidents resulting in the blinding of two pupils, as the model for the evil principal Wackford Squeers in *Nicholas Nickleby*. Later that same year, he visited the industrial city of Manchester to survey the working conditions of factory laborers. What he found "disgusted and astonished" him. "I mean to strike the heaviest blow in my power for these unfortunate creatures," he wrote in a letter to a friend, and he later came through on his word with the publication of *Hard Times,* an indictment of the evils of the industrial revolution.

Nineteenth-century communist revolutionaries Marx and Engels later asserted that Dickens, together with a handful of other English realists, had "issued to the world more political and social truths than have been uttered by all the professional politicians, publicists, and moralists put together." In real life as in his fiction, Dickens was a tireless champion of humanitarian causes. He penned countless newspaper articles advocating reform of the legal, penal, education, and sanitation systems, made dozens of impassioned speeches on the plight of the poor and, beginning in 1853, began to give public readings of his works that were initially undertaken on behalf of charity.

Dickens in the New World

"I F I TURN INTO THE STREET, I AM FOLLOWED by a multitude. If I stay at home, the house becomes, with callers, like a fair," the besieged author wrote wearily during his first trip to America, undertaken at the height of his popularity in 1842. "I have no rest or peace, and am in a perpetual worry." Dickens had begun his six-month tour of the United States brimming with passionate idealism, expecting the New World to be a model egalitarian society, but he was soon profoundly disillusioned, writing "this is not the republic I came to see; this is not the republic of my imagination."

Upon returning home, he penned his nonfiction travelogue, *American Notes,* in which he recorded his observations on everything from American table manners to conditions in the country's factories, insane asylums, prisons, orphanages, and reform schools. In addition to detailing a host of minor quibbles, he took aim at the young nation's rampant capitalism, con-

During his stay in Boston, Dickens lodged at the **Omni Parker House** hotel and was feted there by Longfellow, Emerson, and Holmes on November 21, 1867. See page 177 for more on the hotel's illustrious literary connections. Four months later, Dickens spoke at a farewell banquet held in his honor at **Delmonico's** in New York City (*www.delmonicosny.com*; 56 Beaver Street).

formity of thinking, and its institution of slavery. Washington Irving, who presided over a banquet feting Dickens in New York, was later said to be so angered by the book that he avoided visiting the author during a subsequent trip to London.

Twenty-five years after his first visit, Dickens undertook another American reading tour and found his second impressions of the country more favorable, spurring him to append a postscript to *American Notes.* In a farewell speech he delivered in New York shortly before sailing back to England, he marveled at "the amazing changes that I have seen around me on every side." Unfortunately, the punishing rigors of the trip—during which he delivered 75 readings between November 1867 and April 1868—caused his already failing health to rapidly deteriorate.

From his first public reading of *A Christmas Carol,* it was clear that Dickens had a gift for mimicry and performance, and that his works—with their distinctively eccentric characters—readily lent themselves to dramatization. The dynamic author nearly became a stage actor before his writing career took flight, and he indulged a lifelong interest in the theater by engaging in amateur theatricals with friends such as writer Wilkie Collins. As one biographer noted, "Without a single prop or bit of costume, by changes of voice, by gesture, by vocal expression, Dickens peopled his stage with a throng of characters." Similarly, his contemporary Thomas Carlyle remarked to him admiringly after attending a reading of *The Pickwick Papers,* "Charley, you carry a whole company of actors under your hat."

The adulation Dickens received during his readings—which became so renowned that hundreds of fans were sometimes turned away—fed his bottomless need for love and admiration. During the last 12 years of his life, Dickens delivered nearly 500 public readings throughout Britain and the United States. (The custom-built reading lectern he used during his performances is on display at the Doughty Street house.) But the physically demanding nature of the readings exacted a heavy toll on the writer. Dickens's exhaustive preparation (he sometimes rehearsed a new reading up to 200 times), his highly emotive style of delivery, and the grueling rigors of months spent on the road may have hastened his early demise at age 58. Flying in the face of his rapidly deteriorating health and ignoring the advice of his friends, family, and physician, Dickens steadfastly continued giving performances up until three months before his passing.

For much of his life, the writer had been plagued by gout, neuralgia, and nervous exhaustion, which he tried to counteract through vigorous exertion, sometimes walking up to 20 miles a day. "Work and worry, without exercise," he wrote to his friend and future biographer, John Forster, "would soon make an end of me. If I were not going away now, I should break down." While returning from a restorative trip to France shortly after penning those words, Dickens suffered a further blow to his fragile mental health in a deadly train crash. "No words can describe the scene," he wrote to Forster of the accident that was to haunt him with "sudden vague rushes of terror" for the remainder of his life. Shaken but miraculously unharmed, he "worked for hours among the dying and dead" in the steep ravine where the train had derailed. He then clambered back into his own precariously dangling carriage to rescue what would be his last completed manuscript, *Our Mutual Friend*. In the book's postscript, he wrote poignantly, "I remember with devout thankfulness that I can never be much nearer to parting company with my readers forever, than I was then, until there shall be written against my life the two words with which I have this day closed this book –THE END."

IF YOU GO: The peripatetic author moved often throughout his life, but of the many residences he occupied during his decades in London, the house at 48 Doughty Street is the only one to have survived. Purchased by the Dickens Fellowship in 1924 and subsequently opened as a museum, the house contains much of its original early 19th-century woodwork, moldings, and fireplaces. Complementing the vast permanent collection of Dickensian furnishings and memorabilia are rotating exhibits highlighting aspects of the author's personal and professional life. The museum regularly hosts special events, and during the holiday season the house is decked in festive finery befitting the author of *A Christmas Carol*. **Charles Dickens Museum** 48 Doughty Street • London, England WC1N 2LX• Tel: (44) 207 405 2127 • *www.dickensmuseum.com* • Open Tuesday through Sunday; closed Mondays except for bank holidays

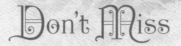

Don't Miss

Among the many evocative Dickensian artifacts displayed at the Charles Dickens Museum are:

◉ The **garret window** from the now demolished residence at 16 Bayham Street in London's Camden Town, where Dickens lived as a young boy. The writer, whose bedroom was located in the garret, recalled the dwelling as "a mean, small tenement with a wretched little back-garden abutting on a squalid court," and it is thought to be the location of Mr. Micawber's house where David Copperfield lodged.

◉ A large **wood-frame grill preserved from the Marshalsea Debtors Prison**, where John Dickens was incarcerated. During this bleak time, he passed on some sage advice to his son: "If a man had twenty pounds a year, and spent nineteen pounds nineteen shillings and sixpence, he would be happy; but that a shilling spent the other way would make him wretched." Thirty years later, the younger Dickens satirized his father by having Mr. Micawber voice the same sentiments to David Copperfield before asking to borrow a shilling.

◉ Dickens's navy blue **Court Suit** with brass buttons and gold piping, which he wore at two royal functions in the months before his death. During his March 1870 private audience with Queen Victoria, he found her "strangely shy" while she described him in her journal as "very agreeable, with a pleasant voice and manner."

◉ Catherine Dickens's **turquoise and gold engagement ring**; she wed Charles Dickens on April 2, 1836, and they produced ten children, but their union was not to last. "Poor Catherine and I are not made for each other, and there is no help for it," Dickens wrote to a friend shortly before they formally separated in 1858.

Dickens died of a stroke on June 9, 1870, five years to the day after the accident. His death was regarded as a national tragedy, and thousands descended on his burial site at Westminster Abbey to pay their respects. "I never knew an author's death [to] cause such general mourning," observed Longfellow from the United States, while Dickens's friend Thomas Carlyle opined, "It is an event world-wide, a *unique* of talents suddenly extinct."

Drink, Dine, and Doze

RULES

35 Maiden Lane • London WC2E 7LB • Tel: (44) 207 836 5314 • *www.rules.co.uk*

London's oldest restaurant, Rules, has been beloved by generations of writers, actors, and mere mortals for its "porter, pies and oysters" for more than 200 years. Other menu staples at the sprawling three-story establishment include traditional British game dishes such as Wiltshire rabbit. Charles Dickens, who attended the theater several nights a week in the surrounding Covent Garden neighborhood, was a regular here, as were writers William Makepeace Thackeray, John Galsworthy, and H. G. Wells. With its classical decor and old-time touches like draft beers served in silver tankards, it's easy to be forgiven for wondering if Dickens himself might wander into the room at any moment.

THE LAMB AND FLAG

33 Rose Street • London WC2E 9EB • Tel: (44) 207 497 9504

Dickens is thought to have imbibed at this wood-paneled 300-year-old pub tucked down an alleyway in London's Covent Garden neighborhood. Despite its Georgian facade, it is one of the few half-timbered buildings to have survived the 1666 Great Fire and was once informally known as the Bucket of Blood due to the bare-knuckle fistfights that were held here.

For more about the **George Inn**, which features in *Little Dorrit*, the **Spaniards Inn**, which features in *The Pickwick Papers*, and **Ye Olde Cheshire Cheese**, a Fleet Street haunt of Dickens and dozens of famed writers, see pages 204 and 206–208.

Seventeenth-century poet John Dryden is said to have been attacked by thugs in the alleyway and the upstairs bar bears his name.

DIRTY DICK'S

202 Bishopsgate • London EC2M 4NR • Tel: (44) 207 283 5888 • www.dirtydicks.co.uk

This Victorian pub is located on the site of a shop owned by 18th-century ironmonger Nathaniel Bentley, who became a dirty, ragged recluse when his fiancée died on the eve of their wedding. Bentley, whose sad deterioration was widely reported at the time, may have been one inspiration for the eccentric Miss Havisham in *Great Expectations*. Left at the altar, Miss Havisham never quite recovered, living in her wedding dress with her clocks stopped at the hour of her intended nuptials.

ELSEWHERE IN THE AREA

THE LONDON OF CHARLES DICKENS WALK

London Walks • www.walks.com • 2:15 p.m. on Fridays

Many Dickensian nooks and crannies known by the author and his characters still abound in the city's narrow alleys and sequestered streets, and the best way to uncover them is on **The London of Charles Dickens Walk**. Among the sites you'll visit are:

"There is little enough to see in Furnival's Inn. It is a shady, quiet place, echoing to the footsteps of the stragglers who have business there."

—MARTIN CHUZZLEWIT

- The former site of **Furnival's Inn**, where Dickens lived while beginning his first novel, *The Pickwick Papers*. The building was demolished in the late 19th century and is commemorated with a Dickens bust and plaque.
- Before becoming associated with the legal profession, the area known as **Middle Temple** was occupied by the Knights Templar. Pip has chambers at the 16th-century Middle Temple Hall in *Great Expectations* (incidentally the location where Shakespeare's first production of *Twelfth Night* was staged), and Middle Temple features prominently in *Barnaby Rudge*.
- **The Old Curiosity Shop** is thought to be the oldest shop in central London and is purported to be the location where Little Nell and her grandfather resided in the eponymous

novel. Although the claim is unsubstantiated—in fact the shop's name was changed subsequent to the novel's publication—Dickens lived and worked nearby and is thought to have visited on several occasions.

CARLYLE'S HOUSE

24 Cheyne Row • London SW3 5HL • Tel: (44) 207 352 7087 • *www.nationaltrust.org.uk/ carlyles-house* • Open Wednesday through Sunday, mid-March through late October

Dickens once said that his contemporary, the Scottish essayist and historian Thomas Carlyle, was the man "who had influenced him most." Carlyle's work held enormous sway during Victorian times, and among the literati who graced the doorstep of his Queen Anne–style home were Dickens, Tennyson, Browning, and philosopher John Stuart Mill. Mill once infamously arrived bearing all that was left of the manuscript for volume one of Carlyle's lengthy historical tome *The French Revolution*—a single burned scrap of paper (on display at the house today). The philosopher's maid had mistaken the manuscript for garbage and set it alight. Devastated, Carlyle later confessed that he felt like a man who had "nearly killed himself accomplishing zero."

Carlyle's historical treatise, *The French Revolution*, inspired Dickens's fictional account of the events surrounding the 1789 uprising in *A Tale of Two Cities*. Likewise, Carlyle's works on social criticism influenced Dickens's novel *Hard Times*, which he dedicated to the essayist.

The 300-year-old home is a time capsule of the decades he and his wife, Jane, spent there, from the soundproof attic study where he toiled to the walled garden where they relaxed with their beloved dog Nero.

FARTHER AFIELD

CHARLES DICKENS BIRTHPLACE MUSEUM

393 Commercial Road • Portsmouth, Hampshire PO1 4QL • Tel: (44) 239 282 7261 • *www.charlesdickensbirthplace.co.uk* • Open daily April through September

On February 7, 1812, John and Elizabeth Dickens welcomed their son Charles into the world at this modest dwelling on England's

While living near Portsmouth, Arthur Conan Doyle practiced medicine and wrote his first Holmes adventure, *A Study in Scarlet*. At the **Portsmouth Museum**, the exhibit "A Study in Sherlock" features items related to the writer and his famous detective (www.portsmouthcitymuseums.co.uk).

southern coast, little suspecting their youngster would achieve international renown less than 30 years later. Today, the birthplace home re-creates the lower middle-class surroundings the Dickens family would have known. Among the memorabilia on display are the elegant couch on which the writer spent his final hours before dying at his grand house in Kent, his death certificate, and his parents' rent book, recording—unsurprisingly—that they were in arrears.

DICKENS WORLD THEME PARK

Leviathan Way • Chatham Maritime, Kent ME4 4LL • Tel: (44) 870 241 1415 • www.dickensworld.co.uk • Weekends only

Dickens lived the happiest years of his childhood in the Kentish town of Chatham in southeastern England, where the family moved when he was five. The site where John Dickens once toiled in the Naval Dockyards is now the Dickens World Theme Park, which plunges visitors into the depths of a Dickensian London that's fun for both the young and the young at heart. Visitors must book a guided tour, a 90-minute interactive experience led by actors in period costume.

BLEAK HOUSE BROADSTAIRS

Fort Road • Broadstairs, Kent CT10 1EY • Tel: (44) 1843 865 338 • www.bleakhousebroadstairs.co.uk

Every summer for almost 14 years Dickens decamped with his family to the seaside resort town of Broadstairs, finding the "brisk and bracing" sea air beneficial to his health. For much of that time, he resided in Fort House, an "airy nest" above the harbor. Decades later, the dwelling was re-christened Bleak House as some believe it inspired John Jarndyce's home in the novel of that name. Today, the writer's summer retreat is a guest house and wedding venue; visitors checking into the Charles Dickens Room have use of the light-filled study where

Dickens penned portions of his autobiographical novel, *David Copperfield*. Tours of the study are offered, as well as afternoon tea in the Great Expectations Dining Room. Broadstairs is about a 90-minute train ride from London.

DICKENS HOUSE MUSEUM

2 Victoria Parade • Broadstairs, Kent CT10 1QS • Tel: (44) 184 386 1232
• *www.dickensfellowship.org/broadstairs* • Open daily April through October

While summering in Broadstairs in 1850, Dickens wrote several chapters of *David Copperfield* and based the protagonist's aunt, Betsey Trotwood, on the kindly and charming Mary Pearson Strong. Her house, described in the novel as "a very neat little cottage with cheerful bow-windows," is now the Dickens House Museum. *Copperfield* fans will immediately feel at home in the parlor, furnished exactly as described and depicted in the novel by renowned illustrator Phiz. Other rooms contain Dickens ephemera, such as a mahogany sideboard that once belonged to the author, prints drawn by Phiz, and letters Dickens wrote from Broadstairs extolling the virtues of "Our English Watering Place."

The **Broadstairs Dickens Festival** (*www.broadstairsdickensfestival.co.uk*) featuring a grand parade in Victorian dress and other events is held each year during the third week of June.

"We are three sisters":

CHARLOTTE, EMILY, AND ANNE BRONTË
IN HAWORTH, WEST YORKSHIRE, ENGLAND

WORKS BY THE BRONTËS

Agnes Grey by Anne Brontë (1847)

Jane Eyre by Charlotte Brontë (1847)

Wuthering Heights by Emily Brontë (1847)

The Tenant of Wildfell Hall by Anne Brontë (1848)

Shirley by Charlotte Brontë (1849)

Villette by Charlotte Brontë (1853)

The Professor by Charlotte Brontë (1857)

Brontë Parsonage Museum

"Wuthering Heights was hewn in a wild workshop," Charlotte Brontë declared of her sister Emily's famed (and only) novel. The fierce, impassioned tale takes place against a backdrop for which Emily had "a particular love": the brooding, windswept moors where she spent the majority of her all-too-brief life.

In Haworth and on the surrounding moors, the Brontë sisters found fertile ground for their literary imaginings.

Home to the Brontë sisters was a Georgian parsonage in the West Yorkshire village of Haworth, where their father, Patrick, was appointed curate in 1820. An industrial town on the edge of a vast expanse of rugged moorland, it was "a strange, uncivilized little place," according to Charlotte. In contrast, present-day travelers drawn to Haworth step into a charming village with historic stone architecture and cobbled streets, much of which Charlotte might even find familiar.

A bibliophile's first stop should be the **Brontë Parsonage Museum**, the beautifully restored sanctum where the wordsmiths lived and wrote. Then follow in their footsteps to *Wuthering Heights* territory, the fabled moors where Emily's story of love, rivalry, and revenge plays out. A several-mile walk along the dramatically scenic landscape—snow-covered in winter and dotted with heather that blooms purple in summer—leads by a waterfall the Brontës often visited and then on to **Top Withens**. These stone ruins of a remote farm are credited as being the geographical setting of Wuthering Heights, "the name of Mr. Heathcliff's dwelling. 'Wuthering' being a significant provincial adjective, descriptive of the atmospheric tumult to which its station is exposed in stormy weather," Emily writes in the novel.

While the sisters flourished creatively in Haworth, the family was beset by personal tragedy during their time there. The year after moving into the parsonage Mrs. Brontë died of cancer, leaving behind six children under the age of eight. The traumatic loss affected the family deeply and later reverberated in Charlotte and Emily's novels. The title character in Charlotte's *Jane Eyre* is an orphan, and nearly all of the children in *Wuthering Heights* become motherless as well.

Heartbreak again befell the Brontës when Charlotte, Emily, and their older sisters, Maria and Elizabeth, attended the Clergy Daughters' School in Cowan Bridge. The school's unheated rooms, harsh disciplinary methods, and unhygienic kitchen practices led to the deaths of Maria and Elizabeth, who returned to Haworth suffering from tuberculosis (then called consumption). The two girls died within a month of each other, leaving nine-year-old Charlotte the eldest child in a motherless household. Understandably, she looked back on her time in Cowan Bridge with great bitterness, recasting the Clergy Daughters' School as the bleak and foreboding Lowood School in *Jane Eyre*.

Close in age and temperament, the four remaining Brontë children—Charlotte, Emily, Anne, and their brother, Branwell—were companionable playmates, often roaming the moors and inventing fanciful stories together. When a set of toy soldiers arrived at the parsonage for Branwell, they conjured for them the fictional kingdoms of Gondal and Angria with their own unique history and geography. In what were some of their earliest writings, the siblings immortalized the soldiers' adventures in stories and poems they penned in diminutive booklets (some of which are on display at the Brontë Parsonage Museum).

From an early age, the sisters cherished the dream of becoming published authors, with Charlotte longing to become "forever known." The need to earn a living took precedence, though, and a series of jobs as governesses and teachers left little time for creative pursuits. Emily in particular struggled with the loss of her freedom. "Liberty was the breath of Emily's nostrils; without it, she perished," explained Charlotte. Emily returned home after just six months away from Haworth and became the stay-at-home daughter, assisting with the family's cooking, cleaning, and housekeeping.

Anne Brontë struggled as well, working for the dreadful Inghams at Blake Hall. Tormented by her disobedient young charges, she was let go after only nine months. She had better luck in her next post at Thorp Green, where she remained for five years and was eventually joined by Branwell, who tutored the family's son. Anne's experiences in the two households laid the groundwork for her debut novel, *Agnes Grey*, an exposé of the ill treatment that governesses endured at the hands of their wealthy employers.

To escape servitude, Charlotte persuaded her sisters to set up their own small school in Haworth. In preparation, she and Emily traveled to Brussels to study French, an experience that proved to be a watershed moment in Charlotte's life. Their brilliant literature teacher, Constantin Heger, quickly recognized the sisters' talents and drew out their literary abilities.

Charlotte formed a passionate but unrequited attachment to Heger, her "dear master," and she poured her unfulfilled longing into her novels. *Jane Eyre*, the tale of a governess who falls in love with her dark and disturbing employer, was an exorcism of Charlotte's own feelings for an older, unobtainable man. Her novel *Villette* is even more autobiographical: partly set at a boarding school in a fictional city based on Brussels, it portrays a woman's infatuation with her Belgian colleague.

When Charlotte returned to Yorkshire, she continued to hold a torch for Heger and penned him a series of emotional letters. At first he responded politely, but the more ardent her appeals became, the more he distanced himself. Finally, he tore up her missives and threw them away unanswered. As his correspondence dwindled, Charlotte lamented, "I lose my appetite and my sleep—I pine away."

Charlotte's consternation about the unanswered letters paled in comparison to another misfortune the sisters suffered. Their school proved an abject disappointment and failed to attract a single student. Meanwhile, Anne was forced to resign from Thorp Green after Branwell's scandalous affair with their employer's wife came to light. Returning home to Haworth, he descended into a spiral of alcoholism and drug addiction.

Four of Charlotte's letters to Constantin Heger (written in French) can be viewed on the British Library's website (*www.bl.uk*). Three were torn up, presumably by Heger, and then rescued from a wastebasket and pieced together by his wife.

A welcome distraction from the sisters' miseries came in the autumn of 1845, when Charlotte stumbled on a cache of Emily's poems. She believed the verses "had a peculiar music—wild, melancholy and elevating" and that they deserved a wider audience.

Initially, Emily was furious at the invasion of her privacy, but her temper cooled after Anne admitted that she, too, had been writing poems in secret. At Charlotte's urging, the sisters published a joint volume of poetry funded from their own meager savings. Several of Charlotte's poems were also included in the collection, which was published pseudonymously under the names Currer, Ellis, and Acton Bell. "We did not like to declare ourselves women," explained Charlotte, citing a fear "that authoresses are liable to be looked upon with prejudice."

While the book of poems sold only two copies, the dismal sales didn't discourage the sisters from pursuing other literary endeavors. Each night after their father retired, they gathered in the dining room and paced around the table, reading aloud from their novels-in-progress and brainstorming plot ideas. After her sisters' deaths, Charlotte continued the comforting custom on her own, unable to sleep without the nightly ritual.

Although Charlotte's first novel, *The Professor,* failed to attract a publisher, *Jane Eyre* made its author, "Currer Bell," an instant celebrity in 1847. "The story quickly took me captive," declared publisher George Smith, who read the manuscript in one sitting and accepted it for publication the next day. The novel follows spirited Jane Eyre from a hardscrabble childhood through her position as governess at a remote manor house and romantic relationship with her enigmatic employer, Mr. Rochester. The title character's independent nature intrigued readers, helping to make the book a runaway success and spurring a rival publisher to rush out Anne's *Agnes Grey* and Emily's *Wuthering Heights.*

Smith also published William Makepeace Thackeray, who once irked Charlotte Brontë by mistakenly introducing her to his mother as "Jane Eyre."

The uninhibited characters, passionate intensity, and moral ambiguity of *Wuthering Heights* deeply polarized its audience. While the story's power and originality were undisputed, critics also found it "coarse and loathsome." One review was particularly harsh: "How a human being could have attempted such a book ... without committing suicide before he had finished a dozen chapters, is a mystery," opined *Graham's* magazine.

Anne's *Agnes Grey* made far less of a splash, overshadowed by her sisters' more sensational novels. "It leaves no impression at all," remarked one reviewer. Her second novel, *The Tenant of Wildfell Hall,* achieved more notoriety. Despite being branded revolting and immoral—or perhaps because of it—the story of a young wife who defies convention and leaves her abusive, alcoholic husband proved popular with the public.

Contrarily, the sisters' decision to publish under pseudonyms drew increased attention to their identity. "Who are the Bells?" reviewers demanded to know. Many were convinced the authors were female, and one rumor claimed the novels were written by a single person. Charlotte and Anne attempted to dispel the myths by traveling to London to meet their publishers.

"We are three sisters," Charlotte told the startled George Smith in 1848, clarifying the identities of Currer, Acton, and Ellis Bell. Several moments passed before Smith finally understood that he was indeed meeting the author of *Jane Eyre.* He took an instant

IF YOU GO: Purchased by a wealthy textile magnate for the Brontë Society in 1928, the parsonage remains much as it did two centuries ago when the sisters paced the dining room brainstorming plot ideas. Visitors looking to do more than meander through the parsonage on their own can book a VIP Tour and Treasures Session; a member of the curatorial team takes participants behind closed doors to see items not currently on public display.

Head to Haworth during warmer weather months so that your visit to Brontë Country can include a leisurely walk on the moors. Haworth is located in West Yorkshire, eight miles west of Bradford and three miles south of Keighley. The nearest mainline railway station is in Leeds. **Brontë Parsonage Museum** Church Street • Haworth • Tel: (44) 153 564 2323 • *www.bronte.org.uk* • Open February through December; hours vary seasonally

Don't Miss

◉ In the parsonage dining room is the **black sofa** on which Emily took her dying breath on the afternoon of December 19, 1848, refusing to see a doctor until it was too late. At her side when she died was her mastiff, Keeper, who followed her funeral procession to the burial vault.

◉ Throughout the house are paintings by Branwell Brontë, including **a replica of a rare portrait of the novelist sisters together**. (See page 244.) In the background is an eerie blank space where Branwell later painted himself out. The original is in the National Portrait Gallery in London (*npg.org.uk*).

◉ The room where the diminutive Charlotte died now displays her tiny **dresses and shoes**, which visitor Virginia Woolf found "so touching that one hardly feels reverent in one's gaze." (Charlotte stood at under five feet tall and was painfully self-conscious about her short stature and plain appearance.)

◉ Enjoy a picnic or read a book in the **Brontë Meadow**, adjacent to the museum, and take in the picturesque landscape—a perfect introduction to the novelists' territory, especially if you don't have time for a lengthy walk on the moors.

◉ The **ink-blot stained table** where Charlotte, Emily, and Anne created their stories has been restored to the parsonage dining room. The museum purchased the table in 2015, a century and a half after it was auctioned off following Patrick Brontë's death. Note the large candle burn and small "E" carved on its surface.

liking to the sisters, whom he described as "two rather quaintly dressed little ladies, pale-faced and anxious looking." When he proposed introducing them to London's literary society, the sisters demurred and insisted on maintaining their anonymity.

Upon their return to Haworth, the excitement of the London excursion was tempered by Branwell's diminishing health. His opium and alcohol addiction had masked the warning signs of consumption, and now the disease had him firmly in its grasp. He died in September of that year, and Emily became ill with it soon afterward.

Ever the stoic, she declined medical help or even homeopathy, which she claimed "was only another form of quackery." Charlotte tried to cheer her dying sister with a hard-found sprig of heather from the winter moors, but Emily no longer recognized her favorite flower. Growing steadily weaker, she passed away in December 1848 at only thirty years old. "I thought it very possible she might be with us still for weeks; and a few hours afterwards, she was in eternity," Charlotte wrote to a friend after her sister's death. "Yes; there is no Emily in time or on earth now."

SKY AND EARTH: "Nothing you ever read about [the Brontës] can make you know them until you go there," American novelist and short story writer Sarah Orne Jewett stated to a friend after visiting Haworth in 1898. At the time she was there, the parsonage where the sisters lived had not yet been turned into a museum. "The present vicar resents pilgrims to the shrine of the Brontë family, but he didn't bite us," she humorously reported. Despite the less-than-warm welcome, she had a pointed message for the cynics who told her not to bother trekking to her much-admired literary idols' home: "Never mind people who tell you there is nothing to see in the place where people lived who interest you. You always find something of what made them the souls they were, and at any rate you see their sky and their earth."

The **Sarah Orne Jewett House Museum and Visitor Center** is preserved in South Berwick, Maine, the author's birthplace and longtime home. Jewett drew on her native terrain in her fiction, setting *The Country of the Pointed Firs* and other works along or near Maine's southern seacoast (*www.historicnewengland.org*).

The Brontë Connection

The Brontës' wild literary imaginings were quick to attract the attention of fellow wordsmiths near and far from the Yorkshire moors. Elizabeth Barrett Browning, living in Italy, remarked on *Jane Eyre*'s spontaneous and free-thinking qualities. Across the pond in Massachusetts, Emily Dickinson procured a copy in secret, knowing her father would disapprove of the provocative tale, and found the story "electric." She was an ardent admirer of the Brontës' poems and novels, intrigued by the innovative psychological fiction written by women.

Later, Dickinson penned the poem "Charlotte Brontë's Grave" after the English author's death and requested that Emily's verse "No Coward Soul Is Mine" be recited at her own funeral. Closer to home, Charlotte's untimely passing prompted Englishman Matthew Arnold—who had met her while both were holidaying in the Lake District—to publish "Haworth Churchyard," a tribute to the Brontë sisters, in a popular magazine.

In the ensuing decades, the Brontës continued to inspire and influence other writers. Virginia Woolf's article "Haworth, November 1904" appeared in *The Guardian,* her first published piece. Some fifty years later, in 1956, newlyweds Sylvia Plath and Ted Hughes—she was an American, he hailed from Yorkshire—ventured to Haworth. They spent a day visiting the Brontë parsonage and rambling on the moors. Each poet later wrote a work titled "Wuthering Heights."

Plath crafted her darkly haunting version in 1961, one year before she split with Hughes and seventeen months before her suicide. Hughes's poem "Wuthering Heights," in which he compares his wife to the mythic and tragic Emily Brontë, appeared the year he died in 1998 in the collection *Birthday Letters.*

Plath is buried in **St. Thomas' Churchyard** in the West Yorkshire village of Heptonstall, where Hughes grew up. His ashes were scattered at a remote location in Devon, England, his longtime home. Like the Brontë sisters, Hughes is commemorated with a memorial in **Poets' Corner** in London's Westminster Abbey.

The Brontës' sorrows continued when Anne was felled by consumption mere months after Emily's death. She died in the coastal town of Scarborough, where Charlotte had taken her to have one last look at the sea. Grief-stricken, Charlotte returned to Haworth, writing mournfully, "I am free to walk on the moors; but when I go out there alone, everything reminds me of the times when others were with me, and then the moors seem a wilderness, featureless, solitary, saddening."

Charlotte found solace by immersing herself in her novel *Shirley*. "The faculty of imagination lifted me when I was sinking," she confided to her publisher. *Shirley* was written with her beloved Emily in mind. The story's free-speaking titular character is the kind of person Charlotte believed her sister might have been under wealthier circumstances.

After *Shirley*'s publication, Charlotte wrote a biographical notice to accompany her sisters' novels, hoping "to give a just idea of their identity." It was the first public confirmation of the authors' gender and brought an end to three years of speculation. The notice also attempted to exonerate the Brontës from the accusations of coarseness that had been leveled at their work. By portraying Emily and Anne as tragic figures who had led quiet, blameless lives, Charlotte hoped "to wipe the dust off their gravestones, and leave their dear names free from soil."

She pointedly refused to reprint *The Tenant of Wildfell Hall*, the novel that had shocked critics the most, dismissing it as "an entire mistake." Her actions, though well intended, forever cast Anne in the shadow of her more famous sisters.

With only her elderly father for company, Charlotte grew intensely lonely and finally succumbed to the persistent proposals of her father's curate, Arthur Bell Nicholls. "My destiny will not be brilliant, certainly, but Mr. Nicholls is conscientious, affectionate, pure in heart and life," wrote the 38-year-old bride-to-be shortly before her wedding.

Although Charlotte entered into her marriage with misgiving, she blossomed in her role as Arthur's wife and described her husband as "the best earthly comfort any woman had." But her newfound happiness was fleeting, as the same dark fate that claimed her sisters found her, too. Pregnant and weakened by severe morning sickness, Charlotte caught a chill while walking on the moors and declined rapidly. She lapsed into delirium and passed away in 1855, just nine months after her wedding.

No sooner had Charlotte breathed her last than tourists were beating a path to Haworth, anxious to see the places made sacred by the sisters' presence and explore the landscapes they described so vividly in their novels. Charlotte had observed this phenomena even when she was still alive, writing to a friend, "Various folks are beginning to come boring to Haworth, on the wise errand of seeing the scenery described in *Jane Eyre* and *Shirley*."

By the time Virginia Woolf visited West Yorkshire a half century later, the village and the atmospheric moors had become synonymous with the three gifted sisters. "Haworth expresses the Brontës; the Brontës express Haworth," Woolf noted. "They fit like a snail to its shell."

DRINK, DINE, AND DOZE

BLACK BULL PUB
119 Main Street • Haworth

At the top of a steep cobblestone street in the center of Haworth is the cozy, 300-year-old watering hole where the Brontës' wayward brother, Branwell, frequently whiled away the hours. Though a talented painter and poet, he was unable to hold a steady job and increasingly found solace in alcohol and opium. In an alcove up the stairwell, his favorite chair has been given pride of place.

ASHMOUNT COUNTRY HOUSE
Mytholmes Lane • Haworth • *www.ashmounthaworth.co.uk*

A few minutes' walk from the Brontë parsonage, this charming bed-and-breakfast with sweeping views of the moors was once home to Dr. Amos Ingham, the Brontë family physician.

ELSEWHERE IN THE AREA

BRONTË WATERFALL AND CHAIR

"We set off, not intending to go far; but though wild and cloudy it was fine in the morning; when we got about half-a-mile on the moors, Arthur suggested the idea of the waterfall . . . It was fine indeed; a perfect torrent racing over the rocks, white and beautiful!" —Charlotte Brontë letter, November 29, 1854

A 2½ mile walk through wild heather moors leads to the Brontës' favorite destination, "the meeting of the waters." There, Emily would recline on a slab of stone, known locally as the Brontë chair, to play with tadpoles in the water.

BRONTË COUNTRY WALKS

Explore the Brontë waterfall, Top Withens, and other landmarks in the Haworth countryside with the **Walkers Map** available at *www .bronte.org.uk/visit-us/explore-bronte -country*. **Helen's Heritage Walks** (*www.helensheritagewalks.co.uk*) offers personalized, private Brontë-themed excursions around Haworth and elsewhere in West Yorkshire, including sites related to *Wuthering Heights* and *Shirley*.

HAWORTH PARISH CHURCH (ST. MICHAEL AND ALL ANGELS CHURCH)

Church Street • Haworth • *www.haworthchurch.co.uk*

The church where the Brontë children's father, Patrick, once presided as curate was later rebuilt, but the 15th-century clock tower still rising by the building was there in his day. All of the Brontës—except for Anne, who died in Scarborough while taking a sea cure—are interred in a tomb beneath the present church. Inside the place of worship, near where the family pew once stood, a pillar above their burial vault has an inscription commemorating the Brontës.

THE PASSIONATE BRONTËS TOUR

Haworth • Tel: (44) 774 910 8105 • *www.bronte walks.co.uk* • Thursday, Saturday, Sunday

While walking along Haworth's historic cobbled streets, hear all about the village's most famous family. Guides use the Brontës' own letters, poems, and stories to illuminate their literary achievements, shed light on their personal passions and tragedies, and reveal what life was like in this tiny Yorkshire town during their day.

FARTHER AFIELD

PONDEN HALL

Stanbury • *www.ponden-hall.co.uk*

West of Haworth is 17th-century Ponden Hall—now a bed-and-breakfast—believed to be the model for the Linton residence, Thrushcross Grange, in *Wuthering Heights*. The house also inspired architectural and interior descriptions of Wuthering Heights, the Earnshaws' abode and later Heathcliff's home. According to local lore, a tiny, single-paned window on the house's gabled east side is said to be where Catherine's ghost scratches at the glass trying to gain entry inside at Wuthering Heights. She tells the tale's narrator that she has been lost for twenty years. "I'm come home," she says mournfully. "I'd lost my way on the moor!"

BRONTË BIRTHPLACE

Thornton • *www.delucaboutique.co.uk*

Charlotte, Emily, Branwell, and Anne were all born in this stone cottage during the five years the family resided in Thornton. The dwelling is now a café, Emily's by De Luca Boutique, which retains some of the historic features—like the fireplace in front of which the future novelists came into the world.

ANNE BRONTË'S GRAVE

St. Mary's Churchyard • Scarborough • www.scarborough-stmarys.org.uk

Suffering from consumption, Anne passed away in 1849 in Scarborough, a town on the North Sea coast in North Yorkshire. Rather than have her sister buried in Haworth, Charlotte chose to "lay the flower where it had fallen." When she visited her sister's grave, she was dismayed to find erroneous information on the tombstone. All but one of the five errors were subsequently corrected, leaving only the mistaken listing of Anne's age as 28 rather than 29.

NORTON CONYERS HOUSE & GARDENS

Wath near Ripon • Tel: (44) 176 564 0333 • www.nortonconyers.org.uk

• House open on select days

While visiting this medieval manor house in North Yorkshire, Charlotte Brontë is thought to have heard the legend of an insane woman once confined to its attic, a fate she later had befall Rochester's wife in *Jane Eyre*. A blocked staircase connecting the first floor to the attic rooms was discovered in 2004, arousing interest in Norton Conyers as inspiration for Rochester's home, Thornfield Hall. Another possible model for Thornfield is **North Lees Hall** (*www.peakdistrict.gov.uk*), an Elizabethan manor owned by the Eyre family and with its own story of an imprisoned madwoman.

A Sacred Place:

VICTOR HUGO IN PARIS, FRANCE

SELECTED WORKS BY VICTOR HUGO

The Last Days of a Condemned Man (1829)

The Hunchback of Notre-Dame (1831)

Les Misérables (1862)

Toilers of the Sea (1866)

The Man Who Laughs (1869)

Ninety-Three (1874)

Notre-Dame de Paris

To celebrate the marriage of his son, the Duke of Orléans, in 1837, King Louis-Philippe held a lavish banquet at the palace of Versailles. Among the distinguished guests attending the festivities in the opulent Hall of Mirrors was Victor Hugo, who had a memorable encounter with the newly wed Duchess of Orléans. "The first building that I visited on coming to Paris," she said to him, "was your church."

Paris was the longtime home of Victor Hugo, and the city's famed medieval cathedral is the primary setting of his novel *The Hunchback of Notre-Dame*.

The church that intrigued her is **Notre-Dame de Paris** (Our Lady of Paris), one of the City of Light's most resplendent landmarks. The soaring Gothic edifice, evoked in the pages of Hugo's *The Hunchback of Notre-Dame,* is adorned with stained-glass windows, flying buttresses, statues of saints and gargoyles, and two looming bell towers. The cathedral's striking, filigreed facade and dramatic location on a small island in the River Seine are rivaled only by its colorful past. The first stones were laid in 1163, with construction lasting for two centuries. Over the years, Notre-Dame has played witness to pivotal moments in the city's history—soldiers prayed there before embarking on the Crusades, rebels vandalized it during the French Revolution (an era that briefly saw the church turned into a secular Temple of Reason with busts of philosophers replacing those of religious figures), and in 1804, Napoleon I boldly crowned himself emperor within its hallowed interior.

Visitors today find an exquisitely well-preserved example of medieval architecture, but it took a great deal of imagination for the Duchess of Orléans and other early literary travelers to conjure up the magnificent structure that dominates the narrative in *The Hunchback of Notre-Dame*. During the 18th and 19th centuries, the church fell into disrepair—shunned by Parisians who viewed it as a shabby relic from a barbaric past—until the auspicious event that proved to be its saving grace. *Hunchback's* publication in 1831 sent droves of tourists in search of "Victor Hugo's cathedral" and inspired the city to

"We recognized the brown old Gothic pile in a moment; it was like the pictures," wrote Mark Twain in *The Innocents Abroad*. "We stood at a little distance and changed from one point of observation to another and gazed long at its lofty square towers and its rich front." About the statues perched on Notre-Dame's facade, he said, "I wish these old parties could speak. They could tell a tale worth the listening to." For more about Twain, see pages 124–31.

restore the monument that had been given the starring role in the dramatic and poignant story.

Set against a vividly rendered backdrop of 15th-century Paris, the novel brims with larger-than-life characters such as the cathedral's deformed and reclusive resident, Quasimodo, who faithfully rings the bells housed in its towers. The church's cavernous confines are also home to a malevolent archdeacon and alchemist, Claude Frollo, who first sees the ethereal Esmeralda in the shadows of the great cathedral and sets in motion a nefarious scheme to possess the gypsy dancer. Quasimodo saves Esmeralda from certain death and she, too, finds shelter within the towers until even the church's warm embrace provides no sanctuary. After the lives of these three figures tragically intersect, it is only the character of Notre-Dame that escapes unscathed.

When Hugo began penning *The Hunchback of Notre-Dame,* he was well-acquainted with the "vast symphony of stone"—particularly with its 200-foot-tall bell towers, which he would often climb to take in the vista of Paris sprawling below. "No view in the world," he writes in the novel, "could be more magical, more airy, more enchanting." Then as now, trekking to the top of the towers requires fortitude to climb the more than 400 steps. "To the spectator who reached this pinnacle in a breathless condition," writes Hugo, "all was at first a dazzling sea of roofs, chimneys, streets, bridges, squares, spires, and steeples. Everything burst upon his vision, at once—the carved gable, the steep roof, the turret hanging from the angles of the walls, the 11th-century stone pyramid, the 15th-century stone obelisk, the round bare tower of the donjon-keep, the square elaborately wrought tower of the church, the great, the small, the massive, and the light."

Using the view from atop the cathedral's tower as a virtual map, Hugo relays the history of Paris, founded as a fishing village by the

Gallic Parisii tribe on the Île de la Cité more than 2,000 years ago. The story's omniscient narrator points out still familiar landmarks, from the Louvre palace to the city's oldest bridge, Pont Neuf, to the Hôtel de Cluny (today a museum housing medieval artifacts). The narrator also notes two particularly memorable sites: "the sharp spire" of the cathedral Saint-Sulpice, where the writer's marriage was solemnized, and the Place Royale (now the Place des Vosges), where he would later reside.

Hugo often ambled through the city's streets—"To err is human, to stroll is Parisian," he wrote in his novel *Les Misérables*—particularly in the evenings accompanied by friends. Infatuated with history and architecture, he took to exploring the old sections of Paris around Notre-Dame. Using the cathedral as the centerpiece of a novel was an idea he had considered for some time, but it wasn't until the summer of 1830—under duress from his publisher—that Hugo began writing *The Hunchback of Notre-Dame*. More than a year after the novel's original due date, Hugo purchased a new bottle of ink, outfitted himself in a gray knit body stocking, and locked away his street clothes to avoid the temptation of going out. He closeted himself with his novel and later wrote to an acquaintance, "I am head over ears in *Notre-Dame*. I fill sheet after sheet, and the subject grows and lengthens before me to such an extent that I am not sure whether my manuscript will not reach the level of the towers."

Along with breathing new life into the medieval cathedral, *The Hunchback of Notre-Dame* was a boon for the career of its creator. At the time of its publication in 1831, 29-year-old Hugo had already achieved widespread fame in France for his poetry, plays, and novels. The book appeared in the wake of the successful staging of Hugo's play *Hernani,* which had caused a stir on opening night when the writer's swashbuckling band of followers and fellow writers (among them Honoré de Balzac) shocked patrons at the Comédie Française theater with their outlandish outfits and raucous behavior like stomping and

Hugo disliked the title of the English translation of *The Hunchback of Notre-Dame* (it was originally called *Notre-Dame de Paris: 1482*), which shifted the emphasis of the story from the "sublime and majestic building" to its bell ringer, Quasimodo.

clapping during the performance. The boisterous group was referred to as Romantics for their revolutionary style of writing—vivid, passionate dramas set against historical backdrops. *Hernani* reportedly received the most enthusiastic reception since the staging of Voltaire's acclaimed plays a century earlier—but not from everyone. The play upset traditionalists who were offended by its use of pedestrian language and its melodramatic plotting. One went so far as to threaten the writer, who received a letter imploring him to "withdraw your filthy play, or we'll do you in."

Fearing a riot if they shut down the production, government censors allowed the play to continue. *Hernani* established Hugo as the leader of the Romantic movement (a term he equated with freedom of expression and creativity), and on the heels of this triumph—which partly accounted for the delay in the novel's appearance—came *The Hunchback of Notre-Dame.* As had *Hernani,* the novel defied the tenets of classical literature by combining elements of the grotesque with the sublime (like the deformed Quasimodo living in the majestic cathedral), having historic figures share the page with fictional characters, and forgoing formal speech for plain talk. *The Hunchback of Notre-Dame* was written for the general population, not for literary critics, and it both horrified and delighted readers. British actress Fanny Kemble recorded in her diary in January 1832, "Victor Hugo has set my mother raving. She didn't sleep all night, and says the book is bad in its tendency and shocking in its details; nevertheless, she goes on reading it."

Translated into dozens of languages, *The Hunchback of Notre-Dame* further broadened Hugo's literary reputation and made him the most famous living writer in Europe. It also brought him monetary reward, which allowed the writer, his wife Adèle, and their four children to move into a grand residence at 6 Place des Vosges in 1832. Located in the picturesque Marais district, the Place des Vosges is the oldest square in Paris and distinctive for its elegant redbrick and white stone 17th-century buildings.

The historic aspect of the Place des Vosges appealed to Hugo, who resided there in a stately town house for 16 years. In the elegant salon, he entertained writers, artists, and other luminaries, among them Alexandre Dumas and British novelist Charles Dickens. After an 1847 visit, Dickens described See pages 71–72 for more about Alexandre Dumas and pages 228–43 for more about Charles Dickens. Hugo's abode as "a most extraordinary place, looking like an old curiosity shop, or the Property Room of some gloomy vast old Theatre." Dickens wasn't far off the mark. Hugo's decorating tastes tended toward the dramatic—red damask, tapestries, paintings, antiques, and pieces of armor—and he had learned from set designers how to achieve a look of opulence at modest cost.

The **Maison de Victor Hugo** is now a museum that illuminates different periods in the writer's life, from his childhood to his exile from Paris to his last days. On display are Hugo's inkwell, the amateur artist's drawings, and other items such as a painting given to him by the Duke and Duchess of Orléans. The museum features re-creations of the scribe's bedroom in his last Parisian residence at 130 Avenue d'Eylau and a Chinese-themed room he designed for the home of his mistress, Juliette Drouet.

While living in the Place des Vosges in 1845, Hugo began working on *Les Misérables* but stopped partway through penning the tale to devote himself to politics. In 1848, an uprising led to the overthrow of the monarchy and the establishment of a republic, with Hugo elected a member of its Constitutional Assembly. From an early age, the writer had demonstrated political inclinations and often promoted humanitarian principles in the pages of his literary works. By later life his royalist sympathies had given way to more liberal views, and the act of taking up a political mantle allowed him to speak out for democracy and champion causes such as freedom of the press, abolition of the death penalty, the establishment of universal free education, and the alleviation of poverty.

Hugo delivered impassioned speeches advocating conciliation within the fledgling government, often putting himself in harm's way in streets simmering with violence. He publicly backed the presidential candidacy of Louis-Napoleon Bonaparte (nephew of the previous ruler), who staged a coup d'état after his election and eventually

Don't Miss

◉ Follow in Hugo's footsteps and **climb the towers of Notre-Dame**. After a trek partway up the north tower and across a platform (where the infamous gargoyles await), the vertical climb continues to the very top of the south tower. Although the panorama differs from that seen by "the ravens who lived in 1482," as Hugo writes in *The Hunchback of Notre-Dame*, the bird's-eye view of Paris with its winding river and decorous architecture is impressive.

◉ The tower trek offers an up close look at two intriguing sites: the spiral staircase leading to **"Esmeralda's cell"** (located in the bookstore) and **the cathedral's largest bell**, housed in a wood-beamed room. Although Quasimodo single-handedly rang *le bourdon* (the great bell), about 16 men were actually needed to complete the task. Today it's electronically operated.

◉ The Maison de Victor Hugo's unusual **Chinese-themed drawing room**—adorned with a colorful lantern hanging from the ceiling, an elaborately wrought mantelpiece, and an array of furniture and delicate china—is a testament to the writer's penchant for interior decorating. The room is a re-creation of one Hugo designed for his longtime mistress, Juliette Drouet, in her house on the island of Guernsey, where she joined him during his exile.

◉ One of the writers who turned out for the opening of Hugo's play *Hernani* was Honoré de Balzac. At a hilltop Parisian abode, now the **Maison de Balzac** (47 Rue Raynouard), he worked on *The Human Comedy* in a sun-filled study dressed in a monk's robe. Still there is the desk that had, he wrote to his longtime companion, Madame Hanska, "witnessed all my thoughts, anguish, suffering, despair, joys, everything!" After Balzac's passing in 1850, Hugo, who served as a pallbearer at the funeral, remarked in a eulogy, "His death has smitten Paris."

declared himself Emperor Napoleon III. In response, Hugo formed a Committee of Resistance and became a wanted man. He fled Paris in secret and remained in exile for 19 years, but his pen never stilled. Along with political tracts and volumes of poetry, Hugo returned to writing *Les Misérables,* which was published to great fanfare in 1862. While *The Hunchback of Notre-Dame* touches on his humanitarian concerns, it was in *Les Misérables* that the writer overtly set forth his liberal political and social views, particularly in the personage of Jean Valjean, a man who suffers injustice at the hands of the government and later uses his wealth to help those less fortunate.

When Hugo returned to Paris on September 5, 1870, after the fall of Napoleon III's empire, thousands of well-wishers gathered at the Gare du Nord train station to welcome him back to his beloved city, which had undergone immense changes in the long years of his absence. Napoleon III had galvanized a redevelopment effort, mostly as a military measure, which included widening the city's streets and

IF YOU GO: Hugo and his family resided on the second floor of an elegant town house in Paris's Place des Vosges from 1832 to 1848. The residence-turned-museum is located in a square built by King Henri IV that was the site of jousting tournaments and other royal spectacles. **Maison de Victor Hugo** 6 Place des Vosges, 4e • 75004 Paris • Tel: (33) 1 42 72 10 16 • *www.maisonsvictorhugo.paris.fr* • Closed Mondays

Notre-Dame, Hugo's muse, is a marvel of medieval architecture both inside and out and remains as awe-inspiring today as it was to Quasimodo. "The cathedral was not only company for him," writes Hugo in the tale, "it was the universe; nay, more, it was Nature itself. He never dreamed that there were other hedge-rows than the stained-glass windows in perpetual bloom; other shade than that of the stone foliage always budding, loaded with birds in the thickets of Saxon capitals; other mountains than the colossal towers of the church; or other ocean than Paris roaring at their feet." **Notre-Dame Cathedral** 6 Place du Parvis, 4e • 75004 Paris • Tel: (33) 1 42 34 56 10 • *www.notredamedeparis.fr* • Open daily; limited accessibility to cathedral during services creating open spaces (such as the Place du Parvis in front of Notre-Dame). The writer once again became a voice for democracy, gaining election to the new republic's Senate in 1876, and playing an instrumental role in preventing the sitting president from creating another dictatorship.

February 26, 1881 (marking the beginning of Hugo's 80th year), was celebrated as a national holiday. More than 600,000 people filed past the writer's home on the Avenue d'Eylau, where he watched the procession from a window with his two grandchildren by his side. In July of that year, the street was renamed Avenue Victor-Hugo in his honor.

The writer's birthday spectacle was trumped only by the grandiosity of his funeral, one of the most elaborate in modern French history. Hugo passed away on May 22, 1885, after a bout with pneumonia. His last days were covered by the international media, and after receiving news of his passing, the Senate and Chamber of Deputies suspended their session as a sign of national mourning. The pauper's coffin requested by Hugo was displayed beneath the Arc de Triomphe the night before his funeral, which took place on June 1 with the pomp and circumstance normally reserved for heads of state. A procession of two million mourners escorted the simple cart bearing Hugo on his last journey through the streets of Paris to the Panthéon—his final resting place in the city where, he once said, "the beating of Europe's heart is felt."

DRINK, DINE, AND DOZE

PAVILLON DE LA REINE

28 Place des Vosges, 3e • 75003 Paris • Tel: (33) 1 40 29 19 19

• *www.pavillon-de-la-reine.com*

Located on the Place des Vosges, this regal hotel sits across the square from where Hugo once resided. A less expensive Right Bank option is the **Hotel Victor Hugo** (19 Rue Copernic; *www.victorhugohotel .com*) near the location of his last residence on Avenue Victor Hugo (named in his honor during his last years) and the fountain-bedecked Place Victor Hugo.

LE PROCOPE

13 Rue de l'Ancienne-Comédie, 6e • 75006 Paris

• Tel: (33) 1 40 46 79 00 • *www.procope.com*

Hugo is among the many scribes who have feasted at this famed restaurant, and he mentions it in his novel *Ninety-Three*. See page 198 for more on Le Procope.

LAPÉROUSE

51 Quai des Grands Augustins, 6e • 75006 Paris • Tel: (33) 1 43 26 68 04

• *www.laperouse.com*

Hugo frequented the restaurant Lapérouse located in a 17th-century town house along the Seine. The exterior is decorated with colorfully rendered panels while the interior features Belle Époque decor, including a number of opulent private dining rooms. Other notable literary figures who patronized Lapérouse include George Sand, Émile Zola, and Gustave Flaubert.

LE GRAND VÉFOUR

17 Rue de Beaujolais, 1e • 75001 Paris • Tel: (33) 1 42 96 56 27

• *www.grand-vefour.com*

Chandeliers and gilt-edged mirrors create a sumptuous atmosphere at this 18th-century restaurant situated on the edge of the Palais Royal garden. Napoleon and Josephine Bonaparte dined here years before Hugo patronized the regal establishment.

ELSEWHERE IN THE AREA

PANTHÉON

Place du Panthéon, 5e • 75005 Paris • *www.paris-pantheon.fr* • Open daily;
hours vary seasonally

Hugo's remains are interred in this secular temple in the Latin

Enduring Exile

ON DECEMBER 11, 1851, Victor Hugo disappeared from Paris, wearing a disguise and traveling under the pseudonym Jacques Lanvin. The outspoken political critic boarded a train bound for Brussels and began a life of exile.

In his first book, the poetry collection *Odes et Poésies Diverses*, the 20-year-old writer stated, "The poet on earth, a voluntary exile, must console humanity; he must fight injustice." Twenty-six years later, after Louis-Napoleon re-established the monarchy and the government began smashing printing presses, Hugo became a leading voice of opposition and was no longer safe in France.

After arriving in Brussels, Hugo wrote the politically charged tract *Napoléon-le-Petit* (Napoleon the Little), in which he ridiculed the emperor. The pamphlet, printed on thin paper and smuggled into France in sections hidden in the linings of garments and in hollow busts of Louis-Napoleon, was enthusiastically received.

The French government had issued an edict against libel emanating from Frenchmen abroad, and the publication of *Napoléon-le-Petit* made it too dangerous for Hugo's family to remain in France, forcing them to join him in exile. Before leaving Paris, his wife auctioned off their furniture, books, and other possessions, including Hugo's prized antiques collection.

In the ensuing years, Louis-Napoleon made two public appeals for French exiles to return, but Hugo remained steadfast in his convictions. "When freedom returns," he said, "I shall return." The *New York Tribune* declared, "His voice is that of free men everywhere."

During his exile, Hugo lived first in Brussels and then on the British Channel isles of Jersey and Guernsey, returning to France after the fall of Louis-Napoleon's empire in 1870. At the train station in Brussels, as he purchased a ticket to Paris, he confided to a young writer accompanying him, "I have been waiting for this moment for 19 years."

Quarter. The mausoleum's interior is ornamented with columns, murals, and a dome, from which hangs Foucault's famous pendulum.

Those buried in the Panthéon's labyrinthine crypt include Voltaire and Rousseau. Hugo shares cell number XXIV with Émile Zola and Alexandre Dumas in a wing dedicated to "Martyrs of the Revolution."

ST.-SULPICE

Place St.-Sulpice, 6e • 75006 Paris • Tel: (33) 1 46 33 21 78

Hugo married his childhood sweetheart, Adèle Foucher, in this 17th-century cathedral on October 12, 1822. Like Notre-Dame, St.-Sulpice features two bell towers. Among its treasures are a magnificent pipe organ and frescoes by Delacroix in the Chapel of the Holy Angels.

30 RUE DU DRAGON

6e • 75006 Paris

This building in the St.-Germain-des-Prés quarter was the site of 19-year-old Hugo's bachelor lodgings, where an inscription commemorates his stay. (This is a private building and can only be viewed from the outside.)

124 AVENUE VICTOR-HUGO

formerly 130 Avenue d'Eylau, 16e • 75116 Paris

Although the original building has since been replaced, an etching of Hugo's visage memorializes the location of his last residence in Paris. (This is a private building and can only be viewed from the outside.)

FARTHER AFIELD

VICTOR HUGO MUSEUM

Quai Victor-Hugo • 76490 Villequier, France • Tel: (33) 2 35 56 78 31 • *www.museevictorhugo.fr* • Open Wednesday through Monday; closed during lunch and on Sunday mornings

Tragedy touched Hugo's life when his eldest daughter, 19-year-old Léopoldine, drowned in a boating accident in Villequier, France, along with her husband, Charles Vacquerie, who died trying to save her. Hugo was vacationing in Spain and France at the time and learned of their deaths while reading a newspaper. This stately former residence of the Vacqueries pays homage to both families, including Hugo's friend, the writer Auguste Vacquerie.

MAISON LITTÉRAIRE DE VICTOR HUGO

Château des Roches • 45 Rue de Vauboyen • 91570 Bievres, France • Tel: (33) 1 69 41 82 84 • *www.maisonlitterairedevictorhugo.net* • Open Saturday and Sunday afternoons, March through November

This manor house outside Paris, where Hugo and his family often vacationed, belonged to an acquaintance famous for his literary salons. The estate is now a shrine to its famous guest, with original editions of Hugo's works, photographs, and other mementos. A tea room is located in the former music room.

HAUTEVILLE HOUSE

38 Hauteville Street • St Peter Port, Guernsey GY1 1DG • Channel Islands • Tel: (44) 148 172 1911 • *maisonsvictorhugo.paris.fr* • Open April through September, closed one day per week

In a white stone house overlooking the coast on the isle of Guernsey, Hugo spent 14 years of his nearly two-decade exile. He arrived in 1856 and set about decorating the manse with sumptuous wall coverings, mirrors, figurines, and other items he acquired in antiques shops on the island, and the house remains much as Hugo left it. Here he completed *Les Misérables* and wrote the novel *Toilers of the Sea*, in which he included a message to the place and people who sheltered him: "I dedicate this book to the rock of hospitality, to this corner of old Norman land where resides the noble little people of the sea, to the Island of Guernsey, severe and yet gentle." The house was shown to visitors when Hugo was away, and during the summer of 1867, nearly a thousand bibliophiles toured the writer's residence.

More information about Hugo in Guernsey, including guided walks, is available at *www.visitguernsey.com/victor-hugo*.

VICTOR HUGO HOUSE

37 Rue de la Gare • L-9420 Vianden, Luxembourg • Tel: (352) 26 87 40 88
• *www.victor-hugo.lu* (French only) • Closed Mondays

Hugo ventured to this small town in northeast Luxembourg near the German border on numerous occasions, and the house in which he resided on his last stay in 1871 is now a museum honoring him. Looming over the village is Vianden Castle, constructed from the 11th to the 14th centuries and restored in 1977.

THE LEGACY OF *LES MISÉRABLES*: Victor Hugo's *Les Misérables* was an international phenomenon on its publication in 1862. Following an ambitious marketing campaign, the novel was sold in Paris, Amsterdam, London, Madrid, Turin, St. Petersburg, and other cities, and within a decade was published in some 40 countries. Along with *The Hunchback of Notre-Dame*, this epic tale (the manuscript of which was in a trunk that almost went overboard during the writer's move from Jersey to Guernsey) remains Hugo's best-remembered work.

***LES MISÉRABLES* LOCALES IN PARIS:** In the fragrant environs of the **Luxembourg Garden** (6e), where "flower-beds shed forth balm and dazzling beauty," Marius first sees Cosette, who is sitting on a park bench talking with her adoptive father, Jean Valjean. While living in a nearby residence years earlier, Hugo would often stroll the garden and compose poems.

After a student uprising turns violent, Jean Valjean saves the life of the injured Marius by carrying the young man through Paris's sewer system. It's possible to explore this "subterranean labyrinth" at the **Paris Sewers Museum** (Les Égouts de Paris) and, like Hugo's characters, disappear "into the secret trap-door of Paris." Quai d'Orsay, where Pont d'Alma meets the Left Bank, 7e; tickets sold at a freestanding booth • Tel: (33) 1 53 68 27 81 • Closed Thursdays and Fridays and two weeks in January

A Shot in the Dark:

JAMES JOYCE IN DUBLIN, IRELAND

SELECTED WORKS BY JAMES JOYCE
Dubliners (1914)
A Portrait of the Artist as a Young Man (1916)
Ulysses (1922)
Finnegans Wake (1939)
Stephen Hero (1944)

JAMES JOYCE MUSEUM

"I want to give a picture of Dublin so complete that if the city suddenly disappeared from the earth it could be reconstructed out of my book," James Joyce ambitiously confided to a friend while writing his groundbreaking masterpiece, *Ulysses*. And indeed the famed Irish novelist succeeded at this enormous task, despite having written the book from afar several years after forsaking his "dear, dirty Dublin" for life as a nomadic expatriate in 1904.

An imposing stone tower outside of Dublin—today home to the James Joyce Museum—was immortalized in *Ulysses* after the writer's brief and memorable stay there.

Early in Joyce's youth, events conspired to ignite in him a burning sense of injustice and disappointment that would later fuel the indignant passion coursing through his work like the River Liffey flows through Dublin (a river which incidentally became a character in his final novel, *Finnegans Wake*). As a boy of nine, Joyce and his younger siblings were jarred from their comfortable middle-class existence when financial crisis struck due to the spendthrift ways of their father. The family was forced to forsake their large house in an upscale seaside village south of Dublin for humble inner-city lodgings, and young Joyce was temporarily removed from school until tuition money could be cobbled together.

Events in the country's political life also took a turn for the worse when popular Irish Parliament member Charles Parnell (known as "Ireland's Uncrowned King") was persecuted by the moralistic Irish church and citizenry for his adulterous affair with Kitty O'Shea. Subsequently, the failure of Ireland's 1893 home rule bill—which Parnell had staunchly and adroitly campaigned for—was attributed in large part to the politician's deposal. Passage of the bill would have boosted the status of Catholic nationalists like the Joyces, whose fates and fortunes were irrevocably intertwined with the establishment of an Irish Free State.

The precocious nine-year-old Joyce—in a fit of pique—wrote a poem speaking out against Parnell's detractors. Increasingly, as the author entered young adulthood, he came to see the politician's persecution as a gross betrayal by his countrymen that had ruined

Ireland's chances for peaceful independence. In the eyes of Joyce, small-minded prudery had obscured the greater cause of uniting for Irish autonomy. (This same prudery could later be blamed for the belated U.K. edition of *Ulysses* 14 years after its initial publication by Shakespeare and Company in Paris.)

Young Joyce and his father came to associate these political events with the family's reversal of fortunes, perhaps because John Joyce had been dismissed from his government job and received an inadequate pension on which to raise ten children. He was never thereafter regularly employed, and following a series of hasty moves in flight from creditors, the family suffered the final disgrace of taking up residence on the north side of Dublin's River Liffey. The river served as a physical demarcation line between the city's genteel classes and its more hardscrabble inhabitants.

This thrust into the seamier side of life contrasted sharply with the soft-focus world of Joyce's privileged childhood. As he once wrote bitterly to Nora Barnacle, the woman who became his lifelong companion, "How could I like the idea of home? My home was simply a middle-class affair ruined by spendthrift habits." But instead of letting the indignity of the experience cripple him, Joyce, not unlike Charles Dickens before him, made use of it in his work to convey the harsh social and economic realities of his time.

After decades of decline and economic stagnation, Dublin at the turn of the 20th century was a city of grinding poverty and crushing despair. Its traditional industries such as textiles had collapsed, leaving in their wake rampant unemployment. With the wealthy fleeing to the suburbs, the city's elegant Georgian town houses fell into disrepair and became overflowing tenements.

From this cauldron of discontent—both in Dublin and across the country—came the Irish literary revival, a movement led by poet W. B. Yeats that was aimed at fostering national identity by reviving Irish folklore in new artistic works. Joyce largely shunned the flourishing movement, which he saw as insular, provincial, and introverted. He felt literary truth lay not in looking at Ireland through the glorified

For more on Yeats, see pages 39–41.

lens of the past but in examining the modern Irish experience with realistic and unflinching rigor, as he did in his early short story collection *Dubliners*.

Unfortunately, the book hit so close to home that its publisher feared libel suits as well as controversy over passages perceived as indecent, and its publication stalled for nine years. In typical emphatic fashion, Joyce implored the publisher to move forward. "I seriously believe that you will retard the course of civilization in Ireland by preventing the Irish people from having one good look at themselves in my nicely polished looking-glass," the author wrote to his editor in 1906.

It was in this "nicely polished looking-glass" that Joyce strived to reflect the lives of ordinary people and their everyday habitats. As he pointed out in a letter to his brother Stanislaus, "When you remember that Dublin has been a capital for thousands of years, that it is the 'second' city of the British Empire, that it is nearly three times as big as Venice, it seems strange that no artist has given it to the world." It fell to Joyce, then, to undertake the task, and he did so upon a canvas writ large in his epic novel *Ulysses*.

In its pages, he set out to capture the sights, sounds, and smells of Dublin's "dailiest day possible" through the eyes of prototypical Dubliner and middle-aged advertising salesman Leopold Bloom. To avoid confronting his wife about her infidelity, Bloom busies himself with his travels around the city. Over the course of a single day on June 16, 1904 (a date that Joyce chose to mark the occasion of his first outing with Nora Barnacle), Bloom's simple activities, such as breakfasting and attending a funeral, bring his character—and the city he calls home—into focus.

Shortly after the book's publication, Joyce wrote in his notebook, "To-day June 16, 1924 . . . Will anyone remember this date?" A century later, thousands of literary pilgrims set out on the city streets each year on **Bloomsday**—June 16—to celebrate his bourgeois everyman hero by following in Bloom's fictional footsteps.

The hub for all things Joycean is Sandycove Point on the southern edge of Dublin Bay, For more on **Bloomsday**, see page 148.

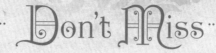

Don't Miss

◉ Courageous swimmers can join members of the Sandycove Bathers Association (established in 1880) at the **"Forty-Foot,"** a deep seawater inlet located on the rocky outcropping in front of the James Joyce Tower. Buck Mulligan braves the same cold waters in the opening chapter of *Ulysses*, and poet W. B. Yeats was allegedly persuaded to take a swim there while visiting the tower's real-life resident, Oliver St. John Gogarty.

◉ At the top of the tower, gaze out to the north on the far side of the bay to **Howth Head**, where Leopold Bloom proposed to his wife, Molly, on the hill that overlooks Dublin Bay.

◉ James Joyce Museum curator Robert Nicholson has held his post since 1978 and is one of the world's foremost Joycean scholars. With his book *The Ulysses Guide: Tours Through Joyce's Dublin*, bibliophiles can undertake their own literary odyssey in the city.

◉ The museum's collection includes two issues of *Time* **magazine** (from 1934 and 1939) featuring James Joyce on the cover. These photography sessions produced the only known color photos of the writer.

◉ In the museum's tall glass display case containing some of James Joyce's personal possessions, don't miss the **necktie once shared by Joyce and Beckett**. "I gathered from Samuel Beckett himself that he was in Paris and needed a tie, so Joyce brought him to his wardrobe and opened it up to display a huge collection of ties, from which he selected one to give to Beckett," says Nicholson. "Beckett presented the tie to the museum in 1979."

site of the 40-foot granite tower where the writer briefly stayed and later chose to set the opening scene of *Ulysses.* The imposing stone structure now houses the **James Joyce Museum,** founded with contributions from filmmaker John Huston and opened on Bloomsday 1962 by Sylvia Beach, the novel's original publisher and owner of the renowned Parisian bookstore Shakespeare and Company. The Joyce Tower is one of a string of similar Martello towers built along the Dublin coast in the early 19th century, designed as defensive forts during the threat of Napoleonic invasion.

For more on Sylvia Beach's Shakespeare and Company, see page 116.

Much later, the tower became a rental residence where Joyce's sometime friend, Irish poet and medical student Oliver St. John Gogarty, took up occupancy in 1904. Gogarty, who had previously loaned the impoverished novelist money, generously extended an invitation for him to stay at the tower. But prior to his arrival, Joyce managed to spoil his reception by insulting his host and the whole of the Irish literary establishment in his satirical poem "The Holy Office," which derided his writerly colleagues for their lack of artistic honesty.

Nonetheless, Gogarty honored his invite to Joyce, but relations between the two in the tower's close confines rapidly deteriorated. Within a week, Joyce was forced to beat a hasty retreat in the middle of the night under mysterious circumstances. Purportedly, Gogarty had fired a gun over his bed in reaction to a nightmare about a crouching panther, causing a shaken Joyce to flee in fright. Shortly thereafter, Joyce and Nora Barnacle made the decision to leave the repressive atmosphere of Ireland for the more enlightened shores of continental Europe, where they were to spend the rest of their lives in self-imposed exile. The reasons for his flight can perhaps best be summed up in the declaration made by his alter ego in Joyce's semiautobiographical *A Portrait of the Artist as a Young Man:* "I will not serve that in which I no longer believe, whether it call itself my home, my fatherland, or my Church."

Though Joyce's stay at the tower may have been brief, the setting and the illustrious incident that transpired there were forever immortalized in *Ulysses,* which recasts Gogarty in the insensitive personage of "stately, plump Buck Mulligan," who condescendingly mocks Joyce's fictional doppelgänger Stephen Dedalus in the book's opening scenes.

Today the 200-year-old tower that hosted the real-life twosome and their fictional counterparts still stands as a stalwart protector of this chapter in Dublin's literary history. Visitors can follow the narrow spiral staircase leading up to the open-air gun platform at the top, where Buck Mulligan and Stephen Dedalus took in the panoramic views of Dublin Bay before breakfast, vividly remarking upon the appearance of "the snotgreen sea. The scrotumtightening sea."

Downstairs, "the gloomy doomed living room of the Tower," known as the "round room," has been refurnished to match its simple appearance as described in *Ulysses*. Two small window slits and a heavy door formerly accessed by way of an outside step-ladder provided "welcome light and bright air" to its occupants, relieving the smoke and fumes spat out by the coal cookstove. A large ceramic black panther stands guard in front of the hearth, alluding to the nightmare Dedalus frets over in the book and which in real life provoked the gun blasts compelling Joyce to leave the tower.

At the bottom of the spiral staircase underneath the round room, visitors can view photographs and portraits of the bespectacled,

IF YOU GO: To get there: Take the DART (Dublin Area Rapid Transit) train from Dublin's Pearse Station and alight at Sandycove (approximately 25 minutes from Dublin city center). The James Joyce Tower and Museum is about a 15-minute walk from the Sandycove station. When exiting the station, turn right, and then left on Link Road. Once you reach the sea front, the tower is visible off to the right. While following the waterfront road toward the tower, keep an eye out for a stone memorial with a quote from *Ulysses* and a tree planted in Joyce's honor. **James Joyce Tower and Museum** Sandycove, County Dublin • Tel: (353) 1 280 9265 • *www.jamesjoycetower.com* • Open daily year-round mustached author along with one of Oliver St. John Gogarty. Several of Joyce's personal possessions are on display at the museum as well, including his prized guitar (he was a renowned music lover), his waistcoat (made by his grandmother), his cigar case (he favored Austrian cheroots known as Virginias), the last cane he used, and his traveling trunk.

An entrance hall at ground level was added to the three-story tower in 1978 to make room for the museum's steadily growing collection of memorabilia, including the voluminous number of letters written by Joyce to his relatives, friends, and publishers. Also on display are rare early copies of *Ulysses,* the most famous being a deluxe edition illustrated by Matisse, which invoked the writer's ire. Rather than illustrating scenes from Joyce's novel, the famed French painter incongruously chose to depict six episodes from Homer's mythical *Odyssey,* whose structure is cleverly paralleled in *Ulysses.* When questioned about his decision, the artist admitted, "*Je ne l'ai pas lu*— I didn't read it."

Among Joyce's writerly compatriots who delved into his famously challenging novel (in which he once boasted of inserting "so many enigmas and puzzles that it will keep the professors busy for centuries") opinion was divided. In a college term paper, future playwright Tennessee Williams summed it up as "a great deal of dullness. Then some dirt. Then more dullness," while young Ernest Hemingway, who was residing in Paris when *Ulysses* was first published, proclaimed it "a most god-damn wonderful book."

Although critical reception to Joyce's work may have been mixed, one truism remained constant throughout his career. Despite having spent most of his adult life abroad, he continued to depend exclusively on the Irish city of his youth—and the ordinary people who populated it—for his subject matter. Rationalizing his single-minded focus, Joyce explained, "If I can get to the heart of Dublin, I can get to the heart of all the cities of the world. In the particular is contained the universal."

Walk in the footsteps of Joyce, Beckett, Shaw, Kavanagh, and other Irish literary greats on the **Dublin Literary Pub Crawl**. See page 155 for more information.

Drink, Dine, and Doze

DAVY BYRNES PUB

21 Duke Street • Dublin 2 • Tel: (353) 1 677 5217 • *www.davybyrnes.com*

In Episode Six of *Ulysses,* Bloom enters this famed "moral pub" owned by eponymous publican Davy Byrne and buoys his flagging spirits with a glass of burgundy and a Gorgonzola cheese sandwich. Today, visitors can do the exact same thing while gazing at murals of Joycean Dublin. Those who don't fancy Gorgonzola can sample regional delights such as smoked Irish salmon, traditional Irish stew, or fish and chips. Playwright Samuel Beckett reportedly lived in an apartment above Davy Byrnes for a short time.

Elsewhere in the Area

DALKEY CASTLE AND HERITAGE CENTRE

Castle Street • Dalkey, County Dublin • Tel: (353) 1 285 8366

• *www.dalkeycastle.com* • Closed Tuesdays

A short distance south of the Joyce Tower lies the Irish Heritage Town of Dalkey, which has many literary associations from past and present. James Joyce taught history in the Clifton School on Dalkey Avenue for a term in 1904 and later had Stephen Dedalus do the same in Episode Two of *Ulysses.*

Other local writers affiliated with the town include Tony Award–winning playwright Hugh Leonard; internationally acclaimed novelist Maeve Binchy; Nobel Prize winner George Bernard Shaw, as well as J. M. Synge, Flann O'Brien, and Samuel Beckett.

For more on George Bernard Shaw, see page 10.

The Dalkey Castle and Heritage Centre, comprising a 15th-century towerhouse, a 10th-century church and graveyard, and a modern exhibition area with a Writers' Gallery, pays homage to the town of Dalkey's medieval history as well as to the literary greats who have walked its streets.

DUBLIN WRITERS MUSEUM

18 Parnell Square • Dublin 1 • Tel: (353) 1 872 2077

• *www.writersmuseum.com* • Open daily

In a stately town house on one of the city's famed Georgian squares, the Dublin Writers Museum traces Ireland's rich literary legacy, starting with storytelling in Celtic times and ending with 20th-century giants Yeats, Joyce, and Beckett. (Look for Beckett's custom-designed telephone with a special button to exclude incoming calls.) Also spotlighted are female Irish wordsmiths like novelist Maria Edgeworth, whose works inspired Sir Walter Scott and Jane Austen, and playwright Lady Augusta Gregory, a co-founder of Dublin's Abbey Theatre.

Upstairs, the Gallery of Writers features an enormous collection of busts and portraits, along with Joyce's beloved piano. A visit here can easily be combined with a stop at the James Joyce Centre (see below), which is approximately two blocks away.

JAMES JOYCE CENTRE

35 North Great George's Street • Dublin 1 • Tel: (353) 1 878 8547

• *www.jamesjoyce.ie* • Open year-round, days and hours vary

This lovingly restored 18th-century Georgian town house is home to the sole remaining item salvaged from Leopold Bloom's now demolished home that formerly stood at 7 Eccles Street—its front door. Writer Patrick Kavanagh said, "I hereby declare this door shut," when he unveiled it on Bloomsday 1967 in its prior location at the Bailey Restaurant on Duke Street. Also on display is the writing desk from the Parisian apartment of Joyce's friend Paul Leon, where the novelist wrote much of his final work, *Finnegans Wake*.

The Joyce Study re-creates the circumstances in which Joyce and Nora lived while the author was working on *Ulysses* in Trieste, Zurich, and Paris from 1914 to 1922. Interactive computers allow visitors to explore the book's content while short documentary films shed light on Joyce's life and the controversy surrounding his famed novel's publication.

Although the writer never lived in this house, it has a Joycean connection that helped save the building from demolition. One of the many real-life Dubliners who peopled the pages of *Ulysses* was Denis J. Maginni, who ran a dance academy here for 15 years. In the Wandering Rocks episode, Joyce depicts Maginni, "professor of dancing &c," as showily attired in a "silk hat, slate frockcoat with silk facings, white kerchief tie, tight lavender trousers, canary gloves and pointed patent boots."

JAMES JOYCE WALKING TOURS

James Joyce Centre • *www.jamesjoyce.ie/events/tours*
• Tours run three times weekly April through September and on Saturdays the rest of the year

The best way to get a sense of the city as Joyce knew it is to take one of the walking tours offered by the James Joyce Centre. Tours vary weekly, and depending on the tour, you may re-trace the Lestrygonians episode of *Ulysses*—in which Leopold Bloom makes his way through the city on his way to the National Library—or visit sights such as the Gresham Hotel, the setting of the final and most memorable scene of the short story "The Dead." Tours depart from the James Joyce Centre and last approximately 90 minutes.

NATIONAL LIBRARY OF IRELAND

Kildare Street • Dublin 2 • Tel: (353) 1 603 0200 • *www.nli.ie*

Episode Nine of *Ulysses* takes place here, and it is also the location where James Joyce ended up after walking all the way to Dublin in the early-morning hours of September 15, 1904, following the shooting incident at the tower. The Library hosts a wide array of events such as lectures, poetry and music recitals, workshops, and children's storytelling sessions.

Bohemian Rhapsody:

FRANZ KAFKA IN PRAGUE, CZECH REPUBLIC

SELECTED WORKS BY FRANZ KAFKA

The Metamorphosis (1915)

The Trial (1925)

The Castle (1926)

Amerika (1927)

Kafka: The Complete Short Stories (1971; several of these
stories were published individually during Kafka's lifetime)

FRANZ KAFKA'S PRAGUE

"Prague does not let go . . . this dear little mother has claws," 19-year-old Franz Kafka wrote to a friend in 1902, vividly capturing the tortuous relationship he had with the city of his birth. Although he may have often dreamed of escape, the "golden city" seemed to exert a magnetic pull on the author, who made no real attempt to abandon it until the final years of his life.

Kafka loved the streets, parks, and palaces of the city, and his yearning to break free had little to do with Prague itself and everything to do with escaping the suffocating presence of his father and his soul-destroying office job. Although the "city of a thousand spires" is not mentioned by name in any of his major works, biographers agree the location is often implied in Kafka's haunting, claustrophobic settings, many of which match descriptions of places he wrote about in diaries and letters. The surreal landscapes and maze of contradictions navigated by his characters are physically embodied in Prague's winding cobblestone streets and its startling juxtapositions of Gothic, Renaissance, baroque, and art nouveau architecture.

While echoes of Kafka now lurk around every corner, during his lifetime the author was little known. The bulk of his writing was published posthumously, and his status as a Jew and native German speaker marked him—and others in his position—as interlopers in their own city. Much like Kafka himself, who struggled to find his place in the world, Prague at the turn of the 20th century was in the throes of an identity crisis. The erstwhile Bohemian capital was home to Czech, German, and Jewish populations, which coexisted uneasily and sometimes violently. Anti-Semitism kept the Jewish minority from being accepted as either purely German or purely Czech, leaving them precariously perched on society's fringes.

Given the divisive cultural climate that surrounded him, it's unsurprising that themes of alienation permeate much of Kafka's writing, particularly his most complex and influential novel, *The Castle*. In the work, a man known only as K. is plunged into a nightmarish world of circuitous logic and Byzantine bureaucracy when he's summoned to work as a surveyor by a castle overlord. Denied access to the mysterious castle officials and unable to confirm if his job even exists, K. finds himself trapped in an unwelcoming purgatory, accepted by neither the villagers nor the castle administrators. A landlady sums up his hopeless position by assailing him, "You are not from the castle; you are not from the village; you aren't anything. Or rather unfortunately, you are something, a stranger, a man who isn't wanted."

While Prague's isolating atmosphere of the period is unmistakably imprinted on *The Castle,* it is unknown whether **Prague Castle** itself— hovering over the city like a vigilant mother—was the inspiration for the novel's physical setting. With origins dating back to the ninth century and a size spanning 110 acres, the sprawling complex—comprising palaces, towers, gardens, a basilica, and a cathedral—is the world's largest medieval castle. Although Kafka briefly lived within its confines in a narrow alley where alchemists plied their craft, he also visited other castles in the Bohemian countryside that may have inspired him.

One component of Prague Castle more definitively linked to Kafka's work is its imposing Gothic cathedral, **St. Vitus**, whose reaching spires give the castle its distinctive profile. It is thought to be here where chapter nine of Kafka's novel *The Trial* unfolds in a shadowy and immense cathedral "bordering on the limit of what human beings could bear."

While Kafka often blurred Prague's physical reality beyond recognition in his writing, he drew more directly on his biographical reality. Max Brod, the author's closest friend and later biographer, noted that "whole chapters of the novels *The Trial* and *The Castle* derive . . . from the atmosphere Kafka breathed in the Worker's Insurance Accident Institute" where the author spent 14 years working as an insurance claims officer. The stagnating case files he handled and his frequent contact with wronged workers inspired the dehumanized worlds and maze-like bureaucratic machinery portrayed in much of his fiction. While the job was necessary to earn a living, he continually resented the time it stole from his real passion: writing. As he lamented in his diary, he led "a horrible double life from which there is probably no escape but insanity."

Kafka's tortured emotional state and the frequent emphasis his writing placed on hopeless conflict against authoritarian oppression was a by-product of his lifelong struggle to gain acceptance from his tyrannical father, Hermann Kafka. As the author wrote in his *Letter to Father,* a hundred-page handwritten missive that he never sent and which was published posthumously: "My writing was all about you; all I did there, after all, was to bemoan what I could not bemoan upon your breast."

His father cast a long shadow over his life, instilling in Kafka immense reserves of self-loathing and doubt, which likely contributed to the depression, neuroses, and physical ailments that plagued him over the years. From an early age, writing was both a respite from his troubles and a vital creative outlet, although Kafka was rarely satisfied with his work and published little during his lifetime.

Kafka idolized poet Johann Wolfgang von Goethe, and in the summer of 1912 he pilgrimaged to Goethe's baroque manse in Weimar, Germany. The renowned poet spent the last 50 years of his life there, until his death in 1832 (Goethe Residence; www.klassik-stiftung.de/en).

He was equally unforgiving with his perceived personal and physical weaknesses, characterizing himself as "fretful, melancholy, untalkative, dissatisfied, and sickly" as well as downright repulsive. "I was afraid of mirrors because . . . they showed an inescapable ugliness," he wrote in a 1911 diary entry. Belying his sense of defectiveness, friends found him reserved yet brimming with passionate intensity and witty, incisive observations. Women were frequently drawn to him and he was engaged three times (twice to the same woman). Despite his romantic aspirations, Kafka never started a family of his own, declaring himself "spiritually incapable of marrying." Instead, the permanent bachelor spent 31 of his 40 years living with his parents in apartments surrounding Prague's **Old Town Square**.

"My whole life is confined to this small circle," he once mused to his Hebrew teacher as he surveyed what is arguably Europe's most architecturally stunning plaza. Built on the site of Prague's medieval marketplace, Old Town Square has remained largely unchanged for centuries. The Gothic town hall and its astronomical clock marking time with mechanical apostles, the spiky-topped Our Lady Before Týn Church, and the effusive baroque Kinský Palace were among the distinctive icons that formed the boundaries of Kafka's front yard.

The author was born in a modest tenement on the square's northwest corner on the fringes of Prague's Jewish quarter. During his youth, the overcrowded buildings and narrow streets of what was then a Jewish ghetto were razed in the interest of sanitation. In their place, modern art nouveau apartment buildings were constructed to house the city's newly emergent bourgeoisie. Although only echoes of the old quarter remained, Kafka eloquently noted in conversation with a friend that "the dark corners, the mysterious little lanes, blind windows, filthy courtyards, noisy taverns, and secluded bars still live within us."

Though later in his life Kafka's search for an identity would lead him to Zionism (a then nascent movement stemming from the ongoing discrimination faced by European Jews), the Kafkas were only a nominally observant Jewish family. On holy days, they would attend the nearby **Altneuschul** (Old-New Synagogue), built in the 13th century.

As Hermann Kafka's successful haberdashery business flourished, the Kafkas moved several times to increasingly grander quarters, often around the square's perimeter. For seven years, the Kafkas resided at the Renaissance-era **House U Minuty** ("at the minute") on the square's southwest side, today part of Old Town Hall. Some of the author's earliest memories are of his dreaded daily sojourn from this apartment to the German elementary school accompanied by the family's cook, one of several servants charged with his care while his parents were consumed with running their business.

Walking through the square and along Týnská Street, the cook, "a small, dry, skinny, sharp-nosed, hollow-cheeked woman," would torment her young charge by threatening to inform his teachers of wrongdoings. In a letter to a friend decades later, Kafka recalled how in terror, he "held onto the doorframes of shops, onto the cornerstones . . . [while] she dragged me further, assuring me that even this she was going to report to the teacher." Although he dreaded school because he feared failure, his worries were unfounded and he eventually went on to graduate from the German university in Prague.

While he may have characterized himself as melancholy, Kafka was far from a brooding, reclusive writer. With his best friend Max Brod and other close acquaintances, he frequented the city's many vibrant cafés, lecture halls, and theaters. As a respite from the indoor drudgery of his office work, he loved taking long walks through the city, delighting in its parks and architectural treasures. On one such walk, he lingered over the baroque statues of saints lining the Charles Bridge and noted in his diary the perfection of "the remarkable light of the summer evening together with the nocturnal emptiness of the bridge." (The same bridge his alter ego Josef K. would later be led across before his execution in *The Trial*.)

As he entered his 30s, Kafka began to seek independence by living on his own for the first time, but the noise in two successive apartments drove him to distraction. In the summer of 1916, he embarked on an apartment hunt with his favorite sister, Ottla. "I didn't anymore believe in the possibility of real peace," wrote the author, who suffered from insomnia and an extreme sensitivity to noise, "but all the same I went in search of it." The search eventually ended at **22 Golden Lane**, a tiny cottage on the grounds of Prague Castle. Although he initially found the house "small, dirty and uninhabitable," Ottla rented it and Kafka was soon won over by its charms, writing excitedly to his then fiancée: "It suits me down to the ground. To sum up its advantages: the lovely way up to it, the quiet there . . . it is something special to have one's own house, to shut in the face of the world the door, not of your room, not of your apartment, but of your own house."

Kafka continued to write at Golden Lane after moving into a larger and more modern apartment at the Schönborn Palace (today the location of the U.S. embassy) on Tržiště Square. Here the author suffered a hemorrhage that marked the beginning of his battle with tuberculosis. Over the next seven years, his rapidly deteriorating health necessitated lengthy leaves of absence from his job, and he spent increasing amounts of time away from Prague convalescing in sanatoriums.

It wasn't until two years before his death that Kafka began work in earnest on his masterpiece *The Castle,* which was never completed. In the final year of his life, he decamped to Berlin and felt, at last, that he had escaped his demons. "I have slipped away from them," he wrote to Max Brod. "This moving to Berlin was magnificent, now they are looking for me and can't find me, at least for the moment."

But Kafka's newfound peace was short-lived. The tuberculosis soon spread to his larynx, making eating and speaking increasingly difficult. Demonstrating his typical dark humor even while wracked with pain on his deathbed, he implored his doctor, "Kill me, otherwise you are a murderer." He passed away in an Austrian sanatorium on June 3, 1924, remaining in many ways as enigmatic as *The Castle* itself, which stopped mid-sentence with no definitive ending.

Even such an ambiguous sense of closure would not have been possible if Kafka's dramatic instructions had been carried out: "Dearest Max, my last request: Everything I leave behind me . . . in the way of diaries, manuscripts, letters, sketches, and so on, [is] to be burned unread." Fortunately, Brod overrode this directive, believing that his friend's merciless self-critical nature was behind the request, and he proceeded with the publication of Kafka's three unfinished novels: *Amerika, The Trial,* and *The Castle.*

Today, Prague's **Franz Kafka Museum** continues the work of Brod and others who refused to let Kafka slip anonymously into the night. Reflecting the dichotomies of the author himself, the exhibition is divided into two spheres. The first, "Existential Space," brings Prague's influence on Kafka into focus through a chronology of manuscripts, photos, and correspondence. The second space, "Imaginary Topography," invites visitors to go underground into a bleak and hallucinatory Prague as seen from Kafka's point of view, re-created through an interplay of images, sound, light, and larger-than-life installations such as rows of filing cabinets.

The museum peels back layers of enigma surrounding Kafka's life and work, demonstrating why he—much like Prague

Kafka's unfinished novel *Amerika,* a coming-of-age story of an immigrant in the land of opportunity, was heavily influenced by Dickens's *David Copperfield.* For more on Charles Dickens, see pages 228–43.

itself—defies easy categorization. One indisputable truism remains, as a friend of the author eloquently observed: "Kafka was Prague and Prague was Kafka. Never had it been Prague so perfectly, so typically, as during Kafka's lifetime, and never would it be so again."

Drink, Dine, and Doze

CAFÉ LOUVRE
Národní třída 22, New Town • Prague 1, 110 00

• Tel: (420) 2 2393 0949 • *www.cafelouvre.cz/en*

This Parisian-style café has been a gathering center for the Prague literati since 1902. Kafka often met with others in the city's literary circle here, including his closest friend, Max Brod.

CAFÉ SLAVIA
Smetanovo nábřeží 2, New Town • Prague 1, 110 00

• Tel: (420) 2 2421 8493 • *www.cafeslavia.cz*

During the Communist era, this Viennese-style art deco coffeehouse became a meeting place for Prague intellectuals, including playwright and future president Václav Havel.

IF YOU GO: Housed on the left bank of the Vltava River in the shadow of both Prague Castle and the Charles Bridge, the Franz Kafka Museum has a number of items not to be missed:

◉ The last known photograph of Kafka, dating from 1923–24
◉ The last letter Kafka wrote to his parents, the day before he died
◉ The original handwritten manuscript pages from *The Trial* and *The Castle*
◉ Kafka's haunting inkblotlike drawings, discovered in the 1960s, capturing scenes from *The Trial* that convey the utter hopelessness of Josef K.'s situation

Franz Kafka Museum Cihelná 2b, Malá Strana • Prague 1, 118 00

• Tel: (420) 2 5753 5507 • *www.kafkamuseum.cz* • Open daily

Don't Miss

⊙ Follow in Kafka's footsteps on the **Franz Kafka Walking Tour** offered by Prague Special Tours (*www.prague-special-tours.com*). Alternatively, visit the Kafka-related sites listed below at your own pace. (All are private properties viewable only from the exterior.)

⊙ **Franze Kafky 3** (formerly U Radnice 5), Old Town Square: Kafka was born here on July 3, 1883. Located on the ground floor is a tiny Kafka exhibition.

⊙ **Sixt House,** Celetná 2, Old Town Square: The Kafka family lived in this medieval building from 1888 to 1889.

⊙ **House U Minuty** ("at the minute"), StaromĐstské námĐsti 2, Old Town Square: The Kafka family had an apartment here from 1889 to 1896. Adorning the facade are beautiful Renaissance-era murals.

⊙ **The House at the Three Kings,** Celetná 3: The Kafkas lived on the first floor of this Gothic building for nearly ten years, and it was here that Kafka first began writing.

⊙ **House at the Unicorn,** StaromĐstské námĐsti 18, Old Town Square: The home of Berta Fanta, a pharmacist's wife who played a key role in Prague's turn-of-the-20th-century cultural life by hosting salons where intellectuals such as Kafka and Max Brod gathered.

⊙ **Franz Kafka Monument:** Located on the border of Prague's Jewish quarter, this 12-foot-tall bronze statue of a headless figure with Kafka sitting on its shoulders was inspired by the author's early short story "Description of a Struggle."

Elsewhere in the Area

22 GOLDEN LANE
- Prague Castle, Hradcany • Prague 1, 119 08
- Tel: (420) 224 373 368 • *www.hrad.cz/en*

Only 11 of the original 24 toy-like houses remain on this narrow cul-de-sac in Prague Castle where alchemists worked in the 16th century. Number 22 is the small cottage that Kafka's beloved sister Ottla rented and which he used as a quiet retreat to write. Today the ground floor houses a small bookshop.

ST. VITUS CATHEDRAL
- Prague Castle, Hradcany • Prague 1, 119 08
- Tel: (420) 224 373 368 • *www.hrad.cz/en*

Prague's largest cathedral, founded in 1344, is presumed to be the locale where chapter nine of *The Trial* is set. Hans Christian Andersen visited in 1841 and spoke of it wondrously: "Aloft on the mountain, with prospect over city, river, and wood-grown isles, lies old Hradschin [Prague Castle]. The church here contains the body of Saint Nepomuk in a magnificent silver coffin. What pomp within, what splendid scenery without!"

OLD-NEW (ALTNEUSCHUL) SYNAGOGUE
- Červená Námĕsti • Prague 1, 110 00 • *www.synagogue.cz*
- Closed Saturdays

Dating from the 13th century, this vaulted medieval synagogue is the oldest in Europe still in active use. Kafka "yawned and dozed away the many hours there" as a young boy with his father on holy days.

NEW JEWISH CEMETERY (NOVÝ ŽIDOVSKÉ HŘBITOVÝ)
Izraelská Žižkov • Prague 3, 130 00 • Tel: (420) 2 2623 5216 • Closed Saturdays

Kafka is buried at plot number 137 along with his parents in this large cemetery that was opened in 1890 on the outskirts of Prague.

FARTHER AFIELD

TEREZÍN

Czech Republic 411 55 • Tel: (420) 4 1678 2227 • *www.terezin.cz/en*

Forty miles northwest of Prague, the town of Terezín (also known by its German name Theresienstadt) was the site of a Gestapo concentration camp in World War II. Of the 144,000 Jews sent there, including Kafka's favorite sister, Ottla (who later died at Auschwitz), only 17,000 survived.

Kafka's two other sisters were transported to Poland's Łódź ghetto, where they are thought to have perished with their families. Kafka's parents passed away a decade before the war's outbreak and were spared the same grim fate as their daughters.

Organized excursions to Terezín can be booked through the tourist office or, alternatively, public buses leave from Prague's Florenc station.

THE PAGES OF PRAGUE: While echoes of Kafka permeate Old Town, just over the Charles Bridge in the shadow of Prague Castle lies the rich literary territory of his predecessor Jan Neruda, known as "the Czech Dickens." Neruda embraced realism and immortalized the streets, houses, and people of the Little Quarter (Malá Strana) where he grew up while poking fun at the Prague bourgeois and promoting the rebirth of Czech nationalism. Today the narrow cobblestone street leading up to Prague Castle has been renamed **Nerudova Street** in honor of the writer, who lived at number 47 in the **House at the Two Suns**.

Much of the work of later Czech writers was influenced by the country's turbulent post–World War II politics both before and during the Communist era, including the early work of exiled existentialist Milan Kundera and famed dissident Václav Havel, whose absurdist plays often satirized Communist bureaucracy.

Family Ties:

LOUISA MAY ALCOTT IN CONCORD, MASSACHUSETTS

SELECTED WORKS BY LOUISA MAY ALCOTT

Flower Fables (1854)

Hospital Sketches (1863)

Moods (1864)

Little Women (1868)

Little Men (1871)

Work: A Story of Experience (1873)

Jo's Boys and How They Turned Out (1886)

The Inheritance (written 1849, discovered and published 1997)

Orchard House

After the publication of Louisa May Alcott's *Little Women* in 1868, curiosity-seekers descended on the small town of Concord, Massachusetts, to see the locale depicted in the popular novel—and perhaps catch a glimpse of its author. The boldest bibliophiles made their way to **Orchard House**, the Alcott family home, where publicity-shy Louisa would sometimes pretend to be a servant when she answered the door.

Home to Louisa May Alcott, Orchard House in Concord was the setting for her novel *Little Women.*

Present-day travelers to Orchard House will find a warm welcome as they immerse themselves in the life and times of Meg, Jo, Beth, and Amy March, the beloved characters in *Little Women*. It was here in this modest, brown clapboard dwelling on Concord's Lexington Road that Louisa penned her semiautobiographical novel 150 years ago. Her fictional portrayal of the Marches mirrors many of her experiences growing up in 19th-century New England, and *Little Women* aficionados will find much about Orchard House that is familiar.

Louisa drew heavily on her family members and their home for details about the characters and the setting, and the similarities between the Alcotts and the imagined Marches are striking. Eighty percent of the furnishings and possessions in Orchard House belonged to the Alcotts, blurring the line between fact and fiction. Indeed, it seems as if Louisa and her sisters might, at any moment, enter a room and entertain visitors with one of their lively dramatic performances. Or it could just as easily be the outspoken, tomboyish Jo, Louisa's alter ego in *Little Women,* who takes to "the boards." Louisa worked her love of theatricals into the story line, making for several memorable scenes as aspiring writer Jo pens, directs, and acts in the plays along with her three siblings—whose real-life counterparts were Louisa's sisters Anna, Elizabeth, and May. (Sadly, Elizabeth Alcott never lived at Orchard House. She died from the lingering effects of scarlet fever shortly before her family took up residence in their new home.)

Louisa's youngest sister, May, was an artist (like *Little Women's* Amy), and the first glimpse of the house's interior begins in what was once her art studio. There, a short film provides an overview of the family and their place in Concord's vibrant history. Before becoming a haven for the leading literati of the mid-1800s, this colonial-era town played a pivotal role during the Revolutionary War. It was here that American patriots clashed with British troops at the town's North Bridge in 1775, igniting the first battle of the Revolutionary War with what Concord resident Ralph Waldo Emerson later referred to as "the shot heard round the world" in his poem "Concord Hymn."

Emerson, whose grandparents had made their home in Concord, settled there in 1834, and he in turn drew other writers and intellectuals to the bucolic town 20 miles west of Boston. Collectively they became known as the New England transcendentalists, and their predominant belief was that one could achieve a higher level of spirituality through nature and reason.

For more about philosopher and writer Ralph Waldo Emerson, see pages 62–64.

The transcendentalists advocated nonconformity and being true to one's self, a sentiment embraced by one of the figures Emerson convinced to move to Concord—Louisa's father, educator and philosopher Amos Bronson Alcott, whose penchant for nonconformity regularly left him unemployed and his family in dire financial straits. The Alcotts moved frequently in Massachusetts and neighboring states according to the dictates of teaching opportunities for Bronson, and they lived in Concord on two separate occasions during Louisa's childhood.

"Wise men and excellent women have no right to live elsewhere," Bronson once declared about Concord, and in 1858 he and his family settled permanently in the town. The purchase of Orchard House was a turning point for the Alcotts, proving to be the transient family's most permanent home. "Much company to see the house. All seem to be glad that the wandering family is anchored at last. We won't move again for twenty years if I can help it," wrote 26-year-old Louisa in her journal, a practice she began at age 10 and continued until her death at 55. Louisa did indeed live at Orchard House for two decades, dividing her time between nearby Boston, where she sought solitude to write, and her family's residence.

Orchard House is a stone's throw from the abodes once occupied by Alcott family friends Emerson and Nathaniel Hawthorne. These notables, along with Concord native Henry David Thoreau, were among the numerous guests who called at Orchard House, especially on Mondays when the Alcotts regularly entertained. At these festive gatherings, guests were treated to merriments like singing, storytelling, charades, and plays put on by Louisa and her sisters.

Readers of Louisa's illustrious tale will recognize the dining room where the March sisters, too, staged their dramatic performances; the bedroom Jo shared with Meg; and the parlor, "a comfortable old room" where "the fire crackled cheerfully" and the siblings sewed, sang, and read aloud. Each room holds a wealth of secrets that will fascinate devotees of *Little Women* and make those new to the book eager to read the story. On the kitchen table is a breadboard decorated with the image of the Italian artist Raphael, a design created by using a hot instrument to burn the wood (a technique called pyrography, or "poker sketching," which Amy uses in the book, leaving her family in fear she'll burn down the house). A cabinet in Louisa's bedroom holds a copy of Dickens's *The Pickwick Papers*, which inspired the March sisters' secret society, The Pickwick Club. In May's room is a trunk of props and costumes like the ones used by the March girls to enact their dramas, including the pair of russet-colored leather boots Jo wears to portray the hero Roderigo in the opening chapters of *Little Women*.

As Elizabeth (Lizzie) Alcott's health declined, Louisa wrote the poem "Our Angel in the House" in tribute to her sister, praising her "cheerful, uncomplaining spirit." She later recast Lizzie as *Little Women's* Beth.

Modern-day guests at Orchard House who are familiar with *Little Women* will undoubtedly relate to how Louisa felt when visiting London in 1865. "I felt as if I'd got into a novel while going about in the places I'd read so much of," she recorded in her journal after seeing Westminster Abbey and other sites depicted in the works of writers she admired, including Charles Dickens.

Along with a three-dimensional tour through the pages of *Little Women*, visitors to Orchard House are privy to intriguing details about the author, her family, and their home. For instance, Louisa disliked seeing herself in portraits and once quipped, "My pictures are never successes. When I don't look like a tragic muse, I look like a smoky relic of the Great Boston Fire." Her mother was one of the nation's first paid social workers, and her amateur architect father attached a smaller building onto the main residence of Orchard House.

The Alcotts were a civic-minded family, and Louisa was a nurse during the Civil War, traveling to Washington, D.C., to minister to Union troops. Her wartime correspondence to her family became the basis for the nonfiction book *Hospital Sketches*. Later Louisa chose to open *Little Women* during the Civil War, with the four March sisters eagerly awaiting word from their father, who is serving as a Union chaplain in the nation's capital. During her time as a nurse, Louisa was stricken with life-threatening typhoid fever. Doctors treated her with calomel, a common remedy of the period that contained mercury. The mercury poisoned her system and left her in frail health for the rest of her life.

The abolitionist movement and women's suffrage were two causes the Alcotts heartily championed. A century after colonists rebelled against the excessive taxation placed on them by the British crown, Louisa campaigned against what she considered taxation without representation. As a wage-earning, tax-paying citizen, she thought it unjust that she was denied the right to vote. Her determination for reform paid off, and in March 1881, Louisa and 20 other women cast their votes in the Concord school committee elections.

The Alcotts continued to struggle financially throughout the years, often relying on the generosity of family and friends (including Emerson, who contributed to the purchase of Orchard House) to make ends meet. Louisa, who never married, was devoted to her parents and sisters and determined to care for them. She worked a variety of jobs—such as teacher, governess, seamstress, and household servant—to help support the family. She also wrote voraciously, penning children's stories, poems, romances, and gothic tales, many of which were sold to popular magazines and printed anonymously or under a pseudonym. In 1854, she published her first book, *Flower Fables,* a collection of fairy tales she had written when she was 16 for one of Emerson's young daughters.

Louisa's first novel, *Moods,* appeared in 1864, and it failed to garner much support from either critics or the reading public. This lackluster response was due in part to the novel's unconventional ideas about marriage, most notably Louisa's disregard of the traditional view that a married woman must devote herself fully to domestic duties at the expense of self-expression. As she wrote in her journal, "It was meant to show a life affected by *moods,* not a discussion of marriage, which I knew little about, except observing that very few were happy ones." The story's rival suitors, who vie for the affections of a passionate tomboy, are believed to be modeled on Ralph Waldo Emerson and Henry David Thoreau.

Four years later, in 1868, Louisa was approached by a publisher to write a book for girls, an idea she initially resisted. "I plod away, though I don't enjoy this sort of thing," she wrote in her journal after beginning work on what was to become *Little Women.* "Never liked girls or knew many, except my sisters; but our queer plays and experiences may prove interesting, though I doubt it." This time Louisa was determined that her novel be free of controversy in the hopes of greater commercial success—and subsequent financial reward for her family. "My next book shall have no *ideas* in it, only facts, and the people shall be as ordinary as possible, then critics will say it's all right," Louisa recorded in her journal after the publication of *Moods.* Decidedly not idea-free and with characters that many readers would disagree are ordinary, *Little Women* was a tremendous success, selling out its first print run in four weeks. Its publication earned Louisa, who was then 36, not only lasting fame but the monetary means to pay off her family's debts and ensure their financial security.

Little Women would never have been written, though, if Louisa had taken the advice of another publisher, James T. Fields. "Stick to your teaching, you can't write," he told the would-be novelist and then loaned her $40 for classroom supplies. "Being willful," Louisa recounts in her journal, she had a ready reply for Fields. "I won't teach, and I can write, and I'll prove it." Prove it she did. With money earned from the sale of *Little Women,* Louisa repaid her debt to Fields, who admitted he had missed the mark about her writing ability. The novel was so well received that Louisa was asked to write a sequel, and in 1869, *Good Wives* was published. The two parts were later combined and sold as one volume, and through the years the book has never been out of print. Louisa subsequently wrote two additional volumes featuring March family members, *Little Men* and *Jo's Boys and How They Turned Out.*

Four years before the publication of *Little Women,* Louisa set sail for a long-awaited tour of Europe as a nurse-companion to a young woman. Among the places she visited were Paris, Geneva, Brussels, Frankfurt, and London, where she took in the sights—castles, cathedrals, gardens, and "all manner of haunts of famous men and women" such as Milton's house, Thackeray's childhood home, and Bacon's Walk. A century and a half after Louisa May Alcott delighted in visiting the "haunts" of the writers she so admired, readers can do the same in the place where she found inspiration for *Little Women.*

A LITERARY ROLE MODEL: "All of the girls admired Dickens," wrote Louisa May Alcott in *Little Women* about voracious reader Jo March and her sisters. The British author was one of Louisa's favored scribes, and along with *Little Women* she references him and his literary creations in *Jo's Boys and How They Turned Out.* Louisa would often stage plays she adapted from Dickens's works, and in 1856, her poem "Little Nell"—inspired by the character in *The Old Curiosity Shop*—appeared in a Boston newspaper.

On an 1865 tour of London, Louisa visited Furnival's Inn, where Dickens wrote *The Pickwick Papers,* and attended one of his famous dramatic readings. Five years later she penned in a letter, "We heard of Dickens's death some weeks ago and have been reading notices, etc., in all the papers since . . . I shall miss my old Charlie."

For a literary look at Dickens's London, see pages 228–43.

◉ In Louisa May Alcott's bedroom is a **half-moon-shaped desk** built for her by her father. "It's so simple and small," says Jan Turnquist, executive director of Orchard House, "and yet at that desk she produced such extraordinary work."

◉ Throughout the house are **mythological figures, flowers, angels, and other drawings** Louisa's sister May sketched and painted on the walls and furnishings.

◉ "Christmas won't be Christmas without any presents," Jo March says mournfully in *Little Women*. Despite a lack of funds for gifts, the March sisters still evoke the spirit of the holidays. **December is a festive time to visit Orchard House,** where special weekend revelries include crafts, carols, recipes, and a treasure hunt. (Prepaid reservations recommended.)

◉ Available at the Orchard House gift shop (located in the former summer kitchen and woodshed) is **a recipe for Apple Slump.** The writer affectionately referred to her family's home as Apple Slump for the way its slanting floorboards resembled the uneven surface of a cobbler-like dessert made by her mother. At the time of the Alcotts' residence, the property included several acres of orchards, and in lean times the family dined on apples and water.

◉ On the parlor couch, Jo March (like her creator) used a sausage-shaped pillow as a mood indicator. If it stood on end, she wanted to socialize; on its side meant do not disturb. Replica **"mood pillows"** are for sale in the Orchard House shop.

Drink, Dine, and Doze

COLONIAL INN

48 Monument Square • Concord, MA 01742 • Tel: 800-370-9200

• *www.concordscolonialinn.com*

Located on Concord's main square—where Louisa and her sisters watched Fourth of July parades—the Colonial Inn's original structure dates to 1716 and was once a store and a private residence. Today the inn welcomes travelers to sleep and dine in its historic environs.

WALDEN POND STATE RESERVATION

915 Walden Street • Concord, MA • Tel: 978-369-3254

• *www.mass.gov* • Hours vary seasonally

Pack a picnic and head to Walden Pond. Louisa and her sisters regularly visited the scenic area, and even went on nature walks with naturalist Henry David Thoreau. For more about Thoreau's time at Walden Pond and a replica of his rustic cabin, see pages 64–65.

Elsewhere in the Area

CONCORD MUSEUM

200 Lexington Road • Concord, MA 01742 • Tel: 978-369-9763

• *www.concordmuseum.org* • Open daily; hours vary seasonally

IF YOU GO: Concord is a 40-minute train ride from Boston's North Station, accessible via the MBTA Commuter Rail. Orchard House is a 20-minute walk from the Concord train station. The house is shown by guided tour only. Tickets go on sale daily at opening and are on a first-come, first-served basis. It's advisable to call ahead and inquire about pre-booked groups, which can sometimes limit public tours. **Orchard House** 399 Lexington Road • Concord, MA 01742 • Tel: 978-369-4118 • *www.louisamayalcott.org* • Open daily; hours vary seasonally; closed January 1 through 15

In the kitchen at Orchard House is a hand-drawn survey of the property done by Henry David Thoreau. In the Concord Museum, a room devoted to Thoreau includes some of his surveying equipment, an occupation he undertook to supplement his income as a writer.

Also in the Concord Museum are the original furnishings from Ralph Waldo Emerson's study. While growing up in Concord, Louisa May Alcott was a frequent visitor to the Emerson home and often borrowed books from the writer's collection.

MINUTE MAN NATIONAL HISTORICAL PARK

174 Liberty Street • Concord, MA 01742 • Tel: 978-369-6993
• *www.nps.gov/mima* • Grounds open daily from sunrise to sunset

Concord played a pivotal role during the Revolutionary War, and the town boasts several commemorative landmarks. One is the "Minute Man Statue" created by Daniel Chester French, a memorial viewed by Walt Whitman while on a Concord visit. French, whose works also include the seated figure of Abraham Lincoln in the Lincoln Memorial in Washington, D.C., once received art lessons from May Alcott.

THE WAYSIDE

455 Lexington Road • Concord, MA 01742 • Tel: 978-318-7863
• *www.nps.gov/mima/planyourvisit/placestogo* • Open late June through October

The Alcotts lived at The Wayside (then known as Hillside) during their second tenure in Concord. Louisa and her sister Anna, who had a particular flair for acting, turned the barn on the property into a theater to stage their plays. The structure is now the Visitor Center, where an exhibit presents the history of the house, including a time when the Alcotts sheltered a slave on his way to freedom in Canada. The Wayside is the only National Historic Landmark lived in by three literary families: the Alcotts, Nathaniel Hawthorne, and children's author Margaret Sidney.

SLEEPY HOLLOW CEMETERY

Just east of Concord Center on Route 62 (Bedford Street) • Concord, MA 01742

Louisa May Alcott, along with several of her immediate family members, is buried in Sleepy Hollow Cemetery in a section known as Authors Ridge. Louisa passed away in Boston on March 6, 1888, two days after the death of her father. See page 100 for information about other famous scribes laid to rest in the Concord cemetery.

THOREAU-ALCOTT HOUSE

255 Main Street • Concord, MA 01742

This yellow-hued abode was once home to Henry David Thoreau's family and the location where he died on May 6, 1862. It was later purchased by Anna Alcott, Louisa's sister, and the writer lived here for a time. (This is a private residence and can only be viewed from the outside.)

IN GOOD COMPANY: Ralph Waldo Emerson, Henry David Thoreau, Nathaniel Hawthorne, and the Alcotts all called Concord home. They in turn drew famous figures to the town, among them Margaret Fuller, a journalist and author of the influential work *Woman in the Nineteenth Century*, and poet Walt Whitman. The American bard became acquainted with Bronson Alcott and Thoreau (who declared him a "great fellow") while visiting New York in 1856, a year after the publication of *Leaves of Grass*. On an 1881 visit to Concord, Whitman had tea with Bronson and Louisa, who had been curious to meet the poet.

Novelist and essayist Henry James immortalized Concord in his travelogue *The American Scene*, declaring, "Why, you're the biggest little place in America—with only New York and Boston and Chicago, by what I make out, to surpass you; and the country is lucky indeed to have you."

During his 1904 visit, James also went in search of the **House of the Seven Gables** in Salem, Massachusetts, Hawthorne's birthplace and the location of the dwelling that inspired his gothic tale *The House of the Seven Gables*. For a trip through the seaside city, see pages 306-16. For more about Henry James, see pages 137–40, and for Walt Whitman, see pages 46–48.

FARTHER AFIELD

FRUITLANDS MUSEUM

102 Prospect Hill Road • Harvard, MA 01451 • Tel: 978-456-3924
• *www.fruitlands.org* • Farmhouse, Shaker, and American Indian Museums: Open mid-April through early November; Art Museum and grounds: Open year-round, hours vary seasonally

In 1843, Bronson Alcott, along with his family and a small group of followers, began a utopian community called Fruitlands. Louisa May Alcott used their difficult and sometimes humorous efforts to live off "the fruits of the land" as the basis for the satirical story "Transcendental Wild Oats." The farmhouse where the Alcotts lived is part of the Fruitlands Museum, whose collection also includes Louisa May Alcott's dolls, Henry David Thoreau's writing desk and bookcase, a rare 1850 Shaker apothecary cabinet, and American Indian art and artifacts.

20 PINCKNEY STREET

Boston, MA 02114

In 1852, the Alcotts moved into rented rooms at 20 Pinckney Street in Boston, where today a plaque commemorating Louisa May Alcott hangs on the building's exterior. The writer later purchased a home at **10 Louisburg Square**. (Both are privately owned and not open to the public.)

See page 151 for "The Hub of Literary America," a walking tour highlighting Boston's literary history.

Mysterious Manse:

NATHANIEL HAWTHORNE IN SALEM, MASSACHUSETTS

SELECTED WORKS BY NATHANIEL HAWTHORNE

Fanshawe (1828)

Twice-Told Tales (1837)

Mosses from an Old Manse (1846)

The Scarlet Letter (1850)

The House of the Seven Gables (1851)

A Wonder Book for Girls and Boys (1851)

The Blithedale Romance (1852)

Tanglewood Tales for Girls and Boys (1853)

The Marble Faun (1860)

Our Old Home (1863)

The novels *The Dolliver Romance*, *Dr. Grimshawe's Secret*, and *Septimius Felton* were unfinished at the time of Hawthorne's death and published posthumously.

THE HOUSE OF THE SEVEN GABLES

An imposing dwelling with a "mysterious and terrible past" stands sentry in Nathaniel Hawthorne's *The House of the Seven Gables*. "The aspect of the venerable mansion has always affected me like a human countenance," declares the omniscient narrator of the 19th-century gothic tale. "It was itself like a great human heart, with a life of its own, and full of rich and sombre reminisces. The deep projection of the second story gave the house such a meditative look, that you could not pass it without the idea that it had secrets to keep."

This 17th-century seaside manse in Salem was the inspiration for Nathaniel Hawthorne's The House of the Seven Gables.

The manse that inspired Hawthorne, colloquially known today as the **House of the Seven Gables**, is picturesquely situated on the edge of Salem Harbor—a modern-day reminder of the house's foundation in Salem's maritime past. The oldest surviving 17th-century wooden mansion in New England, it was built in 1668 for Captain John Turner I, a wealthy sailor and merchant who earned his fortune at sea. Two subsequent generations of Turners occupied the house before it was sold to Captain Samuel Ingersoll, whose daughter, Susanna, introduced her cousin Hawthorne to the house he would later immortalize.

Although Hawthorne kept the exact location of his novel's fictional abode vague, historical and geographical details identify the setting as Salem, Massachusetts, where the author lived intermittently for the first 45 years of his life. This coastal town 20 miles north of Boston is best remembered for two particular aspects of its past—the 1692 witchcraft trials and its unrivaled prosperity as a shipping port during the great age of sail in the 18th and 19th centuries.

At the time of Hawthorne's birth on July 4, 1804, Salem was at the height of its affluence as a worldwide shipping center for the luxury trade and was referred to as the "Venice of the New World." Ships clustered along its wharves bearing ivory, silk, wine, coffee, tea, spices such as cinnamon and cloves, and other exotic cargo from distant ports like the West Indies, Africa, Spain, and Arabia.

While the city's wharves no longer bustle with shipping activity, thanks to its exquisitely preserved architecture, Salem retains much of its ambiance from Hawthorne's era. Situated among the grand, Federal-style homes fronting the harbor is the stately **Custom House** where Hawthorne once worked inspecting cargo while employed as surveyor of the port of Salem. His former office with its sweeping view of the harbor is a veritable shrine to the Salem native and can be seen during tours of the Custom House.

One block from the waterfront, Hawthorne was born in a modest abode on Union Street. Purchased by his grandfather, a privateer during the Revolutionary War, the Union Street house has since been moved to the House of the Seven Gables complex. As a child, Hawthorne dreamed of being a sailor, though his mother disapproved. Hawthorne's father, a ship's captain, had died of yellow fever in Suriname when his son was only three years old. Following his father's death, Hawthorne, along with his mother and two sisters, moved in with his mother's family at **10½-12 Herbert Street**, where the future scribe occupied an attic room.

After his graduation in 1825 from Bowdoin College in Maine (where classmates included future U.S. president and lifelong friend Franklin Pierce), Hawthorne returned to Salem. His primary residence for the next decade was the Herbert Street house, which he

WHAT'S IN A NAME?: Nathaniel Hawthorne changed the spelling of his last name from Hathorne after graduating from Bowdoin College in 1825. Some biographers claim he made the change to reflect the pronunciation of the name, while others maintain it was an effort to distance himself from Puritan ancestors he felt had tarnished the family's reputation, including his great-great-grand-father John Hathorne, a judge during the 1692 witchcraft trials, and Hathorne's father, who was known to have persecuted Quakers. Hawthorne's two sisters, Elizabeth and Louisa, followed suit and adopted the new name.

dubbed Castle Dismal, where he spent much of his time reading and writing in his top-floor room. "So much of my lonely youth was wasted here, and here my mind and character were formed," he later wrote to his future wife, fellow Salem resident Sophia Peabody. "I sat a long, long time waiting patiently for the world to know me, and sometimes wondering why it did not know me sooner, or whether it would ever know me at all." During this time Hawthorne had stories and sketches printed in magazines and journals, and he published his first novel, *Fanshawe,* anonymously (per the custom of the time) and at his own expense. The novel was not favorably received, and Hawthorne reportedly burned what copies of it he could find. He eventually abandoned the confines of Castle Dismal to assume the editorship of the *American Magazine of Useful and Entertaining Knowledge* in Boston in 1836.

Solitude was a lifelong habit of the shy and sometimes moody Hawthorne, who often refused social invitations. Hawthorne confided to Sophia that "lights and shadows are continually flitting across my inward sky, and I know neither whence they come nor whither they go; nor do I inquire too closely into them." Combined with his striking good looks, Hawthorne's aloof demeanor sometimes served to arouse interest in the enigmatic author rather than act as a deterrent. Herman Melville once called Hawthorne "the shyest grape," and British scribe Anthony Trollope reportedly proclaimed the tall, dark-haired author "the handsomest Yankee that ever walked the planet."

Hawthorne met his future wife at the Peabody family's Salem home, located at **54 Charter Street**, which he later used as a model for residences in his novels *The Dolliver Romance* and *Dr. Grimshawe's Secret.* Hawthorne had been invited to call at the Peabody house by Sophia's eldest sister, Elizabeth Palmer Peabody, who was active in literary and intellectual circles and had heard about the young author after the publication of his well-received story collection, *Twice-Told Tales,* in 1837.

Adjacent to the former Peabody home is a place Hawthorne knew well: the **Charter Street Cemetery**, the city's oldest graveyard. The writer often rambled through the burial ground during his frequent solitary strolls around Salem and endowed several of his characters with names he saw on headstones, including Dr. John Swinnerton in *The House of the Seven Gables*. Eight of Hawthorne's ancestors are laid to rest in the Charter Street Cemetery, among them his great-great-grandfather John Hathorne, who acted as a judge in the Salem witch trials. During those dark days, hundreds of people were accused of witchcraft and 20 were ultimately put to death. Hathorne's zealousness during the proceedings earned him the moniker "the hanging judge," and he is represented in the form of the villainous Colonel Pyncheon in *The House of the Seven Gables*.

Hawthorne drew on this chilling time in Salem's history—and the role played by his ancestor—for the foundation of the novel's story line. During an outbreak of religious fervor gone awry, Colonel Pyncheon accuses fellow townsman Matthew Maule of being a wizard. Just as victims of the Salem witchcraft trials were sentenced to be hanged at Gallows Hill on the outskirts of town, Maule met the same grisly fate on "the hill of execution."

While some historians have hypothesized that the Salem witchcraft trials can be attributed solely to religious hysteria, Hawthorne sets forth a more pragmatic reason in *The House of the Seven Gables*: greed. Colonel Pyncheon seeks to gain a desirable piece of property owned by Matthew Maule. By instigating Maule's death, he is able to take possession of the land, on which he then builds an extravagant house with seven gables. As he is about to hang, Maule hurls a curse at the colonel, saying, "God will give him blood to drink." The main action in *The House of the Seven Gables* takes place 200 years after Maule meets his unjust end, and as the story unfolds, descendants of both families continue to be affected by the evils of past generations.

Surprisingly, Hawthorne never actually saw the seven gables that characterize his fictional residence. At the time he visited, four of the gables had been removed to reflect current architectural styles, but he learned of its former appearance from his cousin, Susanna, who had inherited the Salem mansion. The abode's original seven-peaked exterior has since been restored, and guided tours of the house relay the histories of the seafaring families who lived there. Aspects relating to the novel it inspired are also highlighted, while various features that have been added to the house aid the imagination in conjuring up Hawthorne's tale. A replica of a cent shop mirrors the one Hepzibah Pyncheon operates in the novel, and a re-creation of Maule's Well is situated in the colonial-style gardens bordering the house (although the well is, in fact, too close to the sea to have provided fresh water).

The cadence of the phrase "seven gables" intrigued Hawthorne. "The expression was new and struck me very forcibly," he penned in a letter to an acquaintance. "I think I shall make something of it." The vivid impression the house had made on Hawthorne was crucial; at the time he wrote the novel, he was no longer residing in Salem but rather in the Berkshire Mountains in western Massachusetts. There he drew on his memories of the house to create an enigmatic backdrop that suited the fantastic and supernatural elements of his story, like a centuries-old family curse, ill-gotten land on which pristine well water inexplicably turns "hard and brackish," and a mirror "fabled to contain within its depths all the shapes that had ever been reflected there."

In a January 1851 letter to his publisher, Hawthorne wrote, "My House of Seven Gables is, so to speak, finished; only I am hammering away a little on the roof, and doing a few odd jobs that were left incomplete." Hawthorne finished construction on the tale, and *The House of the Seven Gables* was published in April of that year. Following on the heels of his enthusiastically received novel *The Scarlet Letter* (which For more about Henry James, see pages 137–40. Henry James declared "the finest piece of imaginative writing yet put forth in this country"), it cemented Hawthorne's reputation as a preeminent writer of the day.

It was the publication of *The Scarlet Letter* in 1850 that inadvertently led to Hawthorne's final departure from Salem, and the writer was never again to reside in the city of his birth. An essay included in the volume with the novel, titled "The Custom-House," ignited the ire of many of Salem's residents. Hawthorne had used his pen and wit to skewer the city officials and partisan politicians who were behind

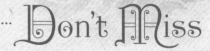

Don't Miss

◉ October is a spookily festive time to visit the House of the Seven Gables when **two dramatic events** take place. During the "Spirits of the Gables," the novel's characters come to life in the house. At the Nathaniel Hawthorne Birthplace, "Legacy of the Hanging Judge" reenacts the Salem witch trials, highlighting the part played by the writer's ancestor. Tickets are required and can be purchased at *www.7gables.org.* (Be sure to plan your trip early. Salem is a popular Halloween destination.)

◉ Stroll through the **beautiful gardens** next to the House of the Seven Gables. In the novel, Hawthorne devotes an entire chapter to "The Pyncheon Garden."

◉ The **Nathaniel Hawthorne Memorial**, a bronze statue honoring Salem's literary son, was dedicated to the author in 1925 (Hawthorne Boulevard between Charter and Essex Streets).

◉ Download a free copy of **Nathaniel Hawthorne's Salem: A Walking Tour of Literary Salem** at *www.nps.gov/sama/planyourvisit/brochures.htm.* Three self-guided walking tours illuminate different aspects of the writer's life in Salem—Relations and Relationships, Salem in Print, and the Custom House. They include anecdotes about Hawthorne and highlight points of interest, such as **14 Mall Street**, his last residence in Salem and the location where he wrote *The Scarlet Letter*, and the Greek Revival–style city hall, which appears in the short story "The Sister Years."

◉ **Two "secret" rooms** in the oldest part of the House of the Seven Gables, which dates to 1668, are set to be unveiled. Never before seen by the public, the chambers are expected to open in 2018 to coincide with the 350th anniversary of the house's construction.

his dismissal from the Salem Custom House in 1849 after a change in political regimes. The *Salem Register* accused Hawthorne of being mean-spirited and took him to task for airing his grievances in public.

Hawthorne wrote to his friend, fellow Bowdoin College alumnus and United States Navy officer Horatio Bridge, that he had caused "the greatest uproar that had happened [in Salem] since witch times." Hawthorne added, "If I escape town without being tarred-and-feathered, I shall consider it good luck." The author went on to use his main adversary in the Custom House incident, the Reverend Charles Wentworth Upham, as a partial model for *The House of the Seven Gables'* Judge Jaffrey Pyncheon, a man whose pleasing outward appearance and silver tongue conceal a heart filled with malice and greed. While "The Custom-House" sparked a firestorm of controversy, *The Scarlet Letter* simultaneously received rave reviews, including one in the *Salem Gazette* that declared the novel "thrilling."

Today it has endured as Hawthorne's most famous work, but the author believed *The House of the Seven Gables* to be the better book (and initial sales exceeded those of *The Scarlet Letter*). He confided to Bridge, "I feel that portions of it are as good as anything I can hope to write." For more about Longfellow, see pages 52–54. Henry Wadsworth Longfellow, another former classmate from Hawthorne's alma mater, called the novel "a weird, wild book, like all he writes."

By far the biggest supporter of Hawthorne's literary endeavors was his wife, Sophia. When he lost his job at the Salem Custom House, she responded with characteristic enthusiasm: "Oh, then, you can write your book!" A year later, that book became *The Scarlet Letter*.

Hawthorne is believed to have paid tribute to Sophia (whose pet name was Phoebe) in the personage of *The House of the Seven Gables'* Phoebe Pyncheon, whose cheer infuses the dreary manse with a ray of sunshine and helps rescue its inhabitants from the grip of the past. After Hawthorne read Sophia the last pages of the haunting tale, she issued a prediction for future readers that has been borne out: "How you will enjoy the book, its depth of wisdom, its high tone, the flowers of Paradise scattered over all the dark places."

Drink, Dine, and Doze

···

MORNING GLORY BED & BREAKFAST

22 Hardy Street • Salem, MA 01970 • Tel: 978-741-1703 • www.morningglorybb.com

You can't lodge any closer to the famed gabled dwelling. This lovely bed-and-breakfast is located in a circa 1808 Georgian Federal building across the street from the House of the Seven Gables complex.

TURNER'S SEAFOOD

43 Church Street • Salem, MA 01970 • Tel: 978-745-7665

• www.turners-seafood.com/salem

This restaurant is housed in a historic building that was once home to the Salem Lyceum, a venue for public performances where Hawthorne, who served as corresponding secretary from 1848 to 1849, invited his friends Thoreau and Emerson to lecture. (The reticent Hawthorne never spoke at the Lyceum himself.) On February 12, 1877, Alexander Graham Bell made the first public demonstration of the telephone here as well.

IF YOU GO: Salem is 20 miles from Boston and can be reached by rail, bus, or ferry. For train and bus information, visit *www.mbta.com*. The Salem-Boston Ferry (*www.salemferry.com*) runs late May through late October.

The House of the Seven Gables and its grounds constitute a historic district on the National Register of Historic Places. In addition to the House of the Seven Gables (also known as the Turner-Ingersoll Mansion for the seafaring families who lived there), the complex includes several 17th-, 18th-, and 19th-century structures that were moved to this location for preservation, one of which is **Nathaniel Hawthorne's Birthplace.**

The House of the Seven Gables Complex 115 Derby Street • Salem, MA 01970 • Tel: 978-744-0991 • *www.7gables.org* • Open year-round except for the first two weeks in January • House is shown by guided tour, which are offered periodically during the day

VICTORIA STATION

86 Wharf Street • Salem, MA 01970 • Tel: 978-745-3400

• *www.victoriastationsalem.com*

Harborside dining offers views of the Custom House, Hawthorne's onetime place of employment. The restaurant's British decor is a fitting tribute to his stint as U.S. Consul in Liverpool, England.

Elsewhere in the Area

SALEM MARITIME NATIONAL HISTORIC SITE

193 Derby Street • Salem, MA 01970 • Tel: 978-740-1660 • *www.nps.gov/sama*

Guided tours of Salem Maritime National Historic Site locations are offered year-round; times and content vary according to season. Along with the home of Elias Haskell Derby (believed to be the country's first millionaire) and the *Friendship* (a replica of a 1727 merchant sailing ship), tours encompass visits to the following:

◉ **The Custom House**: Hawthorne worked in this wharfside building for nearly four years after being appointed surveyor of the port of Salem. On display in his former office are his walking stick, pen and inkwell, and a hydrometer to measure the alcohol content of wine and spirits (which only the surveyor was authorized to use).

◉ **The Narbonne House**: 19th-century resident Sarah Narbonne operated a cent shop in this home (sections of which date to 1675), such as the one Hepzibah Pyncheon runs in *The House of the Seven Gables*. At the time, cent shops (which sold candy, sewing supplies, dry goods, and other items) were one of the few business opportunities available to women.

CHARTER STREET CEMETERY

Charter Street between Liberty and Central Streets • Salem, MA 01970

Eight of Hawthorne's ancestors are buried in Salem's oldest cemetery (also known as the Old Burying Point), including his great-great-grandfather, the infamous Colonel John Hathorne. Hawthorne died on May 19, 1864, in Plymouth, New Hampshire, while on a trip with his friend Franklin Pierce. For more about his burial place, **Sleepy Hollow Cemetery** in Concord, Massachusetts, see page 100.

EAST INDIA MARINE HALL

East India Square • Salem, MA 01970 • Tel: 978-745-9500 • *www.pem.org* • Closed Mondays (except holidays)

Now part of the **Peabody Essex Museum,** the East India Marine Hall was constructed in 1825 to showcase objects sailors brought back from their global journeys. Hawthorne (whose father was a member of the East India Marine Society) showed the hall to his friends Emerson, Thoreau, Longfellow, and Franklin Pierce.

SALEM MUSEUM

32 Derby Square • Salem, MA 01970 • Tel: 978-998-2094 • *www.thesalemmuseum .org* • Open daily, June 1 through October 31

Located in the Old Town Hall, the Salem Museum presents themed exhibits exploring different aspects of the city's history—including one on Nathaniel Hawthorne that covers his Bowdoin College years, marriage to Sophia Peabody, Salem links, friendship with Herman Melville, and more.

While living in the Berkshire Mountains, Hawthorne became friends with fellow writer Herman Melville, who dedicated *Moby-Dick* to him. For more about Melville, see pages 73–74.

SCHOONER *FAME*

Pickering Wharf Marina • Salem, MA 01970 • Tel: 978-729-7600 • *www.schoonerfame.com* • Operates mid-May through October; ticket booth at Pickering Wharf

Sail from Salem Harbor aboard the schooner *Fame,* a replica of a fishing vessel turned privateer ship during the War of 1812, to which Hawthorne's family had financial ties. Visitors booking tickets in advance should confirm reservations prior to arrival as private parties are occasionally given precedence over reservation holders.

European Days

AFTER FRANKLIN PIERCE WAS ELECTED PRESIDENT, he appointed Nathaniel Hawthorne—his friend, biographer, and Democratic Party supporter—to the post of U.S. Consul in Liverpool, England, in 1853.

Hawthorne's reminisces of his European days are collected in *Passages from the French and Italian Notebooks of Nathaniel Hawthorne* and *Passages from the English Notebooks of Nathaniel Hawthorne*. In these colorfully rendered journals, he recalls literary travels like visiting Shakespeare's home in Stratford upon Avon, England, and Sir Walter Scott's manor house, Abbotsford, in Scotland.

See pages 5–8 for more about Stratford-upon-Avon and pages 14–15 for Abbotsford.

After resigning as consul in 1857, Hawthorne and his family headed for the European continent, where they resided primarily in Rome. His Italian sojourn became the basis for his fourth and last completed novel, *The Marble Faun*. The story's Roman backdrop depicts landmarks like the Capitoline Museums (the setting of the opening scene), the "wooded and flowery" grounds of the Villa Borghese, the Colosseum, the Pantheon, and the Trevi Fountain.

In Florence, the Hawthornes were entertained by Robert and Elizabeth Barrett Browning at the poets' home, Casa Guidi. In the Tuscan countryside they lodged in a villa that was the model for the sprawling estate Monte Beni in *The Marble Faun*. Hawthorne wrote to his publisher, "I hire this villa, tower and all, at twenty-eight dollars a month; but I mean to take it away bodily and clap it into a Romance."

For more about Casa Guidi, the Brownings' Florentine apartment, see pages 182–83.

Hawthorne began outlining *The Marble Faun* while in Tuscany and started writing in earnest after returning to Rome. Although he admitted to having mixed feelings about the Eternal City, it nonetheless made a vivid impression on him. "Now that I have known it once," he penned in his notebook, "Rome certainly does draw into itself my heart, as I think even London, or even little Concord itself, or old sleepy Salem, never did and never will."

FARTHER AFIELD

....

OLD MANSE

269 Monument Street • Concord, MA 01742 • Tel: 978-369-3909
• *www.thetrustees.org* • Open mid-March through December; grounds open daily

After their 1842 wedding, Nathaniel and Sophia Hawthorne lived in the Old Manse, a farmhouse owned by Ralph Waldo Emerson. The collection *Mosses from an Old Manse* contains stories Hawthorne wrote while living in the Concord abode. For more about the Old Manse, see pages 63–64.

THE WAYSIDE

455 Lexington Road • Concord, MA 01742 • Tel: 978-318-7863 • *www.nps.gov/ mima/planyourvisit/placestogo.htm* • Open late June through October

Nathaniel Hawthorne purchased The Wayside (then known as Hillside) from Bronson Alcott in 1852, and he and his family resided there before and after the seven-year period they spent in Europe. Hawthorne made architectural changes to the house, including adding gables and erecting a three-story tower inspired by one he saw at a Tuscan villa. Accessible via a trapdoor, he used the top floor of the tower, which he called a "sky parlor," as his study.

HAWTHORNE HOUSE

Tanglewood • 297 West Street • Lenox, MA 01240 • Tel: 617-266-1200 • *www.bso.org*

The little red house in the Berkshire Mountains where Nathaniel Hawthorne wrote *The House of the Seven Gables* was destroyed by fire and has since been replaced with a replica. It's now part of the Boston Symphony Orchestra's summer performance venue, Tanglewood, which takes its name from Hawthorne's *Tanglewood Tales for Girls and Boys*. The cottage is not open to the public but can be seen on the grounds of Tanglewood near the Lions Gate entrance. The house is viewable from Hawthorne Road, which can be reached via West Street/Route 183.

Island Time:

ERNEST HEMINGWAY IN KEY WEST, FLORIDA

SELECTED WORKS BY ERNEST HEMINGWAY

The Sun Also Rises (1926)

Men Without Women (1927)

A Farewell to Arms (1929)

Death in the Afternoon (1932)

Winner Take Nothing (1933)

Green Hills of Africa (1935)

The Snows of Kilimanjaro (1936)

To Have and Have Not (1937)

For Whom the Bell Tolls (1940)

The Old Man and the Sea (1952)

A Moveable Feast (1964)

Islands in the Stream (1970)

THE ERNEST HEMINGWAY HOME

Hemingway
resided on the
isle from 1928
to 1939—one
of the most
prolific periods
of his life—and
it provided the
backdrop for his
only novel set
in the United
States, *To Have
and Have Not.*

"You'll be crazy about this place when you see it," Ernest Hemingway enthused to his editor Max Perkins in 1931. The author was referring with more than a hint of pride to the two-story Spanish colonial stone house at **907 Whitehead Street** in Key West, Florida—his first home on U.S. soil after spending most of his adult life abroad. Initially, the sun-drenched isle was just a stopover for Hemingway and his pregnant second wife after they decamped from Paris in 1928. But the many pleasures of America's southernmost city quickly seduced him, and it became the only domestic locale from which he lived and wrote for an extended period of time.

Writer John Dos Passos once visited Key West and is said to have recommended it to Old Hem as the perfect place to "dry out his bones" after a blustery Paris winter and a year punctuated by three bouts of flu, an anthrax infection, an eye injury, and an unfortunate run-in with a glass skylight. The sedate pace and tropical climes of Key West—a remote locale then accessible only via train or ferry—was exactly what the doctor ordered. With just 12,000 inhabitants who eked out a living fishing or rum-running from Havana, the eight-square-mile island was far removed from the grand boulevards and smoky nightclubs of Paris.

For more Hemingway haunts at home and abroad, see pages 117–23 and 209–12.

Though Hemingway playfully dubbed it "the St. Tropez of the poor," Key West more than made up for its lack of sophistication with a rough-and-tumble charm that suited him just fine. With four books under his belt, the celebrated 28-year-old author relished his blissful anonymity on Key West and quickly fell in step with the rhythms of island time.

He spent mornings working on his blockbuster semiautobiographical novel, *A Farewell to Arms,* opining to his editor, "I would like to stay right here until it is done as I have been doing so very well . . . it is such a fine healthy life and the fishing keeps my head from worrying in the afternoons when I don't work." More than just a temporary balm, deep-sea fishing in the turquoise waters off Key West and the nearby islands of Bimini and Cuba was to become a lifelong passion. Details of Hemingway's fishing exploits routinely peppered his Key West correspondence over the next several years: "Caught the biggest tarpon they've had down here so far this season," he wrote excitedly to Perkins two weeks after his arrival. "Sixty-three pounds. The really big ones are just starting to come in."

There was no shortage of locals who relished the joys of this competitive pursuit, and Hemingway quickly assembled a motley crew of regulars who fished together in the afternoons and caroused at night. Many became enduring friends, such as speakeasy proprietor Joe Russell (the model for bar owner Freddy in *To Have and Have Not*) and hardware dealer Charles Thompson (who later accompanied Hemingway on safari and became the basis for Karl in *Green Hills of Africa*). His fun-loving group of cronies, along with the steady stream of visitors he entertained—John "Old Muttonfish" Dos Passos, Max "Deadpan" Perkins, and artist Waldo "Don Pico" Peirce—became known as Hemingway's "Key West mob."

While Old Hem initially chartered fishing vessels or relied on the boats of friends, it was only a matter of time before he added the title of "Captain" to his résumé. His new 38-foot pride and joy was christened *Pilar,* an erstwhile nickname for his wife, as well as the name they'd chosen for the daughter they were destined never to have. *Pilar* became an enduring symbol of Papa Hemingway and a steadfast companion for the next 30 years. With his faithful sidekick, he battled fish that were larger than life: a record-breaking 119-pound sailfish, a 540-pound marlin he landed on his 36th

The *Pilar*'s first captain, Carlos Gutierrez, is thought to have provided the early inspiration for Hemingway's 1952 Pulitzer Prize–winning novella *The Old Man and the Sea*. In February 1939, Hemingway wrote to Perkins of an "old commercial fisherman who fought the swordfish all alone in his skiff [small boat] for four days and four nights and the sharks finally eating it." He added, "I'm going out with old Carlos in his skiff . . . It's a great story if I can get it right. One that would make the book."

birthday, and a 1,000-pound tuna he fought for four hours before losing out to opportunistic sharks.

After extended stints in rental quarters, the nomadic writer and his wife Pauline decided to make their relationship with the island official by settling permanently there in 1931. During one of her house-hunting forays, Pauline had spotted the potential in a derelict 19th-century coral-stone mansion built by a well-to-do shipping magnate. With seed money from her wealthy uncle, the couple purchased the manse on Whitehead Street for $8,000 and began transforming it into a lush tropical sanctuary. "This is really going to be a hell of a fine house," Old Hem wrote to Perkins in December of that year, noting the army of plumbers, roofers, electricians, carpenters, and landscapers that had descended on the property.

Pauline, ever the dutiful wife, oversaw the renovations so that Papa's writing could continue uninterrupted. The house (now a national historic landmark) still bears the stamp of her impeccable taste, from the Portuguese tiles in the breakfast room to the hand-blown chandeliers she installed in place of ceiling fans. Filled with replicas of the Hemingways' original 18th-century Spanish renaissance furnishings, it retains the air of European sophistication bestowed by its worldly former occupants.

On the second floor of a small outbuilding lies Papa's beloved inner sanctum: his writing studio. Decorated with hunting trophies and lined with heaving carpenter-built bookcases, the room is where Hemingway produced all or parts of several works, including *Death in the Afternoon, Green Hills of Africa, To Have and Have Not, The Snows of Kilimanjaro,* and *For Whom the Bell Tolls.* Despite the looming presence of the old Royal typewriter resting on the heavy walnut writing table, Hemingway usually preferred to draft his work in longhand before transferring the pages into type.

The author wrote religiously from early morning until early afternoon each day when he wasn't traveling, distracted by guests, or on one of his extended fishing trips. Upon finishing, he would often take *Pilar* out for a spin or meet up with members of his mob for drinks after doing laps in the 60-foot saltwater swimming pool shimmering in the yard beneath his studio. A later addition to the house (and Key West's first pool), it cost $20,000 to build and was installed while Hemingway was away covering the Spanish Civil War. Legend has it that when Old Hem returned, he threw down a penny in disgust at the exorbitant expense, telling Pauline she may as well take his last cent. She in turn purportedly retrieved it, embedding it for posterity in the cement near the pool, where the shiny 1934 penny rests today.

Nearby on the veranda is the spot where Papa's punching bag was once anchored. An avid boxer and boxing fan, he enjoyed sparring with the local lightweights, whom he paid 50 cents a round to have a go with him in the backyard. He occasionally officiated during Friday night matches at the outdoor ring in the courtyard of what is now the **Blue Heaven Restaurant**. It was on one of these occasions that boxer Kermit "Shine" Forbes famously vaulted over the ropes and took a swing at him, not realizing his target was the famed Ernest Hemingway. Rather than angered, the barrel-chested writer was impressed by Shine's chutzpah in swiping at someone of his sizable proportions and the two became regular sparring partners.

With Ernest's modest writing income handsomely supplemented by Pauline's wealthy family, the Hemingways lived comfortably during the difficult Depression years. Nonetheless, the writer was keenly aware of the plight of Key West locals, who scraped by on government handouts in order to survive. The island's once bustling cigar-rolling trade had migrated to Tampa, while blight had eradicated its sponge industry. With few sources of sustainable employment for its inhabitants, Key West was forced to declare bankruptcy. Its fate was left squarely in the hands of Roosevelt's New Deal politicians, whose solution—for better or worse—was to transform the isle into a tourist destination.

Hemingway was harshly critical of the government's recovery strategy for the island, as well as its mishandling of the great Labor Day hurricane of 1935, in which hundreds perished on nearby Matecumbe Key after a botched evacuation attempt. It was during this time

"What they're trying to do is starve you Conchs out of here so they can burn down the shacks and put up apartments and make this a tourist town."
—TO HAVE AND HAVE NOT

The screenplay for the 1944 film adaptation of Hemingway's *To Have and Have Not*, starring Humphrey Bogart and Lauren Bacall, was co-written by William Faulkner. The two scribes once butted heads when Faulkner condescendingly remarked of Hemingway, "He has never used a word where the reader might check his usage in a dictionary." See pages 33–34 for more on William Faulkner.

of widespread discontent that he wrote *To Have and Have Not,* a Depression-era saga of a charter boat owner forced into smuggling contraband to keep his family afloat. Although Hemingway's novel of domestic social commentary was given a cold reception by critics, it nonetheless sold a sizable 38,000 copies in two months.

But more than his prose, what Papa's adoring fans craved most was a behind-the-scenes glimpse of the larger-than-life writer. They found willing allies in zealous Key West bureaucrats, who listed Hemingway's house as number 18 on a map of "48 Things for a Tourist to See in Key West." In a tongue-in-cheek 1935 *Esquire* article, "The Sites of Whitehead Street: A Key West Letter," Hemingway pleaded his case to the magazine's readers by noting that he was "a modest retiring chap with no desire to compete with the Sponge Lofts, the Turtle Crawl, the Ice Factory, the Tropical Open Air Aquarium, or the Monroe County Courthouse." He added self-effacingly, "This is all very flattering to [my] easily bloated ego . . . but very hard on production." Unfortunately, his pen did not prove mightier than the tourism industry and his house remained a fixture on the island's sightseeing circuit. With the onset of daily flights from Miami and an upsurge in visitors to the island, Hemingway was prompted to erect a six-foot-high brick wall around his property to ward off curious onlookers.

His distaste for tourism is no small irony given the ceaseless flow of tourists breeching his brick barrier and streaming into 907 Whitehead Street today. While Hemingway might have had a few choice words of welcome, visitors are instead greeted warmly by furry felines said to be the descendants of an unusual cat given to the writer by a ship's captain docking on the island. The bequeathed pet, Snow White, possessed six toes, a rare abnormality passed down to the dozens of cats lolling about the house's light-flooded interiors and spacious lawns.

Unfortunately, the Hemingways' happiness during their early island years was not to last. In December 1936, a stunning and ambitious young reporter named Martha Gellhorn was vacationing on Key West when her path fatefully (some claim intentionally) crossed Hemingway's at **Sloppy Joe's** bar. The author, immediately smitten, remained locked in conversation for hours with the journalist femme fatale. Shortly after parting ways on Key West, both sealed their fate by signing on as war correspondents covering the violent clash between Fascist and Republican forces in Hemingway's beloved Spain. Holed up in Madrid's Hotel Florida in the midst of a city under siege, their wartime romance blossomed with the white-hot intensity of the surrounding artillery fire. Hemingway appeared to shrug off his growing detachment from his family in an alarming letter to his mother-in-law: "After the first two weeks in Madrid," he noted, "[I] had an impersonal feeling of having no wife, no children, no house, no boat, nothing. The only way to function." With his Key West life tucked away in the recesses of his mind, Hemingway returned there only twice during the 13 months he spent abroad covering the war.

His eventual homecoming in May 1938 was far from smooth sailing. Tainted by the stain of his affair, his marriage to Pauline teetered on the brink of collapse. The tension between the couple escalated further with Hemingway's erratic behavior, explosive temper, and dark moods. After the adrenaline-rush thrill of a year of living dangerously, the simple pleasures of domestic life on the quiet isle had lost their luster.

Over the course of the next year, the writer's marriage continued to crumble while his feelings for Martha intensified. The Hemingways spent increasing amounts of time apart, with Ernest abandoning Key West permanently in the spring of 1939 and finalizing his divorce from Pauline a year later. "Here in K.W., it got so I couldn't work," he wrote to a friend before decamping to Cuba on *Pilar*. No doubt the domestic tension and ghosts of his carefree past were impeding progress on the powerful and epic novel that he had feverishly begun writing in his second-floor study. Set in war-torn Spain, *For Whom the Bell Tolls* was published in 1940 to enormous critical

Don't Miss

◉ In the backyard of the Hemingway Home rests the world's most famous—and most unusual—**cat drinking fountain**: a former urinal from Papa's favorite watering hole, Sloppy Joe's, inlaid with colorful ceramic tiles and crowned with a giant Spanish olive jar.

◉ What happens to the Hemingway cats after they've passed on to kitty heaven? They're given pride of place in a **tiny backyard cemetery** where many have individual tombstones, including Marilyn Monroe (1986–2004) and Errol Flynn (1999–2005).

◉ Also on the grounds is a diminutive **replica of the main house** (complete with balcony and yellow shutters). The "cat condo" is a purr-fect home away from home for some of the resident felines.

◉ Feline fanciers should stop in the Hemingway Home bookstore, which stocks a unique and colorful array of **cat-themed gifts and souvenirs**. (Mind the dozing kitties while shopping!)

◉ After a tour of the house and grounds, spend some time hanging out with the friendly and entertaining guides on the **front veranda** to hear even more stories about the resident cats and local folklore.

◉ Kick back at Sloppy Joe's or Captain Tony's (the original location of the bar at which Hemingway drank) with a **Papa Doble**, the refreshing grapefruit and lime juice cocktail that was invented by Hemingway at Havana's El Floridita bar. Although Papa's usual drink was scotch and soda, he would occasionally enjoy a namesake libation at Sloppy Joe's.

and popular acclaim, elevating his literary stature to dizzying new heights. Seclusion in Cuba provided Hemingway with the fresh start that he needed to marshal his formidable talents and regain his joie de vivre. With Martha at his side, he moved into La Finca Vigía, an estate on the outskirts of Havana that he was to occupy for the next 20 years.

Although Hemingway's final chapter in Key West failed to have a storybook ending, his years there defined him long after he sailed from its shores. It was during his time on the isle that the macho persona of "Papa" took form: The rugged writer-cum-sportsman who celebrated the cult of manhood through bold pursuits like big-game hunting, boxing, and battling outsize fish. For Papa, Key West was more than just a place to hang his hat; it was an exuberant

IF YOU GO: "We have bought that old house with the iron rails and balconies opposite the lighthouse in K.W.," Hemingway wrote to a friend in May 1931. Built of indigenous coral stone for a wealthy shipbuilder in 1851, the grand two-story house on Whitehead Street had fallen into disrepair by the time it was purchased by the Hemingways 80 years later. No doubt the worldly couple was attracted to the manse's French-Spanish colonial style, which provided the perfect backdrop for the 18th-century Spanish antique furnishings they shipped over from their Paris apartment.

After the couple divorced, Pauline Hemingway retained possession of the house until her untimely death of a brain hemorrhage in 1951. It remained in the Hemingway family until the author's suicide a decade later, when it was purchased by a private owner and opened as a museum. Much care has been taken to preserve the sophisticated look and feel of the house that Pauline had so artfully cultivated. Throughout its airy rooms are antique re-creations of the Hemingways' furnishings, such as an old cigarmaker's chair in Papa's study, a headboard crafted from the gate of a Spanish monastery, and a long walnut dining table like the one at which Papa held court during the couple's lively dinner parties. **Ernest Hemingway Home and Museum** 907 Whitehead Street • Key West, FL 33040 • Tel: 305-294-1136 • *www.hemingwayhome.com* • Open daily way of life and a soul-soothing elixir that became an enduring symbol of his fiery spirit.

DRINK, DINE, AND DOZE

SLOPPY JOE'S

201 Duval Street • Key West, FL 33040 • Tel: 305-294-5717
• www.sloppyjoes.com

"We all used to gather in the evenings at Hemingway's old resort called Sloppy Joe's."
—TENNESSEE WILLIAMS

Originally owned by Hemingway's friend Joe Russell, the origins of Sloppy Joe's date back to December 5, 1933—the day Prohibition was repealed. Prior to then, Russell was a rumrunner who operated an illegal Key West speakeasy. The bar's first location was around the corner (where Captain Tony's Saloon resides today), but it moved to its current address four years after opening due to a rent hike that Russell refused to pay: from three dollars a week to four. Legend has it that a quarrel over ownership of the bar's fixtures led Russell to take leave of the old locale in the middle of the night. He and his loyal patrons, drinks still in hand, are said to have picked the bar clean, carrying the disputed possessions down the block to 201 Duval Street where Sloppy Joe's has operated for more than half a century.

The friendship between Hemingway and Russell blossomed during Papa's early years on the island after the barkeep cashed a $1,000 royalty check for *A Farewell to Arms* when the local bank refused. Russell, whom Old Hem nicknamed "Josie Grunts," was also a charter boat captain and regular Hemingway fishing companion. The twosome often took extended trips out into the Gulf Stream down to Cuba, once reeling in an astounding 54 marlins in 115 days. Hemingway was with Russell in Havana when the latter died unexpectedly of a stroke in June 1941.

For three days each July, Sloppy Joe's celebrates its literary legacy by hosting dozens of bearded hopefuls from all over the world who vie for the coveted first place title in the **Papa Look-Alike Contest** during **Key West's Hemingway Days**.

For more about the annual Hemingway Days festival, see pages 147 and 149.

CAPTAIN TONY'S SALOON

428 Greene Street • Key West, FL 33040

• Tel: 305-294-1838 • *www.capttonyssaloon.com*

Full of character, this unassuming tavern is an authentic slice of old Key West and the original location of Sloppy Joe's during the majority of the time Hemingway spent on the isle. The author and his mob paid regular afternoon visits here, and Hemingway's onetime bar stool has been mounted on the wall for safekeeping. The author immortalized the locale in *To Have and Have Not* as Freddy's, a rough-and-tumble place where "men in dungarees, some bareheaded, others in caps, old service hats and in cardboard helmets, crowded the bar three deep." It was here in 1936 where Hemingway fatefully met Martha Gellhorn, the woman who would become his third wife four years later.

Originally known as the Blind Pig (a generic term used for a speakeasy during Prohibition), it was Hemingway who suggested the name change to Sloppy Joe's. The squat wood-frame building housing the bar dates back to the 19th century and boasts a colorful past with stints as an icehouse (which doubled as the city morgue), cigar factory, and bordello. The bar's namesake is its former owner, the late Captain Tony Tarracino, who was a white-bearded Hemingway look-alike and onetime bootlegger, bookie, gunrunner, and mayor of Key West.

Throughout the years, Captain Tony's has been a haunt of other famous writers, including southern scribes Tennessee Williams and Truman Capote.

LA CONCHA HOTEL & SPA

430 Duval Street • Key West, FL 33040 • Tel: 305-296-2991

• *www.laconchakeywest.com*

Hemingway often recommended this hotel as a place for his many visitors to stay, and Tennessee Williams finished his Pulitzer Prize-winning play *A Streetcar Named Desire* here in early 1947. Today the hotel is on the National Register of Historic Places.

"From my sixth floor window I can see the ocean almost all the way around the island and a breeze comes through all the time," Tennessee Williams wrote from his room at La Concha in a January 1947 letter.

A Flair for the Dramatic

ALTHOUGH BEST KNOWN for his association with New Orleans, southern gothic playwright Tennessee Williams became a regular visitor to Key West in the 1940s and eventually bought a house there a decade later. "Key West had in those days a very authentic frontier atmosphere which was delightful," he wrote of his early time on the island, which he used as a secluded base for writing as well as relaxation. "It's the only place in this country where it's warm enough for me to swim every day of the year. The sky is always so clear and the water's so blue."

He rented a modest clapboard house at 1431 Duncan Street for six months prior to purchasing the property in 1950. Over the years, he added a pool, gazebo, guest cottage, and writing studio, which he called the Mad House. Although he loved the island and admitted that Key West was the most conducive place for him to work, he continued to spend much of his time in hotels and rented apartments in New Orleans, New York, and Europe. Throughout his globe-trotting, he retained his Key West house (which today is privately owned and not open to the public) for more than 30 years until his death in 1983.

"It is the least commercial of the Florida resorts and the swimming is incomparable, better even than Capri," Tennessee Williams wrote of Key West to his friend Carson McCullers in 1948. "There is a small and really nice little society of artists and many pleasant little frame houses like the ones in Nantucket." For more on Carson McCullers, see pages 31–32, and for Tennessee Williams, see pages 36–37.

Other writers in the southern gothic tradition visited Key West during the dramatist's time there, including his good friend Carson McCullers, who stayed with him for several weeks in 1955. Although Papa Hemingway had left town by the time of Tennessee's arrival, the dramatist became friendly with Pauline Hemingway and later met Ernest in Havana at El Floridita, Hemingway's favorite Cuban watering hole. "I had expected a very manly, super macho sort of guy, very bullying and coarse spoken," the playwright wrote in his memoirs about their encounter. "On the contrary, Hemingway struck me as a gentleman who seemed to have a very touchingly shy quality about him."

PIER HOUSE RESORT

1 Duval Street • Key West, FL 33040 • Tel: 305-296-4600 • www.pierhouse.com

Truman Capote visited the isle in March 1975, staying at the Pier House while writing a story for *Esquire* magazine; Tennessee Williams also frequented the hotel's restaurant and Chart Room Bar while living on Key West.

BLUE HEAVEN RESTAURANT

729 Thomas Street • Key West, FL 33040 • Tel: 305-296-8666

• www.blueheavenkw.com

This blue-shuttered 19th-century wood-frame building in the heart of old Key West has a past as colorful as its bright exterior. A dance hall, bordello, and playhouse have occupied the property, and it has hosted cockfighting, gambling, and Friday night boxing matches that were attended and occasionally refereed by Ernest Hemingway. Today it's a popular family-owned restaurant serving up homemade Caribbean fare.

ELSEWHERE IN THE AREA

CASA ANTIGUA

314 Simonton Street • Key West, FL 33040 • www.keywesttravelguide.com

Blame it all on a Model A Ford. Ultimately, the impetus for Hemingway's decade-long stint in Key West may have come in the unlikely guise of just such an automobile—the delayed delivery of which turned a brief flirtation with the isle into a passionate affair. When Ernest and Pauline sailed from Paris to Havana and then onward to Key West in April 1928, they were anticipating taking receipt of a new Model A Ford on the isle in order to journey north. But the car's delivery from Miami was delayed, and the Hemingways were given free accommodation in the Trev-Mor Hotel above the dealership until the belated auto finally arrived. It was at this location where the writer completed *A Farewell to Arms,* sending Max Perkins a telegram: "Working Hard," while falling head over heels for Key West.

Today the building is known as Casa Antigua. The rooms where the Hemingways once stayed are a private residence, although visitors are allowed entry into Casa Antigua's lush tropical garden.

ST. MARY STAR OF THE SEA

1010 Windsor Lane • Key West, FL 33040 • Tel: 305-294-1018
• *www.stmarykeywest.com*

The Hemingways occasionally attended services at this Catholic church and on January 14, 1932, their two-month-old second son, Gregory, was baptized here.

Also baptized at the church in 1969 was an adult resident on the isle, dramatist Tennessee Williams, who was purportedly intoxicated and urged by his brother to convert. "It wasn't my idea," the Episcopalian-born playwright later admitted. "I don't think I really wanted to do it, but that happened during my Stoned Age . . . My real religion is writing."

TENNESSEE WILLIAMS KEY WEST EXHIBIT

513 Truman Avenue • Key West, FL 33040 • Tel: 305-842-1666 • *www.twkw.org*
• Open daily

Tennessee Williams was a part-time Key West resident from 1941 until his death in 1983, and this memorabilia-packed exhibit pays homage to his time on the island. Though celebrated as a playwright, Williams was also an amateur artist, and reproductions of his colorful paintings (which he sometimes gave as hostess gifts) are on display. So is a typewriter he used while in Key West and—intriguingly—documents exploring the controversial circumstances of his death.

CUSTOM HOUSE MUSEUM

281 Front Street • Key West, FL 33040 • Tel: 305-295-6616 • *www.kwahs.org*
• Open daily

Inside this eye-catching, Romanesque-style building—crafted from red stone and originally the island's customs office—are exhibits related to Key West's colorful history, including one devoted to its best-known resident. Biographical information is blended with displays of personal mementos like Hemingway's blood-stained Red Cross uniform, worn during his days as an ambulance driver during World War I, a pair of leather boxing gloves, and a to-do list (one task: buy oranges).

Among the intriguing details shared about Hemingway's Key West days is that he has a marine namesake. During a marlin run in the summer of 1934, he invited members of the Academy of Natural Sciences on board his boat, *Pilar*, to conduct research in the waters between Florida and Cuba. In gratitude, a spinycheek scorpion fish was bestowed with the name *neomerinthe hemingway*.

The next year, *Pilar* and its owner were again pressed into service. After one of the most powerful hurricanes ever recorded hit the Florida Keys, he set out in his boat—which he had zealously guarded the night of the storm—to help with the relief efforts.

Elsewhere in the museum, the stairway walls are adorned with original pen-and-ink drawings by artist Guy Harvey depicting scenes from Hemingway's *The Old Man and the Sea*.

FORT JEFFERSON, GARDEN KEY, DRY TORTUGAS NATIONAL PARK

Tel: 305-242-7700 • *www.nps.gov/drto/index.html*

• Reachable by ferry, boat, or seaplane

Long before they became a national park, the Dry Tortugas were a favorite deep-sea fishing destination for Hemingway. During one outing, he and members of his "Mob," a group of fishing buddies (including editor Maxwell Perkins), were waylaid by a strong tropical storm and marooned at Fort Jefferson on Garden Key for seventeen days. Luckily, their supply of canned goods, coffee, and liquor—supplemented with fresh-caught fish—saw them through until they could safely return to Key West.

Small Town, Big Book:

HARPER LEE IN MONROEVILLE, ALABAMA

WORKS BY HARPER LEE
To Kill a Mockingbird (1960)
Go Set a Watchman (2015)

THE OLD COURTHOUSE MUSEUM

Surrounded by a landscape of cotton fields, red clay roads, rolling hills, and pinewoods, the small town of Monroeville is tucked into a rural pocket of southwest Alabama. Its distinction as the state's literary capital comes from two illustrious writers who have roots in the town: Truman Capote, the author of *In Cold Blood,* and Harper Lee, who used Monroeville as the basis for the fictional Maycomb in *To Kill a Mockingbird.*

"It is and it isn't autobiographical," Lee once said of her Pulitzer Prize–winning novel. "What I did present as exactly as I could were the clime and tone, as I remember them, of the town in which I lived." Much about Monroeville has changed since the Depression-era days of Lee's childhood, the time period that serves as the story's setting. The oak- and crape myrtle-lined street where the scribe spent her youth has given way to suburban sprawl, yet there is one place in Monroeville where time has stood still.

Standing at the center of the town square in both the real and imaginary milieus is an elegant, redbrick courthouse constructed in 1903. Inside the domed edifice adorned with a clock tower is one of the most famous courtrooms in America, immortalized in Lee's novel and in the Academy Award–winning film adaptation of *To Kill a Mockingbird.* (An exact replica of the courtroom was re-created on a Hollywood sound stage.) It's here that Atticus Finch defends an innocent black man accused of raping a white woman in a gripping trial scene that concludes with the heroic lawyer's powerful closing statement in which he declares, "In this country the courts are the great levelers, and in our courts all men are created equal."

As a child, Lee attended court sessions there and watched her attorney father, A. C. Lee—who provided the inspiration for the character Atticus Finch—practice his profession. The Old Monroe County Courthouse is now a museum, with the second-floor courtroom

"Mockingbirds don't do one thing but make music for us to enjoy. They don't eat up people's gardens, don't nest in corncribs, they don't do one thing but sing their hearts out for us. That's why it's a sin to kill a mockingbird."
—To Kill a Mockingbird

restored to its 1930s appearance. Visitors are welcome to explore its spacious confines, from the rows of dark wood spectator benches to the witness stand where Tom Robinson and his accuser, Mayella Ewell, give conflicting testimony in *To Kill a Mockingbird* to the balcony where young Scout Finch watches the trial unfold with Reverend Sykes, her brother, Jem, and their friend Dill.

The inspiration for Scout's scrappy sidekick, Dill, was Capote, who spent much of his first ten years living with relatives in Monroeville after his parents separated. He himself told *Gone with the Wind* producer David O. Selznick, "I am the character called Dill," described by Lee in the novel as "a pocket Merlin, whose head teemed with eccentric plans, strange longings, and quaint fancies." The rough-and-tumble Scout is thought to be in part a depiction of her creator, who was known around Monroeville as a spirited tomboy. A young Lee engaged in fistfights on the playground, preferred overalls to dresses, read voraciously, and called her father by his first name—all traits shared by *To Kill a Mockingbird*'s Scout.

In the **Old Courthouse Museum,** the exhibit **"Harper Lee: In Her Own Words"** details the writer's early years. She was born Nelle Harper Lee in Monroeville on April 28, 1926. (Nelle is Ellen spelled backward in honor of the writer's grandmother and the name by which she was known in her hometown.) The exhibit is told almost entirely in the author's own words, using excerpts from interviews she gave after the novel's 1960 publication, and enlivened with reproduction vintage photographs. The display highlights various aspects of Lee's life and literary legacy, from the similarities between the character of Atticus and her father to her reaction to the book's success and its big-screen adaptation.

A second exhibit, **"Truman Capote: A Childhood in Monroeville,"** comprises letters, family scrapbooks, and memorabilia such as the writer's sailing cap (he was rarely ever outside without a hat), a blue glass vase and plate he told friends were heirlooms from Monroeville, a postcard he sent to his aunt from Russia in 1956, and an invitation to his September 25, 1984, memorial service held at New York City's Shubert Theatre.

The exhibit sheds light on Capote's relationship with Lee, who accompanied him to Kansas in 1959 to aid in researching his true crime book, *In Cold Blood*. It also highlights connections between his fiction and family members he commemorated in print, particularly his cousin Sook, who appears in "A Christmas Memory" and other short stories. Handwritten letters to an aunt in Monroeville are part of the collection, including a missive Capote penned to her in which he revealed, "Yes, it is true that Nelle Lee is publishing a book . . . I liked it very much. She has real talent."

Order is restored in the courtroom every spring when a two-act play based on the book is staged. The first part of the well-acted production takes place in an outdoor amphitheater on the Old Courthouse grounds, where a stage set re-creates the Finch residence, along with those of kindly Miss Maudie, gossipy Miss Stephanie, cantankerous Mrs. Dubose, and the mysterious Boo Radley. The play's second act unfolds in the courtroom with audience members acting as trial spectators seated on the main floor as well as in the balcony.

The stage set is left intact year-round on the Old Courthouse lawn, which is the starting point for the museum's self-guided walking tour: "Monroeville in the 1930s," a guide to the town as Harper Lee and Truman Capote knew it during their childhood years. (Cultivated on the courthouse grounds are 50 varieties of camellias, the type of flower Jem destroys in a fit of pique in Mrs. Dubose's yard in *To Kill a Mockingbird*.) Sites on the walking tour include the building where A. C. Lee once had a law office, the edifice where Capote's cousins ran a millinery shop, the onetime location of the Boulware house— believed to be the model for the Radley residence—and the jail in front of which Atticus and his children dissuade a band of enraged citizens from taking justice into their own hands.

The site of Lee's childhood home on South Alabama Avenue is now occupied by **Mel's Dairy Dream**. A fire destroyed the adjacent abode of the Faulks, Capote's relatives, and a historical marker designates the spot where it once stood. All that remains are the remnants of a rock-walled garden and a fishpool where Scout, Jem, and Dill while away summer hours in *To Kill a Mockingbird*. More recent reminders

"I shall always cherish the memory of my childhood here—I have traveled all over the world and found there is no place like the USA—and truly no place like home."

—TRUMAN CAPOTE

of the novel are two building-side murals depicting notable scenes from the book: the jailhouse encounter and Scout, Jem, and Dill spying on the Radley home.

Both Lee and Capote's affinity for the written word began early. Along with alternating "offices" at each other's houses and creating stories on a typewriter bestowed on them by Lee's father (who gave Capote a pocket dictionary he carried for years), the two were avid readers. "We had to use our own devices in our play, for our entertainment," recalled Lee, whose favored authors included Jane Austen and Robert Louis Stevenson, in a 1964 interview. "We didn't have much money. Nobody had any money. We didn't have toys, nothing was done for us, so the result was that we lived in our imagination most of the time. We devised things; we were readers, and we would transfer everything we had seen on the printed page to the backyard in the form of high drama."

Lee's own life took a dramatic turn when she left law school just shy of obtaining her degree to pursue a career as a writer. Originally intending to follow in the footsteps of her father and sister and practice law in Monroeville, she instead moved to New York City. There, she worked in a bookstore and as an airline reservations clerk before a generous bequest from friends allowed her to take time off to focus on her writing. She penned a number of unpublished short

IF YOU GO: Monroeville's local theatrical production of *To Kill a Mockingbird* takes place annually with a limited number of performances in April and May at the Old Courthouse Museum. Tickets can be purchased at *www.tokillamockingbird.com*. They go on sale March 1 and sell out quickly.

Listed on the National Register of Historic Places, the Old Courthouse Museum is the centerpiece of the town square. Brochures of the self-guided walking tour, "Monroeville in the 1930s," are available in the visitor information room. **Old Courthouse Museum** Part of the Monroe County Heritage Museums • 31 North Alabama Avenue • Monroeville, AL 36460 • Tel: 251-575-7433 • *www .monroecountymuseum.org* • Open Tuesday through Friday 10 a.m. through 4 p.m., Saturday 10 a.m. through 1 p.m.

stories before beginning a novel at the suggestion of a literary agent. The intensely private author, who wrote *To Kill a Mockingbird* over a period of more than two years in Manhattan and Monroeville, had modest ambitions for her inaugural publication. "I never expected any sort of success with *Mockingbird,*" she said in 1964 during one of the last interviews she granted. "I kept at it because I knew it had to be my first novel, for better or for worse."

The 34-year-old author's debut was an immediate sensation, receiving glowing reviews, garnering a Pulitzer and other prizes, and achieving a nearly two-year run on best-seller lists. When the book first appeared, Monroeville residents believed that the world would have little interest in the local happenings in their corner of the Deep South. Lee's publisher cautioned that she temper her expectations about sales, and even her father thought a Monroeville bookshop owner was overzealous for placing a 100-copy order. Instead, *To Kill a Mockingbird*'s eloquent and thought-provoking portrayals of childhood and racial intolerance proved to be universal. As Lee said in 1962, the novel "portrays an aspect of civilization—not necessarily Southern civilization. I tried to show the conflict of the human soul—reduced to its simplest terms."

GO SET A WATCHMAN: The literary world learned of *Go Set a Watchman*, which Harper Lee penned and submitted to her publisher before *To Kill a Mockingbird*, in 2015, after the manuscript's discovery (it was published later that year). In the novel, 26-year-old Jean Louise "Scout" Finch returns in the mid-1950s to Maycomb, where she confronts disturbing realities about the social and political climate in her hometown and about her loved ones. In one scene, Jean Louise visits the eatery that stands where her childhood home once did (today Mel's Dairy Dream), and in another she sits in the courthouse balcony and watches a town council meeting take place on the main floor below. Interspersed throughout the story are flashbacks from her childhood, including a humorous scene in which she, Jem, and Dill stage a mock baptism in a fish pool in the yard where Truman Capote–inspired Dill lived with relatives.

◉ The **annual staging of** *To Kill a Mockingbird* is a unique opportunity to see the novel come to life. The set used in act one of the production is left intact year-round on the courthouse lawn and is an ideal spot for a photo op.

◉ **Take a seat in the courtroom's balcony section,** where Scout, Jem, and Dill sit with Reverend Sykes and watch Tom Robinson's trial unfold in *To Kill a Mockingbird.*

◉ **A memorial to Atticus Finch: Lawyer-Hero**—a bronze plaque set in a rock donated by the Alabama Bar Association as the first of its Legal Milestones monuments—is located near the northeast entrance to the Old Courthouse. Harper Lee declined to attend the dedication ceremony but wrote in a letter to the association, "Please accept my heartfelt thanks for a unique honor. Atticus would have been a bit nonplussed by the tribute, but deeply grateful!"

◉ Part of the Old Courthouse Museum's Harper Lee exhibit is a **documentary featuring interviews with locals who knew the author.** Reminiscences about Lee and the novel include trying to guess which real-life figures inspired her characters and the excitement generated when Gregory Peck came to town to research his role as Atticus Finch.

◉ On display in the Capote exhibit is **a typewriter** on which he worked on the novel *Summer Crossing* (thought to be lost for decades but discovered and published in 2005) during a Monroeville visit. His other works include the true crime narrative *In Cold Blood,* the novella *Breakfast at Tiffany's,* and the debut novel *Other Voices, Other Rooms* (whose character Idabel Tompkins is said to be modeled on Lee). The short stories "A Christmas Memory," "One Christmas," and "The Thanksgiving Visitor" are based on his Monroeville childhood.

Drink, Dine, and Doze

··

BUDGET INN

484 South Alabama Avenue • Monroeville, AL 36460 • Tel: 251-575-3101

At this no-frills motel (then known as the Monroe Motor Court), Harper Lee had a meeting with Gregory Peck. They had hoped to have a private tête-à-tête, but some intrepid teenage girls tracked them down. Lee answered the knock on the door, and Peck graciously complied with their request for an autograph.

DAVID'S CATFISH HOUSE

145 Highway 84 East • Monroeville, AL 36460 • Tel: 251-575-3460
• *www.davidscatfishhouses.com*

Harper Lee was known to indulge in the food at this rustic restaurant, where the house specialty is catfish. The Alabama Bureau of Travel and Tourism designated the catfish and cheese grits at David's one of the "100 dishes to eat in Alabama before you die."

SWEET TOOTH BAKERY

5 West Claiborne • Monroeville, AL 36460 • Tel: 251-575-7040

Located near the courthouse square, this eatery serves up more than just sweet treats. Locals line up for hearty midday fare like fried chicken, smothered pork chops, collard greens, and corn bread. The custom here is to take the main meal, referred to as dinner, at midday, as Atticus and his children do in *To Kill a Mockingbird*.

THE PROP AND GAVEL

42 East Claiborne Street • Monroeville, AL 36460 • Tel: 251-575-7767
• *www.facebook.com/thepropandgavel*

One of Harper Lee's last public appearances was at a luncheon given in her honor at this restaurant by the Old Courthouse Museum. The 89-year-old author was presented with hot-off-the-press copies of the American and British editions of *Go Set a Watchman*.

Christmas Memories

A CHRISTMAS GATHERING IN THE late 1950s was particularly memorable for Harper Lee, who spent the day with friends in New York City. "There was an envelope on the tree, addressed to me," she recalled in a 1961 magazine essay. "I opened it and read: 'You have one year off from your job to write whatever you want.'" Lee used her friends' magnanimous gift to produce no less than a Pulitzer Prize-winning novel.

In 1959, Lee and Truman Capote were asked to Christmas dinner at the home of a prominent lawyer in Garden City, Kansas, where they were researching a quadruple murder that became the story of *In Cold Blood*. The invitation proved to be a turning point, helping pave the way for their acceptance in the town and leading to interviews with key figures in the case.

See pages 31–32 for more on Carson McCullers, and page 195 for Harry's Bar.

Capote had his share of other notable holiday moments as well. One Christmas Eve he joined fellow scribe and Georgia native Carson McCullers at her home in Nyack, New York. "We played old Marlene Dietrich records and drank wine. It was a very southern Christmas—my last southern Christmas up north—and we had all kinds of fried chicken and cakes," he reminisced. "Everybody was very kind about my not giving them a present although they all gave me one." The gifts, Capote claimed, had been stolen when his apartment was robbed earlier that day. The writer's other holiday revelries included a champagne-fueled repast at Harry's Bar in Venice and imbibing a potent cocktail of vodka spiked with red pepper to ward off a winter chill in Leningrad (now St. Petersburg).

One of Capote's favorite places was Switzerland, where he spent several Christmases. "I have a little chalet, very cozy and warm, perched almost on top of an Alpine peak: the view is spectacular—rather like living in an aeroplane," he once described it. "It seems to be in the spirit of everything."

"I started writing when I was eight—out of the blue, uninspired by any example . . . not knowing that I had chained myself to a novel but merciless master."
—TRUMAN CAPOTE

Elsewhere in the Area

ALABAMA SOUTHERN COMMUNITY COLLEGE

2800 South Alabama Avenue • Monroeville, AL
36460 • Tel: 251-575-8271 • www.ascc.edu

The college annually hosts the **Alabama Writers Symposium** in April. The lineup includes author readings, live music, art exhibits, and other events open to the public.

The building housing the college's library features a replica of the clock tower that sits atop the Old Courthouse. Among the works of art on display inside is a series of mixed-media collages created by Alabama artist Nall. The collages include interpretations of *To Kill a Mockingbird* and Capote's works, as well as the legacies of three other famous figures with Alabama ties: Martin Luther King, Jr., Booker T. Washington, and Helen Keller. Located outside the library is the **Writers Fountain** with the names of southern scribes etched in its circular stone border.

Helen Keller's ancestral home, **Ivy Green** (see pages 34–35), is located in Tuscumbia, and Booker T. Washington is buried at Tuskegee University. The educator and former slave is also commemorated at the **Booker T. Washington National Monument** in Hardy, Virginia (www.nps.gov/bowa).

MAKING IT TO MONROEVILLE: The town is best reached by car and is accessible from several major airports: Birmingham (3.5 hours), Montgomery (2 hours), Mobile (1.5 hours), and Pensacola, Florida (1.5 hours). A day trip or overnight venture can be easily combined with a stay in Montgomery or Mobile.

Located in Montgomery, the **Scott and Zelda Fitzgerald Museum** (see pages 110–11) is the only venue devoted to the Jazz Age duo. The **Alabama Shakespeare Festival** (*www.asf.net*) stages the Bard's productions year-round. For more information about Montgomery, visit *www.visitingmontgomery.com*.

The premiere of the film version of *To Kill a Mockingbird* was held in the port city of Mobile, where a superb lodging place is the art- and antique-filled **Berney/Fly Bed & Breakfast** (*www.berneyflybedandbreakfast.com*) on historic Government Street. For more information about Mobile, visit *www.mobile.org*.

California Dreaming:

JOHN STEINBECK IN MONTEREY AND SALINAS, CALIFORNIA

SELECTED WORKS BY JOHN STEINBECK

Cup of Gold (1929)

The Pastures of Heaven (1932)

Tortilla Flat (1935)

In Dubious Battle (1936)

Of Mice and Men (1937)

The Long Valley (1938)

The Grapes of Wrath (1939)

Cannery Row (1945)

The Log from the Sea of Cortez (1951)

East of Eden (1952)

Sweet Thursday (1954)

The Winter of Our Discontent (1961)

Travels with Charley in Search of America (1962)

The Acts of King Arthur and His Noble Knights (1976)

STEINBECK COUNTRY

The rugged stretch of coastline where Monterey Bay meets the Pacific Ocean almost inspired struggling writer John Steinbeck to abandon his craft for a career in marine biology. The stunning seascape and its mysterious underwater world were closely familiar to the scribe, who spent boyhood summers in his family's Pacific Grove cottage a short distance from the water's edge.

John Steinbeck immortalized his hometown, Salinas, in the semi-autobiographical novel *East of Eden* and Pacific Grove and Monterey in *Cannery Row* and *Sweet Thursday*.

Resplendent with Victorian homes, pinewoods, and an annual influx of monarch butterflies, the tranquil town beckoned to Steinbeck time and again throughout his life. As it was for the writer, who took up residence in "the little Pacific Grove house" for six years in the 1930s, the locale makes an ideal—and picturesque—base for exploring nearby Monterey and Carmel-by-the-Sea, as well as the writer's birthplace in the Salinas Valley.

"Pacific Grove and Monterey sit side by side on a hill bordering the bay," wrote Steinbeck in *Sweet Thursday,* the novel in which he brought back the colorful cast of rogues and dreamers first introduced in *Cannery Row.* "The two towns touch shoulders but they are not alike." In contrast to serene Pacific Grove, founded as a Methodist retreat in 1875 and referred to as God's kingdom by the sea, Monterey in Steinbeck's time was a rough-and-tumble industrial town sustained by a sardine canning industry.

Since the 1945 publication of *Cannery Row,* literary travelers have been drawn to Monterey, where a favored attraction along the now-famous street is a small, weatherbeaten building. The diminutive domicile at **800 Cannery Row** was the home and professional domain of self-taught marine biologist Edward F. Ricketts, Steinbeck's closest friend and the inspiration for Doc, the novel's central

Penned after Steinbeck served as a World War II correspondent, *Cannery Row* was, he remarked, "a kind of nostalgic thing, written for a group of soldiers who had said to me, 'Write something funny that isn't about the war. Write something for us to read—we're sick of war.' "

character. "Tourists began coming to the laboratory, first a few and then in droves," recalled Steinbeck. "People stopped their cars and stared at Ed with that glassy look that is used on movie stars."

After laboring over his writing in the Pacific Grove cottage, Steinbeck often rambled the short distance to Ricketts's lab, where the two amateur philosophers indulged in "whiskey and conversation." During the 1930s the lab was a social gathering place for writers, artists, and assorted others, and Ricketts threw parties that sometimes lasted for days. "Life on Cannery Row," reminisced Steinbeck, "was curious and dear and outrageous."

Along with Doc's dwelling, readers came in search of the stomping grounds inhabited by *Cannery Row*'s happy-go-lucky Mack and the boys. Development has since done away with many of their haunts, but standing near the lab are buildings Steinbeck used as models for two memorable establishments. The **Wing Chong Building** at 835 Cannery Row was the site of Lee Chong's Grocery, where the boys stocked up on Old Tennessee brand whiskey (or Old Tennis Shoes as they preferred to call it) and pooled their meager funds to purchase supplies for a surprise party they threw for Doc at the lab. In the space that once housed **La Ida Café** at 851 Cannery Row, sometime bartender Eddie surreptitiously poured leftovers from patrons' drinks into a gallon jug. The result was an "always interesting and sometimes surprising" concoction he took home to imbibe.

Boosted by Steinbeck's spirited book, tourism became the town's new trade after the decline of the canning industry in the late 1940s. The moniker Steinbeck used in the novel, "Cannery Row," was declared Ocean View Avenue's official name in 1958. When Steinbeck returned to Monterey for a visit in 1960, after making his home in New York City for more than a decade, he found the waterfront strip much changed from the days of his past. In place of the canneries that used to "rumble and rattle and squeak" are restaurants, shops, and boardwalk-style attractions, lending a carnival-like atmosphere to the city once known as the Sardine Capital of the World. "They fish for tourists now," Steinbeck observed in his memoir *Travels with Charley*, "and that species they are not likely to wipe out."

Cannery Row's biggest modern-day draw is the 3.3-acre Monterey Bay Aquarium, located on the border with Pacific Grove and a stone's throw from Ed Ricketts's lab. The oceanic wonder is situated on the site of what was the row's largest fish-packing plant, Hovden Cannery, built in 1916 and one of the last to cease operation. In the main entrance of the aquarium, an exhibit about the area's history highlights Steinbeck and Ricketts's storied place in Cannery Row lore—and Ricketts's pioneering contributions to marine biology (his tome *Between Pacific Tides* is still in print). The two would undoubtedly have admired one of the aquarium's premier attractions, a three-story, 28-foot-high kelp forest teeming with sardines, leopard sharks, wolf-eels, and other sea-dwelling specimens.

The Cannery Row area is known as New Monterey, but Steinbeck was equally familiar with the city's historic downtown section. He frequented the watering holes on Alvarado Street and for a time lived in an 1830s adobe house not far from where Robert Louis Stevenson lodged in the 19th century. Monterey and its environs also set the scene for Steinbeck's fourth book, *Tortilla Flat,* his first critical and commercial success, published in 1935. Three previous works, which brought scant fanfare or financial reward, had each been published by a different company hard-hit during the Great Depression. "Every time a publisher accepted one of my books, he went bankrupt. One book was accepted by one publisher, printed by a second and issued under a third," said Steinbeck. "I began to feel like the Typhoid Mary of the literary world."

For more about Stevenson, who appears in Steinbeck's short story "How Edith McGillcuddy Met R. L. Stevenson," see pages 75–78.

Unbeknown to Steinbeck, a cure for his languishing literary career was in the works. A Chicago bookseller had become an ardent fan of the talented young writer and recommended his works to a friend, New York City editor Pascal Covici. After countless rejections that led Steinbeck to lament to Ricketts, "Maybe I am not a novelist," *Tortilla Flat* was taken on by Covici, who remained the eventual Nobel and Pulitzer Prize winner's lifelong editor. The accomplishment of *Tortilla Flat* was a major turning point in Steinbeck's career.

As he wryly noted, "It did have one distinction the others had not: It was not ignored."

The book grew out of Steinbeck's interest in the legend of King Arthur. "I wanted to take the stories of my town of Monterey and cast them into a kind of folklore," said the writer, who modeled the irrepressible Danny and his band of compadres after the valiant Arthur and the Knights of the Round Table. Steinbeck had been fascinated with the mythical medieval figure since receiving a copy of *Le Morte d'Arthur* for his ninth birthday. He and his younger sister, Mary, created a secret language using little-known Middle English words from the story, and with his pony as sidekick, he roamed the hills surrounding his hometown of Salinas and acted out Round Table adventures.

One of the most agriculturally rich areas in the state, the Salinas Valley is located some 20 miles inland from the sea. At the turn of the 20th century, the Steinbeck family journeyed from Salinas to the Pacific coast by horse-drawn carriage while today it's traversed by a 30-minute car ride. The scenic route recalls the opening pages of Steinbeck's ode to the Salinas Valley, *East of Eden,* in which he paints a season-by-season portrait of the land, from the springtime burst of blooms when "the whole valley floor" is "carpeted with lupins and poppies," to balmy summers when the rolling hills turn "gold and saffron and red—an indescribable color."

East of Eden is Steinbeck's self-described magnum opus in which he wove together the history of his mother's ranching family with a fictional story line. "In a sense it will be two books—the story of my county and the story of me," claimed the author. "My wish is that when my reader has finished with this book, he will have a sense of belonging in it. He will actually be a native of that Valley," Steinbeck recorded in a journal he kept throughout the writing process. With its detailed descriptions of people and place, *East of Eden* serves as a splendid introduction to Steinbeck's realm.

Known for regaling friends and family with stories he spun, Steinbeck decided on his intended profession at age 14. After graduating from high school in 1919, he spent the subsequent decade intermittently attending Stanford University (he eventually left in 1925 without a degree) and indulging his wanderlust. He briefly worked in San Francisco and took a steamer to New York City via the Panama Canal, an experience that provided fodder for his first novel, *Cup of Gold,* written in wintertime solitude during a two-year stint as caretaker at a Lake Tahoe residence. Steinbeck also roamed the northern California landscape he reinvented on the page, working as a ranch hand, a laborer, and a chemist at a sugar factory. He gathered anecdotes and impressions the same way he later collected marine specimens with Ricketts. "I'm a shameless magpie," he once described himself, "picking up anything shiny that comes my way—incident, situation, or personality." He translated his findings into the stories of *In Dubious Battle, Of Mice and Men,* and other memorable tales, including his Pulitzer Prize–winning novel *The Grapes of Wrath.*

The Depression-era saga, which chronicles the myriad hardships of the Joad family, had its roots in a series of articles Steinbeck was asked to write for a San Francisco newspaper about the treatment and conditions of farm laborers. He purchased a secondhand bakery wagon and visited migrant camps in the San Joaquin Valley, often pitching in to lend a hand to the sick and starving. His firsthand experiences with the social injustices heaped upon disadvantaged farmworkers added flesh-and-blood humanity to his fictional portrayal of the Joads as they struggle to survive in California after an arduous journey from the Dust Bowl state of Oklahoma, where drought, a poor economic climate, and bad farming practices forced people off their land.

Steinbeck's sympathies for the plight of migrant workers curried him no favor in his native city, where copies of *The Grapes of Wrath,* the best-selling book of 1939, were ceremoniously burned near the library now bearing his name. The book ignited the ire of some Salinas residents, particularly ranchers and bankers who felt they were

Steinbeck's controversial novel had an ardent supporter in Eleanor Roosevelt, who told the press after visiting California migrant camps, "I never have thought *The Grapes of Wrath* was exaggerated." In a note to the First Lady, Steinbeck wrote, "May I thank you for your words. I have been called a liar so constantly that sometimes I wonder whether I may not have dreamed the things I saw and heard in the period of my research."

cast in a poor light. Eventually veneration replaced malice, and when it was suggested in 1957 that Salinas's high school be named after him, the writer was decidedly not in favor of the idea. "If the city of my birth should wish to perpetuate my name clearly but harmlessly," he declared, "let it name a bowling alley after me or a dog track or even a medium price, low-church brothel; but a school!"

Today the writer is lauded in Salinas not with a dog track or bowling alley but with the impressive **National Steinbeck Center**. The brick-and-glass building anchors one end of Main Street in the city's Oldtown section, which is depicted in *East of Eden*. The center's vast John Steinbeck Exhibition Hall is a bibliophile's fun house with interactive exhibits, mini-theaters showing film adaptations of *The Grapes of Wrath* and other works, and an oversize crossword puzzle for testing one's Steinbeck smarts.

The **Steinbeck Festival** takes place every other year in May. See pages 146–47 for details.

Thematically arranged galleries offer an in-depth look at Steinbeck's life, his literary works, and the region. The museum begins with his childhood in Salinas, featuring facts about *East of Eden* as well as the history of lettuce harvesting in the area. Another gallery focuses on *The Grapes of Wrath*, including the controversy surrounding the novel, while "An' Live Off the Fatta the Lan'" (named for Lenny's memorable quote in *Of Mice and Men*) illustrates how Steinbeck drew on his experiences as a ranch hand and a chemist for the Spreckels Company to create working-class characters. Use grooming tools to emulate *The Red Pony*'s Jody Tiflin caring for his horse, visit a re-creation of Cannery Row and the interior of Ed Ricketts's lab, and see the green GMC truck Steinbeck drove around the U.S. in *Travels with Charley*.

Exhibits also illuminate Steinbeck's work as a journalist, from the 1936 articles that became the basis of *The Grapes of Wrath* to his days as a newspaper correspondent in Europe and northern Africa during World War II to dispatches from the Vietnam War. Among the accolades bestowed on Steinbeck were a Nobel Prize in 1962 and, the next year, a Presidential Medal of Freedom, which was awarded

◉ **Stroll along Ocean View Boulevard** in Pacific Grove and take in the view of "the sea rocks and the kelp and the excitement of churning sea water" that Steinbeck vividly conjured in his memoir *Travels with Charley*.

◉ Drop by the Monterey Bay Aquarium and marvel at more than 550 species of marine life. Then explore the area on foot with the self-guided **Cannery Row Audio Tour**, which begins just outside the aquarium and can be downloaded at *www.montereybay aquarium.org*.

◉ **Have lunch** in the elegant ambiance of the Steinbeck House. Menu offerings change weekly and include scrumptious fare like leek and tomato soup and lemon cake with fresh strawberries.

◉ At the National Steinbeck Center, **see the custom-made pickup truck camper Steinbeck christened Rocinante** after the title character's steed in Miguel Cervantes's *Don Quixote*. It was home to the writer and his canine companion during a 34-state journey depicted in *Travels with Charley*.

◉ The self-guided **Historic Oldtown Walking Tour** is a stroll through the Salinas streets Steinbeck made famous. (Brochures are available gratis at the National Steinbeck Center, where the walking tour begins.) Imagine *East of Eden*'s villainous Kate purchasing chocolates at the site where Bells Candy once stood or saunter down Gabilan, the street that lent its name to Jody's horse in *The Red Pony*. Before becoming county treasurer, Steinbeck's father operated the J. E. Steinbeck Feed Store at 332 Main Street. The building that housed the business is now the **Cherry Bean Gourmet Coffeehouse & Roastery**, where one of the java varieties is the Steinbeck Blend.

by John F. Kennedy and presented to the author by Lyndon Johnson after the former President's assassination.

Steinbeck grew up two blocks from where the National Steinbeck Center now stands. Operating as a luncheon restaurant, the **Steinbeck House** is a Queen Anne–style dwelling with gingerbread trim and ornate scrollwork set in a beautifully landscaped yard. Visitors to this restored Victorian showpiece can dine in one of three downstairs rooms where family photographs line the walls and memorabilia such as a clock from the writer's Sag Harbor, New York, home is on display.

In an upstairs bedroom, Steinbeck penned his earliest stories and submitted them to magazines under a pseudonym. "I never put a return address on them," he confided to a friend years later. "I was scared to death to get a rejection slip, but more, to get an acceptance." Eventually the aspiring writer did make his mark on the literary world. When honoring him with the 1962 Nobel Prize for literature, the selection committee noted that his sympathies "go out to the oppressed, the misfits, and the distressed," and added, "In him we find the American temperament also expressed in his great feeling for nature, for the tilled soil, the waste land, the mountains and the ocean coasts." Steinbeck immortalized the places with which he was most familiar through the medium he knew best: books, which he viewed as "one of the very few authentic magics our species has created."

IF YOU GO: The National Steinbeck Center is an excellent place to begin a visit to Steinbeck Country. Be sure to allow ample time to take in the museum's many facets. In addition to the John Steinbeck Exhibition Hall, the center includes a theater where two short films are shown, one about Steinbeck's life and the other a history of the Salinas Valley. The center regularly hosts lectures, readings, and other events, as well as walking tours during the summer. A special celebration is held each year to commemorate the author's February 27 birthday. **National Steinbeck Center** 1 Main Street • Salinas, CA 93901 • Tel: 831-796-3833 • www.steinbeck.org • Open daily

Drink, Dine, and Doze

STEINBECK HOUSE

132 Central Avenue • Salinas, CA 93901

• Tel: 831-424-2735 • *www.steinbeckhouse.com*

• Open for lunch Tuesday through

Saturday, 11:30 a.m. through 2:00 p.m.

(reservations accepted); house tours given the

first Sunday of the month, May through September

This 1897 abode was home to the Steinbeck family for 35 years, and the writer was born here in his parents' first-floor bedroom (now the reception room) on February 27, 1902. After departing for Stanford University, Steinbeck occasionally returned for brief stays and worked on *Tortilla Flat* and *The Red Pony* here while caring first for his ailing mother and then his father. Neither of Steinbeck's parents lived to see him achieve success as a writer, with his father passing away five days before the publication of *Tortilla Flat*.

Owned and operated since 1974 by the nonprofit Valley Guild, the Steinbeck House restaurant is open for lunchtime dining, featuring dishes made from Salinas Valley produce. Afternoon tea is served one day per month. (Proceeds are used for house preservation as well as donated to local charities.) On display in the Best Cellar Gift Shop is the headboard from the bed in which the writer was born, along with his mother's desk and table.

RESTAURANT 1833

500 Hartnell Street • Monterey, CA 93940 • Tel: 831-643-1833

• *www.restaurant1833.com*

Steinbeck occasionally stopped by this adobe house, once a private residence, to see Hattie Gragg. The social maven (said to haunt her former home) regaled the writer with colorful tales of Monterey inhabitants that are believed to have partly inspired characters in *Tortilla Flat*. At Restaurant 1833 (the year of the building's construction), enjoy American fare in Hattie's Room, one of numerous dining spaces, or sip cocktails in the Library.

Travels With Steinbeck

WHEN JOHN STEINBECK DEPARTED Stanford University for the final time in 1925, he left a note for his roommate: "Gone to China. See you again sometime." He intended to make like adventure writer Jack London and sail to the Far East aboard a freighter. Although a lack of seafaring experience kept him from being hired on as a deckhand, Steinbeck had plenty of other adventures throughout his lifetime.

His most famous voyage was the 1960 cross-country trek he made with his French poodle, Charley, a trip that took the pair across 10,000 miles from the East Coast to the shores of the Pacific and back again. His aim, he related, was to "rediscover this monster land." The undertaking is eloquently chronicled in *Travels with Charley*, whose title is a nod to Robert Louis Stevenson's *Travels with a Donkey*.

In 1943, Steinbeck served as a newspaper correspondent during World War II. He covered conflicts abroad for the *New York Herald Tribune*, and even while in northern Africa, the California seascape was ever on his mind. "The sea was the same blue as in Monterey," he recalled, "and it made me very terribly homesick." Four years later, Steinbeck and photographer Robert Capa traveled through the Soviet Union, an experience he recounts in *A Russian Journal*. The writer was allowed to visit the country because its Communist leaders viewed *The Grapes of Wrath* as an anticapitalist treatise.

On his deathbed, Steinbeck confided to his wife that his most cherished memory was their trip to Somerset, England. They rented a cottage and explored the countryside of his childhood hero, King Arthur, for several months in 1959, which lead to the posthumously published *The Acts of King Arthur and His Noble Knights*. "Yesterday I climbed to Camelot on a golden day. The orchards are in flower and we could see the Bristol Channel and Glastonbury too, and King Alfred's tower and all below. And that wonderful place and structure with layer on layer of work and feeling," he wrote to a friend. "I shall go up there at night and in all weather, but what a good way to see it first. I walked the circuit of the ramparts and thought very much of you and wished you were with me."

THE SARDINE FACTORY RESTAURANT

701 Wave Street • Monterey, CA 93940 • Tel: 831-373-3775 • *www.sardinefactory.com*

The deceptively understated exterior of this former cafeteria for cannery workers hides a gorgeous restaurant where dining rooms include a glass-domed conservatory and the intimate Steinbeck Room with historic photos of Cannery Row (and one of the writer) adorning the walls. A more casual lounge area features live piano music on select evenings, and the menu showcases dishes named for Steinbeck's works such as the East of Eden House Salad, Sweet Thursday Desserts, and Tortilla Flat Tapas.

GUEST INN, ASILOMAR

800 Asilomar Avenue • Pacific Grove, CA 93950 • Tel: 831-372-8016
• *www.visitasilomar.com*

This oceanfront conference center and retreat has hotel and guest cottages that are open to the public for overnight stays. On the wooded grounds is the four-bedroom Guest Inn, a cottage formerly owned by Steinbeck's sister, where the writer stayed for several months in 1941 while working on *Sea of Cortez*. Co-written with Ed Ricketts, the tome chronicles their findings during a six-week expedition to the Sea of Cortés (also called the Gulf of California), including the discovery of 35 new marine species.

MONTEREY PENINSULA LODGING: Cannery Row area choices range from easy-on-the-wallet motels to high-end resorts, including the **Spindrift Inn** (*www.spindriftinn.com*), which has some rooms overlooking the historic street and others with ocean views. Nearby in Steinbeck Plaza is the **Cannery Row Monument**, which features a bronzed John Steinbeck seated atop a rock, his friend Ed Ricketts, and other figures representing Cannery Row's sardine-canning-era heyday.

In Pacific Grove, the **Green Gables Inn** (*www.greengablesinnpg.com*) and the **Seven Gables Inn** (*www.thesevengablesinn.com*) are both located on scenic Ocean View Boulevard overlooking the stretch of shoreline Steinbeck once traversed. The Seven Gables has rooms named for Steinbeck and Robert Louis Stevenson.

PINE INN

Ocean Avenue between Lincoln Street and Monte Verde Street • Carmel, CA
93921 • Tel: 800-228-3851 • *www.pineinn.com*

Steinbeck had a rendezvous with an actress at the Pine Inn, only
to be smitten by the friend accompanying her, Elaine Scott, who
became his third wife. This stylish establishment was the first inn
built in Carmel-by-the-Sea, an upscale seaside town with an abundance of boutiques and galleries.

ELSEWHERE IN THE AREA

....

GARDEN OF MEMORIES MEMORIAL PARK

768 Abbott Street • Salinas, CA 93901

"The cemetery was deserted and the dark crooning of the wind bowed the
heavy cypress trees," wrote Steinbeck of the Garden of Memories in *East
of Eden*. The cemetery is the final resting place of the writer, who died of
heart failure at his New York home on December 20, 1968, at age 66. His
ashes rested for two days at his family's Pacific Grove cottage, and the day
after Christmas a memorial service was held at
Point Lobos State Natural Reserve in Carmel.

Legend has it Robert Louis Stevenson used
the coastal landscape of **Point Lobos State
Natural Reserve** (*www.pointlobos.org*) as a
model for *Treasure Island*'s terrain.

Despite his tumultuous relationship with the
town, it was Steinbeck's wish to be buried
in Salinas.

LARA-SOTO ADOBE

460 Pierce Street • Monterey, CA 93940

In 1944, Steinbeck and his second wife, along with their infant son,
took up residence for a short time in "one of the oldest and nicest
adobes" in Monterey, where he worked on *The Pearl*. "It is a house
I have wanted since I was a little kid," he wrote to his editor. "It is a
laughing house."

Now owned by the Middlebury Institute of International Studies
at Monterey, the house is part of the city's annual "Christmas in the
Adobes" (*www.parks.ca.gov*) event. Some 20 dwellings are festively

decorated and awash in candlelight, and holiday revelries include live music and refreshments. Tickets go on sale October 15.

MONTEREY

Ed Ricketts's lab at **800 Cannery Row** is owned by the city of Monterey and is open to the public on select days during the year, such as his May 14 birthday. Other landmarks include **Bruce Ariss Way,** a small thoroughfare off the Row where three restored cannery workers' cottages can be seen.

A **bronze bust of Ricketts** is located on a recreation trail (formerly railroad tracks) that parallels Cannery Row; the spot is where Steinbeck's comrade died after his car was struck by a train in 1948. **A bronze bust of the writer** stands at the entrance to Steinbeck Plaza at Cannery Row and Prescott Street.

For information on Cannery Row and the Monterey area, visit *www.canneryrow.com*, *www.canneryrow.org*, and *www.seemonterey.com*.

TRAVERSING STEINBECK'S TERRAIN: The **Steinbeck Itinerary** on *www.seemonterey.com* suggests what to seek out in three days, from the art deco architecture in Steinbeck's hometown to Fremont's Peak, where he bids farewell to the Salinas Valley in *Travels with Charley.*

Steinbeck Country: Exploring the Settings for the Stories by David Laws is a reference booklet with sites related to the writer, including *The Long Valley*'s **Castle Rock** with bluffs that look like "a tremendous stone castle." Beautifully illustrated, *A Journey into Steinbeck's California* by Susan Shillinglaw is another handy guide while traversing the terrain—and a terrific armchair read afterward. (Both are available for purchase in the National Steinbeck Center shop.)

Take a guided stroll along Cannery Row, the street Steinbeck made famous, with **California Legacy Tours** (*www.calegacytours.com*). Or sign on for the Historic Monterey Walking Tour, which highlights places Steinbeck lived and locations mentioned in his books. Other offerings include Walk in the Footsteps of RLS, focusing on Scottish writer Robert Louis Stevenson and his life-changing journey to Monterey.

In *The Pastures of Heaven*, a group of sight-seers venture along **17-Mile Drive** (*www.pebblebeach.com*), a toll road located between Pacific Grove and Carmel-by-the-Sea. After taking in the dramatic coastal views, they head to the 18th-century Mission San Carlos Borromeo del Rio Carmelo (*www.carmelmission.org*).

PACIFIC GROVE

Steinbeck went from struggling to celebrated scribe while living in his family's Pacific Grove cottage at **147 11th Street** (a private residence) from 1930 to 1936, producing *The Pastures of Heaven, The Long Valley, Tortilla Flat,* and other works. He rewrote *Of Mice and Men* after a zealous puppy "made confetti" of half the manuscript.

Additional locales associated with the writer include **Point Pinos Lighthouse** (*www.pointpinoslighthouse.org*), the oldest continuously operating lighthouse on the West Coast, mentioned in *Cannery Row* and *Sweet Thursday*. In the latter, after being asked by Doc to have dinner, Suzy "mooned away on the path that leads along the sea to the lighthouse on Point Pinos. She looked in the tide pools, and she picked a bunch of the tiny flowers that grow as close to the ocean as they can."

Visit *www.93950.com* for a self-guided driving tour of Steinbeck's Pacific Grove, and *www.pacificgrove.org* for general information about the town.

CARMEL-BY-THE-SEA
TOR HOUSE

26304 Ocean View Ave • Carmel, CA 93923 • Tel: 831-624-1813
• *www.torhouse.org* • Tours given Friday and Saturday

Poet Robinson Jeffers was hands-on when constructing a stone house along the central California coast that inspired much of his work. He apprenticed himself to the building contractor, learning the art of making "stone love stone," and built an accompanying tower by himself. Jeffers's verse earned high praise from Steinbeck, who declared: "His poetry is perfect to me."

Select Index by Locale

Index

Photo Credits

Pages 4, 6, 7, Steven Rendon; p. 10, courtesy Abbey Theatre; p. 12, photo courtesy of The Eugene O'Neill Theater Center/Monte Cristo Cottage; p. 13, National Park Service; p. 14, The Abbotsford Trust; p. 16, Parks Canada; p. 19, The Wordsworth Trust; p. 22, ©National Trust Images/Andrew Butler; p. 27, Brian Schmidt; p. 32, Eudora Welty House/Mississippi Department of Archives and History; p. 33, Rowan Oak, University of Mississippi; p. 36, Brian Schmidt; p. 37, 39, 40, Joni Rendon; p. 42, Keats House/The City of London; p. 45, NPS Photo by Phil Smith, Courtesy of Carl Sandburg Home NHS; p. 46, George Mallis; p. 48, New Hampshire Division of Parks and Recreation. Photo by Ellen Edersheim; p. 50, photo courtesy of Emily Dickinson Museum, Amherst, MA; p. 52, courtesy National Park Service, Longfellow National Historic Site; p. 56, City of Austin Parks and Recreation Department; p. 59, Laura Ingalls Wilder Home Association Mansfield, MO; p. 60, Copyrights AFS / photo Allard Bovenberg; p. 62, Marie A. Gordinier; p. 64, The Department of Conservation and Recreation (DCR), Walden Pond State Reservation. Photo by Kindra Clineff © for the DCR; p. 67, Brian Schmidt, used by permission of Frederick Douglass National Historic Site; p. 68, Pearl S. Buck International; p. 71, Brian Schmidt; p. 78, 80, Steven Rendon; p. 84 Historic Hudson Valley/www.hudsonvalley.org; p. 89, Joni Rendon; p. 90, Aleksey Kolyaskin; p. 98, 101, 104, Steven Rendon; p. 106 copyright Burgh Island 2007; p. 110, Shannon McKenna Schmidt; p. 114, Ritz Paris; p. 116, Brian Schmidt; p. 117, The Ernest Hemingway Foundation of Oak Park; p. 121, Steven Rendon; p. 125, Mark Twain Boyhood Home & Museum, Hannibal, MO; p. 127, Mark Twain House and Museum, Hartford, CT; p. 130, Steven Rendon; p. 133, David Dashiell/The Mount; p. 135, Steven Rendon; p. 145, photo courtesy Tennessee Williams/New Orleans Literary Festival; p. 147, Andy Newman, FL Keys News Bureau; p. 149, The Jane Austen Centre, Bath, UK; p. 156, Shannon McKenna Schmidt; p. 159, The Board of Trinity College Dublin; p. 161, The British Library; p. 162, The New York Public Library; p. 163, Brian Schmidt; p. 164, courtesy Virginia Festival of the Book; p. 167, courtesy Texas Book Festival; p. 167, courtesy Miami Book Fair; p. 168, Steven Rendon; p. 170, Brian Schmidt; p. 174, courtesy Hotel Monteleone; p. 175, courtesy of Personality Hotels/Photo by Nate Bennett; p. 179, Inn BoonsBoro; p. 180, courtesy Library Hotel; p. 183, The Landmark Trust; p. 184, Hotel Gritti Palace Archives; p. 187, Steven Rendon; p. 188, courtesy of L'Hotel, 13 rue des Beaux-Arts, 75006 PARIS – www.l-hotel.com; p. 190, courtesy of Island Outpost; p. 193, Shannon McKenna Schmidt; p. 193, Bloody Brigid cocktail recipe created by John's Grill; named by the California Historical Society; p. 196, Brian Schmidt; p. 198, Steven Rendon; p. 200, Shannon McKenna Schmidt; p. 201, 203, 204, 206, Steven Rendon; p. 209, courtesy of La Closerie des Lilas; p. 215, Bettmann/CORBIS; p. 216, The Jane Austen Centre, Bath, UK; p. 225, Steven Rendon; p. 228, Bettmann/CORBIS; p. 229, Charles Dickens Museum; p. 230, Steven Rendon; p. 237, Joni Rendon; p. 244, DeAgostini/Getty Images; p. 245, 254, 255, Steven Rendon; p. 256, Brian Schmidt; p. 258, Bettmann/CORBIS; p. 259, Brian Schmidt; p. 267, Steven Rendon; p. 272, CORBIS; p. 273, Frank Lynch; p. 281, The Dublin Writers Museum; p. 283, Bettmann/CORBIS; p. 284, 291, 292, Steven Rendon; p. 294, Bettmann/CORBIS; p. 295, used by permission of Orchard House/The L. M. Alcott Memorial Association (photo by John J. Althouse); p. 301, used by permission of Orchard House/The L. M. Alcott Memorial Association (photo by Amy B. Brown); p. 306, Smithsonian Institution/CORBIS; p. 307, Brian Schmidt; p. 319, Bettmann/CORBIS; p. 320, Hemingway Home, Key West: Rob O'Neal Photography; p. 328, used by permission of Sloppy Joe's; p. 329, Steven Rendon; p. 334, Time & Life Pictures/Getty Images; p. 335, Monroe County Heritage Museums; p. 344, Bettmann/CORBIS; p. 345, Brian Schmidt; p. 353, Brian Schmidt